FRENCH PHILOSOPHY IN THE TWEN

In this book Gary Gutting tells, clearly and authoritatively, the story of French philosophy from 1890 to 1990. He examines the often neglected background of spiritualism, university idealism, and early philosophy of science, and also discusses the privileged role of philosophy in the French education system. Taking account of this background, together with the influences of avant-garde literature and German philosophy, he develops a rich account of existential phenomenology, which he argues is the central achievement of French thought during the century, and of subsequent structuralist and poststructuralist developments. His discussion includes chapters on Bergson, Sartre, Beauvoir, Merleau-Ponty, Foucault, and Derrida, with sections on other major thinkers including Lyotard, Deleuze, Irigaray, Levinas, and Ricoeur. He offers challenging analyses of the often misunderstood relationship between existential phenomenology and structuralism and of the emergence of poststructuralism. Finally, he sketches the major current trends of French philosophy, including liberal political philosophy, the return to phenomenology, and French analytic philosophy.

GARY GUTTING is Professor of Philosophy at the University of Notre Dame, and a leading authority on twentieth-century French philosophy. He is the author of *Michel Foucault's Archaeology of Scientific Knowledge* (Cambridge University Press, 1989) and the editor of *The Cambridge Companion to Foucault* (1994). His many publications also include *Pragmatic Liberalism and the Critique of Modernity* (Cambridge University Press, 1999).

FRENCH PHILOSOPHY IN THE TWENTIETH CENTURY

GARY GUTTING
University of Notre Dame

CAMBRIDGE UNIVERSITY PRESS
Cambridge, New York, Melbourne, Madrid, Cape Town, Singapore, São Paulo

Cambridge University Press
The Edinburgh Building, Cambridge CB2 2RU, UK

Published in the United States of America by Cambridge University Press, New York

www.cambridge.org
Information on this title: www.cambridge.org/9780521662123

© Gary Gutting 2001

This book is in copyright. Subject to statutory exception
and to the provisions of relevant collective licensing agreements,
no reproduction of any part may take place without
the written permission of Cambridge University Press.

First published 2001
Reprinted 2001, 2002

A catalogue record for this publication is available from the British Library

Library of Congress Cataloguing in Publication data

Gutting, Gary.
French philosophy in the twentieth century / Gary Gutting.
p. cm.
Includes bibliographical references and index.
ISBN 0-521-66212-5 – ISBN 0-521-66559-0 (pbk.)
1. Philosophy, French – 20th century, I. Title.
B2421.G88 2001   194–dc21

ISBN-13 978-0-521-66212-3 hardback
ISBN-10 0-521-66212-5 hardback

ISBN-13 978-0-521-66559-9 paperback
ISBN-10 0-521-66559-0 paperback

Transferred to digital printing 2005

To Anastasia
with love
remembering our first day in Paris, June 20, 1968

Contents

Preface	page xi
A note on references	xiii
List of abbreviations	xiv

PART I: THE PHILOSOPHERS OF THE THIRD REPUBLIC (1890–1940) — 1

1 Fin-de-siècle: the professors of the Republic — 3
   Philosophy and the new university — 3
   Positivism — 8
   Spiritualism: Ravaisson and Renouvier — 9
   Idealism: Lachelier and Boutroux — 14

2 Science and idealism — 26
   Philosophers of science: Poincaré, Duhem, and Meyerson — 26
   Brunschvicg — 40

3 Bergson — 49
   Bergson on the history of philosophy — 51
   Time and free will — 56
   Matter and memory — 60
   Creative evolution — 66
   Religion and morality — 75

4 Between the wars — 84
   Bachelard — 85
   Blondel — 89
   Neo-Thomism and Maritain — 94
   Marcel — 98
   Toward the concrete — 102

PART II: THE REIGN OF EXISTENTIAL PHENOMENOLOGY (1940–1960) — 119

5 Sartre — 121
   Being and nothingness — 128
      Background — 128
      The basic ontological scheme — 131
      Consciousness — 133
      Nothingness and anguish — 137
      Bad faith — 140
      Being-for-others — 144
      Freedom — 147
   Critique of dialectical reason — 151

6 Beauvoir — 158
   Beauvoir and the origins of existentialism — 158
   The second sex — 165

7 Merleau-Ponty — 181
   The phenomenology of perception — 186
      Merleau-Ponty's conception of phenomenology — 186
      The body — 190
      Language — 192
      The Other — 195
      The cogito and the truth of idealism — 197
      Freedom — 203
   Phenomenology and structuralism — 208

PART III: STRUCTURALISM AND BEYOND (1960–1990) — 213

8 The structuralist invasion — 215
   Saussure — 215
   Lévi-Strauss — 221
   Structuralism and phenomenology — 224
   Philosophy of the concept: Cavaillès, Canguilhem, and Serres — 227
   The high tide of structuralism — 234
      Marx and Althusser — 235
      Freud, Lacan, and Kristeva — 238
      Barthes — 244
   Poststructuralism — 249

9 Foucault — 258
   Madness — 264
   Order — 267

	Discipline	278
	Sex	282
10	**Derrida**	289
	Deconstruction	291
	Differance	298
	Is Derrida a skeptic?	304
	Ethics	308
	Religion	313
11	**Philosophies of difference**	318
	Lyotard	318
	Deleuze	331
	Irigaray	341
12	**Fin-de-siècle again: "le temps retrouvé"?**	353
	Levinas	353
	Ricoeur	363
	Recent directions	371

Conclusion: the philosophy of freedom   380
Appendix: philosophy and the French educational system   391
References   394
Index   412

Preface

There is nothing sacred about the century as a unit of time, but there is a relatively self-contained and coherent story to be told about French philosophy from about 1890 to about 1990. In telling it, I have tried to be comprehensive although by no means exhaustive. There are full chapters on the half-dozen figures I regard as of the highest importance and substantial sections on about a dozen other major thinkers. Beyond that, I have let the logic of my narrative, more than any desire for encyclopedic completeness, determine whom I discuss and how. Given the constraints of length, it has been impossible to avoid arbitrary exclusions. Thoughtful readers will regret no more than I that there is little or nothing on André Lalande, Alain, Simone Weil, Pierre Bourdieu, Alain Badiou . . .

My approach has been that of a historically minded philosopher rather than a historian per se. I have, accordingly, paid more attention to the internal logic of ideas than to, for example, social-political contexts, economic determinants, or the psychology of influence. I have, however, tried to give a sense of the flow and interaction of ideas from one thinker to another and to explain, at least in intellectual terms, major changes in views (from, for example, idealism to existentialism and existentialism to poststructuralism). My main goal has been to provide the reader with lucid and fair analyses of what philosophers have thought and of how the thoughts of different philosophers are related. I have also paid some, necessarily limited, attention to the broader intellectual context of French philosophical thought (for example, German philosophy, avant-garde literature, and structuralist social science) and to its dependence on the distinctive French system of education. (The appendix provides a summary of basic facts and terminology that may be useful for understanding references to this system.)

My first four chapters, on the years before World War II, cover much material seldom discussed in English. I hope that readers will see the importance of spiritualism, university idealism, Bergson, and French philosophy of science for understanding the developments of the latter half of the century. I also hope they will come to share my appreciation of the intrinsic philosophical value of what thinkers such as Lachelier, Poincaré, Brunschvicg, and Blondel achieved. My later chapters, covering better-known but often quite difficult philosophers, put a particularly strong emphasis on clarity of analysis. They also defend some controversial judgments about, for example, the centrality of Sartre's *L'être et le néant*, the philosophical importance of Beauvoir's *Le deuxième sexe*, the relatively marginal role of structuralism, and the significance of poststructuralism. The Conclusion presents my view that twentieth-century French philosophy is best read as a sustained reflection on the problem of individual freedom.

I am especially grateful to those who read and so perceptively commented on drafts of this book: Karl Ameriks, Philip Bartok, Frederick Crosson, Thomas Flynn, Anastasia Friel Gutting, and Stephen Watson. Warm thanks also to those who offered their expert assessment of particular chapters or sections: Alissa Branham, David Carr, Jean Gayon, Eric Matthews, Todd May, William McBride, and Ernan McMullin. Philip Bartok deserves special mention both for his acute close reading and his invaluable bibliographical assistance.

I also want to thank the University of Notre Dame's Erasmus Institute, which provided financial support and a splendid intellectual atmosphere for a semester's work on this book. I am especially grateful to the Director, James Turner, and the Associate Director, Robert Sullivan. Thanks are also due for all the stimulation and assistance I received from the 1999–2000 cohort of Erasmus fellows: Terry Bays, William Donahue, Anita Houck, Pamela Jason, Wesley Kort, Daniella Kostroun, Roger Lundin, John McGreevy, and Susan Rosa.

Special thanks are due to Hilary Gaskin, the philosophy editor at Cambridge University Press, who suggested that I write this book and encouraged me throughout its writing, and to Jocelyn Pye for excellent copy-editing.

Finally, as always, by far my greatest debt is to my family: to my children, Tom, Edward, and Tasha, for all the pride and joy they bring; and to my wife Anastasia for the perfect gift of loving and being loved by her.

A note on references

Books and articles are cited simply by title, with full details given in the References. All citations are in English and are from a published translation when one is listed in the References. Otherwise, the English translations are my own. When a text is cited repeatedly, the title is abbreviated (e.g., *EN* for *L'être et le néant*) and page references are given in the main text, the first number referring to the French original and the second to the English translation.

Abbreviations

A	Maurice Blondel, *L'action*
CRD	Jean-Paul Sartre, *Critique de la raison dialectique*
CS	Luce Irigaray, *Ce sexe qui n'en est pas un*
D	Jean-François Lyotard, *Le différend*
DS	Simone de Beauvoir, *Le deuxième sexe*
DSM	Henri Bergson, *Les deux sources de la morale et de la religion*
EC	Henri Bergson, *L'évolution créatrice*
EDI	Henri Bergson, *Essai sur les données immédiates de la conscience*
EDS	Luce Irigaray, *Éthique de la différence sexuelle*
EH	Léon Brunschvicg, *L'expérience humaine et la causalité physique*
EN	Jean-Paul Sartre, *L'être et le néant*
FI	Jules Lachelier, *Du fondement de l'induction*
LI	Jacques Derrida, *Limited Inc.*
MC	Michel Foucault, *Les mots et les choses*
MJ	Léon Brunschvicg, *La modalité du jugement*
MM	Henri Bergson, *Matière et mémoire*
MP	Jacques Derrida, *Marges de la philosophie*
PK	Michel Foucault, *Power/Knowledge*
PP	Maurice Merleau-Ponty, *Phénoménologie de la perception*
PS	Claude Lévi-Strauss, *La pensée sauvage*
QM	Jean-Paul Sartre, "Question de méthode"
S	Maurice Merleau-Ponty, *Signes*
SH	Henri Poincaré, *La science et l'hypothèse*
SR	Jean-Paul Sartre, "Jean-Paul Sartre répond"
TI	Emmanuel Levinas, *Totalité et infini*
VS	Henri Poincaré, *La valeur de la science*

PART I

*The Philosophers of the Third Republic
(1890–1940)*

CHAPTER I

Fin-de-siècle: the professors of the Republic

Abandoning the study of John Stuart Mill only for that of Lachelier, the less she believed in the reality of the external world, the more desperately she sought to establish herself in a good position in it before she died.
(Marcel Proust, *In Search of Lost Time*, IV, 438)

PHILOSOPHY AND THE NEW UNIVERSITY

Writing just after the end of World War I, an acute observer of the French philosophical scene judged that "philosophical research had never been more abundant, more serious, and more intense among us than in the last thirty years".[1] This flowering was due to the place of philosophy in the new educational system set up by the Third Republic in the wake of the demoralizing defeat in the Franco-Prussian War. The French had been humiliated by the capture of Napoleon III at Sedan, devastated by the long siege of Paris, and terrified by what most of the bourgeoisie saw as seventy-three days of anarchy under the radical socialism of the Commune. Much of the new Republic's effort at spiritual restoration was driven by a rejection of the traditional values of institutional religion, which it aimed to replace with an enlightened secular worldview. A principal vehicle of this enterprise was educational reform and specifically the building of a university system dedicated to the ideals of science, reason, and humanism. Albert Thibaudet highlighted the importance of this reform when he labeled the Third Republic "the republic of professors".[2]

Philosophy was at the center of the new educational regime, exerting its influence through the famous "classe de philosophie"

[1] Dominique Parodi, *La philosophie contemporaine en France*, 9–10.
[2] In his *La république des professeurs*.

that was the main requirement for students in French public high schools (lycées) during their last year (when they were seventeen to eighteen years old).[3] The class's modern history went back to regulations of 1809 that reestablished the medieval divisions of philosophy into logic, metaphysics, and morality and stipulated that it be studied for eight hours a week. There was also introduced a division treating the history of philosophy. Around 1830, Victor Cousin[4] added psychology, which soon became the most important element of the curriculum. Also, where the rules of 1809 had given merely a set of recommendations for teaching and a list of authors, Cousin worked out a detailed required structure. The idea was to cover the whole of philosophy, both its problems and its history, in a year-long grand synthesis. Cousin also began the process of laicizing philosophy, by reducing the role of religious questions. His structure stayed in place until philosophy was eliminated from the curriculum of the lycées in 1853 under the Second Empire.

In 1863 philosophy was restored to the lycées and became a required subject for all students in the last year of secondary education.[5] During the First Empire, a lycée education became required for many civil service positions. This meant that, after 1863, the "classe de philosophie" was extremely important for French secondary students, since it was now a key topic on the exam they had to pass to receive their degree (the *baccalauréat*) and be eligible for state employment. Its importance was further emphasized by the reform of 1874, which made philosophy and rhetoric separate divisions, emphasizing philosophy's autonomy and distinctiveness. Moreover, since philosophy was taught only in a single year – the final one – it was presented as the culmination and synthesis of all that had gone before, the "crown", as it was inevitably put, of secondary education. It was not surprising that philosophy soon replaced rhetoric as the course with the highest intellectual status

---

[3] For an overview of the structure of the French educational system, see the Appendix.
[4] Victor Cousin (1792–1867) was minister of education in the 1830s and 1840s under the bourgeois monarchy of Louis-Philippe. His own philosophical position, which he called eclecticism, tried to synthesize French philosophical psychology (deriving from Maine de Biran) with empiricism, Scottish realism, and German idealism. During the mid-nineteenth century, eclecticism had the status of an "official" philosophy in the French university. Cousin was also important as an editor, translator, and historian of philosophy.
[5] For a general discussion of French education in the later nineteenth and early twentieth centuries, see Fritz Ringer, *Fields of Knowledge: French Academic Culture in Comparative Perspective, 1890–1920*. On the role of philosophy in France during this period, see Jean-Louis Fabiani, *Les philosophes de la république*.

and, accordingly, attracted a large number of the brightest students interested in secondary teaching.

Since the main goal of the university teaching of philosophy was to produce teachers for the lycée philosophy class, there was considerable continuity between the content of the two programs. At the same time, the qualifying examination (the *agrégation*) for those who wanted to teach philosophy in the lycées was geared to university-level research rather than merely what we would think of as high-school teaching. The result was a large number of talented lycée teachers with a high level of specialist knowledge in philosophy; and, of course, the best of these went on to take doctorates in philosophy and become university professors.

The French educational system thus gave philosophy a highly privileged place in the Third Republic. There was an audience composed of a general public educated in the rudiments of philosophy, as well as a substantial number of secondary school teachers with specialist knowledge of the subject; and there was a highly elite group of university professors engaged in philosophical research. Accordingly, a faculty of philosophy presided over the "republic of professors". Thibaudet falls into religious language in trying to express the sublimity of the philosopher's role: "The philosophical vocation embodies a principle analogous to a priestly vocation. Anyone who has prepared for the *agrégation* in philosophy . . . has been touched, at some point, like a seminarian, by the idea that the highest degree of human grandeur is a life consecrated to the service of the mind and that the University lets one compete for positions that make it possible to render this service."[6]

Nevertheless, as Ernst Curtius (writing in 1930) emphasized, French culture remained essentially literary. The dominant figures were writers such as Zola and Anatole France, who were outside the university system; and philosophical writing itself was literary in the sense that, as Bergson said, there was "no philosophical idea, no matter how profound or subtle, that could not be expressed in the language of everyday life [*la langue de tout le monde*]".[7] Curtius, imbued with German idealism's conception of philosophy, saw the

---

[6] *La république des professeurs*, 139.
[7] Cited by Ernst Curtius, *The Civilization of France: An Introduction*, 100. Fabiani notes, however, that "during the period 1880–1914 there were no close connections between professors of philosophy and avant-garde writers" (*Les philosophes de la république*, 115). As we shall see, that changes with the generation of the 1930s.

French as surrendering the philosophical enterprise "to literary form and average intelligence" and thought this was why, although "in Germany intellectual culture may be philosophical, in France it can be literary only".[8]

The university philosophy of the early Third Republic (before World War I) had both the strengths and the weaknesses of its privileged status. The high level of talent and the informed critical audience sustained a professional solidity that contemporaries favorably (and rightly) contrasted to the eloquent vagaries of Victor Cousin's eclecticism and Hyppolite Taine's positivism, which had dominated the Second Empire. Also, universal philosophical education and the high social position and connections of professors gave philosophy a strong influence on the general French culture. Scientists such as Henri Poincaré (brother-in-law of the philosopher Émile Boutroux) showed a particular interest in philosophical issues. Marcel Proust (a groomsman at Bergson's wedding), was a friend of Léon Brunschvicg, his fellow lycée-student in the philosophy course of Alphonse Darlu. The strong philosophical content of the writings of André Gide and Paul Valéry is often remarked; and the work of André Malraux, who studied philosophy with Alain (the pseudonym of Émile Chartier), the most famous of all lycée teachers, has been characterized as "the thought of Alain transposed into the novel".[9]

But privilege also encouraged intellectual complacency and damped the creativity that can rise from radical questioning by less socially secure thinkers. With the arguable exception of Bergson, the philosophers of the early Third Republic worked within a relatively narrow band defined by their training in the history of thought, their bourgeois moral ideals, and the political realities of their time. Curtius stretches the point to the maximum:

[French philosophy's] conservative Humanism could not endure either the Pantheism of a world-intoxicated ecstasy, nor the transcendental idealism of the creative spirit, nor the knowledge of salvation which desires redemption and depreciates the value of the world, nor the moral criticism of an heroic will to power. A Hegel, a Schopenhauer, a Nietzsche are unthinkable in France.[10]

On the other hand, eschewing the ecstasies of Germanic metaphysics – and the attendant drive for strong originality – allowed the

---

[8] *The Civilization of France: An Introduction*, 99–100.
[9] Jean Guitton, *Regards sur la pensée française, 1870–1940*, 59.
[10] *The Civilization of France: An Introduction*, 104.

French professors to create a fruitful circle of sensible conversation, focusing on a small set of key topics and grounded in a common formation and strong mutual respect. Such conversation was carried out in the *Revue de métaphysique et de morale* (founded by Xavier Léon and Léon Brunschvicg in 1893) and in meetings of the closely related Société Française de Philosophie (founded in 1901). The degree of shared understanding that could be assumed is most striking in André Lalande's project of a *Vocabulaire technique et critique de la philosophie*. This volume, which went through eleven editions between 1900 and 1926, offered detailed definitions of the full range of philosophical terms, finally formulated by Lalande but informed by commentary from most of the leading philosophers of the period. (Lalande's proposed definitions were discussed regularly at sessions of the Société, and the comments of members are printed beneath the *Vocabulaire*'s entries.) The work came remarkably close to its goal of "achieving accord among philosophers – as much as possible – on what they understand by. . . philosophical terms".[11]

Focused and fruitful, if not drastically creative, early Third Republic philosophy was rather like much contemporary analytic philosophy (or medieval scholasticism), though far less technical and rigorous and far more accessible to the general culture. Such thought is not likely to make new epochs, but it is an effective contribution to the civility and rationality of the age in which it finds itself.

Politically, the philosophers of the Third Republic, like other members of the new university, occupied an interesting and important position.[12] Their social status and position as government employees obviously made them part of the establishment, but since they had typically been born into intellectual families (with parents who were teachers, writers, physicians, etc.) they were less inclined to identify with the conservative values of the wealthy bourgeois class. (They had, in Pierre Bourdieu's terms, much more cultural capital than economic capital.) Accordingly, professors as a whole formed an influential class of liberal supporters of the Third Republic's ideals, with those with the highest level of intellectual status generally the most liberal. So, for example, in the Dreyfus affair, which split France

---

[11] *Vocabulaire technique et critique de la philosophie*, ix.
[12] See Fritz Ringer, *Fields of Knowledge: French Academic Culture in Comparative Perspective, 1890–1920*, 219–25.

at the turn of the century, the majority of professors at the Sorbonne and the École Normale Supérieure supported Dreyfus, and this support was particularly strong among philosophers.

Reflecting the Third Republic's secular liberalism, the central concerns of its philosophers were science, human freedom, and the relation between the two. Unlike the German idealists, who felt themselves possessed of intuitive or dialectical modes of knowing that far outstripped the plodding efforts of empirical science, these philosophers saw their reflections as grounded in an accurate understanding and appreciation of scientific results. On the other hand, even those closest to a positivist acceptance of the ultimate cognitive authority of science rejected empiricist epistemologies of scientific experience in favor of a rationalist active role for the mind. In a parallel way, construals of freedom typically avoided the determinism or compatibilism favored by empiricism and the subordination of the individual human will to an idealist absolute spirit. Because of this lack of sympathy with the dominant traditions of both Germany and Britain, French thought was very nearly autonomous during this period.[13]

POSITIVISM

Surveys of philosophy in France from 1870 to 1920 almost always employ a standard division of their subject into three schools: positivism, spiritualism, and idealism. These are useful categories for understanding the problems and approaches of the period, but they are much less helpful as classifications of individual thinkers. This is particularly so for positivism. The term was first used by Auguste Comte (1798–1857) to characterize his effort to develop a philosophy based on only the plain (positive) facts of experience – of which science provides paradigm examples – and to avoid metaphysical hypotheses. It came to be applied to any view that privileged empirical science over metaphysical thought. A "positivist" might well hold strongly scientistic views such as Humean empiricism or materialistic reductionism, but not necessarily. Many positivists

---

[13] Similarly, there was little foreign interest in French philosophy. Harald Höffding, for example, in his comprehensive history of modern philosophy, omits any treatment of French philosophers of the latter half of the nineteenth century, noting that, although they are important in the thought of their own country, "they have brought no new principles to bear on the discussion of problems" (*A History of Modern Philosophy*, 486).

rejected Comte's exclusion of theoretical entities, such as atoms, from science, and Comte himself maintained the irreducibility of biology and sociology to physics and chemistry. Later, leading positivists such as Ernest Renan and Hyppolite Taine painted grand visions of historical progress that were with some plausibility labeled Hegelian. This represented a broadening and dilution of positivism as it became more a general intellectual orientation than a well-defined philosophical position. In the mid-nineteenth century, positivism was still a major force, but its main proponents were literary figures such as Renan and Taine rather than academic philosophers. From 1870 on it was rejected by every major philosopher.[14]

Nonetheless, the positivist spirit survived. It was a major motivation for extending the methods of the natural sciences to the human domain, leading to the seminal work of Durkheim in sociology and of Pierre Janet in empirical psychology.[15] Such work did not assume or imply that all knowledge was scientific, but it did constitute a challenge to anti-positivist arguments that the specifically human domain was not open to empirical understanding. Other vital legacies of positivism were the development, by Poincaré and Duhem, of philosophy of science as a separate subdiscipline and the central role accorded detailed discussions of the history and results of science by virtually every major figure from Boutroux to Brunschvicg and Bergson. Indeed, by the 1930s Bachelard could respectably maintain that philosophy, while not reducible to science, should be identified with the philosophy of science.

SPIRITUALISM: RAVAISSON AND RENOUVIER

Spiritualism has a good claim to be the national philosophy of France. It is rooted in Descartes' assertion of the epistemic and

---

[14] One thinker who did defend a strong positivist position in the early 1900s was Félix Le Dantec (1869–1917). Parodi briefly summarizes his views in his survey of the contemporary scene; but then, in place of his usual critical assessment, he merely remarks, "it would be pointless to criticize such work" (*La philosophie contemporaine en France*, 57). The marginal place of positivism is also suggested by the two pages devoted to it in Lalande's *Vocabulaire*, in contrast to the four pages on spiritualism and the nine on idealism.

[15] For a long time, there was no sharp distinction drawn between psychology/sociology and philosophy. Even well into the twentieth century, Durkheim, Janet, and similar thinkers were routinely regarded as philosophers and included in standard surveys such as Parodi's *La philosophie contemporaine en France* and Isaac Benrubi's *Les Sources et les courants de la philosophie contemporaine en France*. Even today, the work of sociologists such as Pierre Bourdieu and Bruno Latour has a strong philosophical component.

metaphysical primacy of thought but does not require his mind–body dualism. The view is, in fact, consistent with any ontology that allows for these two central assertions: that the value of human existence derives from the higher mental faculties (both intellectual and affective) of individuals; and that these faculties are neither reducible to material processes (including sense experience) nor assimilable to a higher level of reality (the absolute). Spiritualism is thus an assertion of the metaphysical and ethical primacy of the individual mind (*l'esprit*), against the claims of materialism, empiricism, and certain sorts of idealism.

One of the earliest and most influential spiritualists was François Maine de Biran (1766–1824). Arguing against Locke, Hume, and, especially, Condillac and the *Idéologues*, he maintained that empiricist reductions of mental life to the flow of passing sense impressions were refuted by our experiences of willing (*effort voulu*), which reveal a persisting self continually straining against bodily resistance. In these experiences, a unified self or mind is revealed through what Maine de Biran calls our *sens intime* (inner awareness). Such inner experiences of human freedom remained the foundation of later spiritualist cases for the ultimate autonomy and value of the individual.

The spiritualist legacy reached early twentieth-century French philosophy primarily through Félix Ravaisson (1813–1900). Ravaisson never held a university chair (Cousin, who had initially helped advance his career, blocked the appointment). But he exercised major influence through a series of administrative positions: inspector of libraries, general inspector of higher education, and, most important, chair of the committee that set and graded the *agrégation* examination in philosophy. His interest in art led to scholarly work on Da Vinci and on ancient Greek sculpture and an appointment as curator at the Louvre, where he carried out a major restoration of the Venus de Milo.

In 1867, Ravaisson published his *La philosophie en France au XIXe siècle*, a report commissioned by the French government on the occasion of the Exposition of 1867. Surveying the history of French philosophy after 1800, he noted the dominant place of Comte's positivism and of its main rival, the eclecticism of Victor Cousin. Ravaisson argued that both these positions had failed and that exigencies of fact and argument were driving French philosophy toward the spiritualism that Maine de Biran had developed but his contemporaries ignored. Ravaisson predicted a new philosophical epoch dominated by what he called "spiritualistic realism or positivism"; that is, a philosophy that gives priority to spiritual "facts" in the same way that ordinary realism and positivism do to perceptual and scientific facts. Such an epoch would, he said, have as its "generating principle the consciousness that mind [*l'esprit*] has of itself, a self recognized as an existence from which all other existences derive and on which they depend, and which is nothing other than its own activity".[16]

His prediction was entirely correct. By 1890 Ravaisson's books were, in Parodi's words, "the breviaries of all the young philosophers"[17] and the philosophical agenda was being set by thinkers such as Lachelier, Boutroux, and Bergson (all students of Ravaisson at the École Normale), who were strongly sympathetic to the spiritualist view.

If, as Comte had famously said, materialism is the claim that the higher can be explained by the lower, spiritualism claims to explain the lower by the higher. Here, of course, the higher is the mind, but not the Cartesian mind that includes any experience whatsoever. The spiritualist mind is the locus of only the higher mental functions such as intelligence, will, and aesthetic appreciation. It does not include lower forms of mentality (e.g., sense perception and emotions), associated with our "animal" nature. The mind or spirit is, then, the locus of the "properly human" dimension of our experience. The project of spiritualism is, first, to describe, accurately and in detail, our experience of ourselves as spiritual beings; and second, to show that everything else (the realm of nature) is subordinated to and dependent on spirit. True to Maine de Biran's seminal descriptions, Ravaisson and his followers made freedom the fundamental feature of the mind, thereby placing creative action at the root of all reality. Whereas Maine de Biran understood freedom primarily in terms of the effort exerted by the will, Ravaisson emphasized the desire (and therefore the love of the good) behind this effort, a desire he saw as ultimately directed toward the perfect goodness of the Christian God.

Although Descartes can be readily regarded as the first French spiritualist, since he gave clear epistemic and metaphysical priority to intelligence and volition, Ravaisson replaced the Cartesian

---

[16] *La philosophie en France au XIXe siècle*, 275.
[17] *La philosophie contemporaine en France*, 29.

dualism of mind and matter as separable substances with a distinction between mental life and nature as two interdependent poles of activity. (Here he was influenced by the later philosophy of Schelling, with whom he had studied in Munich,[18] and by Aristotle's doctrine of form.[19]) This was the basis for his own introspective study of our experience of habit, a topic suggested by both Maine de Biran and Aristotle. Following Maine de Biran, he saw habit as a paradigm example of the union of the creative free agency of mind with the repetitive stability of the material world. In moving from knowledge based on explicit reflection to a habit of implicit understanding (as a cook might at first make crepes by meticulously following a recipe but later come to toss them off "by second nature"), we go from an external relation to the objects of our knowledge to "an immediate understanding in which object and subject are fused".[20] Here we are not far from the intuition of Bergson, who wrote an elegant and perceptive appreciation of Ravaisson when he succeeded him in the Académie des Sciences Morales et Politiques.[21]

Spiritualism was typically a conservative position, a comfortable intellectual niche for supporters of an elitist bourgeois politics and Catholic Christianity. But there was a more radical variant, that of Charles Renouvier (1815–1903), which, though always relatively marginal, eventually exerted significant influence. Renouvier was a student at the same time as Ravaisson at the École Normale. He was very active in politics at the time of the 1848 revolution but became disillusioned after Louis Napoléon's coup in 1851 destroyed hopes for a socialist democracy. He abandoned politics for philosophy, although he did later edit and publish a journal, *La critique philosophique*, aimed at a general intellectual audience. Renouvier never held an academic position (he had sufficient inherited wealth to

---

[18] We should not make too much of the personal contact with Schelling. As Bergson tells us, Ravaisson spent only a few weeks in Munich. Also, Schelling spoke French badly and Ravaisson was not much better at German. See Henri Bergson, "Notice sur la vie et les oeuvres de M. Félix Ravaisson-Mollien", in *La pensée et le mouvant*, reprinted in *Oeuvres*, 1458.

[19] Ravaisson first made his name with a two-volume commentary on Aristotle's *Metaphysics* (1837). He viewed Aristotle as the true founder of spiritualist philosophy because, even more than Plato, he overcame empiricism and materialism, by making forms the causes of the movements of real existents and locating formal perfection in the mental lives of individual intelligences. On this and other aspects of Ravaisson's thought, see Émile Boutroux's very helpful "La philosophie de Félix Ravaisson", in his *Nouvelles études d'histoire de la philosophie*, 194–220.

[20] Félix Ravaisson, *De l'habitude*, 37.

[21] Henri Bergson, "Notice sur la vie et les oeuvres de M. Félix Ravaisson-Mollien", in *La pensée et le mouvant*, reprinted in *Oeuvres*.

Fin-de-siècle: the professors of the Republic 13

make a profession unnecessary). After the coup, he left Paris for the south of France, where he had been born, and, working there in relative isolation, wrote continuously until his death in 1903, producing one of the largest oeuvres in the history of French philosophy.[22]

Renouvier tied his philosophy, which he characterized as "neo-criticism" (or, sometimes, "French criticism"), to that of Kant, although he does not seem to have penetrated very deeply into Kant's thought, which was more a starting-point than a continuing inspiration. What he took from Kant was mainly the idea of our phenomenal experience as structured by intellectual categories that are conditions of the possibility of this experience. He rejected Kant's noumenal world, maintaining that the phenomenal realm is the sole reality. He also saw phenomenal reality as fundamentally relational, excluding substance from the list of categories (and including becoming) and making relation the basic category of which all others are forms. These empiricist tendencies were, however, balanced by the addition of categories with a stronger metaphysical content than Kant's. Specifically, Renouvier introduced finality (purpose) and personality as essential structures of the phenomenal world. This led him to the characteristic spiritualist emphasis on the creative choices of individual minds as the driving force of reality.

Renouvier's ethical and political thought reflects the centrality of individual freedom.[23] But freedom is also a crucial epistemological category for him, since he holds that experience, even as informed by the system of categories, does not entirely determine what we must accept as the truth. Our judgments, from the lowest perceptions to the highest metaphysical speculations, always involve an irreducible element of free choice. Spiritualists such as Ravaisson were uneasy with this epistemological indeterminism and even more so with Renouvier's religious views.[24] His relativism left no place for a being of absolute perfection, such as the Christian God, and he also rejected the idea of an actual infinity – quantitative or qualitative – as incoherent. On the other hand, Renouvier thought that the

---

[22] Renouvier's most important work is his four-volume *Essais de critique générale*, Paris: 1854–64.
[23] William Logue, *Charles Renouvier: Philosopher of Liberty*, emphasizes Renouvier's ethics and politics and provides some useful historical background.
[24] Ravaisson offers a guardedly sympathetic treatment of Renouvier in his *La philosophie en France au XIXe siècle*, 110–18. This was probably the beginning of an awareness of Renouvier's work in the wider intellectual community.

impossibility of an actual infinity required a beginning of the universe in time and accepted personal immortality as necessary to make sense of moral obligations. This led him to assert the existence of God as creator and moral ideal, but he insisted that this being was finite in both knowledge and power (which finitude, he thought, provides the only plausible solution to the problem of evil). Moreover, God's creative role is consistent with human freedom since he is, as Renouvier put it, a "creator of creators".[25] Renouvier's heterodox theological views underlay his vigorous practical opposition to the power of the French Catholic Church, an opposition focused during the 1870s and 1880s in his journal, *La critique philosophique* (and its supplement, *La critique religieuse*), which followed a strongly anti-Catholic editorial policy.

Renouvier's lack of a position in the educational establishment, along with the unorthodoxy of his views, limited his influence on French philosophy. But the vigor of his thought – not to mention the huge amount he published over a period of sixty-one years – had an undeniable impact. He attracted a small group of disciples (and the strong admiration of William James) and eventually received some very belated official recognition, including election to the Académie des Sciences Morales et Politiques in 1900, at the age of eighty-five. His most important direct influence was on the work of Octave Hamelin, who offered a detailed analysis of Renouvier's work in his Sorbonne course of 1906–7 and whose own powerful philosophical system was strongly informed by Renouvier's work.[26]

IDEALISM: LACHELIER AND BOUTROUX

Mainline spiritualist thought had a natural tendency to idealism (and, indeed, Ravaisson sometimes called the view he championed idealism). But spiritualism allows the denial of the key idealist claim that ultimately only minds exist and is committed to a genuine plurality of individual persons and, especially, to a distinction between finite human minds and the infinite God that created them. (Hence the attraction of spiritualism for Catholic thinkers, including Ravaisson, Lachelier, and Blondel.) We need, therefore, to distin-

---

[25] Address to the Edinburgh Philosophical Society (1914), cited by J. Alexander Gunn, *Modern French Philosophy*, 294.
[26] Octave Hamelin, *Le système de Renouvier*. Hamelin also wrote important studies of the "systems" of Aristotle and Descartes.

guish at least between spiritualism and the absolute idealism of a Fichte or a Hegel.

In any case, idealism in France derived from appropriations of Kant, not Hegel, who had little influence there before the 1920s.[27] There were no translations of Hegel until 1859 (twenty-eight years after his death), and it was not until well into the twentieth century that full French versions of major books such as *The Phenomenology of Spirit*, *The Science of Logic*, and *The Philosophy of Right* were available. Even Kant's influence was slow in developing and became important only with Jules Lachelier (1832–1918), who presented a Kantian account of scientific reasoning in his thesis, *Du fondement de l'induction*, defended in 1871 and published the next year.[28]

Lachelier's thesis is an elegantly written *tour de force*, which, in the space of about 100 pages, expands an analysis of the problem of induction into a comprehensive idealist view of reality. The problem of induction is that of finding and justifying principles that warrant the move "from knowledge of facts to knowledge of the laws which order them" (*Du fondement de l'induction* [*FI*], 3/1). He endorses the common views that the conclusions of an inductive inference assert more than its premises and so cannot be grounded in the principles of deductive logic, and that inductive inferences require a principle of efficient causality, guaranteeing that the same phenomena will follow whenever the same antecedent conditions occur. But he argues that induction also requires a principle of final causality.

Efficient causality tells us only that *if* conditions are the same, the same results will follow. Successful induction also requires that we know that the conditions are the same. We can, of course, know from observation that conditions now *seem* to be the same as they were previously. But this gives no assurance that there are not *unobserved* conditions that make the situation different than it was previously. Lachelier gives the example of the biological law that members of a given species generally produce members of that same species. If all we knew was that the same phenomena follow if the

---

[27] Octave Hamelin (1856–1907), mentioned above, combined the spiritualism of Renouvier with something like Hegelian dialectic in his well-regarded *Essai sur les eléments principaux de la représentation* (1907). But Hamelin died early and his Hegelian tendencies had no extended influence.

[28] The index to Ravaisson's *La philosophie en France au XIXe siècle* shows the continuing dominance of pre-Kantian influences. It lists 6 references to Hegel, 7 to Kant, but 43 to Leibniz.

same conditions occur, "we would have to limit ourselves to asserting that the product of each generation would resemble its progenitors *if* all the required conditions come together". To go further and maintain that the new generation will actually be of the same species as the previous, we must also know that "all these conditions do in fact come together" (*FI*, 11/5). Since we cannot generally know this by direct observation, we must assume that there is a principle of order at work that guarantees the stability of species by maintaining the same conditions of generation. By such a principle, a feature of a whole (the stability of a species) determines the developments of its parts (the generation of individual organisms). Such determination is, according to Kant's definition, an instance of final causality. Although this example is biological, the point also holds for chemical and physical systems. Without a principle of final causality, we would know only a world of (efficient) causal relations among objects defined entirely by those relations. We would have no access to the familiar world of substantial objects that are the enduring instantiations of natural kinds.

There are, then, two principles required for successful inductive inference: one of efficient causality, "in virtue of which phenomena form a series wherein the existence of the preceding determines the existence of the following," and one of final causality, "in virtue of which these series, in their turn, form systems, in which the idea of the whole determines the existence of the parts" (*FI*, 12/6). But is there any way to justify these principles?

Lachelier thinks we can do so by showing that the principles are essential to the "concrete and particular acts by which thought constitutes itself while seizing immediately upon reality" (*FI*, 14/7). But neither empiricism nor rationalism can make the case. If, with empiricists, we hold that knowledge is merely of phenomenal appearances, then – as the failure of Mill's justification of induction shows – any argument for induction will have to be from phenomenal experience and therefore valid only if circular. If, on the contrary, as rationalists maintain, knowledge is of sensorily inaccessible things-in-themselves, then induction could in principle be justified on the basis of truths about the structure and stability of the substances or causes beneath appearances. But we have no access to such substances and causes, and evocation of them is merely "the assertion of a problem transformed into its solution" (*FI*, 36/20). (Lachelier also maintains that, even if there were, say, an intellectual intuition of things-in-themselves, this would still give them only as they appear to us intellectually at a given moment, not as they are apart from our experience of them.)

There is, however, another alternative, based on the Kantian claim "that whatever may be the mysterious foundation beneath phenomena, the order in which they follow each other is exclusively determined by the requirements of our own thought". To see if Kant might be right, Lachelier says that we should try to establish the two principles of induction "by showing that if they did not exist then human thought would not be possible" (*FI*, 42/23). A successful demonstration will confirm Kant's view of the active role of the mind in knowledge and justify induction.

Thought is about the phenomena (sensations) of our world. But a thought is not itself another phenomenon nor is it about just one phenomenon. It requires a subject, distinct from the succession of phenomena, that exists as a unity over against this succession. Traditional (pre-critical) views locate this distinctness and unity in the thinking subject's existence as a metaphysical substance separated from the world it experiences. But, given this separation, there is no way to understand how thought could ever know the world outside of it. It would have to remain enclosed in its own autonomous existence. For knowledge to be possible, thought must rather be a unity in virtue of its relation to the world of phenomena; that is, thought must be one precisely because it unites the succession of phenomena into a single world that is the object of its experience and knowledge. The unity of thought is not that of an autonomous metaphysical act but that of a form providing coherence and hence intelligibility to the flux of sensations.

Reflection on our experience immediately reveals that one aspect of this coherence and intelligibility is the single time and space in which phenomena occur. But, Lachelier argues, space and time alone are not sufficient to unify phenomena into a coherent world. Phenomena existing in the same space and time could still occur in total independence of one another and never provide a coherent object for thought. Phenomena must also be unified through their interconnection by laws of necessary causal succession. Such laws of efficient causality provide the unity needed for phenomena to be coherent objects of thought. "Thus, all phenomena are subject to the law of efficient causes, because this law is the only foundation to which we can attribute the unity of the universe, and in its turn this unity is the supreme condition of the possibility of thought" (*FI*, 47/ 26).

Lachelier further maintains that the phenomenal world, precisely because it is governed by efficient causality, must be a mechanistic world; that is, a world consisting entirely of motions determined by their antecedent motions. Phenomena occur in space and time; consequently their unity must be a unity that exists through space and time. But the only possible form of unity through space and time is continuous movement, understood as continuous change of spatial location over time. All phenomena must be movements. What we have, then, is a system of movements governed at every point and moment by strict laws of efficient causality: a mechanistic universe. Our Kantian turn seems to have led to what Lachelier calls an "idealistic materialism" (*FI*, 69/38). But we have not yet taken account of the role of final causality.

It might seem that we cannot effect a Kantian derivation of final causality since the distinctness and unity of the subject (and hence the possibility of thought) are guaranteed by efficient causality alone. But Lachelier maintains that the unity so guaranteed is "incomplete and superficial" (*FI*, 76/42). This is because an object given simply as part of a mechanical system of efficient causes is not given as a full-blooded thing in its own right (an instance of a structured kind) but only as, so to speak, a place-holder in the causal network. It has no intrinsic content but exists only through its causal relations to other items in the network. This corresponds to the point made above, in our analysis of inductive inference, that efficient causality by itself guarantees only that the same results follow from the same conditions, not that the same conditions will regularly recur; regular recurrence is necessary for the stability of enduring kinds. This sort of stability (or, equivalently, a world of things with enduring natures) is, as we have seen, guaranteed only by a principle of final causality. Lachelier acknowledges that thought could exist in the diminished world of mere efficient causality. But he maintains that this would be a "purely abstract existence", because it would be in a world with no substantial content. Such an existence "would be, so far as thought is concerned, a state of illusion and death" (*FI*, 79/44). He therefore concludes that the fully real (concrete) existence of consciousness requires a principle of final causality.

The reality of final causality radically transforms Lachelier's picture of the world. The truth of cosmic reality is not "idealistic materialism", which in fact expresses merely the abstract mechanical skeleton of a robust purposive nature. Movement still conforms to the patterns of mechanical laws, but it is now seen to be ultimately derived from forces that express the world's intrinsic teleology. These forces are not intervening outside causes; they flow directly from the internal organization of natural objects. Indeed, Lachelier insists that force is not a thing in itself but "only the tendency of movement toward an end" (*FI*, 93/51). Most important, the priority of (teleological) force over movement implies the priority of freedom over determinism. An end cannot externally determine the means (movements) that bring it about because the end does not exist until the means have produced it. Rather, "the means dispose themselves in the order fitted to realize the end" (*FI*, 87/48). Consequently, finality requires that the forces informing natural movements be spontaneous tendencies to the relevant ends. On the abstract level of efficient causes, the purely quantitative formal structures of natural developments are still mechanically determined. But the qualitative content of concrete things is the contingent product of spontaneous activity.[29]

Mere spontaneity is not full freedom. Every part of nature enjoys a certain freedom (and hence life and even thought) in that its goals are achieved by its innate tendency toward them, not by mechanistic determination. But freedom in its full sense consists "in the power of varying one's purposes and in conceiving new ideas" (*FI*, 97/53-4). Animals act with a freedom limited to the precise means of fulfilling goals set for them by nature, as when a bird chooses materials and locations for its nest. Rational beings such as humans, however, employ intelligence not just to achieve pre-given goals but also "to conceive an infinite number of pure ideas which our will then undertakes to realize externally" (*FI*, 98/54). Freedom properly understood is not, as so many philosophers have thought, the will's unconstrained choice of means of action; it is rather the intellect's invention of new goals of action. Lachelier argues that freedom in this sense is required by the principle of final causality "since the systematic unity of nature could not be realized except as the result of original invention and creations properly so-called" (*FI*, 97/54).

We see, then, the transformation effected by the need to include

---

[29] In his *Études sur le syllogisme*, Lachelier argues that the syllogism provides the appropriate logic for the qualitative while mathematical logic (including the logic of relations) is appropriate for the quantitative.

the principle of final causality in our account of knowledge and the world: "the realm of final causes, by penetrating the realm of efficient causes without destroying it, exchanges everywhere force for inertia, life for death, freedom for fatality" (*FI*, 101/56, translation modified). The result is no longer the "idealistic materialism" of the world as a nexus of efficient causes but what Lachelier calls a "spiritualistic realism", in which mechanism is subordinated to finality and "every being is a force, and every force is a thought which tends toward a more and more complete consciousness of itself" (*FI*, 102/56, translation modified). Lachelier's final insistence on "realism" rather than "idealism" reflects not an assertion of a reality independent of thought – he remains an idealist in rejecting this – but rather an insistence on the metaphysical autonomy of individual persons, which he refuses to assimilate to any absolute thought. This keeps open a path to Lachelier's Catholic commitment to an afterlife of personal salvation and immortality. But this is not a path that he thinks can be traveled by philosophical reflection since on it we "cross, by an act of moral faith, beyond the boundaries both of thought and of nature" (*FI*, 102/56).

Lachelier published very little beyond his thesis on induction,[30] but his influence was immense, particularly through his teaching at the École Normale, where he was *maître de conférences* (a post roughly equivalent to a Reader at a British university or an American associate professor) from 1864 to 1875, and, like Ravaisson, through his later position as chair of the committee that set the *agrégation* in philosophy. His writing and teaching set high standards of conceptual subtlety and rigor and also made serious engagement with Kant *de rigueur* among his pupils, including, most prominently, Boutroux and Bergson.[31]

Émile Boutroux (1845–1921) dominated the academic philosophy of the Third Republic through World War I. He followed his teacher, Lachelier, as *maître de conférences* at the École Normale (1877–86), where he taught Bergson, Blondel, and Durkheim. He

---

[30] We should, however, mention his famous article, "Psychologie et métaphysique" (translated as "Psychology and Metaphysics" in *The Philosophy of Jules Lachelier*), first published in 1885, in which Lachelier develops his idealism via a description of psychological experience (developed in opposition to positivist reductionism) and with a particular emphasis on the role of the will.

[31] Bergson was not formally a student of Lachelier, since he did not enter the École Normale until 1878, three years after Lachelier stopped teaching there. But Lachelier was a strong influence on Bergson, who dedicated his doctoral thesis to him.

formulated his major philosophical ideas in his thesis, *La contingence de les lois de la nature* (1874). His later work consisted of reformulations of these views (particularly in *De l'idée de loi naturelle dans la science et la philosophie contemporaine* [1895]) and numerous important studies in the history of philosophy (from 1888 to 1902 he was professor of the history of modern philosophy at the Sorbonne). Boutroux was also a leading figure in "official" French academic life, a role that, perhaps, led to his writing, in 1915, *Philosophy and War*, one of those unfortunate books connecting German aggression with German philosophy.[32]

Boutroux shared the general concern with the tension between science and freedom. He endorsed Lachelier's picture of a world in which free and purposive creativity had priority over the abstractions of scientific causality but was dissatisfied with Lachelier's Kantian willingness to accept a total scientific determinism for the phenomenal world. Because our lives are led in this world, Boutroux argues, this concession to determinism means that any given human action is the necessary product of past actions. Perhaps I have a noumenal nature (or character) that has been created by a choice outside the deterministic network. But then my freedom has been entirely spent in the creation of this character, which becomes the determining cause of all my individual actions. "A strange doctrine", he concludes, "one that regards . . . repentance, conquests of self, struggles between good and evil, as but the necessary events of a drama the issue of which has been decided upon beforehand". Moreover, Boutroux adds, even this character cannot be properly regarded as my free creation. As a part of the intelligible (phenomenal) world, it too must belong to a deterministic system. The Kantian effort at reconciliation of freedom and determinism succeeds only in placing freedom and hence "morality in a sphere inaccessible to human consciousness". As a result, "this hypothesis would prevent us from passing any moral judgment either on others or on ourselves".[33]

Boutroux concludes that the assertion of human freedom must be at the expense of a deterministic view of phenomena; to justify the claim that we are free, we must establish that the phenomenal world described by science is indeterministic. To say that the world is

[32] For an American example of this genre, see George Santayana, *Egotism and German Philosophy*.
[33] *La contingence de les lois de la nature*, 169, 170.

indeterministic is to say that the laws governing it are not necessary. Here Boutroux has in mind three senses of necessity: the analytic necessity of logical truth, the synthetic a priori necessity of Kantian truths about the conditions of possible experience, and the empirical necessity of de facto constant correlations.

He undertakes to show that, in all of these senses and at every level, there is no necessity in the world. His approach is nothing if not comprehensive and systematic.[34] It begins by distinguishing a series of six successively more specific levels of description. The first level (that of "being", in Boutroux's terminology) is simply that of an aggregate of separate individuals. Subsequent levels correspond to further specifications of these individuals. The second level (that of "genera") adds that the individuals have natures allowing them to be divided into qualitatively similar classes; the third (that of "matter") makes the individuals material beings, extended in space and time; the fourth (that of "bodies") adds that they are structured material substances, for example, atoms or compounds of atoms; the fifth (that of "life") that they are organisms; the sixth (that of "man") that they are intelligent. For each level, Boutroux argues that there is neither external nor internal necessity; that is, the level is not required to exist in virtue of a preceding level (external necessity), nor, given its existence, are there necessary laws governing its development (internal necessity). In so arguing, he must, of course, show that there is no external or internal necessity of any of the three types (analytic, synthetic a priori, and empirical). He must, then, provide six arguments against necessity for each level, for a grand total of thirty-six arguments. There are, however, just a few basic patterns to Boutroux's arguments.

These patterns are well illustrated in his treatment of being, the first level of reality. Here we begin with nothing more than a collection of individual beings and do not assume that they are intelligent, alive, substantial, material, or even grouped into distinct genera. Boutroux's first question is about external necessity: is there anything outside the realm of actual being (in the realm of mere possibility) that requires the existence of a collection of beings? Certainly, there is no analytic necessity, no contradiction in asserting that a given collection of beings does not exist. An existent is a

---

[34] Mathieu Schyns offers an excellent account of Boutroux's sometimes difficult argumentation in *La philosophie d'Émile Boutroux*.

synthesis of possibility and actuality (the actualization of a possibility), and there is no logical necessity for any such synthesis. Nor can it be maintained that the very possibility of experience requires the actuation of a specific set of possible beings. In the domain of experience, the possible is simply that which may or may not be given as an object of experience. Our experiential knowledge (science) tells us about connections that exist among the actualized possibilities, but the mere fact of experience does not require that certain possible beings be actualized. Nor, finally, is it possible to argue that we know as a matter of empirical fact that any of the objects of our experience *had* to be actualized.

So the existence of beings is a contingent fact, not an externally imposed necessity. But, given this existence, are there necessary laws for the development of a collection of beings (i.e., internal necessity)? Boutroux first argues that there can be no question of a logical necessity because developmental laws require us to think of the beings they govern as in certain respects stable and unchanging, whereas the mere idea of a collection of beings is consistent with their being in random flux. As to the possibility of a Kantian a priori causal connection, Boutroux agrees that the idea of a productive cause would have to be a priori, since it goes beyond anything given in our experience. But he notes that, precisely for this reason, we have no basis for postulating a metaphysical connection that is not grounded in experience. It might be maintained that there is still the empirical necessity of a scientific law, which is revealed by experience and does determine that one phenomenon follow upon another. But Boutroux argues, first, that even an exact correspondence between cause and effect would not prove a necessary connection. Even if, for example, observation of gases showed that the product of pressure and volume was always exactly equal to a constant multiplied by temperature, this might merely show that gases have always behaved this way; deviations might still be possible. But more important, he argues, is the fact that our observations are never able to show the exact validity of a law. We measure pressure, volume, and temperature only up to a certain range of uncertainty, and connections between these phenomena may be indeterminate precisely within this range.

Boutroux deploys similar arguments for the higher levels of reality. He excludes logical necessities of existence or developmental laws by showing that each successive level involves new features and laws that are not implied by the preceding levels. For example, a world of non-material genera and species is discontinuous, whereas a world of matter is extended and hence continuous; and matter may vary in size and position without changing qualitatively, so that the qualitative laws of non-material genera cannot determine purely quantitative relations among material entities. Kantian a priori claims of existence or causal connection he rejects by showing that our actual experience of phenomena does not support such claims. For example, although metaphysicians may understand the solubility of sugar in water in terms of unobservable powers informing these two substances, scientific observation reveals only that there is a constant correlation between sugar's melting and its being put into water. Finally, Boutroux rejects claims of empirical necessity by arguing, first, that experience never excludes the possibility that a given level of object might not exist. For example, even if we knew that living cells were the products of certain chemical reactions, we would not know that such reactions had to occur or that cells did not merely happen to follow from them. And Boutroux always excludes the empirical necessity of laws by appealing to the inexactness in our knowledge of the correlations they express. For the case of organisms, he suggests that the laws governing them (e.g., the law of adaptation, which says that species vary to survive in new circumstances) are so imprecise that biology does not in fact constitute a positive science.

Boutroux's defense of indeterminism has a distinctly positivist, anti-Kantian, anti-idealist bent. He takes for granted the authority of scientific descriptions, rejects logical analysis of concepts as irrelevant to questions of truth about the world, and insists on an empiricist reading of immediate experience that replaces Kantian necessities with Humean correlations. This positivist bent is even more obvious in *De l'idée de loi naturelle dans la science et la philosophie contemporaine*, where Boutroux makes his case by a direct analysis of scientific results rather than by abstract philosophical argumentation.[35] But his account is also relentlessly anti-reductive, with each successive level of reality distinguished by new traits (the continuity of matter, the self-determination of life, the moral freedom of human beings) that cannot be explained via "lower" categories. Moreover,

---

[35] Here, as we shall see, Boutroux's views have important similarities to those of his brother-in-law – with whom he also had close intellectual contacts – Henri Poincaré.

the distinctive features of each ontological level are always further and richer achievements of freedom. Boutroux deploys positivist epistemology in the service of spiritualist ontology. Ravaisson and Lachelier might well question his means, but they would agree with his result.

CHAPTER 2

Science and idealism

> It's like the rules of logic or scientific laws, reality conforms to them more or less, but remember the great mathematician Poincaré: he's by no means certain that mathematics is a rigorously exact science.
> (Marcel Proust, *In Search of Lost Time*, III, 149)

The narrative of French philosophy during the first two decades of the twentieth century consists of three intertwined stories: the development of philosophy of science as an independent discipline, the solidification of university idealism in the philosophy of Léon Brunschvicg, and the brilliant rise of Bergson's spiritualist metaphysics. This chapter treats the first two topics, and the following chapter is devoted to Bergson.

PHILOSOPHERS OF SCIENCE: POINCARÉ, DUHEM, AND MEYERSON

Although French philosophers firmly rejected positivism, they still recognized the centrality of science for philosophical reflection. Lachelier and Boutroux, in particular, insisted on the need to construct a unified account of nature that showed how the truths of science and of human freedom combined in a coherent whole. Such a synthesis involved exhibiting the limitations of science (indeterminism, absence of finality) that require us to complement it with metaphysical accounts if we are to describe the full concreteness of reality. This enterprise of developing a metaphysics of nature called for serious philosophical reflection on scientific knowing, which in turn required a thorough acquaintance with the methods and results of science. Moreover, the survival of the Comtean idea that science had to be understood as a historical phenomenon[1] led to a rapid development of the epistemology of science, a historically based effort to understand the structure of science as a cognitive enterprise. In principle, the new epistemology of science could have remained entirely subordinated to the goals of the metaphysics of nature. In practice, it emerged as more and more an autonomous study of science in its own terms, with decreasing concern for including scientific results in a synthetic metaphysical view of nature as a concrete whole.

The move to autonomy is perhaps clearest in the philosophical reflections of Henri Poincaré (1854–1912). As a distinguished mathematician and scientist, Poincaré had little training in philosophy and no interest in the spiritualist and idealist orientation of philosophers such as Ravaisson and Lachelier. (Neither are mentioned in his three main books on philosophy of science, and even Bergson receives only one passing reference.) On the other hand, Poincaré was well aware of current philosophical issues about the nature and limitations of science and was very sympathetic to the ideas of Boutroux, his friend and brother-in-law, about the contingency of laws. Poincaré's writings on methodological topics set a model for a new philosophical approach to science, one that placed a high premium on careful discussion of the conceptual foundations of particular theories and, on this basis, developed sophisticated analyses of the key concepts of observation, law, theory, and explanation. He was, along with Mach and Duhem, a founder of the philosophy of science that became so central in twentieth-century analytic philosophy.

Poincaré was, however, less naively empiricist than the early logical positivist philosophers of science who came after him. Reflecting the Kantianism of his milieu, he acknowledges the role of theoretical interpretation in scientific observation, and his sophisticated conventionalism gives the mind an active role in the constitution of empirical objects and truth. But his work derives more from reflection on scientific practice than from philosophical principle, leading him, for example, to different accounts of conventions in geometrical axioms, empirical generalizations, and theories; and his a priori categories, such as simplicity, are more a function of pragmatic utility than of transcendental conditions of experience.

---

[1] In the first lesson of his *Course in Positive Philosophy* (1830–42), Comte had emphasized the need to trace "the course actually followed by the human mind in action, through the examination of the methods really employed to obtain the exact knowledge that it has already acquired" (*The Essential Comte*, 32).

Among Poincaré's most important views are his account of the roles of hypotheses in science and his defense of the objectivity of scientific knowledge. In *La science et l'hypothèse*, he distinguishes several kinds of hypotheses, each with a distinctive and essential role in scientific inquiry (*La science et l'hypothèse* [*SH*], 3/28). The first kind comprises general claims testable by observation. They are essential to science's project of foreseeing the future, an enterprise inconsistent with the popular view of science as simply a body of certain facts, proven by observation. General empirical hypotheses are by their very nature an extrapolation beyond what observation gives and so are always open to refutation by subsequent experience. They are most often explicitly formulated generalizations, supported but not logically entailed by experimental data; for example, Kepler's laws of planetary motion, based on Tycho Brahe's observations of the solar system. There are also unconscious hypotheses of this sort, unthinking assumptions, often engrained in our language, about how nature must behave. (Poincaré cites examples from Ampère's work on electrodynamics and notes the value of rigorous mathematical formulations in bringing such assumptions to light.) Poincaré notes that scientists should try to make hypotheses one at a time, so that they will know just what has been refuted by a negative experimental result. (Duhem, as we shall see, will question whether this is in fact possible.) Poincaré argues that a falsified hypothesis is not a failure of science. A scientific hypothesis is formulated on the basis of what we have reason to expect, and the failure of our expectations points to the existence of a new phenomenon that represents an advance in our knowledge. He also distinguishes a subclass of empirical hypotheses that are "perfectly natural and from which one can hardly escape" (*SH*, 187/135). Examples of such assumptions (no doubt often unconscious precisely because they are so natural) are that the influence of very distant bodies is negligible, that quantitative effects vary continuously with their causes, and that nature behaves according to basic principles of symmetry. Such hypotheses, for all their obviousness, may turn out to be falsified by observation, although they are so fundamental that "they are the last that ought to be abandoned" (*SH*, 188/135).

Poincaré also thinks that some scientific hypotheses are not empirically testable at all. The most important examples are claims that seem to be substantive empirical hypotheses but turn out to be "reducible to disguised definitions or conventions" (*SH*, 3/28).

Consider, for example, the question of the geometrical structure of physical space. For a long time, there seemed to be no doubt that this was Euclidean, since there seemed to be no coherent alternative to the familiar axioms of Euclidean geometry (such as, for example, that two lines intersect in at most one point). The only question concerned the nature of the necessity of these axioms: were they analytic truths, derivable from the very definitions of basic geometrical terms (as Leibniz held) or were they, as Kant maintained, synthetic a priori truths required as conditions of possible experience? But according to Poincaré, the development in the nineteenth century of alternative, non-Euclidean geometries refuted both of these claims by showing that the Euclidean axioms were not necessary. Such geometries contained axioms contrary to those of Euclid (those of Riemannian geometry, for example, allowed distinct lines to intersect in more than one point) and could, moreover, be proved to be self-consistent if Euclidean geometry was. This put them on a logical and conceptual par with Euclidean geometry.

Of course, even if Euclidean geometry is not the only conceptual possibility, it might seem to be the only one supported by empirical evidence. Do precise measurements not show, for example, that the three interior angles of a triangle add up to 180 degrees? (Non-Euclidean geometries require sums lesser or greater than 180 degrees.) One difficulty with this idea – suggested by Boutroux's treatment of measurement – is that the non-Euclidean nature of physical geometry might be apparent only beyond the limits of the accuracy of our current measurements. But according to Poincaré even unlimited accuracy in measurement could not establish the empirical truth of one geometry over another because we would always be free to reinterpret the metric (that is, the way in which measuring instruments vary in different parts of space) used to make the measurements. Perhaps, for example, if we assume that our measuring rods are perfectly rigid bodies, our measurements will support Euclidean geometry. But the very same measurements will support a non-Euclidean geometry on the assumption that the lengths of our rods vary with their position. (We might, of course, try to measure our measuring rods at various locations – say by timing light rays that we shot back and forth along their length. But the result of these meta-measurements would depend on equally untestable assumptions about the speed and straightness of the light rays.) Poincaré concludes, then, that the question of the geometry of physical space can be resolved only by our specifying a *convention*.

This does not, he insists, put the nature of space up to our arbitrary choice. Our choice of a convention is not a whim; it is based on powerful considerations of convenience (e.g., simplicity). Our choice is free in the sense of not compelled by logic or observed facts, but it is not arbitrary. In fact, Poincaré maintains that "Euclidean geometry is, and will remain, the most convenient" (*SH*, 70/65), not only because of our familiarity with it and its obvious adequacy to everyday experiences, but also because of its greater intrinsic simplicity.[2]

Poincaré also thinks that some of the fundamental principles of physics are conventional. Here we often begin with an empirical hypothesis, say that bodies attract one another in inverse proportion to their distance or that energy is conserved in closed systems. There is considerable evidence for the hypothesis; it has very fruitful consequences and eventually becomes central to our way of thinking about physical phenomena. At this point, we begin maintaining the hypothesis even in the face of contrary evidence. If two bodies seem to move according to something other than the inverse square law, we take this as evidence that there are other forces operative, not that the law is invalid. If energy seems not to be conserved, we assume that the system is not closed. Eventually, what was an empirical hypothesis becomes a principle true by definition, and the rest of our physics is built around it. (We can, of course, decide to cease treating a principle as a definition, but that too is a conventional decision.) Poincaré showed how the history of modern physics supports his distinction between empirical hypotheses and definitional principles.

Poincaré was forced to a careful consideration of the objectivity of science by the writings of one of his students, a brilliant mathematician-turned-philosopher, Édouard Le Roy. Le Roy argued that Poincaré's demonstration of the conventionality of certain scientific principles should be extended to all of science: "the scientist creates [*fait*] the order and determinism that he imagines he discovers in things".[3] Why, after all, can we not extend to all scientific claims the

---

[2] This view has, of course, been proven wrong, at least for the purposes of theoretical physics, by the general theory of relativity, which describes the universe in terms of a Riemannian geometry of variable curvature.

[3] Édouard Le Roy, "Science et philosophie", 513.

analysis that Poincaré gives for the law of gravitation and the conservation of energy? It may seem that this suggestion misunderstands Poincaré's analysis. The conventional character of certain scientific hypotheses was uncovered, in effect, by separating them into two components, one conventional, the other empirical. So, Poincaré points out (*La valeur de la science* [*VS*], 260/334–5), the statement *The stars obey Newton's laws* is broken up into: *Gravitation obeys Newton's laws* and *Gravitation is the only force acting on the stars*. The first component statement may be treated as a conventional definition, but then the second must be regarded as an empirical hypothesis, falsifiable by observation. The latter, then, remains as a claim of fact on which the truth of the Newtonian theory depends.

But such a response will not satisfy Le Roy, who maintains that even scientific facts are created by the scientist: "Far from being imposed on him from outside, scientific facts are, in truth, made [*faits*] by the scientist who asserts them."[4] Here Le Roy's thought, inspired by Bergson, is that the sole reality truly given to the mind is an unstructured continuum of passing time (*la durée*).[5] This continuum is not accessible to the intellect and is revealed only by an extra-intellectual intuition. All the structures of science are imposed by the mind on this continuum: "The facts are carved out [*taillés*] by the mind in the amorphous matter of the Given."[6] If so, there are no objectively given scientific facts, merely the free decisions of the intellect to divide reality up in certain conventional ways. The point of this division is to provide us with rules of action as guides toward practical goals. The rules work, but only because we have formulated them so that they will. As a result, "our calculations are not, properly speaking, true, but they are effective. Their favorable results are less the success of our science than of our action."[7]

Poincaré's immediate response to this extreme claim is that the very success of our rules of action is proof that science is not purely our creation: "If science did not succeed, it could not serve as [a] rule of action." Further, the practical success of science derives from its ability to predict the future. Accordingly, "there is no escape from this dilemma: either science does not enable us to foresee, and then it is valueless as a rule of action; or else it enables us to foresee . . .

---

[4] "Un positivisme nouveau", 145.
[5] See below, chapter 3.
[6] "Science et philosophie", 517.
[7] "La Science positive et la liberté", 338–9.

and then it is not without value as [a] means of knowledge" (*VS*, 240–1/324).

This response is effective in principle, but how do we know that it does not tell against Poincaré as well as Le Roy? Perhaps Poincaré's introduction of convention into our understanding of science undermines the idea of an objective scientific fact and makes even his own position vulnerable to his dilemma. To respond adequately to Le Roy, Poincaré needs an account of the nature of scientific facts.

He has such an account, based on a distinction, acknowledged by Le Roy, between brute facts (*les faits bruts*) and scientific facts. Poincaré's complaint against Le Roy is that he tries to separate entirely the brute fact from scientific work, so that the first exercises no constraint on the second. Poincaré maintains that a scientific fact is simply a translation of a brute fact into a particular (scientific) language and, as such, has to follow constraints imposed by the brute fact. He offers the example of the "facts" about an eclipse of the sun. There is a continuum, beginning with the common-sense fact that it is getting dark, and moving through ever higher levels of scientific interpretation such as, *An eclipse occurred at nine o'clock*, *An eclipse occurred at the time predicted by Newton's laws*, and *The eclipse occurred because of the earth's revolution around the sun*. In fact, even our first "common-sense" fact involves a minimal interpretation of "the impression of obscurity" (*VS*, 245/327), so that it is really this impression rather than the assertion "It is getting dark" that is the brute fact. At each stage beyond the sheer impression of darkness, this brute fact is expressed in increasingly rich and nuanced language. But, Poincaré maintains, each such expression is constrained by the brute fact it is trying to formulate. Granted, we choose to express the fact through the simple qualitative categories of dark and light or through the far more sophisticated categories of the heliocentric theory. But in all cases, given the categories we have chosen, some formulations are better than others (it would not do to say *It is getting lighter* or *The sun is in front of the moon*); and this is because of the controlling role of the brute fact we are trying to express.

This response makes scientific and common sense, but it scarcely resolves the philosophical problems raised by Le Roy's position. For the dispute between him and Poincaré depends on the nature of "brute facts": whether there are any such things and, if there are, whether they have the minimal conceptual structure required to constrain "scientific facts". Resolving such issues would require a much closer probing than Poincaré is prepared to undertake of the precise nature of the concrete experience in which we encounter alleged "brute facts". Such probing will be a high priority for subsequent philosophers of experience such as Bergson and, later, Sartre and Merleau-Ponty. But Poincaré has little interest in the nature of experience, just as he has little interest in Kantian questions about the conditions of possible experience. He is, perhaps rightly, content with our humdrum, common-sense understanding of "fact" and "experience".

Pierre Duhem (1861–1916) was also a prominent scientist (and an even more prominent historian of science), but, unlike Poincaré, very interested in fundamental issues of epistemology and metaphysics. Nonetheless, his work, like Poincaré's, helped constitute philosophy of science as an autonomous discipline. In *La théorie physique* Duhem insisted on a sharp split between the world known by science and the world of metaphysical truth. In his view, the object of science was merely the sensory appearances of things. The real world beneath these appearances – for Duhem a domain of Aristotelian substances – was inaccessible to scientific scrutiny although open to nonempirical philosophical reasoning. Duhem enforced this epistemological dualism with his contention that empirical science has no explanatory capacity. To explain is to trace phenomena back to their real causes in the realm of metaphysical substances. Science, having no access to such causes, can merely formulate and systematize empirical generalizations describing the phenomena.

According to Duhem, scientific practice has often been confused by efforts to use theories to explain. To eliminate this confusion, he distinguishes between the explanatory and the representational aspects of any given theory. What a theory represents are phenomena. Science concerns itself with measurable features of the phenomenal world and associates them with mathematical symbols. These symbols, in turn, are connected to one another in mathematical propositions. The propositions are formed with a view to logical consistency and considerations of convenience (e.g., simplicity). They are also constructed in the hope that conclusions deduced from them will, when translated back into observational terms, accord with experienced phenomena. Duhem insists, however, that there is no reason to think there is one particular set of mathematical propositions observationally superior to all other sets. Many different ways of representing phenomena mathematically would yield interesting and useful conformities with the phenomena. There is, accordingly, no reason to think that the mathematical structures of even the most empirically successful theory tell us what underlies and explains phenomena. Those who speak of theories as explaining phenomena, rather than just describing and predicting them, misunderstand the significance of theory construction. Such misunderstanding leads to a fruitless concern with the details of theoretical structures, based on the false idea that these details provide the deep truth about nature. In fact they are just convenient – and hardly unique – tools for representing phenomena.

Corresponding to Duhem's distinction between experienced phenomena and theoretical representation is his distinction between "practical facts" and "theoretical facts". A practical fact is a description of phenomena in ordinary observational language (for example, *This paperweight is heavy*, or a basic generalization such as *Heavy objects fall to earth when dropped*). A theoretical fact is the translation of the practical fact into a symbolic language (for example, *This body of mass* m *is being acted on by a force* g). This distinction is very similar to Poincaré's between "brute facts" and "scientific facts", but in his *La théorie physique*, Duhem rejects Poincaré's view that the scientific description is *merely* a (convenient) translation of the brute fact.[8] He points out that, just as there are numerous alternative scientific descriptions of any given brute fact, so too there are numerous brute facts with the same scientific description. *There is a current of* n *amps in the circuit*, for example, translates brute facts about the behavior of any number of experimental set-ups for measuring electric current. Poincaré admits this but says that it merely reflects the variety of laws connecting currents with different ways of measuring them. Duhem agrees but maintains that this shows that our theoretical description of the brute fact as a current in a circuit is not a mere translation but a complex theoretical interpretation of the fact. His conclusion is that theoretical facts are not basic scientific truths; they are already complicated instruments of calculation that have no truth value in their own right.

It follows directly that scientific laws and theories cannot be

---

[8] See Duhem's comments on Poincaré's distinction in *The Aim and Structure of Physical Theory* [*La théorie physique*], 149–51.

regarded as simply inductive generalizations from observed (practical) facts. The initial scientific descriptions of such facts already assume a theory about them. But Duhem does not see this as showing that laws and theories are, as Le Roy maintains, the arbitrary creations of our minds. As we have seen, laws and theories can be rejected if they have consequences that, when translated back into the language of practical facts, turn out to be false. Of course, Duhem also famously holds that there can never be a decisive refutation of any single theoretical hypothesis because any empirically meaningful deduction will require several hypotheses to derive its conclusion. (There will, for example, be hypotheses giving theoretical descriptions of our measuring apparatus or stating the absence of various distorting forces.) Any empirical refutation will show only that at least one of the relevant hypotheses is false. Duhem's point here, however, is not the skeptical one that no test can justify rejecting a hypothesis. He is simply noting the inadequacy of pure logic to ground such a rejection. There is, he says, such a thing as "good sense", which enables us to make rational judgments about cases "that do not fall under the hammer of the principle of contradiction".[9] It may be difficult for scientists to achieve consensus about such cases, but eventually there will emerge a shared judgment about what it is rational to conclude.[10]

Duhem's account of science is, as he emphasizes, strictly positivist in the sense that it rejects any underlying ontology for scientific theories. The metaphysical content of science is nothing beyond the common-sense world given in the "practical facts" of ordinary experience. Theories function simply as instruments of calculation without revealing the reality beneath the appearances of ordinary experience, which is why they have no explanatory force. Scientific results are, therefore, strictly independent of any metaphysical claims: they can neither establish nor refute any theory about the real natures of things. But Duhem thinks nonetheless that we can

---

[9] *The Aim and Structure of Physical Theory*, 217.
[10] On a related issue, Duhem agrees with Poincaré that there are cases of theoretical principles that are not open to empirical refutation because they come to have the status of definitions. But he rejects Poincaré's view that there are some principles (e.g., the axioms of Euclidean geometry) so entrenched in our thought that we could never reject them. "The history of physics shows us that very often the human mind has been led to overthrow such principles completely, though they have been regarded by common consent for centuries as inviolable axioms" (*The Aim and Structure of Physical Theory*, 212).

have knowledge of the reality beneath appearances and that, moreover, scientific results are not irrelevant to that knowledge.

Developing a metaphysical account (or, as Duhem often puts it, a cosmology) requires first of all close attention to the practical facts given in experience, apart from any theoretical interpretations. These common-sense truths are the fundamental data of metaphysics. The trick is to separate them from the theoretical accretions that we so easily confuse with the plain truth. Here is required the finesse of the subtle and imaginative mind (*l'esprit de finesse*), as opposed to the logical rigor of the geometrical mind (*l'esprit géométrique*).[11] Given an adequate grasp of the practical facts, pure reason can penetrate to an understanding of the metaphysical reality lying beneath them. For Duhem, the core of Aristotle's philosophy of nature is still the best expression of metaphysical truth, although this truth must be separated from the mass of outdated science that Aristotle and his successors built up around it.

Duhem recognizes our inveterate tendency to move from the predictive success of scientific theories to a belief that they are true, to assume, as he puts it, that our most successful theories provide a "natural classification" of objects, rather than just a convenient but dispensable system of conceptual organization. He insists that this move is a matter of faith rather than knowledge; ontological inferences from even the best current theory are ungrounded, since the problems of the moment often require theoretical structures that will have to be subsequently abandoned. But he also agrees that it is possible to construct good metaphysical arguments from the history of science, when, as in fact happens, this history exhibits a convergence toward a single unified theory of all natural phenomena. There is absolutely no empirical, scientific reason to explain or expect such convergence – no reason why adequate description of the phenomena should not require two or more mutually irreducible theoretical systems. But the fact of convergence supports the conclusion that there is a coherent reality underlying the world of appearances. Moreover, Duhem maintains, there will be an analogy between the scientific theory that gives an ideally adequate description of phenomena and the cosmology that explains why the phenomena are as they are. With a thorough grounding in

---

[11] For Duhem's version of this Pascalian distinction and his application of it to the history of science, see *The Aim and Structure of Physical Theory*, chapter 4.

the history of science, we can discern an overall direction in the development of theoretical structures, from which we can make an educated guess about what would be the nature of an ideally adequate theory. His own reading of the historical data was that the convergence is not toward modern atomistic theories but toward a generalized thermodynamics strongly analogous to Aristotelian natural philosophy.

Duhem's endorsement of Aristotelianism is not unconnected with his Catholic religious faith. Certainly, he saw his belief as requiring a "spiritualist" metaphysics such as he found in Aristotle and his medieval successors, as opposed, say, to a metaphysical materialism or naturalism. Nor did Duhem deny that it was important to his faith to show that there could be no contradictions between Catholic doctrines and scientific results. But he insists that his view of science was developed in complete independence of his religious commitment and should be entirely convincing to nonbelievers. In this sense, it is not, as Abel Rey suggested, the "physics of a believer".[12]

Duhem's positivist rejection of science as explanatory and realistic was challenged by the work, likewise deeply informed by the history of science, of Émile Meyerson (1859–1933). Meyerson first argues that explanation has been the consistent aim of science throughout its history. Scientists from Aristotle through Galileo and Newton to Maxwell and Einstein have tried to discover the true nature of physical reality and to use this as a basis for explaining observed phenomena. Duhem, of course, agrees but sees the drive for explanation as a dead-end that has distracted scientists from their true business of describing phenomena. But according to Meyerson, when scientists "describe" phenomena they are really replacing the inadequate interpretations of common sense with more accurate scientific interpretations. He accepts the distinction between brute or practical facts and theoretical or scientific facts and agrees with Duhem that the distinction is between two different interpretations. "The scientist *makes* scientific facts and not brute facts", but, in

---

[12] Abel Rey, "La philosophie scientifique de M. Duhem", 44ff and 133ff. Duhem's response, "The Physics of a Believer", is included as an appendix to *The Aim and Structure of Physical Theory*. Édouard Le Roy was likewise a strongly committed Catholic (although, unlike Duhem, he was a strong opponent of scholastic Aristotelianism). He also insisted that his hyper-conventionalist view of science did not derive from his religious faith. On the other hand, Le Roy's extension of his conventionalism to religious dogmas, which he presented as merely rules for guiding action, resulted in his views being included in Pius X's condemnation of modernism (in his encyclical "Pascendi gregis" of 1907).

making a scientific fact, the scientist "has exactly followed the same process which common sense employed in creating the brute fact" and has thereby produced an improved version of practical facts.[13] The resulting theoretical facts are, therefore, better descriptions of physical reality and, as such, have the ontological significance that Duhem accords to practical facts: they are data from which we must construct a metaphysical cosmology. It follows that this construction is carried out not by transempirical metaphysics but by theoretical science itself.

Meyerson's realistic view of theory is intimately connected to his famous thesis that to explain is to identify. According to this thesis, to explain a phenomenon scientifically is to identify it with a theoretical description that replaces our common-sense description. So, for example, the kinetic theory explains heat by identifying it as the motion of molecules, and electromagnetic theory explains the current in a circuit by identifying it with the flow of electrons. Meyerson supports this thesis through detailed historical studies of chemical and physical theories, studies that challenge Duhem's positivist histories.[14] He also uses the thesis to argue that a surd of irrationality underlies the scientific enterprise. Since to explain is to identify, a total explanation of the universe would require reducing it to a sheer undifferentiated unity. This, however, contradicts the plurality of objects that always confronts science and that, accordingly, poses an impassable limit on rational explanation.

Despite important disagreements among themselves, Poincaré, Duhem, and Meyerson represent a single new and distinctive approach to philosophical reflection on science. They are positivist in their effort to avoid metaphysical assumptions and empiricist in their insistence on the central role of observation and experiment. But their positivism does not extend to the dogmatic elimination of all metaphysical inquiry and their empiricism is a sophisticated sort that allows for the mind's active role in the constitution of both theory and experience. They also all emphasize the need for philosophers of science to operate out of an intimate acquaintance with the actual practice of science, both historical and contemporary. Not only the spirit of their approach but also many of their specific

---

[13] Émile Meyerson, *Identity and Reality*, 378.
[14] These studies are found both in *Identité et réalité* and, especially, in *De l'explication dans les sciences*. Later, in *La déduction relativiste*, he supports his views by an analysis of Einstein's theory of relativity.

formulations of problems and solutions are directly relevant to contemporary discussions, and their thought has maintained a significance outside of France unusual in French thinkers of their period.

At the same time, its positivism and empiricism separated the new philosophy of science from the spiritualism and idealism that continued to define mainline French philosophy in the Third Republic. The separation was deepened by the specialized training in science and its history that the new discipline required.[15] Bergson and Brunschvicg combined traditional interests with specialized work on scientific issues. Eventually, however, French philosophy of science became a nearly autonomous domain, respected and influential in the French university, but, especially after the rise of existential philosophy, mostly left to a small circle of specialists. Gaston Bachelard and Georges Canguilhem were, as we shall see, important figures in the general education of successive generations of students at the Sorbonne. But, apart from the exceptional case of Michel Foucault, they had relatively little influence on existentialist and post-structuralist philosophers dominant from the 1940s on. Outside of France, after the rise of logical positivism, philosophy of science took a formal, non-historical turn for which the French tradition was uncongenial. The French in turn were disdainful of what they saw as the naive epistemological foundationalism of logical positivism and its insensitivity to the actual practice of science. Later, when the historicist reaction against positivism took hold, English-speaking philosophers of science rediscovered major themes articulated long before by the French tradition, such as the theory-ladenness of observation and the irreducibility of scientific rationality to logic. But by then the two approaches were too far apart for fruitful interaction. The French could hardly share the excitement of what they rightly saw as old news;[16] and the British and Americans had scant interest in discussions which, if they read them at all, lacked

---

[15] Also relevant here is the fact that Poincaré, Duhem, and Meyerson were all, in different ways, outsiders to the close community of the philosophers of the Third Republic. All were trained in science rather than philosophy. Duhem, at least partly because of his conservative religious and political views, never received a call to Paris and remained throughout his career at the provincial university of Bordeaux. Meyerson was born in Lublin, Russia (now Poland), educated in Germany, and never held a teaching position in France.
[16] When George Steiner chided Foucault for (in *Les mots et les choses*) not mentioning Kuhn, Foucault responded that he had instead cited a thinker who had anticipated Kuhn, Georges Canguilhem ("Foucault responds 2", 60).

the analytic clarity and rigor to which they were accustomed and that ignored logical positivist philosophy of science as hardly worth refuting.[17]

BRUNSCHVICG

Léon Brunschvicg (1869–1944) was the leading representative of university idealism. As a professor of philosophy at the Sorbonne from 1900 to 1939, he exercised immense influence, and every aspiring French philosopher, from Marcel to Sartre and Merleau-Ponty, had to come to terms with his thought. Brunschvicg was famous as an editor of Pascal and a historian of philosophy (particularly that of Spinoza), but the heart of his work was the "critical idealism" he developed and defended throughout his career. The root and foundation of critical idealism is his thesis, *La modalité du jugement*, completed when Brunschvicg was only twenty-eight years old. What might seem to be merely a specialized monograph on modality is in fact an outline of an entire philosophy.

Brunschvicg's idealism is based, first of all, on a thorough rejection of the thing-in-itself. He finds no sense in the idea that we could have any knowledge of something as it exists entirely apart from its relation to our knowledge. "Knowledge is not an accident that is added on from outside a being" but rather "constitutes a world that is the world for us", for "a thing outside of knowledge would be by definition inaccessible, indeterminable, that is to say equivalent for us to nothing" (*La modalité du jugement* [*MJ*], 2). Further, Brunschvicg does not reject external, material realities in favor of an internal, spiritual reality. A substantial subject of experience would be just as much a thing-in-itself as the external substances posited by realism. A consistent idealism must see *all* beings as the objects of a thought that is itself a function or act of thinking, not an independently existing thing.

Whereas natural sciences are concerned with the objects of thought, philosophy is concerned with thought itself, the intellectual activity through which objects are presented to (constituted for) us. It

---

[17] Anglophones may also have been put off by the fact that, during the 1960s and 1970s, a number of French students of philosophy of science (or, as the French say, *l'épistémologie*) were followers of Louis Althusser's structuralist Marxism, which appropriated some key concepts of Gaston Bachelard, by then the most influential French philosopher of science. See below, chapter 8.

may seem that characterizing the activity of thought as "intellectual" begs important questions about its nature, but Brunschvicg is prepared to argue that thinking is identical with judging, the quintessential intellectual activity. Since philosophy itself is an example of intellectual activity, it follows that it is an essentially reflective enterprise: "Intellectual activity becoming aware of itself [*prenant conscience d'elle-même*] . . . – that's what philosophy is" (*MJ*, 4).

Brunschvicg tries to establish his central claim that thinking is judging by arguing that the other two traditional elements of thought, concepts and reasoning, are reducible to judgment. Philosophers have perennially argued over whether concepts should be defined by their extension (nominalism) or by their comprehension (realism). But according to Brunschvicg the premise of this venerable debate is wrong. There is no need or possibility of reducing a concept to either the individuals that fall under it or the properties that describe those individuals. Rather, a concept is precisely the *linking* of a certain set of properties to a certain set of individuals. "To conceive *man* is to unite together certain characteristics and certain individuals [and] to assert these characteristics of these individuals." But such an assertion is precisely what is meant by a judgment, so "we can say without paradox that to conceive is to judge" (*MJ*, 8).

We are inclined to think that deductive reasoning is a matter of connecting two or more judgments so as to derive yet another judgment. Now a connection of two judgments cannot be itself a judgment, since a judgment unites two terms (a subject and a predicate), not two judgments. So it would seem that an instance of deductive reasoning must be something other than a judgment. Brunschvicg, however, maintains that deductive reasoning is not a matter of connecting two or more judgments but of making a single judgment. Consider, for example, a standard syllogism: All philosophers are just; Socrates is a philosopher; therefore, Socrates is just. On Brunschvicg's analysis, this syllogism expresses the single judgment, *Socrates is just*. The two premises of the syllogism merely explicate this judgment by noting, first, that the characteristic *being just* (the predicate of the judgment) is included in the characteristic *being a philosopher* and, second, that Socrates (the subject of the judgment) is an instance of the general subject, *a philosopher*. Because of this, the judgment, *Socrates is just*, can also be expressed as *This philosopher* (i.e., Socrates) *has the characteristic of being a philosopher* (which includes being just). When we reason deductively, we begin with the first form of the judgment (expressed in the premises) and conclude with the second form. But the conclusion is not a new judgment, just a "new expression of a judgment that was already in my mind" (*MJ*, 19). In this way, reasoning is revealed as just a matter of making a judgment (Brunschvicg develops similar analyses for other syllogistic figures).

Having established that to think is to judge, Brunschvicg turns to the question of what a judgment is. It is, first of all, an affirmation, an assertion that something is the case. The deep philosophical issues arise when we ask what "is" means in a given judgment. Since Aristotle, philosophers have agreed that judgments vary depending on whether what they affirm is necessary existence, actual existence, or possible existence. Brunschvicg accepts this distinction of the three modalities of judgment (hence three meanings of "is") but maintains that the significance of these modalities cannot be discovered by a merely formal (logical) analysis of the language in which they are expressed. Understanding the forms of judgment requires us to answer fundamental metaphysical and epistemological questions of being and truth.

Brunschvicg begins by noting that, in some cases, judgment seems to be a matter of our awareness of the internal connection between two ideas. When, for example, I judge that *the sum of the interior angles of a triangle is two right angles*, the "is" of my judgment expresses the necessary intellectual connection between the two terms connected. Such a judgment expresses the unity that the mind finds between two notions that are only verbally separated and are in themselves mutually implicated. Here Brunschvicg will say that judgment takes the "form of interiority", since its "is" expresses the internal unity of ideas. In other cases, however, my judgment seems to have nothing to do with the internal connections of ideas but rather expresses the brute fact that something exists in reality, that, for example, *this thing exists here and now*. In such a case, "is" does not express a unity required by the mind's understanding but a "shock of reality" that the mind must simply accept without understanding: "it is the impossibility of the intellect's penetrating to the interior of what it represents in order to analyze and understand it that obliges [the intellect] to stop short [*s'arrêter*], to posit being, that is, to recognize the fact that *that is*" (*MJ*, 88). Here judgment takes the "form of exteriority", its "is" expressing not the

Science and idealism

internal necessity of intelligible thought but the undeniable givenness of an external reality.

Brunschvicg's acceptance of this givenness does not mean that he is abandoning idealism. Like Fichte (from whom he takes the expression "shock of reality"), he is prepared to argue that the very exteriority of external objects is just the way they are given to (constituted by) the mind. But there nonetheless remains an unbridgeable epistemological gap between what can be known simply through the mind's internal reflection and what requires the jolt of external experience.

Brunschvicg emphasizes that pure interiority and pure exteriority are merely ideal forms, limiting cases of judgment, which in reality is always a mixture of the two. This means that our effort to discover the truth of reality cannot be a matter, as some idealists have thought, of the mind's reflectively intuiting or deducing its own intellectual content. Such an enterprise will yield only fragile abstractions that cannot sustain the shock of reality. At the same time, Brunschvicg of course rejects the empiricist error of believing that the truth lies simply in what the mind passively receives from outside. Truth and reality are rather expressed in "mixed judgments" through which what has been given so far in experience is interpreted through the best intellectual framework so far developed by the mind. Since both the most precise experience and the most accurate interpretations of it are achieved by science, it follows that the philosophical pursuit of truth and reality must take the form of historical reflection on science's development of increasingly adequate judgments.

It is this conclusion that justifies Parodi's characterization of Brunschvicg's thought as a union of positivism and idealism ("positivisme idéaliste").[18] The positivism consists in his claim that we know the truth by experiencing the historical progress of science, the idealism in his corresponding insistence that this history is the record of the mind's constitution of ever more successful frameworks for the interpretation of experience. The truth is derived from reflection on the life of the mind, but the mind itself is encountered as a positive

---

[18] Dominique Parodi, *Philosophie contemporaine en France*, 425, 430. Parodi notes the similar positions of Louis Weber (*Vers le positivisme absolu par l'idéalisme*), and of Alain (pseudonym of Émile Chartier). Alain (1868–1951) was an exceptionally charismatic teacher, who, at the Lycée Henri IV in Paris (1909–33), influenced a generation of students that included Simone Weil, Raymond Aron, and Jean-Paul Sartre.

reality in human history of science, not as an esoteric ahistorical object of philosophical insight.

Brunschvicg's early views on judgment, truth, and reality provide the guiding thread for the three massive historical studies that constitute the bulk of his life's work. The first was *Les étapes de la pensée mathématique* (1912), which follows the entire history of mathematics and of mathematically inspired philosophy from the ancient Greeks through twentieth-century logicism and intuitionism. Brunschvicg rejects the idea that mathematics is a pure study of merely ideal relations and instead views it as essentially tied to our efforts to understand the world. His history shows how novel mathematical ideas emerge from the mind's creative efforts to make sense of our experience of the world: "nature puts the mind to the test; the mind responds by constituting mathematical science."[19] At the same time, Brunschvicg follows the work of philosophers – particularly, Plato, Descartes, Leibniz, and Kant – inspired by the mathematical achievements of their times. He acknowledges the resulting advances in philosophical understanding but denounces the philosophical systems that present those results as the final word on the nature of reality, arguing that the subsequent history of mathematics always creates new ideas that undermine the old systems. The only philosophical conclusion supported by the history of mathematics is Brunschvicg's own anti-systematic view of the mind responding to ever new and unpredictable "shocks" of nature with its own new and unpredictable interpretations.

A second volume, *L'expérience humaine et la causalité physique* (1922), develops the same general viewpoint, this time through a study of scientific and philosophical conceptions of causality. It concludes that history undermines the pretensions of both the philosophies of nature of absolute idealists such as Hegel and the philosophies of science of other modern philosophers such as Descartes and Kant, but supports the more modest claims of Brunschvicg's philosophy of thought (*philosophie de pensée*). As he uses the term, a philosophy of nature offers a view of the natural world, derived entirely from philosophical insight and reasoning, that claims to be independent of and superior to the empirical constructions of natural scientists. Whereas both ancient and early modern philosophers saw an intimate connection, if not identity, between philosophical and

[19] *Les étapes de la pensée mathématique*, 569.

scientific efforts to understand the world, the philosophy of nature, first fully developed by German idealists of the early nineteenth century, claimed to be able to "achieve, on its own, through original procedures, the system of things that scientists have not been able to achieve" with their mathematical and experimental methods (*L'expérience humaine et la causalité physique* [*EH*], 544). Brunschvicg rejects this project as "a chimera", refuted by its obvious inconsistency with scientific truths and explained by the human desire for "dogmatic speculation that seeks simple and definitive systems" (*EH*, 545).

By contrast a philosophy of science quite properly does not seek "truths beyond the plane of scientific verification; it limits the horizon of human knowledge [*connaissance*] to the results furnished by science [*savoir scientifique*]" (*EH*, 546). Such philosophies – especially in the form of Kant's critique or Comte's positivism – effectively oppose systems of dogmatic metaphysics. But they go wrong in thinking that, from the de facto science of their time, they can extract final truths that must define the framework of all subsequent science. Brunschvicg notes how often, during the last century, developments in pure mathematics – and even more in mechanics and physics – "have blithely ignored [*jouées comme à plaisir*] the alleged limits imposed on them in the name of [Kantian] criticism or of positivism" (*EH*, 546). (In this regard, Brunschvicg finds Einstein's general theory of relativity particularly revolutionary.)

Brunschvicg's own "philosophy of thought" balances the claim that only science can provide the definitive account of reality with a realization that the content of its account cannot be extracted from the science of any given time. What is required instead is historical reflection on the full sweep of science as it has developed over the last 2500 years: "science considered apart from its history [*devenir*] is an abstraction". The philosophy of thought hopes to show that this history is not a mere "aggregate of disparate and diverging opinions". Its project is to employ a "total knowledge of the curve followed [by science] up to now ... to project the light of a new reflection onto the previous phases of thought and ... in particular to clarify the relative position of the present". The result will be "a philosophy of human history" that will "define the direction [*sens*] of the drama in which humanity has found itself engaged since it first became aware of its contact with things" (*EH*, 552).

Brunschvicg speaks of his philosophy of thought as being "progressive" and in tune with the "rhythm of progress" (*EH*, 552). Given his strong claims about the unpredictability of the future direction of science, it is hard to see how even the most well-informed history could give us a real sense of where science is going in the long run. But Brunschvicg thinks there is something substantial that can be said about the moral and religious progress of humankind, a progress that he sees as intimately connected with the development of science and which he treats in his third magnum opus, *Le progrès de la conscience dans la philosophie occidentale* (1927).

Brunschvicg's view of progress is rooted in the account of practical judgments that he developed in *La modalité du jugement*. There he argued that practical judgments should be understood as parallel to theoretical judgments. Corresponding to the distinction between the form of exteriority and the form of interiority (that is, between judgments about experientially given facts and judgments about the internal relation of ideas), there is a distinction between judgments concerning happiness, which depend on the external world, and judgments of morality, which, following Kant, Brunschvicg sees as deriving from "internal conditions tied to a rational principle" (*MJ*, 217). Likewise, just as theoretical judgments are in fact always a mixture of exteriority and interiority, so our practical judgments always combine considerations of happiness and of morality. Just as scientists must apply a priori intellectual frameworks to the given facts of experience, so we must apply the a priori principles of morality to the given passions and desires of our concrete existence. "In the two cases, the task of judgment is the same: it faces us with a given nature, either as external world or as individual character." Just as in the theoretical realm scientists "destroy bit by bit the illusions born from sensible representations", so in the practical realm moralists "denounce the contradictions of human nature and the vanity of its spontaneous will". More generally, moral principles and the principles of mathematics are both characterized by a "rational purity and universality" that is gradually extended to various levels of physical and social reality (*MJ*, 221).

Brunschvicg insists that these parallels are not simply an artifact of his mode of exposition. They express the "higher truth" of the "unity of the human mind [*l'esprit*]". Although our analyses distinguish "knowledge and action, theory [*speculation*] and practice, life does not know this distinction" since "theoretical matters [*démarches spéculatives*] are intimately tied to practical matters, which continue and presuppose them" (*MJ*, 221). Since Brunschvicg identifies the mind with the activity of judgment, the only difference between theory and practice lies in the object of the judgment, not in the nature of the judgment itself, which is in either case a creative structuring of pregiven materials. Even more importantly, the attainment of theoretical truth and of moral goodness both require the same central virtue: a rigorous pursuit of the universal by renouncing all personal perspectives and interests.

Here it is important to take account of Brunschvicg's emphasis on freedom. In its own right, the mind is entirely free to construct whatever laws and norms it chooses. In both science and ethics, "there is nothing outside of freedom"; "consciousness is the creator of moral values, as it is of scientific values and of aesthetic values".[20] Its "existence is to develop in conformity to the law that it imposes on itself".[21] In both science and morality, the mind is essentially creative: "In all domains, the heroes of the spiritual life are those who, without referring to outdated models . . ., have cast ahead of themselves lines of intelligence and truth that are destined to create a moral universe in the same way that they have created the material universe of gravitation or of electricity."[22] Thus far, Brunschvicg sounds like a proto-existentialist, and there surely are some anticipations of Sartre in his formulations. But he goes on to insist that the development of both science and ethics requires that the mind's freedom be directed toward a universal, objective viewpoint; he never makes the key existentialist move of giving individual consciousness ontological and ethical priority over this viewpoint.

Brunschvicg sees the epistemic and the moral progress of humanity as intertwined. Just as we have moved from the perspectival limitations of sense perception toward universal laws valid for all observers, so we have moved from moral ideals limited to our own social groups to an ideal of love for all humans. The history of humanity is the history of its progress to unity, both cognitive and ethical.[23]

As Brunschvicg sees it, this progress has involved sloughing off many of the elements of traditional religion. The development of

---

[20] *Le progrès de la conscience dans la philosophie occidentale*, 715, 705.
[21] *L'idéalisme contemporain*, 32.
[22] "Vie intérieure et vie spirituelle", 146.
[23] Hence Brunschvicg's title, *Le progrès de la conscience*, intends both meanings of the French *conscience*: consciousness and conscience.

critical idealism shows that the idea of God as a transcendent being, entirely independent of our minds, is incoherent. Further, the apparatus of institutional religion – its rites, creeds, and codes – have been impediments to the free development of thought. To this extent, there should be no place for "religious consciousness" in the future history of humanity. Brunschvicg does allow, however, for a reformulation of religious language in defensible terms. This requires an understanding of God not as a superhuman personage, causally involved with the world, but as a value, indeed the ultimate value of truth and love, the unity toward which human history is converging.

CHAPTER 3

Bergson

> For the truths which the intellect apprehends directly in the world of full and unimpeded light have something less profound, less necessary than those which life communicates to us against our will in an impression which is material because it enters us through the senses but yet has a spiritual meaning which it is possible for us to extract.
> (Marcel Proust, *In Search of Lost Time*, VI, 273)

The strong focus of the early Third Republic's philosophers on science is hardly unusual. The identity of philosophy has always been intimately associated with that of science. We can think of philosophy's premodern period as the time, before the scientific revolution, when it was identical with science, when philosophy was simply the enterprise of understanding the world in all its aspects. The scientific revolution destroyed this identity by showing that there was at least one domain – knowledge of the material world – where philosophy's methods of rational insight and logical argument were not adequate. Here, it was gradually discovered (and, of course, anticipations of the discovery can be traced back to the very beginnings of Greek inquiry) that the empirical method of testing conjectures by observing whether their consequences were true was far superior. No doubt philosophy, considered simply as our search for truth, could be regarded as employing this method. Then what the modern world has come to know as science would still be part of philosophy. But this is mere contingency of words. The determining historical fact is that philosophy came to be identified with employments of reason other than the empirical, prediction-driven procedures of science. The future of philosophy, in the wake of these procedures, depended on the value of these other employments of reason.

It is not, therefore, surprising that roughly from the time of

50   *The Philosophers of the Third Republic (1890–1940)*

Descartes, the critique of science became a major philosophical concern. Explicitly or implicitly, every modern philosophical enterprise has had to guarantee a place for itself by showing that there is something for it to know that escapes the grasp of empirical science.[1]

There have been many vehicles for staking out the domain of philosophy, from Descartes' dualism through the positivists' analytic-synthetic distinction. But one of the most persistently attractive has been the claim that philosophy can and should root itself in an experience with an *immediacy* or *concreteness* that escapes the abstractions required for successful empirical science. Here the general thought is that the precision required for rigorously testing hypotheses requires us to ignore certain aspects of our experience that are not open to scientific (e.g., quantitative) formulation. The claim (or hope), however, is that philosophy is capable of giving us an epistemically adequate access to the experience that science must ignore. The appeal to a distinctive realm of philosophical experience is prominent in the French spiritualist tradition and especially in the work of its greatest representative, Henri Bergson (1859–1941).[2]

Since Bergson's mother was English, he spent considerable time visiting her relatives and grew up with a native fluency in English. But his education was entirely in the French system. He entered the École Normale in 1878 (where he was a classmate of Jean Jaurès and Émile Durkheim), passed the *agrégation* in 1881, and received his doctorate in 1889. For many years Bergson taught at lycées, particularly two elite Parisian schools, the Lycée Louis-le-Grand and the Lycée Henri IV. He never held a university professorship but did teach at the École Normale before being elected to a chair at the Collège de France in 1900, where his lectures became the rage of fashionable Paris. He had immense influence not only on philosophers but also on French writers such as Proust, Valéry, and Péguy, as well as many British and American modernists; psychologists such as Pierre Janet and Jean Piaget; political theorists such as Georges Sorel; and avant-garde artistic movements such as Cubism, Fauvism, and Futurism. Unlike other French philosophers of the time,

---

[1] Some philosophers, such as Quine, hold a methodological naturalism that assimilates their enterprise to empirical science. However, for them, the fact that we still continue to talk of "philosophy" – if we do – reflects only the contingent genealogy of certain discussions or the sociological classification of certain groups of inquirers. Philosophy has no irreducible epistemic status.

[2] On Bergson's relation to spiritualism, see Dominique Janicaud, *Une généalogie du spiritualisme français*.

Bergson gained an international reputation; he received the Nobel Prize for literature in 1928. He was also active in diplomatic affairs, working for the entry of the United States into World War I and, after the war, serving on the League of Nations' Commission for Intellectual Cooperation. Bergson's health (particularly, crippling arthritis) forced him to retire from his chair in 1921 and eventually from most other public activities. Shortly before his death he refused a personal exemption offered by the Vichy regime to its anti-Semitic laws and insisted on registering as a Jew.

BERGSON ON THE HISTORY OF PHILOSOPHY

Toward the end of his most influential book, *L'évolution créatrice* (1907), Bergson offers a critical sketch of the history of philosophy in its relation to science that provides an excellent introduction to his philosophical project. Bergson sees science as essentially tied to what he calls the "cinematographical method" (*L'évolution créatrice* [*EC*], 773/357). By this he means that science views reality not as a continuous flux (the duration that it in fact is) but as a series of instantaneous "snapshots" extracted from this flux. In terms of a simple but fundamental example, science derives from a mind-set that makes Zeno's paradoxes both inevitable and unsolvable. Its end is the control of nature and thereby more effective action in the world. Now action, Bergson maintains, is always directed from a starting-point to an end-point and has no essential concern with whatever comes between the two. Therefore, the focus of science on action leads directly to its cinematographic view of reality.

It may be readily accepted that such a construal makes sense for ancient science, which divided the world into a discontinuous series of qualitatively distinct essences or natures and for which, as Bergson puts it, "physics is but logic spoiled" (*EC*, 765/347). But what about modern science, which rejects the qualitative approach and conceptualizes the world as a continuous manifold, open to the technique of the differential calculus? Bergson recognizes the distinctive character of modern science but does not see it as abandoning the division of the natural flux into isolatable moments. Modern science abandons not the ancient division of nature into moments but the ancient assumption that certain of these moments are privileged over others, in favor of the democratic view that science must be able to describe nature from the standpoint of any one of its moments. Thus, the ancients saw the motion of a falling body as intelligible in terms of the privileged moment of its *telos*, its return to the earth to which it was naturally inclined. Galileo, by contrast, developed a kinematics for which "there was no essential moment, no privileged instant" and for which "to study the falling body is to consider it at it matters not what moment in its course" (*EC*, 775/360).

Accordingly, ancient and modern physics do not differ over the assumption that the flux of nature is divisible into discrete elements. They differ only on whether there is an intrinsically privileged division or an equivalence of all possible divisions. Bergson compares the difference to that between an ancient sculptural aesthetic for which the horses on the Parthenon frieze are caught at a moment that distills the essence of their gallop and a modern photographic aesthetic that sees all instantaneous snapshots of the gallop as equally valid representations (*EC*, 776/361). From this difference follow the modern emphasis on quantitative rather than qualitative descriptions and the modern concern with laws rather than concepts. But the essential scientific view of nature as a succession of fixed moments, as opposed to our lived experience of continuous time, remains in place.

It may be objected that modern science has given time an essential role, making it the independent variable in all its equations, whereas ancient science took a fundamentally static view of nature. Aristotle thought he had understood planetary motion adequately when he conceptualized it as circular (and even Ptolemy did not pretend to provide a physical explanation of celestial motions). But Kepler was not content with his discovery that planetary orbits were elliptical. He required laws that described how the planets traveled through these orbits over time. Bergson admits this modern enthronement of the temporal but maintains that the time in question is not the continuous flux of duration but a spatialized, immobile surrogate for it:

> In contrast with ancient science, which stopped at certain so-called essential moments, [modern science] is occupied indifferently with any moment whatever. But it always considers moments, always virtual stopping-places, always, in short, immobilities. Which amounts to saying that real time, regarded as flux, or, in other words, the very mobility of being, escapes the hold of scientific knowledge. (*EC*, 779–80/366)

It appears, then, that even modern scientific accounts fail to catch the essential movement of lived time. We might have expected, accordingly, that modern philosophy, which was deeply concerned with finding itself a distinctive place in a cognitive realm more and more dominated by science, would have grounded itself precisely on lived duration. We might have expected a philosophy that rejected the "cinematographical method" and focused on the "flux itself of duration" of which "science neither would nor could lay hold" (*EC*, 784/372). Certainly, "this conception of metaphysics is that which modern science suggests" (*EC*, 785/373).

However, although Bergson finds some hints of such a construal of philosophy, he maintains that, on the whole, this was not the direction taken by Descartes and his successors. One reason was the abiding influence of the ancient view of reality, which made "time a degradation, and change the diminution of a form given from all eternity" (*EC*, 786/374). This view had led to metaphysical systems, from the Eleatic to the Aristotelian, that, despite their differences, privileged eternal, spiritual structures and regarded the world of matter and change as inessential and ultimately unreal. Even Aristotle, who so resisted the Platonic separation of form from matter, ended by in effect combining all the forms into one, which he identified with the self-thinking "Thought of Thought" and established as the ultimate unmoved cause of all motion. Modern metaphysicians were strongly inclined to "repeat with the new science what had been tried on the old"; that is, to view the new world of mechanized matter in the same way that the ancient metaphysicians had viewed their world of eternal forms: as a complete and unified system encompassing all truth and all reality. Admittedly, given its essential role as independent variable, time could not be simply reduced to an unreal status. But, since the modern view treated time as nothing more than a fourth spatial dimension,[3] it could readily be viewed as having no creative efficacy, as merely the vehicle for the automatic unrolling of a nomologically determined sequence.

According to Bergson, the direction modern philosophy took is the natural direction of the human mind, given its evolutionary orientation toward practical action. A metaphysics of duration is a precious theoretical truth, but not one for which we are adapted. "The science of matter proceeds like ordinary knowledge",

---

[3] The spatialization of time becomes explicit only in Minkowski's formulation of special relativity, but Bergson sees it as implicit in modern science since at least Galileo.

perfecting and extending it but not altering its fundamentally cinematographic bias (*EC*, 779/365).

Descartes himself, according to Bergson, shows some inclination to the new metaphysical possibility in his separation of the mind as free agent (and God as continuous creator) from the universal mechanism of the external world. His dualism may well be incoherent, but it at least represents a bow to the reality of duration. By contrast, Spinoza and Leibniz, insisting on total systematic unity, return fully to the spirit of ancient metaphysics and refuse the new path suggested by the limitations of modern science. They transform the determinism that is a plausible methodological or heuristic rule of the new science into "a fundamental law of things" (*EC*, 788/378). The ancient system of *concepts* is merely replaced with a modern system of *laws*. Bergson sums up the essential similarity of ancient and modern metaphysics as follows:

> The resemblances of this new metaphysics to that of the ancients arise from the fact that both suppose ready-made – the former above the sensible, the latter within the sensible – a science one and complete, with which any reality that the sensible may contain is believed to coincide. *For both, reality as well as truth are integrally given in eternity.* Both are opposed to the idea of a reality that creates itself gradually, that is, at bottom, to an absolute duration. (*EC*, 794/384–5)

In Kant, however, Bergson finds an important tendency (not, admittedly, ever properly developed) to a new metaphysics. He agrees that, from one point of view, Kant's philosophy "is only a continuation of the metaphysics of the moderns and a transposition of the ancient metaphysics". Certainly, "the philosophy of Kant is ... imbued with the belief in a science single and complete, embracing the whole of the real" (*EC*, 795–6/387). Bergson does not, accordingly, read Kant as a critic of metaphysics as such. But he does see Kant as developing an extremely important criticism of the modern metaphysics of Spinoza and Leibniz. The germ of this criticism is a distinctive feature, noted above, of modern science as opposed to ancient: the focus on laws rather than concepts. Laws, Kant argues, are relations between two terms, and "a relation is nothing outside of the intellect that relates" (*EC*, 796/387). Since, then, as modern science tells us, the phenomenal universe is a system of laws, it follows that the "phenomena have passed through the filter of an intellect". So far he is in agreement with the modern rationalist metaphysicians, who, however, go on to identify this intellect with that of God, the infinitely good and powerful source of the universe. Kant notes that there is no need to go so far, that the unification required for phenomena to be governed by laws might be provided by the human intellect. To this extent, "the criticism of Kant consisted chiefly in limiting the dogmatism of his predecessors, accepting their conception of science and reducing to the minimum the metaphysics it implied" (*EC*, 797/388–9).

If this were all of Kant's thought, he would offer merely a more modest and defensible – but, for Bergson, still misguided – version of modern metaphysics. But at the same time that he substituted human for divine intelligence as the source of the forms of our knowledge, Kant also insisted on a distinction between these forms and the matter of knowledge. The relations constituted by the intellect are, for him, between terms that have "an extra-intellectual origin". Contrary to Spinoza and Leibniz, Kant "affirmed . . . that knowledge is not entirely resolvable into terms of intelligence" (*EC*, 797/389).

Bergson argues that this extra-intellectual cognitive matter could and should be identified as the duration he regards as the content of our lived experience and of a new type of metaphysics. Kant, however, passed by this open door because he "believed this matter to be either coextensive with intellect or less extensive than intellect" (*EC*, 798/390). Rather than seeing the matter of knowledge as extending beyond its forms and providing the richer reality from which they are abstracted, he insisted that intellectual forms exist independently of matter, which had no role except to receive their imprint.

As Bergson sees it, Kant subordinated matter because, despite the critical bent of his philosophy, he never questioned science itself. "The criticism of our knowledge of nature that was instituted by Kant consisted in ascertaining what our mind must be and what Nature must be if the claims of our science are justified; but of these claims themselves Kant has not made the criticism." Kant held back from the critique of science because "he took for granted the idea of a science that is one, capable of binding with the same force all the parts of what is given, and of co-ordinating them into a system presenting on all sides an equal solidity" (*EC*, 798/390). In so doing, he ignored the fact that, as we move from the merely physical to the vital and then the psychical, science becomes less adequate as an account of our experience, that it becomes "less and less objective, more and more symbolical" (*EC*, 798/390).

Formulated in terms crucial for both Kant and Bergson, Kant's view is that all our *intuitions* are "sensuous, or, in other words, infra-intellectual". That is to say, for Kant, immediate experience yields knowledge only to the extent that it conforms to the structures of the intellect; beyond these structures it offers only the non-cognitive stuff from which knowledge is constituted. Kant thus ignores the possibility, exploited by Bergson's philosophy, that there might be a supra- (or ultra-) intellectual intuition (*EC*, 799/391) that would provide direct knowledge of concrete life and thought.

Such life and thought are not things-in-themselves lying beyond our experience but the very stuff of that experience in its most immediate form, the stuff from which the world of the intellect is an abstraction. This stuff of immediate experience is Bergson's duration, the lived passage of time that pervades our lives. Bergson's philosophical project consists in the articulation of our experience of duration, the contrast of this experience with our standard ("spatialized") modes of experience and thought, and the reassessment of fundamental philosophical questions in the light of this articulation and contrast.

TIME AND FREE WILL

In Bergson's first book, his doctoral thesis *Essai sur les données immédiates de la conscience*, defended and published in 1889, his ultimate concern is with the problem of freedom. But the basis for his treatment of freedom is laid down by a detailed account, in the two opening chapters, of the nature of psychological states, including, for example, feelings of pleasure or pain, emotions of anger or pity, perceptions of external objects, and aesthetic enjoyment. He begins with the common-sense view that such states are qualitative but capable of different degrees of intensity, that they succeed one another in time, and that later members of temporal series are causally determined by prior members. His ultimate claim is that the so-called problem of freedom arises from confusions implicit in this common-sense picture, confusions Bergson thinks he can eliminate by presenting a better description of the qualitative nature of psychological states and of their temporal character.

No one will deny that we experience psychological states as intrinsically qualitative, but Bergson rejects the common idea that they are also somehow intrinsically quantitative because we can speak of them as "greater" or "lesser" in intensity. Discussing a wide range of cases, he argues that such quantitative language must refer either to the quantitative features of a state's external cause (as when one drum-beat is louder than another because it was produced by a greater force) or to the greater involvement of the state in our organic or psychic life (as when a pain is greater than another because it affects more of the body or when one grief exceeds another by intruding into more parts of our life). The alternative to Bergson's view is to try to think of psychological states as intensive quantities, irreducibly qualitative but still subject to the categories of mathematical measurement. But, according to Bergson, there is no coherent way of combining quality with measurability, and therefore no consistent conception of the intrinsic quantitative intensity of a quality. Further, as we shall see, trying to deploy such a conception leads to unsolvable problems regarding human freedom.

The mistake of thinking of psychological states as quantitative is compounded if, as philosophers often do, we go on to think of the temporal succession of a multiplicity of such states as a whole made up of discrete, countable elements. There is no doubt that psychological states exist in time, coming, in some sense, one after another. But we are unfortunately inclined to think of this temporal duration as a matter of distinct elements, each existing at a given point of time, preceding and succeeding other distinct elements existing at other given points of time. Thinking this way makes time nothing more than a locus that unites a multiplicity of discrete psychological states into a quantifiable (e.g., countable) whole. But this is to reduce time to a form of space: a container in which are gathered a set of discrete and homogeneous elements; that is, separate complete units that share a fixed nature enabling us to group them together for purposes of enumeration. Such a reduction denies what is given in our immediate experience of our psychological states as temporal; namely, "a wholly qualitative multiplicity, an absolute heterogeneity of elements which pass over into one another" (*Essai sur les données immédiates de la conscience* [*EDI*], 149/229). As existing in time, psychological states are aspects of a continuous flux of novelty in which nothing is ever fixed, complete, or separate. In this flux, anything that we can say exists "now" also incorporates into a qualitative whole everything that we can say is "past", a whole that is itself being incorporated into the new synthesis of the "future".

Common sense and, especially, science misdescribe psychological states by trying to apply the categories of quantity and extension to what is in fact irreducibly qualitative and temporal. This misrepresentation derives from our tendency to assimilate quality to quantity and duration to extension. This assimilation is, as we have seen, well justified in the context of practical action, which concerns only reaching a given goal from a fixed starting point and has no interest in the reality of the interval in between. But the needs of action abstract from the concrete reality that we experience when we withdraw ourselves from practical needs and seek disinterested truth. Further, on Bergson's view, many of the traditional problems of philosophy derive from an attempt to describe the qualitative duration of concrete reality through the quantitative abstractions of science. The result is a confusion of duration and extension that leads to unresolvable aporiae.

Bergson maintains that the traditional problem of freedom is a paradigm example of such confusion. The problem arises from the suggestion, apparently contrary to our experience of ourselves as free agents, that all our actions are determined by antecedent causes. Determinists maintain that determining causes exist and make our actions unfree. Non-determinists either deny that such causes exist and maintain that our actions are uncaused and therefore free (libertarianism) or they agree that determining causes exist but argue that their existence is consistent with the freedom of the actions they produce (compatibilism). According to Bergson, however, all these positions share the false assumption that the self (the agent) can be properly described as a succession of separate psychological states (feelings, thoughts, volitions) that *could* be related by causal connections. (Bergson calls this the "associationist" view of the self, referring to the associationist psychology of Hume and other empiricists.) This associationist view is false because, as we have seen, the self is not a set of successive independent elements but a unified organic process. It is not a "multiplicity of juxtaposition" but a multiplicity "of fusion or interpenetration" (*EDI*, 107/162). It makes no sense to speak of causal relations within such a multiplicity because there are no elements that can be properly separated out as causes or effects.

On the other hand, a description of the self that accords with the "immediate givens of consciousness" shows it to be an organic whole that creatively produces its future, and this production is precisely what we mean by freedom. At the deepest level, our "states of consciousness cease to stand in juxtaposition and begin to permeate and melt into one another, each to be tinged with the colouring of all the others". Thus, "each of us has his own way of loving and hating; and this love or this hatred reflects his whole personality" (*EDI*, 108/164). Moreover, "the outward manifestation of this inner state will be just what is called a free act, since the self alone will have been the author of it, and since it will express the whole of the self" (*EDI*, 109/165–6). Here Bergson is close to the Aristotelian notion of agent causality, revived much later in the twentieth century by analytic philosophers such as Roderick Chisholm.[4] Bergsonian duration has no place for the "transient" causation whereby one discrete occurrence is correlated with another in accord with a universally valid law of nature. But it does allow for the "immanent" causation whereby an agent as an organic whole produces an effect. Of course, in contrast to Aristotelian views, Bergson does not see his "agent" as a stable substance but as a developing synthesis within the ever-changing flux of duration.

Bergson's view of freedom allows for the sort of inversion of cause and effect that is characteristic of the account Sartre offers more than half a century later.[5] Thus, Bergson describes cases in which "it happens that we weigh motives, we deliberate, although our decision has already been made. An internal voice, scarcely perceptible, murmurs: 'Why this deliberation? You know the result and you are quite certain what you are going to do'" (*EDI*, 104/158). In fact, although Bergson presents this as just one kind of case that is inconsistent with the associationist account of action, it would seem to be a general model for him, as it is for Sartre, since his durational view of the self cannot allow for the isolation of antecedent motives or reasons as the causes of our actions. At the same time, Bergson's view differs from Sartre's because it identifies consciousness with the psychological self and does not posit the entirely transparent awareness, separate from the self, that is the locus of Sartre's radical thesis of entirely unconstrained freedom.

This difference with Sartre is particularly apparent in Bergson's view that freedom is a matter of degrees and that, in fact, "fully free actions are very rare". More often, what we do is the product of a habitual response to stimuli that has no connection with the

---

[4] A. R. Lacey notes this similarity in his *Bergson*, 85.
[5] See the discussion of Sartre on freedom in chapter 5, below.

"fundamental self" (*moi profond*) (*EDI*, 110/168) of durational experience. This is because most of the time we operate not on the level of duration but on the level of the intellect's abstract spatialized categories. When, for example, my alarm clock rings, it might happen that "I might receive this impression σὺν ὅλῃ τῇ ψυχῇ [with my entire soul], as Plato says; I might let it blend with the confused mass of impressions which fill my mind; perhaps in that case it would not determine me to act". But most often the ringing of the alarm does not "disturb . . . my whole consciousness" but operates on a superficial level as an impression that I mechanically associate with the idea of getting up in the morning. Then, "the act follows the impression without the self interfering with it. In this instance I am a conscious automaton." Bergson acknowledges that "the majority of our daily actions are performed in this way" and that "it is to these acts, which are very numerous but for the most part insignificant, that the associationist theory is applicable" (*EDI*, 111/168). In a free action, by contrast, "the deep-seated self rush[es] up to the surface" and breaks through the "crust" of mechanical habits (*EDI*, 111/169). Such an action "does not . . . express . . . some superficial idea, almost external to ourselves, distinct and easy to account for" (*EDI*, 111/170). Rather, it "agrees with the whole of our most intimate feelings, thoughts and aspirations, with that particular conception of life which is the equivalent of all our past experience, in a word, with our personal idea of happiness and of honor" (*EDI*, 112/170).

Unlike Sartre, then, Bergson does not have the problem of making even the most trivial actions radical expressions of a fundamental project. Such expressions are as rare as they are important, and the vast majority of our actions are either entirely mechanical or at least only very partial expressions of the durational self. Bergson notes that, in this regard, his view of freedom "does not have the absolute character that spiritualism sometimes ascribes to it" (*EDI*, 109/166, translation modified).

MATTER AND MEMORY

Bergson's second book, *Matière et mémoire*, was published in 1896, seven years after the *Essai sur les données immédiates de la conscience*. As the subtitle (*Essai sur la relation du corps à l'esprit*) indicates, its focus is the relation of the body to the mind. At the core of Bergson's position is what we might call (although he did not) his pragmatic view of the body, that "the body is an instrument of action, and of action only". The obverse of this view is that bodily events and states – including those of the brain – have no role in our representation of the world. The force of these claims becomes clear in Bergson's accounts of the two cognitive phenomena to which the body is most obviously relevant (and where, therefore, the question of its relation to the mind as locus of knowledge is most pressing): perception and memory. According to him, "there is only a difference of degree, not of kind, between the so-called perceptive faculties of the brain and the reflex functions of the spinal column" (*Matière et mémoire* [*MM*], 356/225). Both brain and spinal column serve simply to transform external excitations (e.g., sense stimulations) into motor responses (actions). The only difference is that in reflex action these responses are generally causally necessary whereas in perception they are "more or less freely chosen" (*MM*, 356–7/225). As for memory, Bergson maintains that the brain does not, as is often thought, "store up" images of the past. It merely responds to present stimuli in a manner similar to past responses. It is the locus of what Bergson calls "habitual memory" (in contrast to the "pure memory", which, as we shall see, he attributes to the mind alone).

As Bergson sees it, all the standard responses to the "mind–body problem" fail because they insist on treating perception and memory as instances of pure (i.e., representational) knowledge and therefore have to treat the body, which has an obvious role in both perception and memory, as somehow capable of representing the world. Materialists, for example, must see knowledge as achieved once the body (brain) attains the relevant representational state. But then they have no explanation for the epiphenomenal existence of mental states, which can be nothing more than the useless duplication of physical states. Idealists, on the other hand, locate knowledge entirely in the perceptions (representations) of the mind, so that even my body is real only as an object of my experience. But even idealists must accept scientific results about the role of brain-states in sense-experience. They will, of course, regard such states not as independently existing things but as themselves objects of possible perceptions. But then they will have to admit that this very restricted set of possible perceptions is mysteriously correlated with my ordinary perceptions of the external world; that is, they "must suppose . . . an inexplicable correspondence between my real perception of things and my possible perception of certain cerebral movements which do not in any way resemble these things" (*MM*, 358/226–7). (More generally, Bergson thinks that "this is the reef on which all idealism is wrecked: there is no possible transition from the order which is perceived by our senses to the order which we are to conceive for the sake of our science" (*MM*, 358/227).)

The inadequacies of materialism and idealism might seem to constitute a proof of dualism. But if dualism is formulated in the standard representationalist way, it will reduce to either materialism or idealism. For I will have to regard brain-states as either the cause or the occasion of my mental representation of an object. If they are the *cause*, then they are sufficient to produce my representation, and consciousness becomes merely epiphenomenal. If, on the other hand, brain-states are merely the *occasion* of my mental representation, they have no essential role in knowledge, and we are back on the road to idealism (*MM*, 358/227). However, Bergson thinks that dualism can be formulated so as to avoid the mistake of making perception a representation of the world.[6]

He develops his account in terms of the *image*, a notion he deploys in a way he thinks avoids both realistic[7] and idealistic views of matter. He intends this description to catch the standpoint of "common sense", which would be equally puzzled by the idealist claim that the things we see and touch exist only for the mind and by the (scientific) realist claim that these objects exist independently but have none of the "secondary" qualities (color, texture, etc.) common sense attributes to them. In Bergson's usage, an image is "a certain existence which is more than that which the idealist calls a *representation*, but less than that which the realist calls a *thing*" (*MM*, 161/9). This, he says, reflects the common-sense view in which "the object exists in itself, and, on the other hand, the object is, in itself, pictorial, as we perceive it: image it is, but a self-existing image" (*MM*, 162/10).

---

[6] Bergson does not explicitly consider the possibility of similarly reformulating materialism and idealism, but such reformulations would seem to be non-starters. Representation must enter into our account of cognition at some point, and materialists, who can have no recourse to independent higher cognitive functions, must therefore make our most basic perceptions representative if knowledge is to be possible at all. Idealism is stuck with a representationalist approach from the beginning, since it must regard knowledge as entirely located in the intentional structures of the mind.

[7] As will soon be apparent, "realism" here means the view that we might characterize as a "scientific realism", which holds that external objects exist independently of consciousness but only as described by scientific theories, not as perceived in ordinary experience.

In order to develop a non-representationalist account of perception, Bergson proposes that we regard the body as a "center of action" (*MM*, 359/228). It receives "vibrations" from the external world into its "perceptive centers". These vibrations may well be said to somehow "represent" the world, but they do not constitute my perception of it (for one thing, I do not experience these vibrations, which are revealed only by neuro-science). On the other hand, science shows that the function of the vibrations "is solely to prepare the reaction of my body on neighboring bodies, to sketch out my virtual actions". There are certain aspects of external bodies that matter for my reactions to them and others that do not. Perception is nothing more than my body's selection, effected through the mechanisms of afferent and efferent nerves, of those features of other bodies that are to be taken account of in its actions in the world. The function of perception "is to eliminate from the totality of images all those on which I can have no hold, and then, from each of those which I retain, all that does not concern the needs of the image which I call my body" (*MM*, 360/229).

What Bergson has so far described is merely what he calls "pure perception". Pure perception is an abstract limit-case of what we ordinarily mean by perception, since it does not include the body's perceptions ("affections" or "sensations") of its own inner states or, more important, our memories of previous perceptions. Sensations are of far less importance for Bergson than they are for many empiricist and idealist philosophers, who see them as the epistemic basis of our knowledge of the world. Bergson, on the contrary, sees sensations as nothing more than perceptions of my own body that color, in a peripheral way, my perceptions of other bodies. Such sensations "far from being the materials from which the image is wrought, will then appear as the impurity which is introduced into it, being that part of our own body which we project into all others" (*MM*, 365/235).

Memory, however, is another matter. Here Bergson does not mean the habitual memory whereby the body itself reacts as it has previously to past stimuli. He is referring, rather, to pure memory, in the sense of "the representation of an *absent* object" (*MM*, 366/236).[8]

---

[8] A good example of Bergson's distinction is given by the case of learning to recite from memory a poem by reading it over twenty or thirty times. My reciting of the poem so learned is an instance of habitual memory. My memory of each separate reading of the poem is an example of pure memory. See *Matter and Memory*, 79–80.

Whereas pure perception is essentially a function of the body (a center of activity, not of representation), pure memory, according to Bergson, is essentially a function of the mind (in its capacity for representation). To establish this claim, he closely scrutinizes the data of empirical physiology and psychology to show that they exclude the view, commonly held, that memories are stored in the brain. If memories were stored in the brain, then "characteristic lesions of the brain would correspond to definite gaps in memory" (*MM*, 367/237). But according to Bergson no such correspondence exists. When definite gaps in our memory occur, for example when we suffer from "an amnesia in which a whole period of our past existence . . . is abruptly and entirely obliterated from memory", this is not triggered by "any precise cerebral lesion". Conversely, when there is a distinct localized brain lesion (for example, in certain cases of aphasia), there is not a loss of a specific set of memories but rather a partial diminution of the "whole faculty of remembering" (*MM*, 367/237). The locus of memory, therefore, is not the body but the mind: "With memory we are, in truth, in the domain of spirit" (*MM*, 370/240).[9]

We are also in the domain of duration. Memory – that is, "pure memory", independent of the body – is simply our experience of the continuous, heterogeneous flow of time that Bergson sees as fully concrete reality. Because it is total immersion in duration, which in turn is the whole of our temporal reality, Bergson maintains that pure memory contains recollection of literally all our past experience. Of course, we are explicitly aware of only a small part of this past at any given time, so it follows that the largest part of our pure memory is unconscious.

Matière et mémoire is not, however, particularly concerned with exploring the domain of duration and pure memory for its own sake. This is a major theme of *L'évolution créatrice*, particularly in its discussion of intuition. But in the earlier book Bergson is more interested in how pure memory intersects with pure perception to constitute our ordinary experience as mind–body composites. Entirely pure memory (full immersion in duration) is a rare, entirely spiritual achievement, one most of us attain only fleetingly. Pure

---

[9] Bergson's claims would need at least some serious reformulation in the light of later developments in neuroscience. See Jean Delacour, "Matière et mémoire, à la lumière des neurosciences contemporaines" and other essays in Philippe Gallois and Gérard Forzy (eds.), *Bergson et les neurosciences*.

perception is an ideal limit, corresponding to an instantaneous engagement of the body (controlled by the brain) with other bodies, entirely abstracted from temporality (*MM*, 373/244). Actual perception of our everyday world is a synthesis of pure perception and pure memory. For Bergson, it is this synthesis that constitutes the union of mind and body.

The synthesis occurs when the mind "inserts" into a present perception memories that resemble the perception, thereby enriching it and giving it temporal thickness. Bergson cites the simple example of what happens when we read. Psychological experiments prove that we do not actually read "letter-by-letter". Rather, "our mind notes here and there [on the page] a few characteristic lines and fills all the intervals with memory-images which, projected on the paper, take the place of the real printed characters and may be mistaken for them" (*MM*, 248/103). On the lowest level, a purely physical perception of the shapes "ca" and "le" may, when supplemented with a relevant memory (of the connecting "nd"), yield a perception of the sign "candle". Further memories will then be supplied, corresponding to past uses of "candle", that specify its semantic meaning. A higher level might insert memories that add a specific emotional tone to the perception, and a still higher level might infuse it with a symbolic religious significance. Bergson speaks, therefore, of the infinity of "planes of consciousness", corresponding to all the different levels of what we might call the "interpretation" of perception by memory. In this terminology, Bergson will call pure perception the "plane of action" and pure memory "the plane of dream".[10] When both are included, the planes of consciousness encompass the whole of human experience, from the ideal limit of a purely physical response to our world, through the various modes of conceptualizing that world for practical purposes, to the intuitive apprehension of the final reality of duration itself.[11]

It may seem that nothing Bergson has said, original and perceptive as it might be, really addresses the key question of just how mind and body interact. Even if we grant him that this interaction

---

[10] "Dream" here signifies detachment not from reality but from the practical world of action.
[11] On the central role of the notion of planes of consciousness in *Matière et mémoire*, see Frédéric Worms, "La théorie bergsonienne des plans de conscience: Genèse, structure et signification de *Matière et mémoire*", in Gallois and Forzy (eds.), *Bergson et les neurosciences*, 85–108. See also Worms's *Introduction à* Matière et mémoire *de Bergson*.

reduces to the insertion of memories into perception, how are we to understand the "insertion" of a spiritual memory into the physical process of perception? To this Bergson would no doubt reply that the question itself derives from an inappropriate reification of memory and perception. It assumes a metaphysical separation of material brain and immaterial memory that must be somehow bridged. But this is a misleading picture. Concrete experience does not present the interaction of independent entities belonging to distinct ontological categories. Rather, it presents an organic experiential whole of which what we call mind (memory) and body (brain) are abstract dimensions. Experience does not reveal an ultimate metaphysical duality that the "union" of mind and body must overcome. Instead, mind and body are each aspects of the same metaphysical reality, the reality he will later call the "vital impetus" (*élan vital*). Admittedly, however, neither of Bergson's first two books, restricted as they are to issues of philosophical anthropology, develop (even if they somehow require) this sort of comprehensive ontology. This Bergson tried to supply in his next book, *L'évolution créatrice* (1907).

CREATIVE EVOLUTION

Here Bergson takes as his topic the most basic of all metaphysical questions: what does it mean to exist? He begins, however, with our experience of our own existence, the one case for which our access to existence is "internal and profound" (*EC*, 495/3). Given what Bergson has already said about duration, it is no surprise that he sees existence as a matter of temporal development, understood as a process of self-creation: "for a conscious being, to exist is to change, to change is to develop [*se mûrir*], to develop is to go on creating oneself endlessly" (*EC*, 500/10).[12] But can this characterization be extended to all reality?

Early on, Bergson seems to have thought that it could not. In his first book he says: "Thus, within our ego, there is succession without mutual exteriority; outside the ego, in pure space, mutual exteriority without succession" (*EDI*, 72–3/108).[13] But by the time of *L'évolution*

---

[12] Here I have altered the English translation of *se mûrir*. The text has "matures", which strikes me as having too much of an ethical connotation.
[13] There are, however, other passages in the *Essai* that suggest something like duration in the external world. For example: "We certainly feel . . . that although things do not endure as

créatrice, Bergson had come to regard temporal succession as an "undeniable fact, even in the material world" (*EC*, 502/12). If, he says, I mix some sugar in some water, "I must, willy-nilly, wait until the sugar melts". Further, the time I wait is not the physicist's mathematical time, for which all that matter are the beginning- and end-points, with no consideration given to the interval in between. The time "coincides with my impatience, that is to say, with a certain portion of my own duration . . . It is no longer something *thought*, it is something *lived*" (*EC*, 502/12–13). Bergson also notes that the assumption of a totally isolated system, necessary for the complete mathematicization of time, is always only an idealization. There is always a thread of connection between any system and the rest of the universe, and "it is along this thread that is transmitted down to the smallest particle of the world in which we live the duration immanent to the whole of the universe". Bergson therefore concludes that "there is no reason . . . why a duration, and so a form of existence like our own, should not be attributed to the systems that science isolates, provided such systems are reintegrated into the Whole" (*EC*, 503/14).[14]

Moreover, within the physical world there is a special class of isolated systems that have the characteristics of duration. These, of course, are organisms, the life that Bergson thinks we can make the primary model for his generalization of duration to all reality. Arguing against reductionism on scientific grounds, Bergson maintains that the *individuality* of an organism, its existence as an autonomous biological system, requires the "continuity of change" and "preservation of the past in the present" that are characteristics of the duration we find in consciousness. The only remaining question is whether life also involves the "invention, [the] unceasing

---

we do ourselves, nevertheless there must be [in them] some [incomprehensible] reason why phenomena seem to succeed one another instead of being unfolded all at once" (*EDI*, 137/209–10). (The bracketed terms correspond to words in the French that are not translated in the English version, *Time and Free Will*.)

[14] Extending duration to the world described by physics raises the question of how duration relates to time as understood by science, in particular Einstein's theory of relativity. Bergson addressed this question in *Durée et simultanéité*. He argued that, properly interpreted, relativity theory is entirely consistent with his philosophy of duration. He also argued that his philosophy requires the constancy of the velocity of light characteristic of relativity and offered a solution to the famous "twin-paradox". Bergson's discussion was the occasion of a great deal of controversy, and it is now generally agreed that there are mistakes in his interpretation of relativity, although some commentators insist that his work is nonetheless an important contribution to our understanding of the theory. See A. R. Lacey, *Bergson*, 59–66 and Milic Čapek, *Bergson and Modern Physics*, 238–56.

creation" of consciousness (*EC*, 513/27). If so, then life will be the perfect model for extending the duration of consciousness to reality as a whole. We will then be able to plausibly think of the entire universe as an organic whole, not just existing but "enduring".[15]

But first Bergson needs to show that life shares the creative novelty of conscious duration. Here he turns to evolution (or, as he terms it, "transformism"). His ultimate goal is to show that the fact of evolution must be seen as the product of a dynamic impulse, the *élan vital*, that is the principle of all life. This impulse will be the creative force within duration, now regarded by Bergson as the highest metaphysical principle.[16]

But in order to establish the role of *élan vital* Bergson must first exclude the standard understandings of evolution in terms of mechanism and finalism. A mechanistic theory of evolution, such as Darwin's formulation in terms of natural selection, presents functionally unified structures (e.g., the eye of a vertebrate) as the ultimate outcome of a vast multiplicity of small changes, each occurring for reasons independent of the ultimate outcome. Like many other critics, Bergson points out that an immense number of variations is necessary and no proper subset of them is sufficient for sight. It is monstrously improbable that all of these variations just happened to occur simultaneously, but it is equally improbable that

[15] Bergson is also concerned with the traditional metaphysical objection to a metaphysics of duration: that if process is the ultimate reality, it is impossible to explain why there is something rather than nothing, since only a self-existent absolute, free from change, can provide such an explanation. Bergson thinks this objection falsely assumes that we have a coherent concept of "nothing" in an absolute sense. On the contrary, he argues, "nothing" always means "something else", that is, something other than what we needed or expected. We have no idea of sheer absence (nothingness), merely of the relative absence implied by another presence. Therefore, the question, "Why is there something rather than nothing?", is meaningless (*EC*, 728–47/299–324). Bergson thinks this mistake underlies a wide range of metaphysical and epistemological errors.

[16] Interestingly, Bergson says that his philosophical case does not strictly require accepting evolution (transformism) as a fact. Even if it were proven "that species . . . have arisen by a discontinuous process", the similarities of species and the parallels established by embryology and anatomy would remain. On the basis of these similarities and parallels, Bergson thinks, "biology could and would continue to establish between living forms the same relations and the same kinship as transformism supposes today" (*EC*, 515/29). It would just be that the connections were "ideal", not the outcome of physically real evolutionary processes, although, given the data of paleontology, we would still have to admit that connected forms appeared successively, not simultaneously. But even without a physical process of evolution, this chronological realization of a sequence of logically connected organisms would be as much of evolution as he needs for philosophical purposes. For "an evolution *somewhere* would have to be supposed", whether this were, for example, in a "creative Thought" that generates the universe or in some "plan of vital organization immanent in nature, which gradually works itself out" (*EC*, 515–16/30).

they just happened to occur one after another and, more important, just happened to be retained over eons as features of the organism. Darwinians will try to rescue the latter alternative by suggesting that each successive variation provided its own distinct advantage, but there is simply no evidence that this was the case. The blind forces of mechanism thus prove incapable of explaining the functional structures of organisms.[17]

But Bergson's rejection of mechanism goes much deeper than this standard attack on its explanatory adequacy. As he sees it, mechanism's failure is not just a matter of its inability to account for some recalcitrant facts. The fundamental problem with mechanism is its defining assumption that the biological world is a construction out of diverse parts. This is true of the things human craft produces, but it is not so for biological nature. "A mere glance at the development of an embryo shows that life goes to work in a very different way. *Life does not proceed by the association and addition of elements, but by dissociation and division*" (*EC*, 571/99). Organic processes, in other words, are not processes of *manufacture*, in which simple elements are combined to produce a complex whole; they are processes of *organization*, in which initially given structures (e.g., a fertilized egg) "explode" into a new structure.

Bergson maintains that the traditional rival of mechanism, finalism, assumes the same fundamental picture of organic nature. Positing a purpose (final cause) outside a biological process will explain, as mechanism cannot, how the process achieves its outcome. But the explanation is based on the same inadequate idea, employed by mechanism, of simple parts assembled into a complex whole. Finalism merely provides an analogue to the worker who does the assembling. This is an advance on mechanism's effort to have the parts somehow assemble themselves, but it involves the same misconception of biological processes. "Finalism thus understood is only inverted mechanism. It springs from the same postulate" (*EC*, 528/45).

The picture shared by mechanism and finalism is one for which life never produces anything genuinely new. The outcome of any biological process is always already present, either in the mechanical forces that will produce it or in the ideas or forms that guide these

---

[17] For responses to this sort of objection to Darwinism, see Philip Kitcher, *Abusing Science: The Case Against Creationism*.

forces. In rejecting this picture, we see that life does indeed include the novelty – in addition to the continuity and historicity – needed to place it in the realm of duration. In other words, life, like consciousness, is an expression of the vital impetus (*élan vital*).

Bergson's cosmology is based on two fundamental features of the vital impetus. First, it never operates outside of a context (environment) defined by brute material givens of which it must take account. (Bergson's analogy here is with a road that, even though its ultimate direction is not determined by the landscape, will have to wind and slope to conform to "the ups and downs of the hills" (*EC*, 582/114).) Thus, the fundamental ontological given is not the vital impulse alone but the vital impulse situated in an inert matter that it strives to mold. Second, the vital impulse is a tendency to creative development but not to any particular line of such development. There is no prefixed plan according to which it acts; its direction varies contingently over time. Moreover, the impulse does not have only one direction; it is a drive toward varieties of development and so forks into an indefinite diversity of paths (like, Bergson says, artillery shells bursting in the sky in an endless tree of branching explosions (*EC*, 578/109)). Evolution displays progress of a sort, but not the finalist's progress of the gradual realization of a predesigned plan.

More fully, Bergson sees evolution as progressive in two senses. On the most fundamental level, there is "a continual advance in the general direction determined by a first impulsion" (*EC*, 583/116). We can, that is, always trace all the forms of life existing at a given moment back to a single impulse from which they all originate.[18] Moreover, we can distinguish "two or three great lines of evolution on which forms ever more complex, ever more and more high, appear". Between these grand lines of progress there are "a crowd of minor paths in which, on the contrary, deviations, arrests, setbacks are multiplied" (*EC*, 584/116). The "grand lines" were not, however, envisaged ahead of time; they have merely emerged as the most relatively stable achievements of the vital impulse.

One grand line has been that of the plants. This is a conservative direction that avoids "action and choice . . . and arrange[s] to get everything that it needs *in situ*, without going to look for it". Here

---

[18] This, of course, can be true even if there is no absolute beginning of the evolutionary process. Bergson's "first impulsion" need not be a unique act of creation.

the *élan vital* has pursued a "safe, tranquil, and bourgeois existence" but one that is also "torpid". But another grand line has been that of the animals. Here the vital impulse has gone "in the direction of movement and action, movement that is more and more effective, and action that is more and more free; here there is risk and adventure, and also consciousness, with its increasing degrees of depth and intensity".[19] The line of animal development has itself divided into two other grand lines, that of instinct and that of intelligence.

Instinct and intelligence both act by employing instruments, but the instruments of instinct are already available organized bodies (particularly an organism's own), whereas intelligence constructs artificial tools to achieve its ends. As a result, instinct operates immediately, effortlessly, and infallibly; but its range of effectiveness is sharply restricted and inflexible. Intelligence, by contrast, requires effort and reflection, trial and error, and will never achieve the efficiency of an automatic mechanism. But it is open to indefinite improvement and highly adaptable to variable situations. Whereas instinct operates on the principle that there is just one solution to a given problem (that embedded in the instinctive reaction), intelligence is based on the need to survey and choose from a range of possible solutions. This is why intelligence requires consciousness, which Bergson defines as "an arithmetical difference between potential and real activity"; that is, a measure of the "interval between representation and action" (*EC*, 618/160).

Conscious intelligence thus distances itself from the material instantiation of its objects in order to focus on the formal, relational features that give them distinct positions in the realm of possibilities. Intelligence does not respond to the specific anatomy and physiology of an arm that can be used to reach food but to the general structure (roughly, a long, narrow, solid object) that makes it a useful instrument. This is why intelligence can use a stick in place of or as a supplement to the arm. It is this capacity for formal abstraction that leads the intellect to separate its objects from the continuous flux of duration and to think of them instead as fixed and distinct units available for our use. Moreover, this separation of objects is of great practical value, since it allows us to focus exclusively on the features relevant for attaining our ends. But, at the same time, it results in the

---

[19] *L'énergie spirituelle*, 11; as translated by F.C.T. Moore in *Bergson: Thinking Backwards*, 122.

intellect's cinematographic vision of the world as a discrete series of independent units, as, that is, a spatialized system of material things, stripped of the duration of life.

With this the cosmology of *L'évolution créatrice* returns to and justifies the starting-point of Bergson's philosophy: his insistence that the intellectual categories of science are not adequate to the concreteness of our immediate experience of lived duration. We now see just why and how the intellect, although it is biologically the distinctive human trait, is a limited instrument of knowledge, formed to deal only with inert matter, that has "a natural inability to comprehend life" (*EC*, 635/182, emphasis omitted). But we also see how humans can overcome the limitations of the intellect. For we are creatures of instinct as well as of intellect; and instinct, as we have seen, is directed to the singular, concrete object, that is, to time as duration. Ordinarily, of course, instinct lacks the distance from objects needed for theoretical knowledge of them; its access to duration remains an unreflective sympathy that goes no further than an implicit know-how. But, according to Bergson, it is possible for instinct to become disengaged, for it to "become disinterested, self-conscious, capable of reflecting on its object" (*EC*, 645/194). Instinct then becomes intuition, the privileged vehicle of philosophical knowledge.

Bergson thinks that the possibility of something like intuition is apparent from the reality of aesthetic experience, which grasps the temporal unity of individual objects in a way that normal, spatialized perception does not. Philosophical intuition is the basis of an "inquiry turned in the same direction as art, which would take life in *general* for its object" (*EC*, 645/194).[20] The turn toward generality derives, according to Bergson, from intelligence itself. "Without intelligence, [intuition] would have remained in the form of instinct, riveted to the special object of its practical interest" (*EC*, 646/195). Philosophy is born from a fundamental cooperation between two complementary powers: "There are things that intelligence alone is able to seek, but which, by itself, it will never find. These things instinct alone could find; but it will never seek them" (*EC*, 623/167,

---

[20] Bergson's classic essay on humor (*Le rire*) locates it at the intersection of the lived time grasped by aesthetic and philosophical intuition and the mechanisms of spatialized perceptions. What we laugh at is a concretely existing human being's acting with the rigidity of an automaton (by, for example, falling through a trap door or responding to a question with a mindless literalism).

emphasis omitted). Intuition is precisely instinct directed toward the intellect's goal of general, theoretical knowledge.

Intuition enables us to go beyond the limitations of intelligence, but Bergson insists that we must continue to recognize and even employ the achievements of intelligence. For one thing, intellectual knowledge is epistemically unmatched by philosophy, which "will never obtain a knowledge of its object comparable to that which science has of its own". Indeed, Bergson says that "intelligence remains the luminous nucleus around which instinct, even enlarged and purified into intuition, forms only a vague nebulosity" and that philosophy does not achieve "knowledge properly so called", which is the privilege of science alone. (This high epistemic regard is no doubt what lies behind the careful attention that Bergson always pays to relevant scientific results.) Moreover, philosophy demonstrates the limitations of intelligence by employing intelligence itself to show just where its categories become inapplicable (*EC*, 646/195). Only then does intuition begin to operate philosophically in its own right and "by the sympathetic communication which it establishes between us and the rest of the living . . . introduces us into life's own domain, which is reciprocal interpenetration, endlessly continued creation". But Bergson recalls that even this transcendence of intelligence has been the result of the "push" of intelligence, which insists on getting beyond its limitations (*EC*, 646/195). There is, therefore, no basis for characterizing Bergson's thought as irrationalist or anti-reason, although it does insist on an essential transrational moment at the heart of philosophy.

Bergson is not an anti-rationalist, but he is an anti-intellectualist, particularly in contrast to Brunschvicg, whose insistence on the centrality of judgment and the priority of science make his philosophy aggressively intellectualist. (In *Les étapes de la pensée mathématiques*, Brunschvicg even labeled his position as "mathematical intellectualism".) This raises the question of Brunschvicg's view of Bergson's critique of the intellect, particularly since he was a good friend of Bergson's and always treated his views with the greatest respect.[21] Brunschvicg readily endorses Bergson's "brilliant demonstration" that "the reality of time, in its psychological truth, consists . . . in the individual rhythm of duration, which is . . . constitutive of

---

[21] See, for example, his discussions of Bergson in *Le progrès de la conscience*, chapter 21. In addition this important book is dedicated to Bergson ("in witness of affectionate admiration for the man and of intimate gratitude [*reconnaissance*] for the work").

the interior life".[22] But he does not agree with Bergson's further claim that intelligence can deal with time only by reducing it to a spatialized abstraction. He suggests that this conception of intelligence is "an interpretation of scientific knowledge [*savoir*]" that has been "surpassed by the evolution of human thought". Specifically, it is the understanding of intelligence given in Kant's transcendental aesthetic, which regards the intelligible world (e.g., the quantitative world of mathematics) as "given at a stroke, forever crystallized in a priori forms" and requiring "the sacrifice of what experience reveals . . . of the perpetually mobile and perpetually new in the appearances of the universe". But this is an outdated view, since mathematical physics has progressively developed into "a supple and living instrument, infinitely plastic and infinitely fruitful, intended to capture and to make present – if not to the senses, at least to the intelligence – qualities that escape the infirmity of our organism and our perception".[23] Moreover, Brunschvicg maintains that duration itself has no reality apart from its constitution by intelligence. He cites Lachelier's formulation: "There is time and, therefore, memory only for an intelligence that does not exist in time."[24] Consciousness itself, understood as the activity of judgment, "grasps in itself . . . the flux of universal life . . . in order to restore the freshness and energy of its immediate reality". In this way, "the impulse of consciousness [*élan de conscience*] is . . . an impulse of life [*élan de vie*] that traverses the universe". Indeed, it must be more than an "impulse of life"; it must be an "impulse of intelligence [*élan d'intelligence*]".[25] Thus, Brunschvicg's response to Bergson is that, properly understood, intelligence has all the dynamism Bergson finds in his vital impulse and must, moreover, constitute this impulse as an object of our experience. This is an ingenious effort at an idealist appropriation of Bergson's metaphysics. But, although Bergson never explicitly responded to Brunschvicg on this point, we can readily see that he could never accept his reduction of the cognitive leap of intuition to the gradual historical progress of scientific judgment.[26]

---

[22] Léon Brunschvicg, *L'expérience humaine et la causalité physique*, 570.
[23] Ibid., 571.
[24] J. Lachelier, "Rapport sur la personnalité", 697. Cited in *Le progrès de la conscience*, 655, n. 1.
[25] *L'expérience humaine et la causalité physique*, 655.
[26] On the personal and philosophical relations between Bergson and Brunschvicg, see the reminiscence of Vladimir Jankélévitch, who was the student and friend of both, in his "Léon Brunschvicg".

RELIGION AND MORALITY

Bergson's last book, *Les deux sources de la morale et de la religion* (1932), appeared twenty-five years after *L'évolution créatrice*. Nonetheless, it reads as a direct extension of the previous work's vision to ethics and religion. "All morality", Bergson maintains, "is in essence biological", provided that term is understood in a properly wide sense (*Les deux sources de la morale et de la religion* [*DSM*], 1061/101). What he means is that ethics and religion are not (and should not be) grounded, as philosophers so often think, in intellectual understanding and rational argument; they derive instead from "Life", from the vital impetus as it works in the human species.

This working is from two directions, corresponding to the "two sources" of morality. But neither source derives from the rational, intellectual realm in which philosophers have traditionally sought the basis of ethics. Rather, the sources are, respectively, below reason (infra-rational) and above reason (supra-rational) (*DSM*, 1029/64). The infra-rational source of morality is the pressure of social constraints on individuals, pushing them to behave according to patterns required for the stability of their society. Here, in Bergson's view, we have the human equivalent of the social instincts that produce an ant-hill or a bee-hive. The difference is that, since human intelligence raises us above the level of pure instinct, the mechanism of social constraint consists instead in an overwhelming sense of obligation, itself derived from deeply entrenched behavioral habits. The "habit" of morality – "the habit whose strength is made up of the accumulated force of all social habits" – is the most powerful of all and "the one which best imitates instinct" (*DSM*, 996/26). This most deeply ingrained habit corresponds to "pure obligation" (*DSM*, 1002/33), which defines what Bergson calls "closed morality", the morality that encloses individuals in a given society and closes them off from individuals outside that society.

The pressure of pure social obligation is always, Bergson maintains, restricted to the particular society to which a person belongs; it does not present us with any moral obligation to mankind in general. (Bergson admits that more "civilized" societies will proclaim obligations of entirely general altruism, but he says the behavior of such societies in war-time belies these verbal expressions (*DSM*, 1001/31).) His point is not, however, that morality is relative to a given society but that the "absolute morality" (*DSM*, 1003/34) of universal love for humankind has a source quite different from the pressures of society. This second, supra-rational source Bergson calls "aspiration" and finds in the appeals made to us by exceptional individuals (sages, prophets, saints) who develop moral visions that go beyond the limitations of closed morality and that, in particular, call us to a love of and community with all humans. The morality corresponding to such appeals is "open morality".

While the driving force of closed morality is habit, the driving force of open morality is emotion. Not, however, the mundane emotion of contentment with one's state (which belongs to closed morality) but the enthusiasm and joy that not only accompany but also inspire "the great creations of art, of science and of civilization in general" (*DSM*, 1011/43). The emotions of closed morality are after the fact, responding with approval to a moral achievement previously defined by society. The emotions of open morality are creative, not reactive. Such emotions are the sources of new moral practices and of new concepts rationalizing them, not the endorsement of practices already available. Consider, for example, "the emotion introduced by Christianity under the name of charity". This emotion swept the ancient world and created both a new metaphysics and a new morality, which "express the self-same thing [the emotion of charity], one in terms of intelligence, the other in terms of will" (*DSM*, 1016/49).

Behind Bergson's description of our moral situation lies his response to the perennial philosophical question of the rationality of ethical commitment. He agrees that in one sense this commitment is eminently rational. Both the habitual obligations of closed morality and the emotional appeals of open morality are projected into the realm of intelligence as obvious "first principles". Intelligence then sets about the project of organizing these principles into a self-consistent system (e.g., making commensurate the demands of justice and charity). The result – the typical standpoint of moral philosophy – is a formulation of morality on the "intermediate plane" of intelligence, where the moral life of humanity is viewed as "higher than that of animal society, where obligation would be but the force of instinct, but not so high as an assembly of gods, where everything would partake of the creative impetus". So organized by intelligence, "moral life will be a rational life" (*DSM*, 1047/85).

But, Bergson goes on, none of this shows that "morality has its origin or its foundation in pure reason" (*DSM*, 1047/85). In one sense, a rational deduction of morality is all too easy; in another, it is simply impossible. It is all too easy because just about any principle of action actually employed by human beings will yield at least a rough approximation of morality, simply because it has been formed by the forces that have created moral obligation. So, for example, even if we begin with personal interest, we will find that, since we are social animals to the core, satisfying this interest will require taking account of the welfare of others. Even the most selfish individual will desire the legitimate praise and respect of others. Our very vices are "saturated with vanity, and vanity means sociability", since it requires the good will of others (*DSM*, 1051/90).

On the other hand, a strict deduction of morality from principles not already implicitly moral is out of the question. Kantians claim, for example, that a "deposit" (that is, money or goods entrusted to someone with the understanding that they are to be returned upon request) must be given back when asked for, since otherwise it would not be a deposit. But, Bergson says, if "deposit" means merely the "material fact" of giving someone money with the understanding that it will be returned later, then there is clearly no inconsistency in refusing to return the money. To get a contradiction we must understand "deposit" in a moral sense, for example, as involving a "trust" that, by definition, "must not be betrayed". Then it would be inconsistent to refuse to return a deposit (since the recipient would in effect be saying: "I agree that what you gave me must be given back but I will not give it back"). But this contradiction results only because we have assumed moral obligation from the beginning. Bergson also questions the Kantian assumption that the requirement of self-consistency, essential in scientific and speculative pursuit of the truth, is likewise necessary for human life in general.[27]

In any case, the failure to justify morality rationally is of no significance, since, according to Bergson, regardless of the results of intellectual inquiry, a commitment to morality is inevitable. This is

---

[27] Bergson thinks that what nowadays would be called "teleological" (in contrast to Kantian "deontological") justifications of morality are even more obviously inadequate. For "it is easy to see that no objective ... will impose itself peremptorily as a mere rational proposition". The claim that a given goal must be accepted by a rational being will have no force on someone who is committed to some other goal: "one can always reason with reason, confront its arguments with others, or simply refuse all discussion and reply by a '*sic volo, sic jubeo*'" (*DSM*, 1050/89). Bergson's critiques of justifications of morality would clearly need much more development to be effective against the sophisticated arguments of analytic philosophers (e.g., Alan Gewirth) during the last fifty years. But the main strands of his criticisms are very similar to the points standardly raised against these arguments.

so first on the level of obligation, which is simply a necessity of the biological life of our species. Evolution has made us social creatures and the obligations of closed morality are built into us biologically as part of the organization of the group to which we essentially belong. The aspirations of open morality do not arise from the compulsions of social pressure, but they do derive from the "more or less irresistible attraction" (*DSM*, 1056/96) to a moral ideal stirred by a compelling life in which we see it embodied. In both cases, the ultimate source of morality is the vital impulse. In the first, it acts through the mechanisms that have produced social animals, and we can well imagine nature's remaining content with the stability of the structures of closed morality. But the reality of open morality shows that the vital impulse has, so to speak, renewed itself through the lives of moral heroes ("those geniuses of the will" (*DSM*, 1023/58)). Here the impulse "comes into play directly, and no longer through the medium of the mechanisms it had set up, and at which it had provisionally halted" (*DSM*, 1021/55). Whereas closed morality expresses nature as it has been constituted, open morality expresses nature as constituting itself anew (in Spinoza's terminology, *natura naturans* rather than *natura naturata*) (*DSM*, 1024/58).

Corresponding to the distinction between closed and open morality is Bergson's distinction between static and dynamic religion. In its static form, religion functions to preserve the stability of society against challenges from intelligence. Although human society is analogous to the entirely instinctual societies of ants and bees, it differs in that its individuals are capable of understanding and questioning their situation, a fact that raises the real possibility of refusing social obligations. As Bergson sees it, such refusal can derive either from selfishness (why should I subordinate my interests to those of others?) or from despair in the face of the uncertainties of life and the inevitability of death (since my projects are never sure of success and I am going to die anyway, why does it matter how I behave?). Static religion intervenes with myths about the universe and our place in it that counter such questioning, for example by promising rewards and punishments in an afterlife and offering magical instruments for the control of nature. Bergson's detailed discussion takes account of the then recent anthropological and sociological work of Lévy-Bruhl and of Émile Durkheim but argues against them that there is no distinctive "primitive mentality". We are beyond "primitives" in what we know about the world but have the same desires and fears and so are still susceptible to the superstitions of static religion. "Scratch the surface, abolish everything we owe to an education which is perpetual and unceasing, and you find in the depth of our nature primitive humanity, or something very near it" (*DSM*, 1083/127).

Just as open morality extends moral obligation from a limited community to all of humankind, so dynamic religion moves from the guardian gods of one tribe to a divinity whose love embraces everyone. And, just as open morality spreads from the emotions of heroic ethical leaders, so dynamic religion flows from the experiences of a select group of religious "geniuses", the mystics. The close connection of open morality and dynamic religion is apparent from the overlap between their heroes, especially Christ, whom Bergson sees as the greatest figure in both morality and religion. The connection is all the closer because, Bergson insists, the most perfect form of mysticism involves not just detached contemplation but also practical action in the world. The greatest mystics are those such as St. Paul, St. Joan of Arc, St. Francis of Assisi, St. Teresa of Avila, St. Catherine of Siena, and Christ himself, who profoundly transformed human affairs.

Bergson defines mysticism quite explicitly:

In our eyes, the ultimate end of mysticism is the establishment of a contact, consequently of a partial coincidence, with the creative effort which life itself manifests. This effort is of God, if it is not God himself. The great mystic is to be conceived as an individual being, capable of transcending the limitations imposed on the species by its material nature, thus continuing and extending the divine action. Such is our definition. (*DSM*, 1162/220–1)

So understood, mysticism in its highest form ("complete mysticism") is found only in the great Christian mystics. It is often said that such people are mentally deranged, and they are undeniably susceptible to morbid and hallucinatory states. But Bergson maintains that such pathologies are likely to accompany radical transformations of the soul, and that visions and nervous agitation are only accidentally related to what is at the core of the mystics' experiences: the love of God pervading their entire selves and inspiring them "to complete the creation of the human species" (*DSM*, 1174/234). In the completeness of mysticism, "visions are left far behind" and all that remains is a total and final union with God, "who is acting through the soul . . . with an irresistible impulse that hurls it into great enterprises" (*DSM*, 1172/232). The mystics' love has the same direction as the vital impulse, indeed, "it *is* this impetus itself, communicated in its entirety to exceptional men who in their turn would fain impart it to all humanity". The goal is the paradox ("living contradiction") of turning a biological species, which is precisely a stable product of the vital impulse, into the creative movement of that impulse (*DSM*, 1175/235).

But mysticism faces the same obstacle that always obstructs the vital impetus: the inertness of matter, in this case, the human need for physical sustenance, which takes up almost all our energies and turns us away from higher things. Hinting at an ultimately political direction of his thought, Bergson suggests that the total fulfillment of mysticism's spiritual goal requires "a profound change in the material conditions imposed on humanity by nature" (*DSM*, 1176/236), a change that in the end might be best effected by "a vast system of machinery such as might set human activity at liberty, this liberation being, moreover, stabilized by a political and social organization which would ensure the application of the mechanism to its true object" (*DSM*, 1175/235).[28] Such radical transformations are not immediately possible, and mystics have instead limited themselves to the more feasible tasks of planting and sustaining the mystical flame in established social institutions, particularly those of static religion, mainly by founding religious communities.

As a result, the historical actuality of religion has been neither purely static nor purely dynamic. "We represent religion, then, as the crystallization, brought about by a scientific process of cooling, of what mysticism had poured, while hot, into the soul of man. Through religion all men get a little of what a few privileged souls possessed in full" (*DSM*, 1177/238). Christianity, for example, "has preserved many rites, many ceremonies, many beliefs even" from static religion (along with large portions of Greek philosophy). This was important for its gaining popular acceptance, "but none of all that was essential; the essence of the new religion was to be the diffusion of mysticism" (*DSM*, 1178/238). Bergson, in other words, regards Christianity (and other historical religions) as a vehicle for the popularization of mystical truth, quite parallel to the "high-level popularization, which respects the broad outlines of scientific truth, and enables ordinary

[28] Some of Bergson's further thoughts along these lines are developed in the often surprisingly non-philosophical political and historical comments of the last chapter of *Les deux sources de la morale et de la religion*.

cultivated minds to get a general grasp of it until . . . a greater effort reveals it to them in detail, and, above all, allows them to penetrate deeply into its significance" (*DSM*, 1178/238-9).

Bergson also thinks that mystical experience is a basis for resolving the traditional philosophical problems of the existence and nature of God. Its first contribution is to bring philosophy back to a concept of God that allows him to communicate with us. Any such concept is excluded by traditional philosophical conceptions of God, which are modeled on Aristotle's "motionless Mover, a Thought thinking itself, self-enclosed, operative only by the appeal of its perfection" (*DSM*, 1180/242). Such a being has little or nothing in common with the God of the Greeks or of the Gospels, and a philosophy concerned with it will be irrelevant to the reality of religious life. By contrast, the God of mysticism, offering his love and calling for our own, is precisely at the root of what is most vital in historical religions.

But does the existence of mystical experience give the philosopher reason to believe in the God of which it speaks? The fact that the greatest mystics "have generally been men or women of action, endowed with superior common sense" (*DSM*, 1183/245) refutes the common objection that they are "crazy" and not to be taken seriously. Likewise, the objection that only a few exceptional individuals have had mystical experiences carries, in Bergson's view, little weight. The testimony of mystics has essentially the same status as the reports, which we rightly believe, of those few explorers who have penetrated barely accessible regions of the earth. Moreover, almost all mystics, even from very different religious traditions, agree in their core account of divinity, and these accounts seem due much more to the experiences themselves than to the doctrinal traditions to which individual mystics belong. These considerations make it probable, though not absolutely certain, that the testimony of the mystics is reliable. But Bergson thinks final confirmation comes from the way mystical testimony coheres with the results of independent philosophical investigation. On the one hand, philosophical reflection on evolution (e.g., in *L'évolution créatrice*) shows that we should expect intelligence to be surrounded with a "halo of intuition", which provides some direct contact with the concrete reality of duration. It is from this intuition that we could expect to learn something of "the inner workings of the vital impulse" (*DSM*, 1187/250). Thus, philosophy establishes precisely the niche that is filled by mystical knowledge. On the other hand, mystical experience would seem to be a fruitful guide to continuing the line of thought that led philosophy to the vital impulse. It directs us away from useless metaphysical speculations about the nature of God and helps us develop a conception of divine love (identical with God's reality) as the driving force of the universe. Bergson briefly sketches how this conception suggests fruitful speculations about the nature of creation, the ultimate purpose of the universe, the problem of evil, and the likelihood of immortality.

These speculations, as Bergson himself points out (*DSM*, 1193/256), take him beyond his position in *L'évolution créatrice* and toward a more traditional view of God as creator and of humanity as the purpose of this creation. This helps explain Bergson's move toward Catholicism at the end of his life. He never formally entered the Church, primarily because, although he had never practiced Judaism, he did not want to appear to be renouncing his heritage at a time when Hitler and the Vichy regime were persecuting Jews. But he did express his acceptance of Catholic doctrine and ask that a priest say prayers at his funeral. There is no doubt about the sincerity of this "conversion", but its significance needs to be understood in terms of Bergson's rejection of the scholastic metaphysics implicit in the Church's formulation of its doctrines and, especially, of his view of the limited and essentially instrumental role of religious institutions.

Bergson's long-term influence on French philosophy has been wide but diffuse. The wave of his initial immense popularity rather quickly subsided, and, as we shall see in the next chapter, he did not have a major effect on the young philosophers of the 1930s and 1940s.[29] But he remained a presence in the French philosophical world, and his books are even today required reading for the *classe de philosophie* and the *agrégation*. Further, the substance and, even more, the spirit of his philosophy was passed on to successive generations of students by Vladimir Jankélévitch (1903-85), one of the most popular professors at the Sorbonne, where he taught from 1951 to 1978. Jankélévitch's *Henri Bergson* (1931) is widely regarded as one of the most subtle and penetrating books on Bergson. His own philosophy (developed in, for example, *Traité des vertus* and *Le je-ne-sais-quoi et le presque-rien*) offers a refined and passionate vision of

---

[29] Bergson did have a very strong influence on the work of Pierre Teilhard de Chardin (1881-1955), a Jesuit paleontologist who combined the philosophy of creative evolution with Christian theology in *L'apparition de l'homme*.

moral life that merges Bergsonian metaphysics with an almost existentialist commitment to individual agency and creativity. He avoids, however, any tendency to existential egoism by insisting on the ethical primacy of generosity (a concept in which Sartre was greatly interested in his reflections on ethics). Jankélévitch was an accomplished musician and musicologist, with important books on Lizst, Debussy, and Ravel, and saw music as both symbol and source of the pure and innocent love required by ethical life.

CHAPTER 4

Between the wars

> Meanwhile the philosophers of journalism are at work castigating the preceding epoch, and not only the kind of pleasures in which it indulged, which seem to them to be the last word in corruption, but even the work of its artists and philosophers, which have no longer the least value in their eyes, as though they were indissolubly linked to the successive moods of fashionable frivolity.
> (Marcel Proust, *In Search of Lost Time*, II, 123)

It is quite possible to view French philosophy during the last twenty years of the Third Republic (1920–40) as little more than an extension of the preceding twenty years. All the main figures of the earlier period (Bergson, Brunschvicg, Meyerson, Boutroux) continue to produce major works. Important younger philosophers are usually readily placed in the old traditions. For example, Louis Lavelle and René LeSenne develop a "philosophy of spirit" that has close affinities with the old spiritualism of Maine de Biran and Ravaisson; and Gaston Bachelard continues the tradition of French history and philosophy of science. From this viewpoint, the most original development is that of distinctively Catholic philosophy, both in Blondel's "philosophy of action"[1] and in Maritain's neo-Thomism. But this development remains relatively isolated, precisely because of its strongly sectarian inclinations and is, in any case, still connected to Bergson and the earlier spiritualist tradition.

But although this continuist picture reflects important features of the interwar period, it completely misses the central fact that the period is at root one of undermining and upheaval. This fact is signaled by a striking reversal in the view of Dominique Parodi, who,

---

[1] Blondel's main work, *L'action*, appeared already in 1893, after which he published little until the 1930s, when his revision of *L'action* appeared along with two major companion volumes.

84

as we saw, said in 1919 that "philosophical research had never been more abundant, more serious, and more intense among us than in the last thirty years".[2] Just fifteen years later Parodi opens his new book with a chapter entitled "The Crisis of Modern Philosophy" in which he says: "Over the last thirty years, it has become quite clear that the intellectual disarray is complete."[3] The disarray was due to the radical challenge to the university philosophies of the early Third Republic by the new "philosophy of existence" that was emerging in connection with young intellectuals' fascinations with avant-garde literature and with German philosophy. We will first pause to examine the more continuist work of Bachelard, Blondel, and Maritain and then move to the incipient existential surge.

BACHELARD

Gaston Bachelard (1884–1962) was initially trained in science and mathematics, receiving his *licence* in mathematics in 1912 and his *agrégation* in philosophy only in 1922, when he was thirty-eight years old (though he completed his doctorate in philosophy just five years later). For many years (1919–30) he taught physics and chemistry, along with philosophy, at the *collège* (secondary school) of Bar-sur-Aube, the small southwestern town where he was born and raised. In 1930 he became professor of philosophy at Dijon, and in 1940 was awarded a chair at the Sorbonne, where he became director of the Institut d'Histoire des Sciences et des Techniques. Although Bachelard came to philosophy late and to the Parisian mainstream even later, he was for many years one of the most influential members of the "republic of professors". Along with his successor, Georges Canguilhem, he not only trained an impressive cadre of specialists in the history and philosophy of science but also gave successive generations of students (including future "stars" such as Foucault and Althusser) their basic understanding of the nature of scientific inquiry.

Bachelard's work, with its deep roots in detailed knowledge of the history and current practice of science, immediately associates him with the tradition of Poincaré, Meyerson, and Boutroux. But his basic view of the relation of science and philosophy derives most

---

[2] *La philosophie contemporaine en France*, 9–10.
[3] *En quête d'une philosophie*, 1.

directly from Brunschvicg, who (along with Abel Rey) directed his doctoral work. Like Brunschvicg, Bachelard sees philosophy as having to work out an understanding of reason by reflection on the historical development of science; and, again like Brunschvicg, his work is based on case-studies in the history of mathematics and the physical sciences.[4] On the other hand, Bachelard emphasizes far more than Brunschvicg the role of discontinuity in the development of science and at least tries to avoid a whole-hearted endorsement of idealism over realism.

Bachelard's picture of scientific development centers on his notion of epistemological break (*coupure épistémologique*). Science requires, first of all, a break from our common-sense experiences and beliefs, since it places everyday objects under new concepts and shows them to possess properties not revealed by ordinary sense perception (or even in contradiction with sense perception, as when what seem to be intrinsic qualities, such as color, are reinterpreted as relations to sense organs). But scientific progress also requires breaks from previous scientific conceptions, which, as much as common sense, can become obstacles to our attaining scientific truth. Thus, the viewpoint of Newtonian mechanics became, in the twentieth century, a major obstacle to Einstein's formulation of an adequate account of space, time, and gravitation. Breaking with the Newtonian view initiated a "new scientific spirit" that involved not only new conceptions of the physical world but also new criteria of scientific methodology.[5] Bachelard's treatment of this subject precedes Thomas Kuhn's treatment of "scientific revolutions" by more than thirty years.

Since for Bachelard philosophical conceptions of knowledge and reality are, quite properly, derivative from the best science of their time, epistemological breaks in scientific thought require corresponding revolutions in philosophy. Much of his work is devoted to developing new philosophical views to replace those "outdated" by the progress of science. He proposes, for example, a "non-Cartesian epistemology" (a notion meant to parallel "non-Euclidean geo-

---

[4] On the similarities of Bachelard's thought to Brunschvicg's, see Michel Vadée, *Gaston Bachelard*, especially 229–35. Vadée maintains that Bachelard's debt to Brunschvicg has been ignored by his followers and commentators (in particular, Canguilhem). See also Bachelard's paper, "La philosophie scientifique de Léon Brunschvicg".

[5] See Gaston Bachelard, *Le nouvel esprit scientifique*, as well as his earlier detailed discussion of relativity theory, *La valeur inductive de la relativité*.

metry"), based on a rejection of Descartes' (and many subsequent philosophers') foundationalist privileging of the "givens" of immediate experience. This epistemology will, of course, also be "non-Kantian" in its denial of the eternal validity of categories that in fact are contingent expressions of Newtonian science. Bachelard further suggests the need for a "psychoanalysis of knowledge" that will expose the unconscious role outdated common-sense and scientific concepts play in our thinking.[6]

Bachelard's insistence on breaks and discontinuity might seem to reject Brunschvicg's view of science as an essentially progressive enterprise. Bachelard, however, maintains that progress does not require continuity. Even though there are sharp conceptual and methodological breaks from one scientific worldview to another, we are still justified in speaking of progress because some specific achievements of past science are preserved as special cases within later theories. Once again, Bachelard invokes the analogy with non-Euclidean geometry, which, for example, denies the Euclidean claim that all triangles have 180 degrees as the sum of their interior angles, while admitting a special class of triangles ("Euclidean triangles") for which this is true. In the same way, concepts such as specific heat (developed by Black in terms of the now superseded caloric theory) and mass (as understood by Newton) have been reformulated in the context of later theories.

There is deeper tension between Bachelard and Brunschvicg on the issue of idealism. Bachelard does criticize a position he calls "realism", characterized as the belief "in the prolix richness of the individual sensation and in the systematic impoverishment of abstractive thought".[7] Realism in this sense asserts the epistemic and metaphysical primacy of ordinary sense objects over what it regards as abstract accounts in terms of the theoretical entities of science. Bachelard's critique of realism is in effect an assertion of the ontological primacy of theoretical entities as concrete realities. To this extent, it amounts to a defense of what analytic philosophers of science nowadays call "scientific realism".

Bachelard does not, however, understand this scientific realism as implying a traditional metaphysical realism, which asserts that the objects of our knowledge are entirely mind-independent. He

---

[6] In this regard, see his *La psychoanalyse du feu*.
[7] *La valeur inductive de la relativité*, 206.

maintains a "rationalism" that emphasizes both the active role of the mind in the construction of the scientific concepts with which we describe reality and the richness and specificity of these concepts in contrast to the vagueness and generality of sensations. At the same time, he tries to stay clear of an idealism that would see the world as constituted by pure thought. Truth is not a matter of the mind's creating or constituting the world. It is, rather, the result of the mind's "revision" (*rectification*) by scientific concepts of a world that is already there. Bachelard says, accordingly, that his rationalism is "applied"; that is, the mind never produces its objects ex nihilo but rather applies its concepts to pregiven objects. However, he also emphasizes that objects are not "pregiven" in any absolute sense but are the results of previous applications of concepts. Although Bachelard wants applied rationalism to be a mean between idealism and realism, his refusal to accept objects that exist independent of our conceptions seems to force him back to something very much like Brunschvicg's critical idealism.[8]

Whatever its relation to idealism, Bachelard's applied rationalism also introduces the crucial idea that scientific instrumentation has a central role in the constitution of the physical world. Instruments are, he says, "theories materialized", and a concept is truly scientific only to the extent that it receives concrete reality through a "technique of realization".[9] Husserl's phenomenology describes how the mind constitutes the objects of everyday experience, but we also require a "phenomeno-technics" that will describe the constitution of scientific objects by instrumental technology.

As we have seen, Bachelard's epistemology of science gives ontological priority to the objects of science and presents the domain of ordinary sense experiences and images as obstacles to attaining scientific truth. However, around 1940 (just after his appointment to the Sorbonne chair in the history of science), Bachelard began publishing a series of books that explored the positive significance of prescientific experience.[10] Here he presented the domain of poetic imagination, dominated by the primitive and fundamental images of

---

[8] For a more detailed discussion of Bachelard's philosophy of science, see chapter 1 of my *Michel Foucault's Archaeology of Scientific Reason*. As I argue there (and as we shall see below), Bachelard's thought has considerable significance for Foucault and for other thinkers of his generation such as Louis Althusser and Michel Serres.
[9] *Le nouvel esprit scientifique*, 13, 16.
[10] See, for example, *La poétique de la rêverie* and *La poétique de l'espace*.

fire, air, water, and earth, as central for our understanding and creation of ourselves as human beings. This work had a considerable impact in literary studies (even outside France), and Sartre makes sympathetic reference to it in his book on imagination and in *L'être et le néant* when developing his method of existential psychoanalysis. Bachelard intended his celebration of the poetic as a complement to rather than a recantation of his defense of the ontological priority of science, but he never worked out in any detail the relation between these two aspects of his work.[11]

BLONDEL

The Third Republic was an avowedly secular institution, endorsing Voltaire's view that beliefs in alleged religious revelations were a private matter of the individual conscience and should not intrude into the public domain. Since philosophy claimed to be a model of public discourse, appealing to a common human rationality, it presented itself as a secular enterprise, neutral among all claims of revealed truth. Some philosophers were, of course, religious – Lachelier, Boutroux, and Le Roy, for example, were devout Catholics. But their religion was neither the source nor the justification of their philosophical views. And these views, in turn, although presumably compatible with their religious beliefs, were not presented as foundations or prolegomena to these beliefs. They were Christian philosophers but with no distinctively Christian philosophy.

In his famous thesis, *L'action*, defended in 1893, Maurice Blondel (1861–1949) did not go so far as to employ his Catholic beliefs as premises of his philosophical arguments or to try to derive these beliefs from naturally known philosophical premises. But he did maintain that a proper philosophical understanding of the human condition would show that our deepest aspirations could not be satisfied in the natural realm, that the intelligibility and fulfillment we desire are possible only if the Christian doctrine of salvation through supernatural grace is true. Like Pascal, he set out to show that, whether or not Christianity is true, we ought to hope with all our hearts that it is. In this sense he proposes a Christian philosophy.

[11] See Jean Hyppolite's three essays on Bachelard, collected in his *Figures de la pensée philosophique*, 643–83.

L'action begins with the urgent question: "Yes or no, does human life make sense, and does man have a destiny?" (*L'action* [*A*], 1/1), and this dramatic, proto-existentialist tone is interwoven throughout its complex and sometimes tediously extended philosophical discussions. This tone corresponds, moreover, to Blondel's guiding conviction that his question must be answered by an understanding of our concrete engagement in the world through action, where "action" means the totality of our thought, feeling, and willing in direct relation with their objects. Blondel begins by emphasizing the inevitability of action: at every instant we are, willy nilly, acting (even if we are trying to withdraw from all action). The question is what sort of overall meaning, if any, we must ascribe to our life of action.

It might seem possible to reject Blondel's question, to refuse even to consider whether life has any meaning. Such a rejection, he maintains, entails a "dilettantism" that would endlessly explore a random variety of human experiences and activities with no concern for finding a unified or even consistent pattern in the variety. Here Blondel has in mind the positivist ironism of Renan and Taine, as well as the poetic decadence of Baudelaire. (His view of dilettantism also recalls Kierkegaard's treatment of the aesthetic sphere, but there is no evidence of direct influence, although there are some striking similarities in their discussions.) Blondel has enough empathy with dilettantism to provide a vivid and nuanced evocation of its attitude. But he concludes that the standpoint is ultimately incoherent. Dilettantes claim to have no interest in overall meaning but are in fact committed to understanding everything in terms of their own selfish project of an endless succession of enjoyments. Dilettantism "is a radical egoism that would destroy everything in order to remain alone like a god" (*A*, 16/30), and this deification of the self is precisely the ultimate meaning that the dilettante purports to eschew.

The pessimist (Schopenhauer is explicitly cited as a primary example[12]) accepts the validity of Blondel's question but gives it an entirely negative answer: life has no meaning, and our attitude toward it should be one of pessimistic denial. Putting the point in Blondel's terms of voluntary action, we should will nothing at all, since nothing in life is worthy of our desire, and find contentment in

---

[12] At the time Blondel wrote his thesis, Schopenhauer was very influential in France, although his initial impact was more in the literary than the professional philosophical world. See Jean-Louis Fabiani, *Les philosophes de la république*, 118.

a state of pure "nolition" (Blondel's coinage from the Latin *nolo*, I do not will). Blondel argues, however, that pessimism is, like dilettantism, incoherent, since its project of willing nothing must be parasitic on the willing of some positive reality. Anticipating Bergson's analysis in *L'évolution créatrice*, he argues that there is no absolute conception of "nothing"; negation is always a relative matter of replacing one positive reality with another. There is, accordingly, no coherent object to which an absolute nolition could correspond. This is confirmed, Blondel maintains, by the fact that Schopenhauer's act of renunciation is itself grounded in a positive preference for the state of nolition that he seeks. "Pessimism . . . lets loose an immense and invincible confidence in the omnipotence of the will since the will appears both necessary and sufficient to produce the pain of existence as well as to create the happy annihilation that would not be without it" (*A*, 36/48). He concludes "we could not have either a conception of or a will for nothingness . . . because from the moment we posit the problem of action [that is, the problem of the meaning of human life] the fact is that we already have a positive solution for it" (*A*, 39/50).

The largest part of *L'action* offers a systematic survey of possible positive views of the meaning of life. Blondel follows a minimalist principle[13] of beginning with the lowest degree of positive commitment that would seem capable of explicating what the meaning of life is. Only after he has shown the inadequacy of a lesser degree of commitment does he move on to a higher one. He thus tries to avoid ignoring possibilities for giving life an acceptable sense that fall short of his own view that only the existence of the Christian God will do. Blondel's treatment of the range of positive meanings shows him to be firmly within the French spiritualist tradition. Although his final goal is to support the Catholic faith, his philosophical precursors are not Augustine or Aquinas but Maine de Biran, Ravaisson, Lachelier, and Léon Ollé-Laprune, his teacher at the École Normale.[14]

Blondel begins with the possibility that scientific materialism answers his question of the meaning of life, but he rejects this

---

[13] On this, see René Virgoulay, *"L'action" de Maurice Blondel*, 15.
[14] Blondel's thought does have some strong similarities to that of Augustine, particularly in his treatment of the will, but this seems due to Augustine's pervasive influence on Christian thought in general rather than any specific study of his works by Blondel. Blondel may also have assimilated Augustinian ideas through Malebranche. John McNeill has argued (in his *The Blondelian Synthesis*) for a major role of the German idealist tradition in the development of Blondel's thought, but his case is rather weak.

possibility on the standard spiritualist grounds that consciousness is not reducible to matter. Similarly, he rejects an answer in terms of psychological determinism, arguing that freedom, concretely expressed in action, is an essential feature of consciousness. His claim, in fact, is even stronger. Free action is "the cement of organic life, the bond of individual consciousness" (*A*, 180/175). Blondel even anticipates Sartre's existentialist language: "The substance of man is action; he is what he makes himself."[15] But Blondel insists that the life of the individual alone cannot sustain the meaning we require. Our action inevitably extends to the social world, seeking meaning first in the family, then in the nation, in the community of all humankind, and even in projections of humanity onto idols of superstitious worship.

At every stage, action is driven to seek further levels of meaning because of the gap between what our willing has achieved so far (what Blondel calls the "willed will", *volonté voulue*) and what we most profoundly will (the "willing will", *volonté voulante*). No matter how successful our willing, no matter how extensive the realm of objects it attains, the will (*volonté voulante*) *is never entirely satisfied. This is because, at the very least, our willing itself, the very root of our action, is not something we have willed:*

Suppose that man does everything as he wills it, obtains what he covets, vivifies the universe according to his liking, organizes and produces as he wishes the total ordering of conditions on which he rests his life: it remains that this will itself has not been posited or determined as it is by him ... he wills, but he did not will to will. (*A*, 326/303)

The will is not content that its action be finally derived from outside. Our ultimate desire is to be entirely self-sufficient; to be, in a word, God: "Man aspires to be a god." Once again, Blondel anticipates Sartre. But, unlike Sartre, he does not conclude that our desire to be God is a "useless passion", collapsing under the impossibility of a being that would be both in-itself and for-itself. According to Blondel, the impossibility follows only if we choose "to be god without God and against God". But there is another alternative: "to be God through God and with God" (*A*, 356/328). To take this route is to open myself to the will of another being, but one that is the source of my being and hence of my very will. In union with this being

---

[15] Cited by Jean Lacroix, *Maurice Blondel*, 33.

(God), I can achieve the self-sufficiency that is my ultimate volition. It is this alternative that opens the way to our rebirth in a supernatural order of grace.

Philosophy, according to Blondel, can take us as far as the possibility of this supernatural order. But it cannot tell us whether the order is actual or whether we ought to choose the alternative it would present. The role of philosophy is to "prove that we cannot, in practice, not pronounce for or against this supernatural: 'Is it or is it not?'" Philosophy can even "examine the consequences of one solution or the other and . . . measure their immense disparity. But philosophy can go no further, nor can it say, in its own name alone, whether it be or not." Blondel sees the whole of *L'action* as operating within this limited domain of the philosophical and so respecting the boundary between what is knowable to natural reason and what is grasped only by supernatural faith. Only in the final sentence of the book does he cross the boundary to speak the "one word, . . . which cannot be communicated because it arises only from the intimacy of totally personal action: . . . 'It is'" (*A*, 492/446).

Despite his insistence on the strictly philosophical grounding of *L'action*, Blondel's secular colleagues were not convinced that his project stood independent of his Catholicism. The doubts were thoroughly articulated at the defense of his thesis, where the board subjected him to four hours of intense questioning before awarding a passing grade. More seriously, his appointment to a university position (there was one waiting for him in Dijon) was held up for almost two years because of official doubts about his philosophical independence. He was finally awarded the post only after Boutroux, his thesis director, directly intervened with the minister of education. In any case, Blondel's influence was mostly restricted to Catholic circles and was further limited by his failure to follow *L'action* with any other books for over forty years. It was only in 1934 that he began to publish an immense trilogy, with a revised version of *L'action* preceded by treatises on thought (*La penseé*) and ontology (*L'être et les êtres*). These volumes – as well as *La philosophie et l'esprit chrétien*, published in 1944 – deepen and extend the basic philosophical achievement of *L'action* (which nonetheless remains the best expression of the core of Blondel's thought), but they came too late to have much impact on the general direction of French philosophy.

NEO-THOMISM AND MARITAIN

Even among Catholics, Blondel had much less impact than he might have had, because his work lay outside the modern revival of medieval scholasticism, particularly the thought of St. Thomas Aquinas.[16] The revival began around 1850, led by Mateo Liberatore in Italy and Joseph Kleutgen in Germany.[17] But it took on central importance for Catholics with Leo XIII's encyclical, *Aeterni Patris* (1879), which in effect established Aquinas as the official philosopher of the Catholic Church. One of the first major francophone reactions to the encyclical was Désiré (later, Cardinal) Mercier's establishment of the Institut Supérieure de Philosophie at the Catholic University of Louvain in Belgium, which developed a distinctive school of Thomism that exercised international influence. In France, the Thomistic revival was led by the Dominicans and was especially centered in the order's house of studies, Le Saulchoir (located in Belgium because of French anti-clerical laws). Almost all the important French Dominican neo-Thomists, including Antonin-Dalmace Sertillanges (1863–1943) and Réginald Garrigou-Lagrange (1877–1964), were associated with Le Saulchoir.

For all its vitality, the neo-Thomist movement had little impact outside Catholic – and, in fact, clerical – circles until the work of two Catholic laymen: Étienne Gilson (1884–1978) and Jacques Maritain (1882–1973). Gilson was a distinguished historian of philosophy, who first made his name with a thesis on the scholastic background to Descartes' philosophy, *La liberté chez Descartes et la théologie*, and then went on to write a series of magisterial books on the "Christian philosophies" of Augustine, Bonaventure, and Aquinas. It is in large part due to Gilson that medieval philosophy became and remains a fruitful area of historical studies in France and elsewhere.

Although Gilson's version of "existential Thomism" had an interest that went well beyond historical interpretation, the leading original philosopher of the neo-Thomist movement was Jacques Maritain. Maritain came from an agnostic family and was initially an adherent of Bergson's philosophy. (The story is that he and his

---

[16] Blondel did avoid condemnation by the Vatican, although there were those in the Church who thought his independence of the Thomistic tradition and sympathy for philosophy since Descartes led him into the errors of modernism, condemned by Pius X in 1907.

[17] My discussion of neo-scholasticism – as well as of Gilson and Maritain – is indebted to the excellent treatment provided in Gerald McCool, *The Neo-Thomists*.

fiancée, Raissa Oumançoff, had been in despair at the meaninglessness of modern existence, even to the point of contemplating a suicide pact, but hearing Bergson lecture at the Collège de France, along with an encounter with the writings of Léon Bloy, revived their hope.) In 1906 Maritain (and Raissa, to whom he was by then married) converted to Catholicism. Given the Church's condemnation of modernist thought, he became uneasy with his Bergsonism and for a time considered giving up philosophy. But his wife's confessor, a Dominican priest, recommended that he study St. Thomas Aquinas. Maritain did so and soon became convinced that here was a philosophy superior even to Bergson's and, in fact, capable of preserving the truth in Bergsonism while correcting its mistakes. His first book, *La philosophie Bergsonienne*, was a vigorous (Maritain even later said "violent") attack on Bergson from a Thomistic standpoint.[18]

Maritain's primary disagreement with Bergson concerned the status of the intuition that is our fundamental contact with reality. As we have seen, Bergson's intuition is a supra-rational insight that reveals intellectual categories as abstractions for the sake of practical action. Maritain, on the other hand, insisted that there is an intellectual intuition of being as such that puts us into direct contact with fundamental structures of reality, which is thereby revealed to be intelligible through and through.

Maritain saw these structures as most clearly revealed in Aquinas's metaphysics of act and potency for which reality is a multiplicity of finite substances created and sustained by the infinite substance, God. Every finite substance is contingent (capable of not existing) because of the real distinction between its essence (the potential to be what it is) and its existence (the act of being – *esse* – whereby its essence is actualized). In God, by contrast, essence and existence are identical; his nature or essence is simply to exist. The divine reality is, accordingly, necessarily existent, a pure act containing the realization of all perfection. Maritain's major treatises on metaphysics develop his position on traditional scholastic and Thomistic debates, such as whether the act of being (*esse*) is grasped through an abstract

---

[18] *La philosophie Bergsonienne*, translated as *Bergsonian Philosophy and Thomism*. This is a translation of a slightly revised version of the French work's second edition, along with an added "Essay of Appreciation", consisting of two chapters of Maritain's *Ransoming the Time*, giving his later and less harsh view of Bergson. Maritain's reference to the "violence" of the original book is in the foreword to this translation, p. 5.

concept or through a judgment.[19] Maritain initially agreed with French Dominicans such as Garrigou-Lagrange that being is knowable through concepts. But he later moved toward Gilson's view that being is apprehended in concrete judgments of existence and, also like Gilson, argued that this view showed Thomism to be an authentically existential philosophy.

These discussions of issues so thoroughly sifted by the Thomistic tradition gave little scope to Maritain's capacity for original philosophizing and, in any case, had little impact on those outside the circle of Thomism, who found themselves incapable of the intellectual intuitions on which Maritain's metaphysics was based. But other aspects of Maritain's Thomism were more original and had wider appeal. His epistemology[20] forthrightly rejected the Cartesian idea, which he saw as corrupting modern thought, that philosophy must begin with the contents of consciousness and somehow justify the existence of external objects. To this Maritain opposed a direct realism in the Aristotelian tradition that allowed him to begin with our knowledge of nature and use it as a basis for a philosophical account of knowing. Maritain's naturalism, however, did not follow the lead of modern empirical science – which he saw as dealing with only abstracted mathematical structures – but that of Aquinas's doctrine of intentional species. The intentional species is posited as an essentially relational form, shared by both the object known and the knowing mind; it is that by which we know, not in the sense of an internal impression from which we somehow infer the external object, but in the sense of the psycho-physical connection that constitutes and explains, but does not justify, knowledge as a natural fact. This might seem an unprepossessingly medieval basis for an account of the varieties of modern knowledge. But Maritain ingeniously deployed it to differentiate metaphysical, scientific, religious, aesthetic, and moral ways of knowing in terms of the formal structures of signification distinctive to each. Thus, he could distinguish between the abstract objectivity with which a scientific object is in the mind and the imaginative immediacy of an aesthetic object. Similarly, in the religious realm, he could distinguish the metaphysician's demonstrative knowledge of God from the mystic's experien-

---

[19] Two of Maritain's most important expositions of his metaphysics are *Sept leçons sur l'être*, and *Court traité de l'existence et l'existant*.
[20] Developed particularly in *Distinguer pour unir, ou, les degrés du savoir*.

tial knowledge and explain why the two sorts of knowledge had to be expressed in such diverse languages.

Maritain's most widely influential work was in political theory.[21] Many Thomists had strongly right-wing (e.g., royalist) political views and even supported Charles Maurras' reactionary Action Française movement. Maritain was initially sympathetic to Action Française but supported Pius XI's condemnation of the group and eventually developed a Thomistic defense of liberal democracy. This defense was based on Aquinas's distinction between nature and person, the same distinction used to explain the Trinity as one divine nature shared by three divine persons. As instantiations of human nature we are all members of a community and obliged to follow the dictates of the authorities to produce the common good. But as persons we are also unique individuals created as such by God and with a direct relationship to him. As persons we possess fundamental rights that cannot be subordinated to social goods. Specifically, once we reach the appropriate level of intellectual and social maturity, we have the right to set the basic direction of our lives, without interference from the state. Maritain allows that there may have been times and places where the majority of humans had not reached the requisite level of maturity. But he insisted that in the modern world almost all adults have reached this level, so that traditional forms of authoritarian government are not morally permissible. In this way, his application of Thomistic principles to the modern world entailed the necessity of representative, democratic government. Maritain's case for democracy helped inspire the Christian Democratic movements in Europe after World War II.

For all their skill and originality, the Christian philosophers of the Third Republic had little enduring influence. Gilson and Maritain had a much larger international audience than Blondel, signaled by their later positions at North American universities, but their impact, like his, seldom extended beyond the circle of Catholic thought. This was not because, as some critics claimed, their philosophies simply presupposed Catholic doctrines. Both the philosophy of action and neo-Thomism were scrupulous in separating philosophical claims, defended entirely by natural reason, from religious faith and its theological developments. But the fact remains that the fundamental principles of these philosophies had little

---

[21] See his *Primauté du spirituel*, *Du régime temporel de la liberté*, and *L'homme et l'état*.

appeal to those who were not already committed to Catholicism (or strongly inclined to it). Blondel presents his claims about the will's drive for the infinite as nothing more than a reflective analysis of our experience of the human condition, but his analysis rang true to few who did not already share his religious sensibilities.[22] Similarly, the founding metaphysical intuitions of Maritain's thought were seldom shared by philosophers outside Catholicism. The failure of Catholic philosophy was not that it confused faith with reason but that its reasoning was unpersuasive.

MARCEL

There was, however, a Catholic philosopher whose views were much closer to what was becoming the mainstream and who can even be plausibly put forward as the first French existentialist. This is Gabriel Marcel (1889–1973), who, while Sartre and the other fledgling existentialists were still in school, was publishing careful descriptions of how embodied subjectivity experiences concrete existence, the human situation, the other, and being itself. There is, in fact, no major theme of existentialism that is not treated, thoroughly and perceptively, in his work. Moreover, like the later existentialists, he combined philosophy with literature, writing thirty plays that were produced with considerable success on the Parisian stage.

Marcel's philosophical writing does not take the form of tightly organized treatises. Much of it consists of essays on specific topics or – a distinctive Marcelian medium – journals in which he jotted down his philosophical thoughts as they developed from day to day.[23] His first book, in fact, was a *Journal métaphysique* (1927) in which he recorded his long and complicated move from the metaphysical idealism he had been inclined to as a student to his first formulations of existentialist philosophy. Similarly, his next book, *Être et avoir* (1935), combined further selections from his journals with a collection of essays. Sometimes Marcel emphasized the connection between his

---

[22] As we have noted, Sartre does accept something like Blondel's analysis, although of the two options posed by it he chooses the anti-religious one. I suggest that this is not a counterexample to my thesis but an indication that Sartre's thought is imbued with a negative religiosity, expressed in a vehement denial of the possibility of the faith with which it sees itself faced.

[23] In this Marcel was preceded by the Swiss philosopher and poet, Henri-Frédéric Amiel (1821–81), who had developed his philosophy (a combination of French spiritualism and German idealism) in a voluminous journal.

drama and his philosophy by appending a philosophical essay to the printed version of a play. His one attempt at something like a systematic exposition of his ideas was in the two volumes of his Gifford lectures, *Mystère de l'être* (1951). But even here his discussion often cannot help but go off in intriguing directions that take him beyond his formal structure.

Marcel presents his philosophy as a matter of what he calls "secondary reflection" rather than "primary reflection". Primary reflection is primary only in that it corresponds to the descriptions of our experience that are nearest to the surface and that we are, therefore, most likely to put forward first when we begin thinking about the human situation. It expresses the standpoint of common sense and of science. Primary reflection makes a sharp distinction between the objects of the world and the mind that experiences and knows them. Knowledge is a matter of the mind obtaining accurate representations of what is outside it, and this accuracy requires a distant, dispassionate, totally objective view of things, impartially verified by the facts. Likewise, the body is sharply distinguished from the mind; it is, in fact, just another object in the world (knowable in the same objective way as other objects), although it also plays an essential instrumental role in our knowledge of the external world, since it transmits to the mind the physical impressions made on it by other bodies. The knowledge attained by primary reflection is not only objective but also general, formulated in terms of abstract concepts applicable to entire ranges of similar objects. This generality is expressed by universal laws such as those of natural science.

Marcel has no quarrel with the validity or importance of primary reflection. Its truths – especially the truths of science – are undeniable and essential for our pragmatic dealings with the world. But he vigorously opposes the idea that primary reflection provides the only or the most important truth about our world and our lives. There is also what he calls "secondary reflection" – secondary not in the sense of subordinate or marginal but in the sense of operating at a further, deeper level. Secondary reflection is the inverse, at every point, of primary reflection. Its knowledge is concrete rather than abstract, personal rather than objective, and based on our involvement with the world rather than our separation from it.

The prototype of secondary reflection is our knowledge of the existence of the material world directly present to us. From the standpoint of secondary reflection, we are from the very beginning involved in the material world. I, as a thinker, am also a body (not a separated mind); and, as a body, I have direct access to other bodies. For secondary reflection, the so-called problem of the existence of the external world is a non-starter. This is because the model for secondary reflection is not disengaged contemplation but active *participation*. I know the world not by distancing myself from it for the sake of objectivity but by forming part of it. What such knowledge lacks in objectivity and generality it makes up in immediacy and fullness. Marcel speaks of it as "blinded intuition", where "intuition" expresses the directness and certainty of secondary knowledge and "blinded" expresses its lack of the clarity and distinctness of primary knowledge.

Correlated with the distinction between primary and secondary reflection is Marcel's distinction between problems and mysteries. Primary reflection deals with problems, that is, with precisely formulable questions with answers that can be judged in a public way by clear criteria. A crossword puzzle is a problem, but so are extremely complex scientific questions (e.g., What are the ultimate constituents of matter?) that may take centuries to answer. I may or may not be interested in a given problem, and once it is solved I can turn my attention to something else. Even if I am desperately interested in solving a problem, the solution has nothing to do with who I fundamentally am. By contrast, a mystery is a question that implicates me in my deepest reality. There are no objective criteria for answering it, and no answer can have universal validity. Indeed, it is wrong to think that there is any pre-established answer that I could ever discover. Responding to a mystery is as much a matter of creatively transforming as of discovering some truth about myself. Examples of questions that lead to mysteries rather than problems are: *Am I free?*, *Have I been created by God?*, *Should I despair in the face of death?*, *Do I love this person?*. Such questions are not unanswerable, but they cannot be answered in the manner of a solution to a problem. This is because, in contrast to a problem, a mystery is not something from which I can withdraw to attain an objective perspective. In response to a mystery, I can only try to journey further into a reality that is an essential part of me. Such a journey will simultaneously reveal and create this reality.

The mistake of much philosophical thought is to treat the self, other people, and God as objects about which we pose and solve problems. The true task of philosophy is to abandon this quest for objective knowledge, modeled on science, in favor of creative intuitions of these realities as mysteries of existence (where "existence" means the fullness of concrete reality). Through such intuitions I not only encounter my self in its full existential concreteness; I also encounter other people, not as alien beings but as members with me of a community essential to us all. For Marcel, the fundamental experience of philosophy is not "I am" but "we are". Further, this "we" eventually is seen to involve not just finite creatures but even God. Of course, for Marcel, there is no question of proving the existence of God by logical or scientific argument. That is impossible because it would require that God be just another thing in an objective multiplicity of things. The reality of God must be that of a person (a "thou", as Marcel, like Martin Buber, puts it) with whom I have direct communication; and this communication is not an exchange between separated subjects but a shared life whereby I participate in the divine reality.

The experience of secondary reflection is thoroughly personal in two senses: it is undergone by a person and it is directed toward persons. As such, the experience is fraught with the emotional and moral substance of personal life. Accordingly, Marcel maintains that this experience must take the form of the most fundamental and intense modes of human feeling and values: fidelity (or faith), hope, and love. I become fully aware of myself, of how I am one with others, and how we are all one with God only by opening myself to the world through a faithful, hopeful, and loving life. Some of Marcel's most impressive work consists of his close descriptions of just what is involved in such a life. Faith, he says, is that whereby the self is created, hope is ultimately for salvation, and love involves the affirmation that the beloved shall not die.

Although he has little use for most traditional metaphysics, Marcel gives central place to the key metaphysical notion of being. For him, however, being is not an abstract concept (the most general and therefore empty of all, since it applies to literally everything) or the ground of an intellectual judgment (corresponding to the "is" implicit in any assertion). Rather, being for Marcel is the concrete constant that remains through all the developments and transformations of our experience. It is the ultimate constancy, assurance, and joy in which all reality participates and toward which our faith, hope, and love are ultimately directed. But in seeking being we do not transcend or subordinate the individual beings of our experience. On the contrary, it is only by experiencing our union with being that we can fully appreciate and achieve our union with other beings. Ultimately, in fact, our union with being cannot be distinguished from our union with the supreme being, God.

Despite the priority of his work, Marcel had limited influence on the younger existentialists.[24] As we shall see, they engaged much more with twentieth-century Germans such as Husserl and Heidegger, philosophers to whom Marcel's thought owed little or nothing. Moreover, Marcel was a theist (and, from 1929 on, a Catholic) who emphasized fidelity, hope, and love rather than the absurdity, despair, and conflict that became canonical for Sartre and company. It is as though Marcel's plunge into the lived experience of the human situation revealed to him the polar opposites of what Sartre, Beauvoir, and Camus found there. (Also, his political positions alone, such as support for Franco's Spain, would have alienated these philosophers from him.) As a result, Marcel remained the odd man out among French existentialists.

TOWARD THE CONCRETE

If young secular philosophers ignored Blondel, the neo-Thomists, and even Marcel, they rebelled, sometimes with disconcerting verbal violence, against the entrenched wisdom of their teachers. They were hardly alone, since there was also a related, and more prominent, literary and artistic challenge to the Third Republic's intellectual and cultural establishment. Some of the earliest opposition came from the literary surrealists, led by André Breton, who used "automatic writing" to unleash the irrational, unconscious

---

[24] Merleau-Ponty gives a somewhat different impression: "The moment of our great initiation into the philosophy of existence" occurred "when we discovered Husserl, Jaspers, Heidegger, and Gabriel Marcel" ("The Philosophy of Existence", in his *Texts and Dialogues*, 132). He particularly cites Marcel as the source for the theme of embodiment. But although Marcel was surely known to the young French philosophers (Sartre, for example, read a paper at a colloquium at Marcel's house), it seems likely that Merleau-Ponty himself had a special interest, probably because of his early attachment to the Catholicism Marcel had embraced. Thus, in the sentence quoted from above, Merleau-Ponty also mentions the Catholic journal *Esprit* (edited by Mounier), which published articles on the philosophy of existence, but which was hardly likely to influence non-believers such as Sartre and Beauvoir. It also seems that Marcel's influence on Merleau-Ponty was not very deep or enduring. There is, for example, only one mention of him in Merleau-Ponty's major work, *Phénoménologie de la perception*. As we shall see, however, Marcel did have considerable influence on Paul Ricoeur.

springs of creativity and supported political revolution through a stormy alliance with the Communists.

Of more theoretical significance were the projects of Georges Bataille (1897–1962), who worked as an archivist and librarian while also producing violently erotic novels along with radical philosophical essays and social schemes. Bataille was initially associated with the surrealists but broke with them and was denounced by Breton. He regarded the irrational forces the surrealists were trying to unleash as of far more than artistic significance. All human life and society, he maintained, was based on a primordial experience of violence and transgression, an experience he saw as a contact with the sacred that was smothered by the smooth rationalities of bourgeois society. Bataille's novels evoked and analyzed this experience, which he also explored through anthropological studies of primitive societies. In the latter project he was joined by Roger Callois, a classicist with strong interests in anthropology, and Michel Leiris, a surrealist writer who had done ethnographic field work in Africa. From 1937 to 1939, they ran a biweekly discussion group, called the Collège de Sociologie, devoted to the study of experiences of the sacred. (At the same time, Bataille started a secret society, *Acéphale* [headless], which seems to have tried to revive ancient violent rituals designed to stimulate ecstatic experiences of the sacred.) Bataille also attended Kojève's seminar on Hegel (discussed below), where he was particularly interested in the role Hegel gave negation (violence and destruction) in the progress of history.

Although the young philosophers endorsed Bataille's rejection of bourgeois values and often shared his fascination with violence and transgressive action, they had no sympathy with his radical irrationalism. Sartre strongly criticized him in a 1943 article as "a new mystic",[25] and, like Breton, he had little impact on the development of existentialism. However, as we shall see, there was a great upsurge of philosophical interest in Bataille with the emergence of poststructuralism in the 1960s.

Perhaps the most violent philosophical assault on Third Republic values was Paul Nizan's attack on "the philosophers of the established order", as he put it in the subtitle to his 1930 book, *Les chiens de garde*.[26] "When", he says in a typically vitriolic passage, "one hears

---

[25] Jean-Paul Sartre, "Un nouveau mystique", in *Situations I*.
[26] Nizan was Sartre's close friend at the École Normale and helped promote his early literary writings. Nizan, himself a successful novelist and journalist, was a militant Communist until

M. Brunschvicg [who is Nizan's particular *bête noire*] . . . give a series of lectures on the technique of the transition to the absolute, one fails to see how these bacilli of the mind, these grotesque fruits of the contemplative process, could possibly help the common herd . . . to understand their daughters' tuberculosis, their wives' fits of anger, their military service with all its humiliations . . ., the stinking corruption of their parliaments, or the insolence of the authorities". Nizan sees philosophers' failure to address these social and economic outrages as a sign that they have "betrayed mankind for the sake of the bourgeoisie".[27]

Nizan's militant Marxism gives a political cast to his criticism that was not typical of the early 1930s (Sartre and Beauvoir, for example, were at this time rather unpolitical). But the thought was widespread that the dominant philosophies of the Third Republic had nothing to say about the real issues of human existence. The early writings of Marcel, the polar opposite of Nizan in temperament, style, and politics, equally condemn the vapidity of established philosophy.[28]

Merleau-Ponty provides an even better example. He offers none of Nizan's abuse, and in fact praises Brunschvicg for his "quite extraordinary personal qualities" and as "a man of the first order". But, he says, "as regards pure philosophy, his essential contribution consisted precisely in informing us that we must turn toward the mind, toward the subject which constructs science and the perception of the world". As we have seen, Brunschvicg thought that science could tell us all there was to know about the objects of this mind. The mind itself is, for him, simply the universal reason in which all thinkers participate, and "lengthy philosophical descriptions or explications cannot be made of this mind, this subject".[29] Merleau-Ponty was of course aware of Brunschvicg's account of the various mental functions in *La modalité du jugement*, but he finds Brunschvicg's relentless intellectualization of these functions an

---

1939 (when he resigned from the Party). He was killed in 1940, fighting the German invasion. See Sartre's moving reminiscences in his preface to a reissue of Nizan's 1931 book, *Aden Arabie*.

[27] *Les chiens de garde*, 28–9, 140. This critique reflects Nizan's Marxist tendency to condemn any political stance short of a revolutionary one as reactionary. Brunschvicg, for example, was, like most prominent philosophers, considerably to the left in contemporary French politics.

[28] For example, *Journal métaphysique*, which, however, focuses more on the Anglophone idealists, Royce and Bradley; on Brunschvicg in particular, see the "Introduction" to Marcel's *De refus à l'invocation*.

[29] Merleau-Ponty, "The Philosophy of Existence", in *Texts and Dialogues*, 130.

implausible impoverishment of our lived consciousness. So Brunschvicg has nothing to offer the existential philosopher in either direction: he concedes the world of objects to science, and philosophical reflection on the mind reveals nothing more than an intellectual engine for constituting scientific objects. Moreover, both lacks derive from Brunschvicg's failure to recognize that his mind and its objects are abstractions from the concrete reality of man-in-the-world.

The positive counterpart of the young Turks' critique was a drive *vers le concret* ("toward the concrete"), as the title of a 1932 book by Jean Wahl put it.[30] In contrast to what they saw as the sterile abstractions of rationalist idealism and spiritualism, young philosophers such as Wahl, Marcel, and, later, Sartre, Beauvoir, and Merleau-Ponty sought an approach to philosophy grounded in face-to-face encounters with the fullness of reality. Religious thinkers, so different in most other ways, often shared this orientation of the young secular philosophers. For example, the Russian émigrés Lev Shestov and Nicolas Berdyaev insisted on concreteness and developed existential approaches to religious experience.[31] It was the drive for concreteness that attracted both religious and secular thinkers to the phenomenological philosophies of Husserl and Heidegger. Thus, Jean Hering, a Protestant theologian from Alsace seeking an experiential approach to religion that did not fall into what he saw as the psychologistic subjectivism of recent German theologians, thought that Husserl's phenomenology might be just what he needed. He studied extensively with Husserl at Göttingen and in 1925 published *Phénoménologie et philosophie religieuse*, the first book in French on Husserl. Indeed, much of the earliest French interest in phenomenology was from religiously inclined philosophers and from theologians.[32]

The attraction to phenomenology had little to do with Husserl's ambitions for foundational certainties and scientific rigor. This

---

[30] Jean Wahl, *Vers le concret*.
[31] Here we should mention also Simone Weil (1909–43), an *agrégée* in philosophy (and one of the first women to attend the École Normale), who combined strongly committed leftist social theorizing with intense Catholic theological reflection. See in particular her *L'enracinement*.
[32] For a very helpful, detailed discussion of this religious interest, see Christian Dupont, *Receptions of Phenomenology in French Philosophy and Religious Thought, 1889–1939*. Another early channel for phenomenological thought was Aron Gurwitsch, a Lithuanian Jew who had studied with Husserl and lectured at the Sorbonne during the 1930s on Gestalt psychology and on phenomenology. Merleau-Ponty attended his lectures in 1937.

perhaps explains the tepid reaction of French philosophers to his lecture at the Sorbonne in 1929, which presented the material later published as the *Méditations cartésiennes*.[33] In fact, much of the initial French interest in phenomenology was directed more toward Heidegger than Husserl, and the views of Husserl were sometimes assimilated to those of Heidegger.[34] This tendency is apparent in Levinas's important early study, *Théorie de l'intuition dans la phénoménologie de Husserl* (1930), which explicitly moves away from Husserl's epistemological concerns and toward a Heideggerian emphasis on ontology. There was also serious early interest in Max Scheler's phenomenology of the emotions. Scheler was the first phenomenologist invited to visit France (in 1924 and again in 1926), where he seems to have made a much better impression than Husserl did a few years later. In 1928, Scheler's *Wesen und Formen der Sympathie* (1923) became the first phenomenological book published in French translation. The initial publication in 1947 of Husserl's Sorbonne lectures was in French (translated by Levinas and Gabrielle Pfeiffer), the German original appearing only posthumously, in 1950. But apart from this special case, there was no French version of a major work by Husserl until Paul Ricoeur's translation of *Ideen I* in 1950. And Georges Gurvitch's influential book on contemporary German philosophy, published in 1930, puts more emphasis on Scheler than on anyone else.[35] But it was Heidegger who had the strongest and deepest effect, especially after 1931, when a translation of his *Was ist Metaphysik?* appeared in the avant-garde literary magazine *Bifur*, in an issue edited by Paul Nizan that also contained Sartre's early essay, "Légende de la vérité". The same year, the philosophical journal *Recherches philosophiques* published a translation of Heidegger's "Vom Wesen des Grundes".[36]

The early appearance of Heidegger in a literary forum was no

---

[33] There may also have been a certain amount of Parisian snobbery, since Husserl came across as an unexciting provincial academic (Herbert Spiegelberg, *The Phenomenological Movement*, 403–4).

[34] This perhaps explains the odd story that "when asked soon after the War about his early acquaintance with Sartre, Heidegger did not first remember him by name; then he identified him as 'the Frenchman who had always confused him with Husserl'" (Spiegelberg, *The Phenomenological Movement*, 463, fn. 2).

[35] Georges Gurvitch, *Les tendances actuelles de la philosophie allemande*. On Scheler's reception in France, see Spiegelberg, *The Phenomenological Movement*, 402–3.

[36] However, there were no full French translations of *Being and Time* published until Martineau's version, privately printed in 1985, and Vezin's version, published by Gallimard in 1986.

accident. Heideggerian themes of anguish and nothingness were important in the work of some of the younger French avant-garde writers, which is where young philosophers were likely to have first encountered them. For example, in Raymond Queneau's *Derniers jours* (1936), the hero, who has come from Le Havre to study philosophy at the Sorbonne, is, like Roquentin in *La nausée* (published two years later), overwhelmed in a garden by the nothingness of things. The themes of nothingness and contingency are also central in Paul Nizan's first novel, *Antoine Bloyé* (1933), which, for example, has a phenomenological description of anxiety expressed in Heideggerian terminology. Sartre's *La nausée* fits in naturally with this literary current, quite apart from its origins in distinctively philosophical reflection.[37]

There was, then, a pervasive desire among French intellectuals after the war for modes of experience, thought, and expression that would put them into direct contact with concrete reality; and German phenomenology was exciting because it promised to fulfill this desire. The point is particularly clear in Sartre's initial enthusiasm for Husserl, portrayed in Simone de Beauvoir's famous anecdote. It was 1932, and Raymond Aron, who had just returned from Berlin, where he had been studying Husserl, was talking to Sartre and Beauvoir in a Parisian café, the Bec de Gaz on Rue Montparnasse:

> We ordered the speciality of the house, apricot cocktails. Aron said, pointing to his glass: "You see my dear fellow, if you are a phenomenologist, you can talk about this cocktail and make philosophy out of it!" Sartre turned pale with emotion at this. Here was just the thing he had been longing to achieve for years – to describe objects just as he saw and touched them, and extract philosophy from the process.[38]

Beauvoir goes on to tell how Sartre then bought Levinas's book about Husserl on the Boulevard Saint-Michel "and was so eager to inform himself on the subject that he leafed through the volume as he walked along, without even having cut the pages".[39] Sartre himself recalls this incident in a later interview (but his memory is that Aron pointed to a glass of beer) and explains his enthusiasm by noting that Husserl's method promised a way of talking philosophi-

---

[37] On these examples of early literary existentialism, see Denis Hollier, "Plenty of Nothing", in Denis Hollier (ed.), *A New History of French Literature*, 896.
[38] Beauvoir, *The Prime of Life*, 112.
[39] Ibid.

cally about concrete objects and that "we thought a great deal about one thing: the concrete".[40] Sartre, with Aron's help, arranged to succeed him as a fellow at the French Institute in Berlin.

Sartre's strong response to Husserl is evident in the startling piece he wrote in 1939, "Une idée fondamentale de la phénoménologie de Husserl: l'intentionalité". Sartre contrasts Husserl's view with what he calls the "digestive philosophy" of the French idealists and neo-Kantians (he mentions Brunschvicg and Meyerson), who assimilate objects to "the spidery mind, [which] trapped things in its web, covered them with a white spit and slowly swallowed them, reducing them to its own substance". Husserl, however, "persistently affirmed that one cannot dissolve things in consciousness". For him, "to know is to 'burst toward', to tear oneself out of the moist gastric intimacy, veering out there beyond oneself". Sartre asks us to "imagine for a moment a connected series of bursts which tear us out of ourselves . . . into the dry dust of the world, on to the plain earth amidst things. Imagine us thus rejected and abandoned by our own nature in an indifferent, hostile, and restive world – you will then grasp the profound meaning of the discovery which Husserl expresses in his famous phrase, 'All consciousness is consciousness of something'." Sartre further notes that not only knowledge but also allegedly "subjective" reactions ("hatred, love, fear, sympathy") are intentional. Rather than "floating in the malodorous brine of the mind . . . they are merely ways of discovering the world. It is things which abruptly unveil themselves to us as hateful, sympathetic, horrible, lovable." Accordingly, "Husserl has restored to things their horror and their charm. He has restored to us the world of artists and prophets: frightening, hostile, dangerous, with its havens of mercy and love." Following the Husserlian doctrine of intentionality, "we are delivered from Proust" and the obsession with "internal life". "It is not in some hiding-place that we will discover ourselves; it is on the road, in the town, in the midst of a crowd, a thing among things, a man among men."[41]

Anyone who reacts to Husserl's sober deliberations with such passion is bringing a substantial agenda to the text. Sartre and his contemporaries were looking for something quite specific in the works of Husserl and Heidegger. It was not a question of their

[40] *Sartre by Himself*, 26–7. Sartre also mentions the importance for him and his friends of Jean Wahl's *Vers le concret*.
[41] "Intentionality: A Fundamental Idea of Husserl's Phenomenology", 4, 5.

passively undergoing "influences" from across the Rhine but of their actively appropriating carefully chosen aspects of German thought for their own purposes. As Merleau-Ponty later said, when he and his friends read phenomenology it was not so much a matter "of encountering a new philosophy as of recognizing what they had been waiting for".[42] What they were waiting for was not a more rigorous foundation of knowledge or a return to the question of Being but a philosophical access to the concrete world.

The same point applies to the introduction of Hegel into France between the wars. Hegelian thought had never taken firm root in France before the 1920s, for a combination of socio-political causes (dislike for a thinker perceived as an apologist for the German state) and philosophical reasons (opposition to absolute idealism and neo-Kantian distrust of the obscurities of dialectical thinking). There was occasional interest, but Hegel's writings were not part of the standard university philosophical syllabus. (Sartre recalls Lachelier saying, "There won't be any Hegel as long as I'm around."[43])

One of the first signs of serious French interest in Hegel was Jean Wahl's 1929 book, *Le malheur de la conscience de Hegel*. Wahl's preface sets the tone for the French appropriation of Hegel. "The dialectic", he says, "before being a method is an experience by which Hegel moves from one idea to another". More generally, "at the origin of this doctrine, which is put forward as an interconnected series of concepts, there is a kind of mystical intuition and affective warmth". In sum, "behind the rationalist, we find the romantic"; "this system, in which the concepts seem at first so marvelously controlled and arranged, is in fact the expression of a living experience". Wahl acknowledges that his view of Hegel corresponds better to the formulations of the young Hegel than to those of the mature systematist. But he is not ashamed to prefer youth, maintaining that the strongest objection to "the Hegelian system in its definitive form" is that "rich as it might be, it is not rich enough to contain the multitude of thoughts, imaginings, hopes, and despairs of the young Hegel". And, he adds, a good many criticisms of Hegel tell against his later systematic doctrines but not against "the Hegelian 'vision' itself in its original character of concrete plenitude".[44] Given this

---

[42] *Phenomenology of Perception*, vii.
[43] *Sartre by Himself*, 25.
[44] *Le malheur de la conscience de Hegel*, v, vii. Wahl had earlier discussed Kierkegaard's critique of Hegel in his *Études kierkegaardiennes*.

attitude, it is hardly surprising that Wahl's book focuses on one of Hegel's most vivid and specific descriptions, that of the "unhappy consciousness" in *The Phenomenology of Spirit*. (And it is Hegel's characterization of unhappy consciousness as due to the impossibility of a being-for-itself that is also a being-in-itself that no doubt inspired Sartre's identical description of the human condition.)

Even before the appearance of Wahl's book, Alexandre Koyré had been offering a seminar on Hegel at the École Pratiques des Hautes Études. Koyré's approach was less "existential" than Wahl's but still emphasized the historical and anthropological rather than the ontological dimensions of his thought. (Koyré was also familiar with Heidegger, and made use of his discussion of Hegel and temporality in *Being and Time*.)[45] In 1933, Koyré left to teach in Cairo, and the seminar was taken over by Alexandre Kojève (1902–68). Kojève's seminar, centered on Hegel's *Phenomenology*, continued until war broke out in 1939, and became one of the most important stimuli for French interest in Hegel. Raymond Queneau, Georges Bataille, and Jacques Lacan were regular participants; Merleau-Ponty attended during the academic year 1937–8.[46]

Like Wahl and Koyré, Kojève had no interest in the Hegelian absolute.[47] Moreover, he was more interested in using Hegel as a starting-point for his own philosophical thinking, strongly influenced by Marx (and Heidegger), than in providing a textually accurate account of Hegel's thought. Responding to criticism in *Les temps modernes* from the Vietnamese phenomenologist, Tran Duc Thao, he said his reading of Hegel was a "work of propaganda, designed to shake up people's minds (*frapper les esprits*)".[48] Whereas Wahl's existential interpretation of Hegel focused on the chapter on unhappy consciousness, Kojève's Marxist take gave pride of place to Hegel's

---

[45] On Koyré and Hegel, see Michael Roth, *Knowing and History*, 5–10 and 96–7.
[46] This list is based on the official record of those registered for the course, as reprinted in Roth's *Knowing and History*, 225–7. Roth notes that there were also participants – e.g., André Breton – who had not registered. Jean Hyppolite reports that Raymond Aron (and possibly Jean-Paul Sartre) also attended (see "La 'Phénoménologie' de Hegel et la pensée française contemporaine", in his *Figures de la pensée philosophique*, 231–4).
[47] The views discussed in the following paragraph are those developed in Kojève's seminar, as presented in *Introduction à la lecture de Hegel*. This is a volume of transcripts and notes from Kojève's seminar assembled by Queneau. See also Roth's excellent analysis in *Knowing and History*, part 2. For Kojève's later revisions of his views, see *Knowing and History*, 134–46.
[48] Letter to *Les temps modernes*, October 7, 1948. For a balanced appreciation and criticism of Kojève's interpretation of Hegel, see Jean Hyppolite, "La 'Phénoménologie' de Hegel et la pensée française contemporaine", 235–41.

description of the master–slave relation. He took the desire for recognition by another consciousness as definitive of the distinctively human condition and read the ensuing "battle to death of consciousnesses" in terms of Marxist class struggle. As Kojève sees it, human history begins with the confrontation of two consciousnesses, each desiring above all the other's recognition of its dominance. The ensuing struggle (the "bloody battle") is violent precisely to the extent that the combatants are willing to die in seeking victory. And it is this violence that makes the struggle and its participants human: "the being that cannot risk its life in a struggle for *Recognition*, in a fight for pure prestige . . . is not a truly *human* being".[49] Without this risk, we remain at the level of animals, dominated by the instinct for self-preservation.

The violent struggle ends when one party surrenders, the fear of death outweighing the desire for recognition and domination. Thus we arrive at the subordination of slave to master. It might seem that the slave has merely reverted to the animal level of self-preservation. But Kojève maintains that something much more significant has happened. The slave's surrender does not represent a reversion to biological instinct but a self-conscious awareness of human finitude in the face of death. At least in this Heideggerian way, the slave's surrender involves a decisive advance in consciousness – and one in which the new master does not share. But there are still other ways in which the slave's position is superior. The slave is condemned to work for the master, but this very work involves creative interaction with and mastery over the world. Also, the fact that the slave works to satisfy the master's desires requires an "abstract" grasp of a desire one does not oneself feel as well as a postponement or sublimation of one's own desires. The slave, therefore, becomes the source of the technological power, conceptual understanding, and reflective self-mastery that are the marks of progress in human history. By contrast, the master, whose desires are fulfilled by the slave's work, remains at the animal level of mere satisfaction. The master's sole distinctively human characteristic is the willingness to risk death for the sake of domination. But, as Kojève puts it, this means that the master "can die as man, but . . . can live only as animal".[50]

Applying the categories of master and slave to the historical

---

[49] *Introduction to the Reading of Hegel*, 141.
[50] *Introduction to the Reading of Hegel*, 55.

realities of successive struggles between socio-economic classes, Kojève offers a Marxist interpretation of the entire sweep of Hegel's dialectical history. He ignores Hegel's speculative conception of this history as a series of moments in absolute thought's self-understanding and sees each new level of synthesis as a higher level of human consciousness and achievement produced by the striving of oppressed classes. As history progresses in Marxist fashion, a previously "slave" class successfully rebels and becomes master. This, of course, does not change the essential structure of oppression. But from the creative thought of the slaves there emerges an ideal of equality among all humankind that is opposed to the existing ideal of hierarchical subordination. This develops first in a spiritualized, transcendent form with Christianity and then in a material, temporally realizable form with Marxism. The ideal is a vision of a utopia in which no one is satisfied at the expense of anyone else and all equally achieve the basic human desire of recognition by their fellows. But, in this utopia, the struggle (more abstractly, the negativity) characteristic of master–slave relations also disappears and with it the creative impetus that led humankind to higher and higher levels of consciousness and achievement. The result would be what Kojève called the "end of history" – not a literal ceasing of human existence in time but an end to the dialectical process of synthesis out of negation that has defined what we have so far experienced as our history. With the end of history, humankind ceases to be defined by its future, that is, it is no longer a being that is not what it is but what it will be, and reaches the final stability of egalitarian equilibrium. Kojève does not think that we have already attained this state and indeed insists that the point of Marxist activism is precisely to reach it. But he believes that the state has been given an adequate theoretical characterization by Hegel (understood through Marx) and that the concrete historical process leading to it was initiated by the French Revolution and extended to the whole of Europe by Napoleon's armies.

Kojève contributed to a new interest in Marx as much as in Hegel and influenced literary figures (especially the surrealists and those associated with them, for example, Breton, Queneau, and Bataille) at least as much as philosophers.[51] But although Kojève, along with

---

[51] The published version of Kojève's seminar did not appear until 1947. However, Kojève's translation with commentary of Hegel's "master–slave" discussion appeared as a journal

Wahl, made Hegel a figure to be reckoned with in French intellectual circles, the highly distinctive interpretations they gave him – along with the absence of translations of Hegel's major works – meant that there was no easy access to Hegel in anything like his own terms. Such access became available only in the 1940s, when Jean Hyppolite (1907–68) published his translation of the *Phenomenology of Spirit* along with his detailed, two-volume commentary on the text.[52] Hyppolite's commentary on Hegel was itself strongly colored by the Marxist and existentialist views dominant at the time he wrote it. But, rather than reducing Hegel to either of these standpoints, Hyppolite tried to formulate his position in ways that would make Hegel a significant new voice in contemporary discussions. In this he was fully successful, not only through his translation and commentary but also through his teaching, first at leading Parisian lycées and, from 1954, at the École Normale Supérieure, until he received a chair at the Collège de France in 1962. (His students included Althusser, Foucault, Deleuze, and Derrida.) Hyppolite was not exaggerating when he said that, for the generation of the 1940s and 1950s, "the reading of Hegel's *Phenomenology* was essential, a fundamental reference point". (More mundanely, readings from Hegel became, for the first time, part of the required list for the philosophy *agrégation*.) In particular, Hegel's thought was the "site of encounter between those fraternal enemies, the existentialists and the Marxists", a common ground where "both sides adjusted their positions and, without formally admitting it, softened their rigidity".[53]

We may well wonder why, if the young French philosophers were seeking concreteness, they did not turn to Bergson rather than to Hegel, Husserl, and Heidegger. Merleau-Ponty himself raises this issue in some reflections (in 1959) on the attitude of himself and his contemporaries around 1930:

article in 1939, and Kojève's interpretations were much discussed among Parisian intellectuals.

[52] *La Phénoménologie de l'esprit*, published in 1941 (the first part of the translation appeared in 1939); Jean Hyppolite, *Génèse et structure de la* Phénoménologie de l'esprit *de Hegel*. Sartre provides a striking example of Hyppolite's impact. In *L'être et le néant*, written from the later 30s to early 40s, the citations of Hegel are taken not from the originals but from a French anthology, *Morceaux choisis d'Hegel*, published in 1936 by Henri Lefebvre and N. Gutterman (see Christopher M. Fry, *Sartre and Hegel: The Variations of an Enigma in* L'être et le néant). But Sartre's *Cahiers pour une morale*, written in 1945–7, has obviously profited from Sartre's reading of Hyppolite's translation and commentary.
[53] Jean Hyppolite, "La 'Phénoménologie' de Hegel et la pensée française contemporaine", 236.

If we had been careful readers of Bergson, and if more thought had been given to him, we would have been drawn to a much more concrete philosophy, a philosophy much less reflexive than Brunschvicg's. But since Bergson was hardly read by my contemporaries, it is certain that we had to wait for the philosophies of existence in order to be able to learn much of what he would have been able to teach us. It is quite certain – as we realize more and more today – that Bergson, had we read him carefully, would have taught us things that ten or fifteen years later we believed to be discoveries made by the philosophy of existence itself.[54]

This still leaves us wondering why Merleau-Ponty and his friends did not take Bergson seriously. One reason might have been his increasing affinity for Catholicism, which was clearly emerging by 1932 in *Les deux sources de la morale et de la religion*. From this point of view, the entire story might be summed up in Sertillanges's remark that the Church would never have put Bergson's books on the Index in 1913 had it realized how his thought would look by 1934.[55]

But this explanation is unpersuasive for the very case of Merleau-Ponty, who began his philosophical life with a strong Catholic commitment. Further, counter to Merleau-Ponty's generalization about his contemporaries' lack of interest in Bergson, Sartre says that he himself became a philosopher precisely because of Bergson. Previously interested in literature but not philosophy, he was assigned Bergson's *Essai sur les données immédiates de la conscience* in his *classe de philosophie* and "was bowled over by it. I said to myself, 'Why philosophy's absolutely terrific, you can learn the truth through it'." Sartre goes on to emphasize the grounds of the book's attraction: "It's a book with concrete tendencies, despite appearances, in that it tries to describe concretely what goes on in the conscious mind. And I think it was that, in fact, which oriented me toward the notion of the conscious mind that I still hold today."[56]

But if Bergson's philosophy provided the concreteness Sartre and his friends longed for, it still failed in another key way. It was, as Jean Hyppolite has noted, a philosophy of a "final serenity", a serenity

---

[54] "The Philosophy of Existence", in *Texts and Dialogues*, 132. In another essay, also written in 1959 (and explicitly in celebration of Bergson's centennial), Merleau-Ponty distinguishes between an original "audacious" Bergsonism that created a genuinely new and exciting philosophical vision and a "retrospective or external" Bergsonism that "loses its bite" because its "insights are identified with the vague cause of spiritualism or some other entity". It was, he says, this latter Bergsonism that his generation encountered ("Bergson in the Making", in *Signs*, 182).
[55] Merleau-Ponty cites this remark in "Bergson in the Making", in *Signs*, 183.
[56] *Sartre by Himself*, 27.

arising from an overall view that gives human reality a home in the natural scheme of things.[57] For Bergson, after all, even before his book on religion, our lives are intelligible as products of the *élan vital* that we encounter in our experience of the duration that constitutes the universe. Any alienation or inauthenticity that we might find in the world of objectifying science is overcome in the concreteness of philosophical intuition, which reveals the unity and directedness of the world and places human beings comfortably in it. All of this is entirely opposed to the young philosophers' defining experience of a freedom that must create its own meanings in an intrinsically absurd world. For these philosophers, the concrete truth was not serenity but anguish (*angoisse*). What Bergson lacked, therefore, was a sense of the tragic nature of human existence. His philosophy of life was a way of transcending our existence as individuals, of giving it meaning through its relation to the grand scheme of the cosmos. The founding insight of the philosophy of existence was, on the contrary, that the world provides our lives with no transcendent meaning. (Even Christians like Marcel held that we could reach transcendence only by faith in something supernatural, not through an appropriate relation to nature.)[58] The insistence on the tragic nature of human existence also explains the enthusiasm of the young French philosophers for Heidegger, as well as the idiosyncratic appropriation they made of Husserl's phenomenology and the distinctive slant of their interest in Hegel.

Despite their general lack of enthusiasm for Bergson, Sartre and Merleau-Ponty do often enough take account of his views. But by this time they are already well along the phenomenological road and find Bergson quite deficient. Sartre, for example, criticizes Bergson for failing to provide "a positive description of the intentionality that constitutes [thought]".[59]

Merleau-Ponty's critique of Bergson is a particularly good example

---

[57] Jean Hyppolite, "Du Bergsonisme à l'existentialisme", in his *Figures de la pensée philosophique*, 453. This paragraph is based on this very perceptive article.
[58] Bergson was, nonetheless, an important thinker for Marcel, who dedicated his *Journal métaphysique* to him (and also to W. E. Hocking, the American idealist). But Bergson's philosophy served Marcel more as a general inspiration than as a specific guide. This was so not only because of the naturalism of Bergson's work prior to *Deux sources* but also because Marcel had little sympathy for Bergson's impersonal cosmology of the *élan vital* and because he was uneasy with Bergson's appeal to intuition, an unease reflected in his own paradoxical references to "blinded intuition".
[59] Jean-Paul Sartre, *L'imaginaire*, 85. Sartre is also critical, in *L'être et le néant*, of Bergson's views on temporality and the self.

of the philosophical tensions between the Bergsonian and the phenomenological standpoints. His doubts are directed toward Bergsonian intuition and can be cast in the form of a dilemma. On the one hand, Bergson's intuition may be taken as pretending to "the absolute observer's viewpoint" that would "transcend the world". If so, "Bergson is not fully aware of his own presuppositions and of that simple fact that all we live is lived against the background of the world". If, on the other hand, Bergson in fact avoids this illusion of transcendence and "his philosophy is finally to be understood as a philosophy of immanence", then "he may be reproached with having described the human world only in its most general structures (e.g., duration, openness to the future); his work lacks a picture of human history which would give a content to these intuitions, which paradoxically remain very general".[60]

Moreover, in developing this second horn of his dilemma, Merleau-Ponty objects not merely to the generality of Bergson's account but to its rejection of certain essential structures of lived experience. Bergson rightly rejects the scientific view of reality as a mere "multiplicity of things externally juxtaposed". But his alternative to this view is a "multiplicity of fusion and interpenetration". Specifically, Bergson's duration swallows objects, along with the space and time in which they exist, into an amorphous unity: "He proceeds by way of dilution, speaking of consciousness as a liquid in which instants and positions dissolve." Bergson's mistake is to "seek a solution in ambiguity".[61] Merleau-Ponty maintains that "space, motion and time cannot be elucidated by discovering an 'inner' layer of experience in which their multiplicity is erased and *really* abolished". The problem with Bergson's intuition is that it purports to be a primordial experience, prior to any division between subject and object. Evoking Kant, Merleau-Ponty argues that "external experience is essential to internal experience", that there is an implicit separation of subject and object, of consciousness and world, in even our most immediate experience.

Merleau-Ponty makes the same point in terms of the central Bergsonian notion of time. As Bergson describes it, duration is a concrete unity in which what the intellect distinguishes as past, present, and future are all dissolved. Consciousness, as Bergson's

---

60 "The Metaphysical in Man", in *Sense and Non-Sense*, 97 n.15.
61 On the other hand, Merleau-Ponty, as we shall see, gives ambiguity a central role in his phenomenology of perception.

famous metaphor has it, is a snowball rolling down a hill, gathering the whole of time into a homogeneous unity. There is, according to him, a principle of continuity whereby "the past still belongs to the present and the present already to the past". But then, Merleau-Ponty argues, "there is no longer any past or present". "If consciousness snowballs upon itself, it is, like the snowball and everything else, wholly in the present" and the structures of temporality (past, present, and future) lose all meaning.[62]

To sum up, Merleau-Ponty maintains that if Bergson is offering a description of our actual lived experience in the world, then the description is inaccurate because it dissolves into a unified flux structural elements (past, present, subject, object) that need to be differentiated for our experience to have any meaning at all. The only alternative would be for Bergson to maintain that he has gotten beyond our lived experience and attained a transcendent, absolute standpoint that yields metaphysical truth beyond what is available to lived experience.

Bergson, no doubt, would respond that it is Merleau-Ponty's description of lived experience that is inaccurate. The perception he takes as fundamental is structured by our practical activity in the world and is, therefore, informed by the categories appropriate for action. These categories replace the concrete continuity of life with the more practically effective discontinuities of spatial and temporal moments and separately existing bodies. From Bergson's point of view, the world Merleau-Ponty regards as concrete is in fact an abstraction constituted by intellectualist categories that distort the lived experience of pure duration.

There is little point in speculating as to how Merleau-Ponty (and the other philosophers of existence) might reply to this response. How, in general, can we resolve disputes about what is "really" given in "concrete experience"?[63] In any case, the young philosophers of the 1930s would have found Bergson's world of duration, no matter how concrete in principle, too far removed from the world of everyday life that fascinated them as an object of philosophical description.

---

[62] *The Phenomenology of Perception*, 276 n.1; for Bergson's snowball image, see *L'évolution créatrice*, 4.

[63] I return to this question in my conclusion.

PART II

*The Reign of Existential Phenomenology
(1940–1960)*

CHAPTER 5

Sartre

It is difficult, when one's mind is troubled by the ideas of Kant and the yearnings of Baudelaire, to write the exquisite French of Henri IV.

(Marcel Proust, *In Search of Lost Time*, III, 689)

Overall, Jean-Paul Sartre (1905–80) considered himself a writer more than a philosopher. Almost as soon as he could read, he projected a career as a master of French literature, his idea of what this might mean changing as his taste moved from boys' adventure novels to the classics. In his mid-teens, he decided, following his excitement at first reading Bergson, to study philosophy at the École Normale; but that was because he regarded philosophy as "simply a methodical description of man's inner states, of his psychological life, all of which would serve as a method and instrument for my literary works . . . I thought that taking the *agrégation* exam in philosophy and becoming a professor of philosophy would help me in treating my literary subjects."[1] The idea was that philosophy would provide an intellectual foundation for literature.

When Sartre's philosophical thought developed and, predictably, took the direction of the new philosophy of existence, it is hardly surprising that he maintained a close tie between literature and philosophy. As Merleau-Ponty said in his review of Simone de Beauvoir's first novel, *L'invitée*: "Everything changes when a phenomenological or existential philosophy assigns itself the task, not of explaining the world or of discovering its 'conditions of possibility', but rather of formulating an experience of the world, a contact with the world which precedes all thought *about* the world . . . From now on the tasks of literature and philosophy can no longer be

---

[1] "Interview with Jean-Paul Sartre", in Paul Schilpp (ed.), *The Philosophy of Jean-Paul Sartre*, 6.

separated."[2] But Sartre did not go as far as Georges Bataille, who, after reading Heidegger, declared that, by opening itself "directly on life, philosophy was finally reduced to literature".[3] On the contrary, he insisted on a sharp distinction of the two, at least as forms of expression. Literary style involves "making sentences in which several meanings co-exist and in which the words are taken as allusions, as objects rather than concepts. In philosophy, a word must signify a concept and that one only." That is why, Sartre insists, "I *never* had any stylistic ambition for philosophy. Never, never. I tried to write clearly, that's all."[4]

None of this means that Sartre's literary and philosophical writings form two independent categories. But it does suggest that his novels and plays require a distinctly complex sort of reading as more than illustrations or refinements of philosophical positions. I will occasionally cite Sartre's literary works to make purely philosophical points but will not overstep the limits of my topic and competence by trying to do them justice in their own terms.

The first period of Sartre's career, ending around 1945, with the victory over the Axis, was a triumph of his youthful ambition for philosophical-literary success. By age forty, he had published a major novel (*La nausée*), had two ready to appear (*L'âge de raison* and *Le sursis*), and was a successful playwright (with *Les mouches* and *Huis-clos*). Moreover, quite according to plan, these literary pieces were all in some sense based on his existentialist philosophy, developed in three classic monographs (on the ego, the emotions, and imagination) and a massive systematic treatise (*L'être et le néant*) that was from the first plausibly considered one of the century's major philosophical books.[5]

After the war, two new factors entered Sartre's life. First, his literary success made it economically unnecessary for him to continue his career as a teacher of philosophy. Trained at the École Normale, he had been teaching in lycées, first in Le Havre and Laon

---

[2] "Metaphysics and the Novel", in *Sense and Nonsense*, 27–8.
[3] "L'existentialisme", in *Oeuvres complètes*, vol. XI, 83.
[4] "Interview with Jean-Paul Sartre", in Paul Schilpp (ed.), *The Philosophy of Jean-Paul Sartre*, 11.
[5] See William McBride's fascinating survey of the book's early reviews, "Sartre: les premiers comptes-rendus de *L'être et le néant*". McBride points out that philosophers of the stature of Gabriel Marcel, Alphonse De Waehlens, and Ferdinand Alquié recognized its significance. But Marcel, like some other Catholic critics, saw something Satanic in Sartre's work, citing the "luciferian" character of "this rebellious individuality, drunken with itself" (*Homo Viator*, 256).

and then, during the war, in Paris. He had expected, not without a certain distaste,[6] to follow the standard academic path, perhaps to a position at the Sorbonne. Now financially independent, he broke with the Third Republic's model of the professor of philosophy and worked without professional colleagues and students. This had enormous consequences for his choice of topics and genres, the scope of his audience, and his ability to speak out on controversial issues. Sartre became a public intellectual in a way that his university predecessors could never have been.[7]

In addition, the Second World War politicized Sartre. Previously, he held views fairly standard for a leftist student and shared Nizan's hatred of the bourgeoisie, but was not politically active. His experience of the war, which included mobilization, a stint in German prisoner-of-war camps, and life under the Nazi occupation and Vichy government, convinced him that he had to take an active part in the fight against oppression. During the war he played a modest role in the intellectual resistance, organizing, with Merleau-Ponty, a clandestine group called "Socialism and Liberty". After the war he threw himself into an activist life, using his new journal, *Les temps modernes*, as a vehicle for political polemics as well as for literature and philosophy, and even founding a short-lived political party (The Revolutionary Democratic Assembly). His remaining years were increasingly filled with speeches, petitions, demonstrations, commissions, and foreign travel, all undertaken with a passionate intensity not always equaled by good judgment.

Sartre's new status and commitment could not but have a powerful effect on his philosophical and literary work. The first result was a series of articles in *Les temps modernes*, reprinted in 1947 as a book entitled *Qu'est-ce que la littérature?*. Here Sartre embraced the enterprise of *littérature engagée* ("engaged literature" or, perhaps better, "committed writing"). This he contrasted to the "pure literature" ("art for art's sake") that the end of *La nausée* seems to endorse. *Littérature engagée* is writing that, realizing its essential relation to a

---

[6] See his comments in *Sartre par lui-même*, 34.
[7] Sartre's example was, of course, difficult to follow to the letter but it did engender a fair approximation in the "super-star" academics who emerged in the 1960s. These were thinkers such as Lévi-Strauss, Foucault, and Derrida, who remained connected to the academy but attained a level of public prestige that gave them a freedom and an audience far beyond that of the ordinary professional. It should be noted that Gabriel Marcel, because of family wealth, was in a position similar to Sartre's, and did, in fact, make a name for himself as a playwright as well as a philosopher.

particular historical situation, strives to make its readers aware of and act on the potential for human liberation implicit in that situation. Such writing is not, Sartre maintains, mere propaganda, since it subordinates itself not to any specific ideology but only to the "eternal values implicit in social and political debates".[8] *Qu'est-ce que la littérature?* shows the strains both of hasty, journalistic composition and of conceptual problems its author does not yet have the resources to resolve. But it is an invigorating start of Sartre's long struggle to reconcile his literary vocation with his political commitment.

The new issue of political engagement also had an obvious influence on the next project on Sartre's philosophical agenda, developing the existentialist ethics announced at the end of *L'être et le néant* that would complete that book's ontology of freedom. This sequel was long awaited and even advertised as forthcoming under the title *L'homme*, but Sartre never made good on his promise. Despite over 500 pages of drafts and notes (written between 1945 and 1947 and posthumously published as *Cahiers pour une morale*), Sartre was unable to formulate a satisfactory existentialist ethics. The problem was not, as many critics thought, the inconsistency of his radical view of human freedom with any sense of ethical values. Sartre had suggested, at the end of *L'être et le néant*, that this difficulty could be avoided by taking freedom itself as the ultimate value; and Simone de Beauvoir, in her *Pour une morale de l'ambiguïté*, had sketched out how such a move could generate plausible moral norms. Rather, as Sartre saw it, the problem was one of concreteness. Existentialism might generate consistent universal values, but what could it say about how to behave in a specific historical situation? In *L'existentialisme est un humanisme* Sartre had said that we must always invent our values and that all that mattered was "whether the invention is made in the name of freedom".[9] This might have had some purchase under the occupation, when the moral choice between collaboration and resistance could be seen as a simple alternative between supporting freedom and supporting oppression. But freedom in so pure a form has little meaning in most practical situations, where opposing choices (say between capitalist free enterprise and socialist liberation)

---

[8] *Situations II*, 15.
[9] "Existentialism is a Humanism", 367. Despite Sartre's later disavowal of this lecture – which he rightly thought was given a definitive status inconsistent with its informal nature – it remains not only a very useful introduction to his thought but also an important adumbration of his attitude toward Marxism.

can both plausibly claim the interest of "freedom". So much must have been obvious to Sartre as he took part in the fray of postwar French politics. The problem of an ethics, then, would be to base it on an understanding not of freedom as such but of freedom in a specific human situation. Sartre's failure to develop an existentialist ethics was his failure to find a way of adequately explicating the notion of *situated freedom*.

This failure strongly influenced Sartre's next major intellectual project, his biographical study of the writer, Jean Genet.[10] On one level, this book, *Saint Genet, comédien et martyr* (1952), was intended to show that the "existential psychoanalysis" developed in *L'être et le néant* was superior to Marxist and Freudian techniques of understanding individuals in their totality. But Sartre also presented Genet as a exemplar of existentialist ethics, telling "in detail the story of a liberation"[11] achieved despite the apparently overwhelming forces of bourgeois oppression. It is as if Sartre hoped to at least *show* what he could not articulate philosophically. But he eventually realized that both *Saint Genet* and his abortive ethical project suffered from the same flaw and that this flaw flowed from a fundamental incompleteness in his existentialist vision. The real problem was that the categories of *L'être et le néant*, even as more subtly and concretely deployed in *Saint Genet*, were not adequate for understanding the social and historical dimension of human existence and, especially, how objective, external structures are essential conditions of our existential choices. As Sartre later put it, "It's obvious that the study of Genet's conditioning by the events of his objective history is inadequate, very, very inadequate."[12]

For the five years after the publication of *Saint Genet*, Sartre was mainly occupied in political disputes about the Communist Party. In 1952, outraged by the arrest, on very dubious grounds, of a French communist leader, he decided that, for all its faults, there was no alternative to unrestricted support for the Party: "an anticommunist is a rat . . . I swore to the bourgeoisie a hatred which would only die with me".[13] He announced his new commitment in "The

---

[10] Jean Genet (1910–86), abandoned as a child and raised in orphanages, lived as a thief and prostitute before achieving success with novels and plays that brutally denounced bourgeois society and exalted the lives of pariahs like himself.
[11] *Saint Genet*, 645.   [12] *Situations IX*, 114.
[13] "Merleau-Ponty", in *Situations*, 198.

Communists and Peace" (1952) and for the next four years, although he never formally joined the Party, became little more than a propagandist for the Communists, not only through essays in *Les temps modernes* but also through reports to the Communist journal *Libération* on his trip to the Soviet Union. The result was some of the most embarrassing statements Sartre ever made.[14] His willing role as easily the most influential "fellow traveler" led to harsh breaks with Camus and Merleau-Ponty, both close friends from the days of the Resistance. But in 1956, in "Le fantôme de Staline", he condemned the Soviet invasion of Hungary and once again broke with the French Communist Party. The next year, he began work on the philosophical project he now realized was necessary as a response to the inadequacies of his earlier formulation of existentialism in *L'être et le néant*: a systematic reformulation of existentialism in terms of socio-historical categories derived from Marxism, which he now recognized as "the one philosophy of our time which we cannot go beyond".[15] The result, a tome of over 700 pages entitled *Critique de la raison dialectique*, was published in 1960.

Critique de la raison dialectique was Sartre's last strictly philosophical work. Three years later he published the story of his early childhood, *Les mots*, which turned out to be his last strictly literary work. From 1963 on, apart from his mostly political occasional essays and a number of political and autobiographical interviews, Sartre's only publications were his three massive volumes on the life of Gustave Flaubert, *L'idiot de la famille*, which appeared in 1971–2. His grand philosophical and literary ambitions end in the obsessive lucubrations of a literary biographer. In retrospect, however, the Flaubert project is understandable as a response to the tensions in Sartre's thought that had been increasing since 1945. Literature, not philosophy, had from the beginning been his raison d'être. But how was a literary vocation consistent with the life of political activism to which Sartre was irresistibly drawn after the war? His early notion of

---

[14] For example, his claim in 1954 (in *Libération*) that "freedom to criticize is total in the USSR". He made even more disturbing claims in the 1970s, in support of increasingly radical Maoist student groups, for example, his pronouncement that "a revolutionary regime has to get rid of a certain number of individuals who threaten it, and I don't see any means other than death. They can always escape from prison. The revolutionaries of 1793 probably didn't kill enough" (*Actuel* 28 [February 1973]). Tony Judt, in *Past Imperfect*, provides a detailed discussion and perceptive analysis of the political stands of Sartre (and others), although his discussion of Sartre's philosophical views is sometimes confused.

[15] *Search for a Method*, xxxiv.

littérature engagée proved impossible to defend in a rigorous way; and in any case, Sartre had not been able to sustain a high level of literary creativity in these or any other terms. The first two novels in his projected tetralogy on World War II were published in 1945, but the third volume (*Mort dans l'âme*) did not appear until 1949; and the fourth volume, promised as a portrait of the heroism of the Resistance, remained unfinished, a literary parallel to the failed philosophical project of an existentialist ethics. During the 1950s, Sartre's literary writing was limited to a few not particularly successful plays. *Les mots* was a splendid swan song, a classically crafted, brilliantly ironic masterpiece, his finest achievement since *La nausée*. But Sartre explicitly presented *Les mots* as a farewell to literature that finally exorcised his attachment through a caustic analysis of its origins.

My suggestion is that Sartre found it impossible to follow his literary vocation in a way that was intellectually consistent with his political commitments. But he also found it impossible to give up thinking about literature and struggling to make sense of its role in human existence. The solution was to write, more and more elaborately, about writers. He had, after all, begun with a brief monograph on Baudelaire in 1947. The big book about Genet in 1952 had, as we have seen, other motives too, but after the work on Flaubert we must see it as also a major step in Sartre's fixation on literature. *Les mots* itself is, of course, a literary biography, and functions as a self-reflective prologue to the giant Flaubert enterprise. It is also striking that the three writers, besides himself, whom Sartre analyzes are all writers of "pure literature", just about as far removed as one could imagine from Sartre's own purported ideal of *littérature engagée* but exactly the models that the young Sartre would have emulated.[16]

We will not go wrong, then, in reading *L'idiot de la famille* as the final step in Sartre's personal effort to come to terms with his literary vocation. But it is also, like *Saint Genet*, a concrete exploration and test of Sartre's philosophical ideas, rethinking and applying the conceptual apparatus of *Critique de la raison dialectique*, as the earlier biography did that of *L'être et le néant*. The work even incorporates a final effort at synthesizing Sartre's entire philosophical achievement

---

[16] Sartre also wrote, between 1948 and 1952, *Mallarmé*, a long study of the French poet, part of which has been posthumously published. He seems to have lost the bulk of the manuscript.

since it combines explicitly existential categories such as lived experience (*le vécu*) with the objective socio-historical structures of the *Critique de la raison dialectique*. Unfortunately, the book's extreme length and self-indulgent lack of organization promise the scant impact of what is, in Ronald Aronson's only slightly exaggerated phrase, "a book that nobody will read".[17]

The focus and limits of this study dictate that we look at Sartre's achievement as a philosopher, particularly as it influenced other philosophers of his and the following generation. This means giving central place to *L'être et le néant*, which is, in any case, far and away Sartre's greatest achievement as a philosopher. It is also at the core of all Sartre's subsequent philosophizing, which refines and develops its central theses but never simply rejects them. I will, therefore, concentrate on *L'être et le néant*, although I will also discuss the *Critique de la raison dialectique* as an extension of Sartre's existentialism to the social domain.[18]

BEING AND NOTHINGNESS

Background

Despite his eventual break with university philosophy, Sartre's initiation into the discipline was entirely conventional. Once he resolved to pursue philosophy as a ground for his literary career, he simply followed the course set out by his teachers: "The development of my ideas on philosophy was related to what I was taught at the lycée and at the Sorbonne. I didn't come to philosophy indepen-

---

[17] Ronald Aronson, "*L'idiot de la famille*: The Ultimate Sartre?", in Robert Wilcocks (ed.), *Critical Essays on Jean-Paul Sartre*, 136.

[18] I am also ignoring any new directions that might be indicated by Sartre's discussions with Benny Lévy, shortly before his death, in which he embraces a "hope" that seems in tension with existential despair and suggests an interest in – though by no means an acceptance of – certain religious viewpoints (see Jean-Paul Sartre, *L'espoir maintenant*). The natural – if often merely expedient – response that Sartre's intellectual powers were failing and that Lévy exercised undue influence on the old man may have some point. But Sartre's unequivocal rejection of religion was – as James Collins long ago pointed out (in *The Existentialists*) – a dogmatic postulate rather than a considered philosophical position and would have been an entirely appropriate object of his critical philosophical attention. (See Sartre's own account of what he calls his "separation" from God from childhood in *Les mots*, 97–103; 250–1.) In any case, Sartre never gave these very late ideas thorough critical consideration, and we have no way of knowing how he might have eventually related them to the existentialism that defined his philosophical thought for his entire adult life.

dently of the courses I had . . . In other words, the philosophical education I received all those years was an academic education."[19] His education moved beyond the syllabus only after he discovered Husserl and Heidegger and studied in Berlin from November 1933 to July 1934. This study, he suggests, consisted mainly of a careful reading of Husserl's *Ideen*.[20] His German seems to have been weak, and he did not have significant philosophical contacts in Berlin.

Sartre's early philosophical essays are phenomenological studies, in the Husserlian sense of careful descriptions of the essential natures of specific psychic phenomena. But from the beginning he showed his independence, particularly in *La transcendance de l'égo* (1936), where he rejected Husserl's view that consciousness is the activity of a transcendental ego and argued instead that consciousness as such is an impersonal awareness, with no internal structure that could correspond to an ego. The ego exists, but it cannot be identified with consciousness; it is instead a transcendent being, an object of consciousness, and so a part of the world like any other object.

Sartre's other early essays, on imagination and on emotion, are less radical but still support his earlier thesis that consciousness has no internal structure. Contrary to standard views, Sartre maintains that images and emotions are not somehow "in" consciousness (as, for example, states or attributes).[21] Rather they are simply ways in which consciousness relates to objects outside of it. So, for example, when I (in Paris) imagine what my friend Pierre, who is in Berlin, is doing, I do not form an image of Pierre in my mind but rather turn my consciousness toward the real Pierre, though in an imaginative rather than a perceptual mode. When I imagine a nonexistent thing, such as a centaur playing a flute, there is, of course, a sensory image that is the object of my consciousness. But this image is not *in* my

---

[19] "Interview with Jean-Paul Sartre", in Paul Schilpp (ed.), *The Philosophy of Jean-Paul Sartre*, 9. Note also Jacques Derrida's comment on Sartre and the university: "It is said that he escaped it or resisted it. It seems to me that university norms determined his work in the most internal fashion" (*Points*, 123).

[20] "So there I was in Berlin, reading Husserl and taking notes on what I read . . . [Question:] And in what order did you read Husserl, first the *Ideen*, or did you start with *Logische Untersuchungen*? Sartre: *Ideen*, and nothing but *Ideen*. For me, you know, who doesn't read very fast, a year was just about right for reading his *Ideen*" (*Sartre by Himself*, 29–30).

[21] Sartre published two books on imagination. The first, *L'imagination*, is a critique of standard views of the imagination. The second, *L'imaginaire: psychologie phénoménologique de l'imagination*, presents his own phenomenological account of the imagination and also interprets a range of empirical data on the topic. Both books derive from his degree work in philosophy.

consciousness and, more importantly, the presence of the image is not sufficient for an act of imagination to have occurred (it might, for example, be an object of hallucination, not imagination). As before, the imagining occurs because of the special attitude that consciousness takes toward its object.

Similarly, for me to feel an emotion is not for my consciousness to be infused with a certain affective quality but for it to take up a certain attitude toward the world. Fear, for example, is not a matter of consciousness's being passively overcome by or infused with a feeling of terror; rather, it is consciousness's active effort to exclude (by fleeing, fainting, or going into shock) the object of fear from its experience of the world. As in the cases of the ego and of images, Sartre is concerned to preserve what he sees as the fundamental phenomenological truth that consciousness is an entirely pure, transparent awareness of objects, not a container filled with thoughts, images, and feelings.

From early on, Sartre's philosophical ambitions extended beyond giving Husserlian descriptions of specific regions of phenomena. He wanted to offer a comprehensive ontology, that is, an account of the fundamental categories of being as such, an account based not on conceptual analysis or abstract reasoning but on the concrete descriptions of phenomenology. He wanted, in sum, a "phenomenological ontology", as he put it in the subtitle of *L'être et le néant*. Sartre's interest in ontology may well have some connection with Heidegger's, but the central issues of how the being of consciousness relates to the being of its objects and the place of contingency in the world are rooted in his strongly Cartesian education and in his personal obsessions. If nothing else, the intensity with which these issues are raised in *La nausée* suggests an autobiographical origin. Moreover, in an interview with Simone de Beauvoir, Sartre tells us that both his interest in contingency and his conviction that consciousness could grasp objects just as they are go all the way back to before he enrolled in the École Normale in 1923, well before he knew anything about Heidegger or Husserl.[22] Also, Sartre says he studied Heidegger seriously for the first time while he was a prisoner of war, when he was already writing *L'être et le néant*.[23] On the other

---

[22] See Simone de Beauvoir, "Conversations with Sartre", in *Adieux: Farewell to Sartre*, 141–2 (on contingency) and 157 (on the objects of consciousness).
[23] *Sartre by Himself*, 50–1 (on studying Heidegger) and Simone de Beauvoir, "Conversations with Sartre", 156–7 (on writing *L'être et le néant*).

hand, Sartre obviously found much in Heidegger, as in Husserl, that was to his purposes in *L'être et le néant*.

The basic ontological scheme

L'être et le néant opens with a thorny introduction, given the ironic Proustian subtitle, "A la recherche de l'être" ("in search of being"), which presents Sartre's fundamental ontological categories. He begins by rejecting one form of realism, that which places reality in an underlying substance of which we experience only the appearances. On Sartre's view, a phenomenon (appearance) is relative to the consciousness to which it appears, but it is not relative to any non-appearing being of which it is merely the phenomenal expression (*L'être et le néant* [*EN*], 12/4).

Sartre notes that this construal of the phenomenon eliminates a number of problematic dualisms: of the inner (substance) and the outer (appearance), of (hidden) power and (manifest) act, etc. It also recasts the notion of essence, which is no longer a secret core, accessible only through phenomenal manifestations. Instead, essences appear directly to us: "the essence . . . is simply the connection of the appearances" and so is "itself an appearance" (*EN*, 12/5). This, Sartre says, is the reason Husserl can speak of an "intuition of essences" (*Wesensschau*) (*EN*, 12–13/5).

There still remains, however, one last dualism, that of the finite and the infinite. What Sartre has in mind here is the fact that, although we at any point have experienced only a finite set of appearances of an object, the object itself cannot be reduced to any such finite set. A complete grasp of its reality must refer to the unlimited set of all its possible appearances.

It is at this point that Sartre's discussion becomes explicitly ontological, i.e., concerned with *being*. On the old picture, which thought of the object or its essence as hidden behind its phenomenal appearances, it was natural to take this hidden reality as the *being* of an object in contrast to the merely phenomenal *appearance* to which we have direct access. But Sartre's account cannot make sense of such a contrast between appearances and underlying being. The appearances themselves must be recognized as having being, that is, as fully real in their own right. But, Sartre says, this means that we must ask about the nature of this being, and the first question is whether this being is itself an appearance. Sartre is quite willing to say that it is, since, after all, an appearance (or phenomenon) is simply whatever is manifested to us, and our ability to talk and think unproblematically about the being of appearances surely suggests that it is in some sense manifest to us. (He also notes, with an implicit reference to his novel *La nausée*, that experiences such as boredom and existential nausea directly manifest the being of appearances to us.) We can, then, speak of the "phenomenon of being" and define ontology as the description of this phenomenon (*EN*, 14/7). Here we have the origin and justification of Sartre's project of "phenomenological ontology".

It is, however, crucial that we not think of this phenomenology of being as simply an instance of the standard Husserlian phenomenology of essences. The phenomenology of essences (eidetic phenomenology) is a matter of moving, via imaginative variation, from a particular red to the essence of red (redness). But being is not an essence. It is not, that is, something that an object has but rather, as Kant argued, the condition of an object's having any properties at all. We cannot, therefore, describe the phenomenon of being by beginning with a phenomenon and achieving, through standard phenomenological method, an intuition of the being of that phenomenon as some sort of meaning or essence of the phenomenon. We cannot, in other words, reduce the phenomenon of being to the being of the phenomenon (as we would, for example, achieve an intuition of redness by phenomenological reflection on a red phenomenon, thereby reducing the phenomenon of redness to the redness of the phenomenon). Being is a phenomenon – it appears to us – but not in the manner of ordinary phenomena that are known through an intuition of their essences. In this sense, being is *transphenomenal*.

The above line of thought expresses the fundamental *realism* of Sartre's ontology. It differs from some traditional representationalist realisms by accepting the "phenomenological" view that there is nothing behind the phenomena, that, accordingly, the real is directly given to us (and is only so given) in phenomenal experience. Despite this, as we have seen, Sartre holds that reality (being) is not phenomenal; that, in other words, the reality of the objects of our experience does not consist in the fact that they are phenomenally given to us. The objects themselves are so given (and only so given), but they are not real in virtue of this. Their reality is given in our phenomenal experience, but it is given precisely as independent of our experience. Being, we might say, is in but not of the phenomenal realm. Or, to employ Spiegelberg's deft characterization, Sartre's view is "a combination of a phenomenalism of essences with a realism of existence".[24]

Given the difficulties of formulating with proper nuance this complex phenomenological realism, it may be suggested that Sartre would do better simply to accept idealism. (He thinks that this is what Husserl himself did.) Why not, in particular, push our acceptance of phenomena in their own terms to its limit and agree that the being of an appearance is simply the fact that it appears? This would amount to accepting Berkeley's claim that to be is to be perceived (*esse est percipi*).

But, according to Sartre, this claim cannot be maintained. His argument (which, with an ironic nod toward St. Anselm, he calls the "ontological proof") is based on the intentionality of consciousness so emphasized by Husserl (although, according to Sartre, Husserl did not properly understand it). Intentionality is the essential relationship of consciousness to an object. But contrary to our usual way of thinking, Sartre maintains that consciousness has no positive reality apart from its relation to its objects. Its being is entirely exhausted by its directedness toward its objects. As Sartre puts it, consciousness is nothing other than a "revealing intuition" (*EN*, 28/23). But this makes no sense unless consciousness has an object that exists entirely separately from it. (To say that consciousness reveals itself or that it somehow constitutes the being of its object is to make of consciousness something other than a pure directedness toward its object.) Accordingly, we must recognize a kind of being beyond consciousness: the being of the object of consciousness or, in the terms we used earlier, the being of the phenomenon. This Sartre calls being-in-itself.

In sum, then, Sartre's initial description of the phenomenon of being (as it is directly present to our experience) has revealed two distinct regions of being: the being of the objects of consciousness (*being-in-itself*) and the being of consciousness (*being-for-itself*), to which we now turn.

Consciousness

The rest of *L'être et le néant* consists in the descriptive (phenomenological) filling in of the details of the general ontological scheme

[24] Spiegelberg, *The Phenomenological Movement*, 489.

sketched in the preface. But before turning to that project, it will be helpful to discuss the notion of consciousness that is the keystone of Sartre's analysis. An obvious question is why Sartre thinks philosophy, rather than (or, at least, in addition to) science, should be able to tell us about consciousness. Of course, scientific methods can be applied in one way or another to any subject matter at all, but there is no guarantee that these methods (essentially, the rigorous intersubjective testing of precisely formulated hypotheses) will tell us everything we want to know about a given subject. This would seem to be particularly true of consciousness, the first-person awareness that is our constant and immediate mode of encountering the world and, especially, ourselves. It seems that scientific accounts always leave out something of this awareness; they do not, as Einstein remarked, give us "the taste of the soup". It is easy to conclude too much from this fact. It does not, for example, follow that there is another realm of things outside of those treated by science, for example, spiritual substances such as souls. Nor does it follow that the entire domain of consciousness could never be entirely understood in terms of strictly empirical scientific categories. But at the very least we can say that first-person awareness cannot be ignored. Science must ultimately come to terms with it, and we cannot imagine our lives not centering on it. This is sufficient justification for a project, such as Sartre's, of offering a detailed account of our first-person awareness.[25]

Sartre's fundamental position is this: consciousness is always of something, but it itself is not something. To say that I am conscious implies that there is some object – typically something real, though in some cases something imaginary or illusory – that I am conscious of. Consciousness is, in the language of Husserl's phenomenology, essentially *intentional* – directed toward something else. Intentionality is a relation, but it cannot be understood by analogy with ordinary relations between things in the world, for example, the relation whereby a box is on top of a table or a fish is in a stream. This is because consciousness is not a thing, not a material thing but also not an immaterial thing such as a soul or a spiritual substance. It is not a thing because its entire existence is exhausted by its relation to

---

[25] There is no reason to think that Sartre would reject this minimalist defense of a philosophical study of consciousness, but his own view gives scant room for any significant scientific knowledge of consciousness.

its objects. It has no content or structure of its own. Nor does it take on content or structure by somehow incorporating its objects. Our ordinary talk of what we experience or think about being "in the mind" is misleading. In typical cases (e.g., sense perception, non-deceptive memory) the object experienced exists outside the mind in the real world. But even when, as in imagination or illusions, there is no real object, the object is not literally in the mind. Consciousness is a totally "transparent" intending of its objects and nothing more. In view of this, Sartre is prepared to say that consciousness is *nothing*.

Consciousness is also transparent in another sense. It is always aware, directly and immediately, of itself as consciousness. As Sartre puts it, to be conscious is to be self-conscious. But here we need to be careful. Self-consciousness might seem to mean consciousness of self, where "self" refers to consciousness as an object of awareness like any other. But then consciousness would also be a thing like any other, and this of course Sartre firmly denies. To preserve his insight about self-consciousness without reifying consciousness, Sartre introduces the notion of a special mode of consciousness, whereby consciousness is aware of itself but without encountering itself as an object. This is not to deny the intentionality of consciousness. When I am aware, there is always something other than consciousness that I am aware of; but along with this awareness of an object, there is also always an implicit (sidelong, so to speak) awareness of my consciousness. To mark the difference, Sartre distinguishes two modes of consciousness: thetic (directed toward or positing an object) and non-thetic (not directed toward or positing an object). Consciousness's implicit awareness of itself is non-thetic.[26] Suppose, for example, I am a pharmacist counting out pills for a prescription, intent on not making a mistake in the number. I will have a thetic awareness of the pills that are the focus of my activity. But there will also be a non-thetic awareness of my conscious act of counting. For, if someone asks me what I am doing, I will immediately reply, "Counting the pills", an answer based on an implicit (non-thetic)

---

[26] Sartre also uses the equivalent terms "positional" and "non-positional". He further marks the distinction between thetic (positional) and non-thetic (non-positional) by writing "consciousness (of) self" for the case of non-thetic consciousness, instead of the normal "consciousness of self" that he continues to use for thetic consciousness. (This is particularly important in French, where the "of" cannot be avoided, since even "self-consciousness" must be expressed as "conscience de soi".)

awareness of the consciousness that is explicitly (thetically) aware of the pills.[27]

Because consciousness is always self-aware, Sartre says that it has *being-for-itself*: its very existence involves an internal relation to itself. The objects of consciousness are not self-aware (we will consider the special case of other consciousnesses below). On the other hand, unlike consciousness, objects of consciousness are things, with the presence and solidity of intrinsic content; they have, in Sartre's terminology, *being-in-itself*, which consciousness of course lacks.

Sartre's account seems to ignore an obvious feature of our experience: the person (or psychological self) as the subject of the properties (habits, character-traits, beliefs, inclinations) that define us as individuals. In fact, Sartre does not ignore this obvious reality, but he displaces it. Rather than identifying it with (or situating it within) consciousness, he maintains that the self exists only as an object of consciousness, that it is a part of the world, like any other thing. Our awareness of this self needs, of course, to be sharply distinguished from self-awareness in the sense of consciousness's implicit, non-thetic awareness of itself. To make the distinction, Sartre speaks of consciousness's (thetic) awareness of the self as *reflective consciousness*, and of consciousness's (non-thetic) awareness (of) itself as *non-reflective* consciousness. (The idea is that reflection involves an explicit awareness of the self as a separate object.) Non-reflective consciousness is prior to reflective consciousness; we do not, as Descartes thought, first know ourselves through explicit acts of reflection but through our implicit awareness of our awareness of objects in the world.

We need, finally, to say a bit more about the relation of being-in-itself to being-for-itself. Our ordinary experience is of objects that have a basic intelligibility – a nature or structure that gives them a meaning (e.g., patterned or functional behavior in the natural world, a purpose in our lives). In Sartre's view, however, this intelligibility does not belong to the object in virtue of its most basic reality as being-in-itself. On the fundamental level the object is a brute, un-

---

[27] Sartre also ties thetic as opposed to non-thetic consciousness to his notion of knowledge. When we have explicit awareness of an object, he says we know it. But consciousness's non-thetic grasp of itself he does not regard as knowledge, since there are no propositions about the nature of consciousness that can be formulated on the basis of non-thetic awareness. His view here recalls Russell's distinction between knowledge by acquaintance and knowledge by description.

structured given, merely existing with no intrinsic meaning. On this level we should not, in fact, speak of different things, since the structure necessary for differentiation is not present. There is just sheer indistinct being-in-itself. In the literary phenomenology of Roquentin's vision in *La nausée*, Sartre characterizes the unintelligibility of being-in-itself in terms of *superfluity, absurdity,* and *contingency*. Being-in-itself is meaningful (and divided into discrete, intelligible objects) only insofar as it is the object of consciousness. Consciousness is, therefore, the ultimate source not of the reality of being-in-itself but of its meaning.[28] In *La nausée* Roquentin's central experience (of the chestnut tree in the Bouville park) is precisely of the intrinsic unintelligibility of being-in-itself.[29] On the other hand, we should not be misled into thinking that, because consciousness is the source of meaning in the world, it has itself intrinsic meaning. As sheer transparent awareness, the for-itself has no more intrinsic structure than does the in-itself. The meaning of my consciousness is given only in the self, which, as we have seen, is strictly other than consciousness and possesses meaning precisely as an object of consciousness.

Nothingness and anguish

So far we have been following Sartre's analysis of being in terms of its two modes, being-in-itself and being-for-itself. In turning to the project of "concretizing" his ontology through a series of phenomenological descriptions, Sartre begins by transposing the question of being from the mode of analysis to that of synthesis; that is, he takes as his object of reflection not being-in-itself and being-for-itself separately but the concrete union of the two in the synthesis *being-in-the-world* (*EN*, 38/34).

This has the result of allowing Sartre to proceed by the examination of human conduct ("the conduct of man in the world"), which he says we can discover simply by "opening our eyes" (*EN*, 38/34). This move is methodologically important, since it allows Sartre to supplement the austere logical analyses of abstract ontology with concrete phenomenological descriptions of lived experience. His procedure will be to develop his ontology by describing a series of

---

[28] Here we can recall again Spiegelberg's comment that Sartre holds a phenomenalism of essences (meanings) but a realism of existence (*The Phenomenological Movement*, 489).
[29] *Nausea*, 170–82.

(appropriately chosen) types of human conduct. One issue to which we need to pay careful attention is that of the precise relation between Sartre's phenomenological descriptions and his abstract ontology.

The first result of Sartre's description of our concrete situation (*being-in-the-world*) is *the reality of negation*. Some philosophers (Sartre has in mind Bergson and also Brunschvicg) maintain that we do not encounter negation as an aspect of our concrete situation, that it enters only at the level of propositions (intellectual judgments) about that situation. On this view, we would encounter negation only when we reflect and compare our judgments and the concepts in terms of which they are formulated. So, from immediate experience I would know only positive things such as *snow is white* and *grass is green*; negation would enter only when, reflecting on what I know of snow and what I know of grass, I form the judgments *snow is not green* and *grass is not white*.

Sartre, however, maintains that our very ability to form negative judgments at the reflective level requires that we already have a notion of negativity, and that this notion itself comes from immediate experiences of negation as a given reality. He illustrates the essential nature of such an experience through the example of a particular instance of questioning behavior: my search for a friend, Pierre, in a café (*EN*, 43–5/40–2).

As I enter the cafe, late for an appointment with Pierre, who is meticulously punctual, I at first seem to encounter a fullness of being; everywhere I look there are objects or activities. But, since I am looking for Pierre and worried that he may have already left, each element of this scene falls back, as soon as it begins to present itself, because I see it as not-Pierre. Since my experience is perceptual, it exhibits the standard structure of ground and figure. But in this case, the café itself, with all its contents, becomes the ground against which I experience not Pierre but his absence as a concrete reality.

Sartre introduces the neologism "nihilation" (*néantisation*) to denote the process whereby negation is introduced on the concrete level of immediate perception (as opposed to the reflective level of intellectual judgment). Correspondingly, *nothingness* is his term for the ontological reality of negation that is introduced by nihilation. The fact that my experience of the Pierreless café involves nihilation – of both the absent Pierre and of the café that lacks him – shows that negation exists as a concrete reality. Since this reality is not reducible to that of being-in-itself (which is pure positivity) or to being-for-itself (because nothingness is not conscious) it follows that nothingness is required as a distinct ontological category, in addition to being-in-itself and being-for-itself.

Given this category, we are able to form at will negative judgments that are not specifically based in our experience, for example, that Attila the Hun or Vladimir Nabokov is not in the café. The contrived and trivial nature of such judgments serves only to emphasize the ontological priority of judgments that are grounded in direct experiences of nothingness.

Although Sartre thinks our experience requires nothingness as a basic ontological category, he does not (as he thinks Hegel and Heidegger do) see it as equi-primordial with being. Rather, he maintains that nothingness is logically subsequent to and grounded in being, since there is no sense in speaking of something that exists entirely independent of what is. Nothingness must, therefore, exist like "a worm in the heart of being" (*EN*, 56/56). But how does it arise? Certainly not from itself, through some incoherent self-nihilation, nor from being-in-itself, which is entirely enclosed in its inert givenness. Nothingness must therefore be somehow derived from consciousness (and hence from being-for-itself), a conclusion supported, moreover, by our experience of negations as arising in the face of our expectations and fears. But consciousness is always of being-in-itself and so it must give rise to nothingness by negating being-in-itself.

This negation is not, of course, a matter of literally destroying (annihilating) being-in-itself. Rather, consciousness negates by *withdrawing* from being. Sartre identifies this withdrawal with *freedom*, since freedom is a transcending of the determinism of causal laws and these laws exist only as structures of being-in-itself. Specifically, freedom involves consciousness's ability to withdraw from (revise or even reject) the self, which, as we have seen, is in the domain of objects and so of being-in-itself. Because I am free, I can deny what I am (that is, what I have been up to now) and constitute at any moment a new meaning for my existence as a self. Negation enters the world in virtue of consciousness's choice to make its self *this* and not *that* in relation to the rest of the world. Thus, in terms of our earlier example, Pierre's absence from the café has real force because I have chosen to be a self that is concerned with finding Pierre in the café. If I am indifferent to Pierre's presence, then his absence is apparent only on the level of intellectual judgments, like the absence of Attila the Hun.

I am free simply because I am conscious, for to be conscious is to give meaning to the objects, particularly my self, of which I am aware. In particular, whenever I reflect on myself (on what I have been up until now), I cannot avoid being aware of my freedom and its ability to withdraw from what I am. It follows that, if Sartre is correct, awareness of freedom should be a constant feature of my reflective awareness of myself: whenever I think, as I regularly do, of myself, I must realize my freedom. He calls this awareness *anguish* (*angoisse*). Anguish is not the same as fear, which always has a specific object (a gun, the night, dying). Anguish can, following Heidegger, be called the fear of nothing, but only if, like Kierkegaard, we identify "nothing" with the freedom whereby we nihilate the world, including the self.

The rather dramatic term "anguish" should not lead us to forget that Sartre is talking about an ontological, not a psychological, category. "Anguish" does not in itself refer to, for example, a state of mental agitation (anxiety) but merely to the fact of our reflective awareness of freedom. But neither should we think that anguish has nothing to do with anxiety and related mental phenomena. It is the ontological foundation of a variety of mental states, ranging from certain forms of "diffuse" anxiety to any number of psychological states involving a "repression" of such anxiety – for example, my troubled complacency when I self-deceptively claim that I "have no alternative" in a given situation.

According to Sartre, anguish may be about either what I may reject out of my past or what I may make of myself in the future. An example of the first is my realization as a reformed gambler, passing by a casino, that there is nothing to prevent me from overriding all my good resolutions and motivations and putting my paycheck on a roll of the dice. An example of the second is vertigo, a "fear" of heights grounded not in any real sense of objective danger but in my realization that I could, at any moment, jump over the rail (*EN*, 67–8/69–70, 65–6/66–7).

Bad faith

We are likely to respond to Sartre that anguish is surely not as common as his account implies. But this, he would reply, results from our efforts to flee from anguish, to pretend to ourselves that we are not really free, despite our ongoing consciousness of our freedom. This flight from anguish expresses the widespread behavior of *bad faith* (*mauvaise foi*, sometimes translated as "self-deception"). Sartre does not maintain that bad faith is inevitable, but he clearly regards it as very common, at least in our current social situation, and takes elaborate pains to describe the many varieties and subtleties of its manifestations. These descriptions are designed, first of all, to convince us that, contrary to appearances, consciousness of freedom and the accompanying anguish are constants in our lives. But Sartre also intends his study of bad faith to provide a basis for a deeper understanding of the nature of consciousness as a being capable of such behavior.

The obvious analogy for understanding bad faith is the lie, since "the one who practices bad faith is hiding a displeasing truth or presenting as truth a pleasing untruth" (*EN*, 83/89). But the problem is that a lie requires a duality of deceiver and deceived, whereas I would seem to be a single unified being.[30] To obtain a positive understanding of bad faith, Sartre offers a number of striking phenomenological descriptions. I will focus on the famous example of "a woman who has consented to go out with a particular man for the first time". She knows that her companion is interested in a sexual relationship; she knows that she will fairly soon have to decide whether to sleep with him. This knowledge seems straightforward and unambiguous. Her desires are another matter – "she does not quite know what she wants" (*EN*, 90/97).

As Sartre paints the picture, this woman does not explicitly want a sexual relationship or even to acknowledge the possibility of one. She knows ("is profoundly aware of") the man's desire for her; "but the desire cruel and naked would humiliate and horrify her" (*EN*, 90/97). So should we say that she simply does not desire a sexual relationship? Not exactly. If she were simply uninterested, her clear course of action would be to deflate the present situation (leave, call a friend over to the table, spill something on her companion). Why does not she do this? Because there are things in the situation that she does want. She enjoys, for example, the appreciation and respect her companion shows her – the compliments, the polite gestures, the

---

[30] Sartre maintains that a Freudian appeal to the unconscious to explain bad faith likewise fails to preserve the unity of consciousness.

admiring looks. No problem, we might say. These things are readily available elsewhere – from her friends, from her family. Didn't her father tell her she looked beautiful before she left the house, and didn't her younger sister look at her with admiration? Yes, Sartre says, but that sort of familial response is not what she has in mind. "She would find no charm in a respect that would be merely respect" (*EN*, 90/97). She does, in other words, want to be the object of sexual desire, but at the same time she does not want to recognize the desire for what it is. She wants to maintain a situation in which she is desired but in which she is able to pretend to herself that she is not.

She does this by exploiting the gap between existence and essence (meaning). There is a sense in which a polite gesture or a kind phrase is merely that. She can always say to herself: "He merely helped me with my coat", or "He merely said my dress was lovely." We may urge, "But he meant much more!" But the fact remains that, if you sufficiently circumscribe the action, you lose sight of its ulterior meaning. The woman deceives herself first of all by restricting her attention to the sheer existence of what her companion does and says (its being-in-itself) and ignoring its essential meaning (constituted by his consciousness).

This gambit, however, works only up to a point – the point at which the companion goes beyond anything that can be construed as mere politeness and acts in an unequivocally romantic way. In Sartre's scenario, he takes her hand, a gesture that, again given the conventions of the situation, has an undeniably romantic (and so ultimately sexual) significance. Surely this will destroy the "troubled and unstable harmony which gives the hour its charm" (*EN*, 90/97)? Not necessarily, since there is another level of evasion. His taking her hand makes his intentions unequivocal, but what does that have to do with *her*? She, after all, is not her hand, this thing that happens to be entwined with her companion's and of which she, as an intelligent person who happens to be engaged in a rather deep intellectual conversation, does not even really notice. Here the bad faith is founded on another gap, that between the body and the self. Although there is surely a deep sense in which I am my body (we do not say that the clumsy waiter spilled water on my body but not on me), there are still ways and contexts in which we deny the identity ("he's only interested in my body", "my body isn't what it used to be"). The woman's bad faith plays on this, identifying herself with her body to the extent that this enables her to enjoy her companion's sexual attention, but separating herself from it when it is a question of admitting her complicity with his desire.[31]

Ultimately, bad faith is based on the distinction of being-for-itself and being-in-itself and the essential relation of the two. The woman is able to treat her companion or herself as a being-in-itself, which in one sense each is, while at the same time treating each, when it suits her, as a being-for-itself. In the most basic terms, bad faith is possible because being-for-itself is characterized by a fundamental duality whereby it is both separated from and identified with being-in-itself.

Accordingly, it is always incorrect (ontologically) to treat a conscious being as simply being what it is or as not being what it is not. Rather, a conscious being is, in Sartre's Hegelian formulae, what it is in the mode of not being it (or, is what it is not and is not what it is). There follows the central ontological consequence of Sartre's description of bad faith: bad faith is possible only because consciousness has the peculiar status of being what it is not and not being what it is. It also follows that sincerity (understood as just being what you are) is not possible.[32]

But what are we to make of the apparently contradictory claim that being-for-itself (consciousness) is what it is not and is not what it is? We can put the point this way: The "what it is" is the set of facts true of the entity. The reality of a being-in-itself is exhausted by these facts, but the reality of a being-for-itself lies rather in interpreting (giving meaning to) these facts. As an interpretation of the facts about it, it is not (it goes beyond) these facts, though of course there is a sense in which they are true of it.

A final question: if sincerity is not possible, is there any alternative to bad faith? Sartre thinks there is, in an attitude that he calls "authenticity". Humans are authentic when they recognize – and live out in their actions – the basic truth that they have no essential reality or nature but are fully and solely free agents. If I have this attitude, I will avoid bad faith, because I will always recognize my complex reality as being what I am in the mode of not being it (and hence being entirely responsible for what I am). Authenticity also

---

[31] Feminist critics have objected to what they see as the sexist nature of Sartre's discussion of this example; see, e.g., Toril Moi, *Simone de Beauvoir: The Making of an Intellectual Woman*, chapter 4. For a broader and deeper analysis of Sartre's sexism (and with special reference to his relations with Beauvoir), see Michèle Le Doeuff, *L'étude et le rouet*.

[32] Here Sartre's discussion evokes classic treatments of sincerity in French literature, from Montaigne through Stendhal to Gide.

amounts to a recognition of freedom itself as the sole value of human existence and thus provides a basis for a positive Sartrean ethics. But, Sartre notes (*EN*, 106, n. 1/116, n. 9), these ethical concerns are not part of his project here.

Being-for-others

So far, Sartre's phenomenologies of the concrete realities of man-in-the-world have found a ready ontological context in his two categories of being-for-itself and being-in-itself. But there are, he thinks, realities that require an addition to these categories, realities involving our experience of other people.

Philosophers have typically approached the question of other consciousnesses as an epistemological problem. Their thought is that, since we have no experience as such of another consciousness but are aware of only the other's body, we need some way of arguing from the bodily behavior of which we are aware to the consciousness of which we are not. Other philosophers have maintained that there is no problem of other minds at all. We simply and directly know that there are other consciousnesses and no account need be given of how this is or how it might be justified.

Sartre agrees that there is no sense in arguing for the existence of other minds; the epistemological problem of other minds is a non-starter. But he does think that we can give an intelligible account of how we become aware of others, an account that will provide a basis for understanding the nature of interpersonal relations and that will also require us to add to our ontological categories one corresponding to being-for-others. There is, in other words, an intelligible and important ontological problem of other minds.

Sartre concretizes the problem by a description of behavior that leads to experiences of shame. Suppose, for example, that I have heard some sounds behind a hotel door and stooped to look through the keyhole. Initially, I am, let us suppose, entirely directed to the objects of my interest, so that my consciousness of self is entirely non-reflective (implicit). At this point, there is no room for shame, since I am not aware of a self as an object (reflective consciousness) that I can judge as shameful. But now suppose someone, say a hotel detective, suddenly comes up behind me. I blush with shame and start stuttering an incoherent "explanation" of my behavior. What has happened?

I have suddenly become aware of myself, but in a way we have not previously encountered. Previously, "self-consciousness" meant either consciousness's non-thetic awareness of itself (where the "itself" is sheer transparent consciousness, with no nature or structure) or else thetic (reflective) consciousness of a substantive, psychological self. The consciousness I now have, Sartre says, is non-thetic; it does not involve reflection and so does not present the psychological self that I constitute as my meaning for myself. At the same time, this consciousness is not merely of consciousness as a totally transparent directedness toward its objects. It is of a substantive, contentful psychological self. What is this self, if it is not the self of reflective consciousness? Sartre's answer is that it is the self as it exists for the other, not for me.

More concretely: As I blubber my explanation of why I have been looking through a keyhole, I realize that, no matter what I say, the hotel detective has his own view of what sort of person skulks around hotel corridors looking through keyholes. Regardless of what I think of myself or how I represent myself to him, he will have his own perception of what I am. For another consciousness, I am an object with a nature (perhaps that of a degenerate pervert), just like any other. In shame, my non-reflective awareness of myself is of myself as this object. I am aware of myself as an object for another consciousness. In this awareness, I encounter myself not as having being-for-itself (as a consciousness) or being-in-itself (as an object of my own reflective consciousness) but as having *being-for-others*.

There are two key points about the nature of this awareness of my being-for-others. First, it presents me to myself as what I am for the other. This does not mean that I entirely grasp just how in detail the other sees me (perhaps he thinks I am a silly old man or curious adolescent rather than a degenerate pervert). But I do know that the other has some view of my nature, and that alone is sufficient to establish my awareness of myself as a being-for-others. Also, the being I have for the other is clearly being-in-itself; that is, the other sees me as an object, with a fixed nature, not as the transparent consciousness of a being-for-itself. Indeed, Sartre says, I am unequivocally a being-in-itself for the other. Whereas with respect to my own reflective consciousness I am always what I am in the mode of not being it, for the other I simply am what I am.

Second, implicit in my awareness of myself as an object of the other's consciousness is an awareness of that very consciousness of the other. This, of course, does not mean that I am living the other's consciousness "from the inside", the way the other does; I do not see the world the way the other sees it. But I am directly aware of the *fact* of the other's consciousness. In particular, I am aware of the other as a freedom other than my own. This is especially important because, as we have seen, to be free is to be able to give meaning to the world. The other's freedom is, therefore, a challenge to my hegemony over my world, since I have no control over the meaning that the other may give to objects that we both experience. To take a simple example, the park bench that I see, as I approach it, as just the right place to spend my afternoon reading may be for another person, coming from a different direction, the place where she always eats her lunch. Since we both live in the same world, these different interpretations are the source of real conflicts between myself and others. Potentially most serious are conflicts over the self – between what I am for-myself and what I am for-others. Indeed, as we have seen, the other is most fundamentally encountered as a threat to my understanding of what I am, offering an interpretation of my behavior ("that degenerate pervert") that I am in no position to undermine (although, of course, I counterattack with my own interpretation of the other: e.g., "a petty tyrant"). From this we can see how Sartre arrives at his conclusion that "conflict is the original meaning of being-for-others" (*EN*, 404/475).[33]

Sartre develops this view by discussing a variety of specific modes of interpersonal relations, ranging from romantic love through sadism. Behind each type of behavior, he finds the effort to control, one way or another, the freedom of the other. Sometimes the strategy is an indirect one: to let the other make an object of me (confer on me a meaning, a self, from outside) in the hope that I will not be just one of the many objects in the other's world but the special one that will fascinate and even enthrall the other. Sartre understands the desire to be loved in this way and treats masochism as an extreme development of this desire. But the strategy may also be direct: to

---

[33] *Huis-clos*, Sartre's 1945 play, is commonly read as a striking illustration of this conclusion, with its famous line, "Hell is – other people" always cited. But although the theme of interpersonal conflict is surely present, it is important to keep in mind that the characters are dead in the precise sense of being no longer able to transform their lives by free action. They represent the fate of those who fail to break out of the bourgeois morality that makes human solidarity impossible, but not necessarily Sartre's judgment on the human condition as such.

make the other an object that I can control and even possess. This, for example, is what Sartre thinks is involved in sexual desire.

Freedom

The last part of *L'être et le néant* is concerned with moving from *being* to *doing*. It might seem that this would require yet another expansion of ontological categories. But, on Sartre's analysis, action derives entirely from the freedom of being-for-itself. Doing, therefore, can be understood in terms of the ontology already established. Nonetheless, this section is a proper culmination of *L'être et le néant*, since freedom is, for Sartre, the fundamental truth of human existence.

Sartre loses no time establishing the connection of action to freedom: action is always intentional (not necessarily reflective but with an implicit end or goal); intentional (goal-directed) behavior implies a lack – something not yet present that is seen as needing to be present; but lack is a negation, which, as we have seen, is always the product of consciousness as being-for-itself. In-itself, being is merely pure undifferentiated positivity. Negation appears only in light of consciousness's interpretation of the in-itself.

From this follows the freedom of action. Consciousness, not the world, must be the ultimate motive of an act, since it alone introduces the negation that lies behind action. Nor can we even say that the world (the in-itself) determines consciousness to see it in a negative way; the negativity is all in the interpretation, not in the fact. As the sole source of its action, consciousness is free in every action.

We might agree that the world as such does not determine our actions but still think that there is an internal determination via reasons (rational considerations of the deliberating will) or motives (non-rational causes such as feeling and desires). The idea would be that in acting consciousness is determined not from outside but by these internal factors. This, however, is ruled out from the start by Sartre's fundamental view of consciousness as transparent and empty, not a structure that could "contain" things such as reasons and motives. But Sartre also thinks the point can be directly established by noting that both deliberation and passion are intentional phenomena, always directed toward ends. Thus, to deliberate and reach a rational decision (the traditional province of the "will") presupposes ends for the sake of which the deliberation is carried out. But the presence of an end implies an intention, which, as we have seen, must itself be established by a free choice. So the deliberative exercise of the will presupposes rather than constitutes human freedom. In rational deliberation, the concern is only with means to an already chosen goal.

The same is true of what we call action out of feeling or desire (motives, in Sartre's terminology). This always involves an intended end; fear has the intention of avoiding a danger, ambition of gaining some prize. Since consciousness is the only possible source of a goal, it is the only possible source of the feelings and desires that are determined by goals.

Both reasons (*motifs*) and motives (*mobiles*[34]) are, therefore, themselves results of free choices, not the causes of them. Moreover, both are simply aspects of consciousness's free choice of its goal-directed action. Thus, "the reason, the motive, and the end are three indissoluble terms of the thrust of a free and living consciousness which projects itself toward its possibilities and makes itself defined by these possibilities" (*EN*, 493/579).

Sartre's account makes action not only free but radically and fundamentally free; there is no determination of it from any other source. But this raises the question of whether his analysis confers too much freedom. Surely, we do not experience ourselves as totally and unlimitedly free. On the one hand, freedom is not purely gratuitous caprice; on the other hand, it is surely somehow conditioned by the concrete situation in which I find myself. Sartre agrees with these points, but thinks they can be reconciled with his radical view of freedom. He attempts the reconciliation through discussions of the *fundamental project* and of the *situation*.

A fundamental project is the for-itself's overall orientation toward the world, the comprehensive goal of all of consciousness's free action. The fact that we act in the context of a fundamental project explains why our lives are not a random series of unconnected and gratuitous actions. But we must not think of the fundamental project as something imposed from outside or above; it is itself a free choice, entirely the project of consciousness's decision to see itself and its world in a certain way. The fundamental project is in no way a Trojan horse for psychological determinism. Nor should we think

---

[34] This term is confusingly rendered as "cause" in the Barnes translation of *L'être et le néant*.

that the fundamental project is some sort of Ur-choice or primordial freedom that itself controls more ordinary choices. The fundamental project exists not as a decision separate from my daily actions but only as an orientation constantly renewed in each of these actions. For this reason, it can, in principle, be reversed or replaced at any instant. Radical conversion is a permanent possibility of human existence. As a result, the judgment that a given individual's fundamental project is of a given sort can be made only retrospectively: my project is only what it has been, as a matter of my free choices, up to now. The fundamental project functions as a reified ideal, guiding a human life only from the perspective of a biographical reconstruction, not from the perspective of a life as it is actually lived. But as such an ideal, Sartre made the notion of the fundamental project basic for the "existential psychoanalyis" that he proposed in place of Freud's analysis of the "unconscious mind", a concept that Sartre saw as a self-contradiction.

In terms of future-directed life itself, the project is essentially a measure of the price of acting in one way or another. Of course, I can always keep climbing a mountain or running a race in spite of my fatigue and pain. But eventually this may be at the price of changing the basic orientation of all my choices up until now. Such a change is, nonetheless, always possible. My free acts constitute the fundamental project, not vice versa.

According to Sartre, freedom (action) always takes place in a *situation*. That is, action is always in the midst of and somehow *directed against* being-in-itself. Accordingly, there is always some resistance, some "coefficient of adversity" (a term borrowed from Bachelard) encountered by a free action. Freedom always encounters obstacles. So much is common sense, and Sartre does not deny it. But he says we need to think more deeply about the origin of these obstacles. Being-in-itself may have some totally generic intrinsic inertia that "opposes" our action on it. But the form of opposition that arises in any particular case, the specific obstacles to our freedom in a given situation, derive from the specific intentions of the for-itself in that situation – and therefore from freedom itself.

From the beginning, there has been much criticism of Sartre's existentialist view of freedom. The critics include Sartre himself, who in a 1969 interview commented on his reaction in recently rereading his remark that "whatever the circumstances, and wherever the site, a man is always free to choose to be a traitor or not . . .": "When I read this, I said to myself: it's incredible, I actually believed that!"[35]

Sartre goes on to explain his view (at the time of *L'être et le néant*) as due to the "drama of the war" and its "experience of heroism". I propose, however, that the view of *L'être et le néant* is more complex than the simplifications of a few striking passages might suggest, and that there are internal reasons for the apparent radicality of Sartre's view of freedom in this work. These reasons also suggest that *L'être et le néant* supports a more complex and nuanced view of freedom.

My point derives from methodological features of *L'être et le néant*. As we have seen, the book offers a deft and fruitful combination of conceptual dialectics (system) and concrete existential descriptions (experience). The first represents Sartre's mastery of the philosophical thinking he learned in the French university system and the second his own literary appropriation of Husserl's phenomenology. Throughout the book, Sartre develops a systematic structure in terms of his fundamental ontological categories (being-in-itself, being-for-itself, nothingness, being-for-others, etc.); this is his ontology. At the same time, he shows how concrete descriptions of existential situations (e.g., of negativities, bad faith, interpersonal relations, situated freedom) complement and deepen this structure; this is his phenomenology.[36] This is, overall, a very effective dual approach, but it involves two limitations. First, the abstract ontological categories, dialectically deployed simply in their own terms, are not always adequate to the richness of the phenomenological descriptions. This is particularly apparent in the latter part of the book, where the sharp conceptual separation of being-for-itself from being-in-itself makes it difficult to appreciate the phenomenology of situated freedom. (A similar point holds for Sartre's descriptions of the body and sexuality.) This is essentially due to the fact – of which Sartre is well aware – that his (and perhaps any) ontological

---

[35] Jean-Paul Sartre, "The Itinerary of a Thought" (interview with *New Left Review*, 1969), reprinted in Jean-Paul Sartre, *Between Existentialism and Marxism*, 33–4. The comment to which Sartre is reacting is in the preface to an early collection of his plays.

[36] As we have seen, Sartre's general ontology ultimately derives (in his introduction) from a phenomenological description, in Husserlian terms, of the cognitive relation between subject and object. But this description takes place on a level of generality that sharply separates it from *L'être et le néant*'s later existential phenomenologies of "being-in-the-world". Further, Sartre's development of his ontology is more a matter of abstract reasoning about the categories of being-in-itself and being-for-itself than of describing the nuances of our experience of them.

categories are an abstraction from the concrete situation of man-in-the-world. The proper attitude is obviously to give priority to the phenomenological descriptions and modify the apparent import of the categories accordingly.

But Sartre's treatment of freedom also needs to be put in the context of a clear pattern of development in his phenomenological examples in *L'être et le néant*. As his systematic structures develop, Sartre's experiential examples expand from the hyper-individuality projected onto his objects by the *flâneur* disinterestedly observing café life, to the commitment of a situated agent struggling with the natural and historical worlds. As a result, the early examples join the abstract ontology in supporting a radically disengaged conception of freedom that is not consistent with the later examples.

Once we discount the categorical abstractions and the distorted early examples, *L'être et le néant* provides a much more sensitive and nuanced view of freedom.[37] This is not to deny Sartre's own claims that the book was overly influenced by the extremity of the war and occupation and that he did not really appreciate the social dimension of human existence until after the war.[38] But it also supports Sartre's further contention that his existentialism is fundamentally consistent with the more adequate view of freedom developed in later works such the *Critique de la raison dialectique*.

THE CRITIQUE OF DIALECTICAL REASON

There are at least three useful ways of characterizing the overall project of Sartre's *Critique de la raison dialectique*. First, it is a reformulation of his existentialism, with a view to taking better account of the limitations of freedom and, especially, providing an account of the social dimensions of human reality. Second, it is a rethinking of Marxism (specifically, its theory of social units), designed to avoid the dead end of reductionist and positivist formulations (which Sartre associates especially with Soviet orthodoxy) by incorporating into it an existentialist view of human being-in-the-world. (Sartre thinks, moreover, that this is more in keeping

---

[37] It is also worth noting that Sartre's play, *Les mouches*, which appeared the same year as *L'être et le néant* (1943), has a similarly more developed view of freedom, implicitly distinguishing, for example, between the "light" freedom that everyone has simply by existing and the "heavy" freedom that we take on by engaged action.

[38] Jean-Paul Sartre, *Between Existentialism and Marxism*, 34.

with Marx's own views.) Third, *Critique de la raison dialectique* provides the basis for, in Sartre's words, "a structural, historical anthropology" (*Critique de la raison dialectique* [*CRD*], 9/822); that is, a theory of human society based not on the "analytical reason" of the positive sciences but on the "dialectical reason" Sartre maintains is required for the study of human reality.[39]

We have noted already in *L'être et le néant* an increasing tension between the radical freedom of consciousness that emerges in the early part of the book and the sense of limits on this freedom as the later part situates consciousness in the social and material worlds. *Critique de la raison dialectique* preserves core existentialist views about freedom and its locus in individual consciousness. But it almost entirely abandons the ontological terminology of *L'être et le néant* and develops instead a set of roughly parallel terms that place far more emphasis on the situated and communal nature of human beings. The fundamental transition is from the language of being to the language of practice. Sartre no longer speaks of "being-for-itself", with its connotations of a solitary consciousness, but of "praxis", the action of an agent (individual or group) on the world. (One connecting thread to *L'être et le néant* is Sartre's continuing use of "project" in *Critique de la raison dialectique* to express the choice implicit in any praxis.) Similarly, talk of being-in-itself is replaced by the language of the *practico-inert*, a term that emphasizes not the wholly undifferentiated givenness of the in-itself but rather the resistance to our projects of objects (from artifacts to forms of life) structured by past praxis of ourselves and others. In this regard, Sartre speaks of the "exigency" that is imposed on praxis by the "exis"[40] (inertia) of the practico-inert and that he is even willing to say provides individuals or groups with a (not inevitable) "destiny". Corresponding to the earlier work's notions of negativity and nothingness are the ideas of alterity (any relation of separation, not just the distinction of consciousness from its object) and, more specifically, transcendence (*dépassement*) in the sense of a process of going beyond a given set of material conditions while at the same time, in the manner of Hegel's dialectic, incorporating them. Finally, talk of the other (and being-for-others) is often replaced by a more

---

[39] For a very helpful discussion of Sartre's Marxism and its relation to his existentialism, see Thomas Flynn, *Sartre and Marxist Existentialism*.
[40] Properly, "hexis", but Sartre consistently ignores the Greek rough-breathing mark.

general notion of the Third (*le Tiers*) that constitutes the unity of a group by observing or controlling it.

To get an idea of Sartre's Marxist theory of social structures, we need to look at the main concepts around which he builds his account: need, scarcity, seriality, and the various forms of ensembles (Sartre's most general word for aggregates of human beings, also termed "multiplicities").

Humans *need* things such as food, clothing, housing, and sex in order to survive (that is, to live, and to live as humans). However, our world is one of *scarcity*; it does not always provide sufficient resources to fulfill all our needs (or the needs of all of us). We must struggle to survive and even face the possibility that the needs of some people will be satisfied at the expense of others. Because of scarcity in the face of our need, we live in a situation dominated by the material structures (both natural and, especially, social) that can satisfy our needs. In such a situation, Sartre says, human relations take on an inert and atomized form that he calls *seriality*. An ensemble of individuals may have a common aim (e.g., finding adequate food or giving their children a good education). But because of scarcity, the common aim separates rather than unites them. Rather than seeking food or education for "us", each individual is forced to seek what is needed for "me". Individuals thus become competitors for their shared need and come to see each other as threats.

Sartre's example is that of people waiting in a line at a bus-stop. They form a series dominated by a thing (the bus) that satisfies a need (transportation to work). Although they share this need, it separates them because of scarcity (there may not be a seat for everyone). In this simple case, the separation and isolation are strikingly expressed by the fact that individuals line up for the bus – first come, first served – each in his or her own place. They literally form a series; but even in more complex cases – say that of high school students seeking admission to elite colleges – the concept of seriality applies to their situation of atomized isolation from one another (*CRD*, 468–74/456–61).

What place is there for freedom in this stark description of the human situation? In one sense, we are still entirely free despite the scarcity and seriality imposed by the world. After all, every limitation and constraint derives ultimately from the fact that we have made certain choices; at a minimum, choices to find adequate food, earn a living, stay alive. This of course is the sort of point Sartre emphasized in *L'être et le néant*. But now Sartre makes it entirely clear that there is another basic sense in which we are not free when constrained by material scarcity: we cannot alter the situation constraining us so that it will not be an obstacle to our needs. His language here shows how far he has come from some of the formulations of *L'être et le néant*: "It would be quite wrong to interpret me as saying that man is free in all situations, as the Stoics claimed. I mean the exact opposite: all men are slaves in so far as their life unfolds in the practico-inert field and in so far as this field is always conditioned by scarcity" (*CRD*, 369/331). This does not, however, mean that the situation must be simply endured, that freedom is helpless in the face of the limits imposed by the situation. Sartre's thought is that often (and particularly in the modern world, with its immense capacities for production) scarcity is not due to a literal lack of enough goods but to imbalanced allocations of those goods. Scarcity, in such a case, is not a sheer physical necessity but the product of the social system of production and distribution.

Further, the limitations in our power to transform an unacceptable situation often apply only to the isolated, serialized individual. Alone, I cannot transform the situation; but *we* can, provided that we begin acting as a unified *group* (an ensemble in which the members have reciprocal relations) rather than a mere seriality. So the key question becomes the "revolutionary" one: How can a genuine group, with power to transform an unacceptable social world, emerge from the alienation of seriality?

According to Sartre, a group emerges first as a "group-in-fusion", as a series of individuals coming together for common action for a specific goal, as in the storming of the Bastille. Typically, this process occurs under threat of external danger. In such a situation, individuals continue to see one another as others (in the sense of *L'être et le néant*), but now as others that have the same project. As a result, individuals now act not as individuals but as what Sartre calls "singular incarnations of the common person" (where the "common person" is defined by the shared project). This sort of joint action constitutes the *group* in Sartre's technical sense.

It is, Sartre says, with the emergence of the group that freedom, apparently lost in the alienation of seriality, is recovered. A group can tear down the Bastille, whereas a series of atomized individuals cannot. So, in this account, freedom is fully realized not as private subjectivity but as an objective social structure. Nonetheless, Sartre's existentialism remains the root of his position, since the objective social structure – the group – ultimately derives entirely from the choices of individuals.

But precisely because a group is formed by individual choices, it can break up because of such choices: if enough individuals withdraw from the project, the group dissolves. There are standard techniques, apparent in the history of the French Revolution, for maintaining group stability (e.g., the Oath and the Terror, characteristic of what Sartre called a "pledged group"). But in the long run, the survival of the group will require much more structure and organization than it has "in fusion" or even as the result of promises enforced by terror. This will be especially so when (as in the case of the new revolutionary French Republic) it must survive assaults by powerful forces of entrenched reaction. In particular, the group's individuals will have to be divided into specialized roles, coordinated by a central authority.

As a result, the group becomes an *institution*, in which people identify with their specialized roles (so losing sight of the overall project) and the central authority begins monitoring and controlling individuals to see that they carry out their tasks. In this way, institutionalization reintroduces seriality and people become open to the manipulation of a sovereign. As a result, the oppression that triggered the revolutionary group action returns (the Napoleonic empire, Soviet communism). This leads Sartre to the central problem of political activity: that of forming a stable and enduring revolutionary group that avoids both the alienation and oppression of institutions and the chaos of anarchist spontaneity. This was a major goal of his political activities right after the war.

Sartre's treatment of institutions is also the locus of his reformulation of the central Marxist concepts of alienation and class. Moreover, institutions are characterized by what Sartre calls *structures* (not present in the group-in-fusion). These are socially created systems of inertia that constrain and limit the freedom of our praxis. They are also proper objects of the "analytical reason" of positivist social science.

This last point leads to our third way of characterizing the *Critique de la raison dialectique*, as a "structural historical anthropology".[41]

---

[41] Sartre uses *structurelle*, not the more common *structurale*, perhaps evoking Heidegger's distinction of *existenzial* and *existenziell*, with an emphasis on process rather than on system. See Peter Caws, *Sartre*, 143.

While Sartre, as we have just seen, fully recognizes a domain for the empirical techniques of mainstream social science in the study of human beings, he insists that such techniques cannot give a concrete and comprehensive account of human reality. This is because praxis, the root of the distinctively human, can be understood only in terms of the "progressive-regressive method" of "dialectical reason". This terminology emerges from Sartre's extensive methodological reflections, particularly in "Question de méthode", the long essay included at the beginning of the French edition of *Critique de la raison dialectique* (but published separately in English). The core of Sartre's methodology is based on the view famously formulated by Engels (but equivalent to the description of situated freedom in *L'être et le néant*) that Sartre paraphrases as follows: "men make their history on the basis of real, prior conditions (among which we would include acquired characteristics, distortions imposed by the mode of work and of life, alienation, etc.), but it is *the men* who make it and not the prior conditions" ("Question de méthode" [*QM*], 61/87). (Sartre in fact regards the main body of the *Critique de la raison dialectique* as essentially a thorough explication and justification of this claim – which is why he said that, logically, the "Question de méthode" could have properly concluded the work.)

Sartre's fundamental point is that an account of praxis (human action) solely in terms of its prior conditions (an instrumental account in terms of external causes or even in terms of the reasons and motives of *L'être et le néant*) is possible only if we first have an understanding of the praxis in terms of its overall purpose or meaning. Suppose, for example (*QM*, 96–100/152–9), a friend and I are seated in a room, reading. My friend suddenly gets up, goes to the window, and opens it. I instantly understand this action as an effort to cool off an overheated room.

This understanding is "progressive" (forward looking) in the sense of grasping the future goal that makes my friend's action intelligible. In its wake, I am then able to construct a "regressive" analysis of the action. I can, for example, note that the room was, in fact, quite hot, that my friend was doubtless made uncomfortable by the heat, indeed so much so that she was willing to interrupt her study to alleviate the situation. But, Sartre emphasizes, I construct this "analytic" explanation (or "intellection", in his terminology) only *given* my progressive understanding. Before my friend's action I may have been aware of the heat only as a "confused, unnamed discomfort" (QM, 96/153), not as a specific causal factor able to provoke action, and I certainly had no awareness of any internal effects of the heat on my friend's dispositions. The room, the window, etc. were present as possibly related to an action, but it was the action itself that revealed them as actually operative in this particular case. The heat, for example, was overbearing precisely because my friend acted to alleviate it.

Sartre takes this simple example as a model of anthropological knowledge. There is room for causal or structural analyses of human action from a strictly external viewpoint. But such analyses must themselves be based on a richer internal understanding (in the sense of *Verstehen*) of the action as an intentional, goal-directed whole. This fundamental understanding lies in the domain of what Sartre calls "dialectical reason". As in Hegel and Marx, this notion embraces not only the process whereby we understand reality but also the intelligibility of the object understood. With regard to both poles, "dialectic" refers to a process of *totalization* whereby the elements of reality and of our knowledge of it are unified in a dynamic whole. The heart of Sartre's criticism of reductionist Marxists such as Lukács is that they replace the always unfinished dialectical *process of totalization* with fixed *totalities* that can be grasped through analytic reason.

Just as *L'être et le néant* ended with a promise of an ethics that would complement its phenomenological ontology, so *Critique de la raison dialectique* promised a second volume that would apply its "social ontology" to the course of actual history. Sartre himself never published or even finished this volume; he said he simply did not know enough history to complete it.[42]

---

[42] The substantial fragment that he did complete was published posthumously as volume II of *Critique de la raison dialectique*.

CHAPTER 6

Beauvoir

O mighty attitudes of Man and Woman, in which there seek to be united . . . what the Creation made separate.
(Marcel Proust, *In Search of Lost Time*, v, 97)

BEAUVOIR AND THE ORIGINS OF EXISTENTIALISM

Simone de Beauvoir (1908–86) was born in Paris, where she was raised and spent most of her life. Her mother was a devout Catholic, whereas her father, who embraced the Third Republic's secularism, thought religion appropriate only for women and children. Beauvoir says it was this clash in fundamental parental values that made her an intellectual, concerned with the critical assessment of ideas. Since mothers had control over the earlier education of their children, Beauvoir's pre-university education was at convent schools, where she was a brilliant student but came to resist the intellectual and the moral narrowness of a Catholic education. The family's financial situation (middle-class but financially strained) made a teaching career a natural choice for the bright elder daughter. Moreover, Beauvoir's father's secularism, along with her own desire to escape from religious education, led her to enroll as an undergraduate at the Sorbonne, a state institution (although much of her work was initially done at institutes within the Sorbonne designed for Catholic students).

Although a university education was at this time no longer unusual for a woman, Beauvoir was intent on a specialization in the almost entirely masculine domain of philosophy. She achieved this goal, despite parental opposition, and became only the ninth woman in France to receive the *agrégation* in philosophy. Beauvoir did exceptionally well in her examinations, finishing second only to Sartre, who was three years older than she and re-taking the exam after his failure the previous year. (Beauvoir was also the youngest person to date to pass the exam.) The examiners had a long debate over which of the two should receive first place: "If Sartre showed great intelligence and a solid, if at times inexact, culture, everybody agreed that, of the two, she was the real philosopher."[1]

Despite her obvious ability and the close run with Sartre, Beauvoir concluded that she did not have a philosophical mind on a par with his and decided to pursue literature instead. In this regard, much has been made of an apparently decisive discussion she had with Sartre during their preparation for the *agrégation* exam, a discussion in which she felt he "took apart" her ideas.[2] The experience was not an isolated one: "Day after day, and all day long I set myself up against Sartre, and in our discussions I was simply not in his class."[3]

We need, however, to remember that the "class" Beauvoir had in mind was that of the highest level of creative philosopher. She had, she acknowledged, a remarkable ability to understand philosophical ideas and "penetrated to the heart of a text" more readily than Sartre. But this very facility, she said, was due to her "lack of originality", which made her better able to assimilate others' ideas. As a philosopher, she thought she could have been an excellent expositor and critic but not "a genuinely creative talent".[4] What she means is clear from her response in an interview with Margaret Simons, who expresses doubts about Beauvoir's claim that "she is not a philosopher": "For me, a philosopher is someone like Spinoza, Hegel, etc., or like Sartre: someone who builds a great system, and not someone who loves philosophy, who can teach it, who can understand it, and who can use it in essays, etc., but is someone who *truly* constructs a philosophy. And that, I did not do." She adds that there are, in her sense, perhaps only two philosophers in a century and says that "Sartre, in my opinion, will be one of them".[5] Given this, her turn away from philosophy was a sign less of self-deprecation than of high ambition: "I possessed far too much intellectual ambition to let this satisfy me." She wanted to "communicate the element of originality" in her own experience and "in order to do

---

[1] Annie Cohen-Solal, *Sartre: A Life*, 74.
[2] Simone de Beauvoir, *Memoirs of a Dutiful Daughter*, 364.
[3] Ibid.
[4] Simone de Beauvoir, *The Prime of Life*, 178.
[5] "Beauvoir Interview (1979)", in Margaret Simons, *Beauvoir and the Second Sex: Feminism, Race, and the Origins of Existentialism*, 11.

this successfully knew it was literature towards which I must orientate myself".[6]

Beauvoir did produce one book in the standard philosophical mode, *Pour une morale de l'ambiguïté* (1947), an essay that tries to develop an ethics on the basis of Sartre's existentialism. The book goes much further than Sartre's published works in trying to derive a morality from freedom as the fundamental value. But Beauvoir herself eventually rejected the book's project on the grounds that it tried to "define a morality independent of a social context",[7] and it cannot be regarded as a major achievement. On the other hand, there is a broader sense in which Beauvoir is an important contributor to the philosophy of existence in her novels, her memoirs, and her treatises on social issues. Although basically working out of Sartre's existentialist framework, she offers distinctive views of freedom and interpersonal relations; and, most importantly, in *Le deuxième sexe* she brilliantly deploys and adapts existentialist categories in a very powerful and original expression of feminism.[8]

True to her literary resolve, Beauvoir published three novels during the 1940s: *L'invitée* (1943), *Le sang des autres* (1945), and *Tous les*

---

[6] *The Prime of Life*, 178. Beauvoir adds that the highest levels of philosophical creativity require a "stubbornness" of which "the female condition does not facilitate the development".

[7] *Force of Circumstance*, 67. See above, chapter 5, on Sartre's parallel effort in the 1950s to develop an existentialist ethics in his *Cahiers pour une morale*.

[8] Some scholars have argued that Beauvoir is a major source of the basic ideas of existentialism, in particular, those of *L'être et le néant*. Beauvoir herself was adamant that she had no such role: "On the philosophical plane, I was influenced by Sartre. Obviously, I was not able to influence him, since I did not do philosophy. I criticized him, I discussed many of his ideas with him, but I did not have any philosophical influence on Sartre, whereas he had such an influence on me, that is certain" (Simons, "Beauvoir Interview (1979)", 9). Those who think we should discount such statements point to evidence that Beauvoir had been thinking about such existentialist themes as freedom, bad faith, and, especially, the other before Sartre began writing *L'être et le néant* and even before the two knew one another. Margaret Simons, in particular, has recently cited Beauvoir's diary entries from 1927 to support a "key discovery . . . : Beauvoir's statement of her interest in the philosophical theme, 'the opposition of self and other'" (Margaret Simons, *Beauvoir and the Second Sex*, 186). However, the passages Simons cites are all expressions of fairly ordinary experiences that would find parallels in a great many diaries and novels. They evoke Sartre's account of interpersonal relations simply because they refer to the everyday phenomena his account wants to elucidate. But they do not provide any substantial phenomenological (or otherwise philosophical) analysis of these phenomena. This, of course, is hardly surprising, since Beauvoir, who had just begun her serious study of philosophy during the last year, has nothing corresponding to the rich methodological and ontological apparatus that Sartre brings to his discussion. Moreover, even if, like Simons, we extract an implicit "philosophy of the Other" from Beauvoir's remarks, it bears little resemblance to Sartre's, since, as Simons emphasizes, it eliminates his striking emphasis on the essential conflict between rival consciousnesses.

hommes sont mortels (1946). These are all distinctively philosophical novels, and they raise the question of just what sort of philosophical role a novel might play. In an essay from the same period, "Literature and Metaphysics" (first published in 1946), Beauvoir outlines a literary method of developing and even in a sense testing philosophical theses. "A good novel", she says, "can stimulate imaginary experiences that are as complete and as disturbing as lived experiences".[9] Often, of course, novelists create such experiences merely to support pre-established theses. But novels can also present characters and situations that are independent of conclusions we already hold and that function as independent sources of experiential truth. So, for example, in *L'invitée*, Beauvoir imagines a complex love triangle (based, however, on her experience with Sartre and Olga Kosakievicz) through which she probes the nature of interpersonal relations.[10] And in *Tous les hommes sont mortels*, in order to understand the significance of death and human finitude, she creates a character who has eternal life. In this way, Beauvoir's novels are a continuation of philosophy by other means.

We may ask how what is, after all, simply fiction could have any relevance for philosophical truth. But by the same token, we might wonder what advantage true stories could have, since their truth can easily represent merely contingent features of human existence, with no relevance for its central or fundamental truths. This is the reason traditional philosophy refuses to base its claims on any particular examples, whether real or fictional, and contents itself with the analysis of general concepts. Thinking along these lines, we might conclude that existentialism, which denies that the truth of human existence can be expressed in conceptual abstractions, finds itself in a double methodological bind. In seeking a truth that is both concrete and fundamental it would seem to be after an impossible

---

[9] Simone de Beauvoir, "Littérature et métaphysique", 107.
[10] Edward and Kate Fullbrook, in *Simone de Beauvoir and Jean-Paul Sartre*, make much of the fact that Sartre (and Merleau-Ponty) read an early draft of Beauvoir's *L'invitée* in 1940. But, apart from the fact that we do not have this draft and have no way of knowing how much influence Sartre might have had on its philosophical content, there is the enormous gap, even for an existentialist, between a literary expression of an idea and the detailed analysis and argumentation required for a philosophical development of an idea. Sartre's originality and greatness as a philosopher depend on the way he carried out this development, something that, as Beauvoir repeatedly emphasizes, she did not even try to do. Moreover, if we are looking for novelistic influences on Sartre's thoughts, Proust, in whom he was steeped when attending the École Normale, is probably a much richer source than Beauvoir.

combination of the specificity of actual existence and the generality of abstractions. Beauvoir's suggestion, however, is that the medium of literature provides a resolution of the existentialist's dilemma. Fictional characters and events are the sort of synthesis of concreteness and generality that we need to see beyond the triviality of mere facts without becoming lost in the abstractions of mere concepts. To use Hegel's expression, the creations of fiction are "concrete universals": individual characters and events that embody fundamental truths about our existence. In these terms, Beauvoir's novels are a distinctly original philosophical achievement, although an achievement of quite a different kind from Sartre's in *L'être et le néant*, where phenomenological description rather than novelistic narration supplies the "concrete universal".

Most of Beauvoir's later work was neither narrowly philosophical nor strictly literary. But it can still be read as a response to the existentialist problem of combining concreteness with generality. These writings (from 1949 on) take two main forms: autobiography and treatises on social issues. Her autobiographical project began with three large volumes, published between 1958 and 1963, in which she gives an account of her life from the beginning almost up to the present. The first volume, *Mémoires d'une jeune fille rangée*, traces her development from a little girl devoted to pleasing her parents to an independent woman with a sophisticated philosophical education, fierce literary ambitions and political commitments, and Jean-Paul Sartre as a life-long companion. The following two volumes (*La force de l'âge* and *La force des choses*) recount how she and Sartre survive the war, become prominent cultural personalities, and lead lives in which they maintain their special personal relationship through numerous love affairs, intense political involvements, and constant writing. Nine years later, Beauvoir published a final volume (*Tout compte fait*), which continued the story up to 1972. After Sartre died in 1980 she published, as a coda to the autobiography, a controversial and moving account of his last days (*La cérémonie des adieux*). Here we should also mention the memoir of her mother's last days, *Une mort très douce* (1964), a book that manages to unite clinical realism and existentialist reflection with the sheer emotional power of a child's grief for the loss of a parent.

Beauvoir's autobiographies meet the existentialist demand for a concrete universal in two respects. On one level, they operate in the same way as novels, with characters and events that are specific but at the same time constructed to express the human condition in general. There is, no doubt, more emphasis in an autobiography on keeping to the literal facts, but, apart from our curiosity about the author, there may be little to distinguish a good autobiography from a good autobiographical novel. But there is another level on which Beauvoir's autobiographies have a distinctive value. She and Sartre tried to live their lives on the basis of an existentialist conception of human reality. Beauvoir's narratives have the particular advantage of showing the strengths and weaknesses of this conception in their lives. There is particular focus on their ideal of an intense and permanent personal commitment that, at the same time, recognizes the right of each partner to less central liaisons with others. As Sartre put it to Beauvoir: "What *we* have is an *essential* love; but it is a good idea for us also to experience *contingent* love affairs."[11] The autobiographies provide close scrutiny of the viability of this ideal and raise extremely interesting questions about Beauvoir's own ultimate attitude toward this version of existentialist commitment, especially through the narrative of her love affair with the American novelist, Nelson Algren, and her reactions to Sartre's affairs with a variety of women. More generally, it may be argued that Beauvoir's autobiographies, even more than her own and Sartre's novels and plays, carry out the existentialist project of, in Toril Moi's words, "break[ing] down the distinction between philosophy and life so as to endow life with the truth and necessity of philosophy and philosophy with the excitement and passion of life".[12]

But Beauvoir also carried out the existentialist project in her treatises on social issues. By far the most important of these was her book on women, *Le deuxième sexe*, published in 1949. (There is also a major study of old age, *La vieillesse*, published in 1970.) As we shall see, *Le deuxième sexe* is an encyclopedic survey of every aspect of thought about and treatment of women. The topic is covered in terms of biology, myth, literature, history, politics, and philosophy. How, we may well wonder, can such a project fit into the existentialist demand for individuality and concreteness? The answer is that behind all the abstractions and objectivities of the treatise lies Beauvoir's own developing awareness of the effect her sex had on her life.

[11] *The Prime of Life*, 24.
[12] Toril Moi, *Simone de Beauvoir*, 147.

For a long time, she tells us, she had not regarded it as of any significance. In 1946, when she first began thinking of writing her autobiography, she posed the question of what it had meant for her to be a woman. "At first thought", she says, "I thought I could dispose of that pretty quickly. I had never had any feeling of inferiority, no one had ever said to me: 'You think that way because you're a woman'; my femaleness had never been irksome to me in any way. 'For me', I said to Sartre, 'you might almost say it just hasn't counted'."[13] This indifference to her sex is understandable, given the fact that, by the time Beauvoir went to college, the French educational system had (just) become more or less equally open to women and men and that she had enjoyed immediate acceptance by Sartre and other male members of the young Parisian intellectual elite.[14] Certainly, we can understand how, when she compared herself to most other women, past and present, Beauvoir could think that she existed more or less outside the domain of sexist oppression.

But when Beauvoir thought further about the question (she says it was at Sartre's suggestion), her view changed radically:

> I looked, and it was a revelation: this world was a masculine world, my childhood had been nourished by myths forged by men, and I hadn't reacted to them at all in the same way I should have done if I had been a boy. I was so interested in this discovery that I abandoned my project for a personal confession in order to give all my attention to finding out about the condition of woman in its broadest terms.[15]

It is, then, clear that Beauvoir's general and objective study of women's condition derived from her realization of the significance of this condition for her. Moreover, this realization does not function merely as an external occasion for the writing of *Le deuxième sexe*. Much of the brilliance of the work derives from Beauvoir's ability to infuse her factual and objective study with her consciousness of herself as a woman. The result is a remarkable synthesis – precisely along the lines required by existentialism – of the general and the personal. Finding new and more effective ways of achieving this synthesis is Beauvoir's primary contribution to existentialist thought.

---

[13] *Force of Circumstance*, 94.
[14] At the time Beauvoir began her university education, women were still technically excluded from the École Normale, and Beauvoir did not even try to gain entry. But exceptions to the formal rule were possible, as Simone Weil's admission to the École Normale during this same period shows.
[15] *Force of Circumstance*, 94–5.

Indeed, at present, *Le deuxième sexe* is by far the single most influential work by an existentialist.

THE SECOND SEX

What, Beauvoir asks, does it mean to be a woman? There are two standard answers. Essentialists say that there is a female nature (the "eternal feminine"), while anti-essentialists (nominalists) say that there is no such thing, that women are just human beings, as men are, their "femininity" merely an accidental characteristic no different from having red hair or being over six feet tall. We will not be surprised that Beauvoir rejects the essentialist view, which contradicts the fundamental existentialist claim that existence precedes essence, that the free choices of our consciousness determine what we are. In this sense, her famous formula, "One is not born, but rather becomes, a woman" (*Le deuxième sexe* [*DS*], II: 13/267) is, for her, a philosophical platitude. But Beauvoir also rejects the anti-essentialist view. Being a woman is, at least in our world, not a casual fact, irrelevant to a person's core identity – any more than is being Jewish or black or old. Nor is being a woman simply a matter of one's own choice: precisely how you are a woman may be up to you, but the fact that you are a woman and that this fact makes a great deal of difference is imposed on you by your situation.

Here it is clear that Beauvoir has moved beyond the simplistic existentialist view of freedom that is at least often suggested by *L'être et le néant*. On that view, being a woman could limit my freedom only to the extent that I chose it to be a limitation. Beauvoir, however, recognizes that some features of my situation may well be obstacles to my freedom no matter how I choose. It does not follow that such a feature must always be an obstacle: we can imagine a situation in which being a woman is of no more significance than having blue eyes. But the fact is that in the current historical situation, being a woman does restrict your freedom, no matter how you choose to live your life. This is a significant revision of the naïve existentialist conception of freedom (and, as we have seen, a revision Sartre himself later develops in *Critique de la raison dialectique*).

Beauvoir's understanding of the constraints under which women exist is built around another existentialist category: that of "the Other". The freedom of women is limited (i.e., women are oppressed) because, historically, they have come to be defined as the other of men.

The root of Beauvoir's line of thought here is Sartre's notion of being-for-others. Not only does consciousness exist "for-itself"; it also exists for other consciousnesses that are aware of it as an object. We have seen how Sartre derives from his phenomenology of the other the idea that each consciousness experiences a conflict between itself and any other consciousness, as each struggles to control the other's freedom. Beauvoir starts with this idea but significantly transforms it. First, she moves the notion of the other from the individual to society, speaking of the shared consciousness that one group has of another. Further, whereas Sartre focuses on the way that the other poses a challenge to identity, Beauvoir emphasizes how consciousness uses its view of the other to construct its own identity. It is not just that the other's awareness of us constitutes a challenge to our self-understanding. In addition, our awareness of the other is part of how we understand ourselves. "Thus it is", Beauvoir says, "that no group ever sets itself up as the One without at once setting up the Other over against itself" (*DS*, 1: 16/xxiii). Accordingly, "the category of the *Other* is as primordial as consciousness itself" (*DS*, 1: 16/xxii).

Beauvoir's basic idea, then, is that women exist as an other for men: part of what it means to be a man is not to be a woman. This alone, however, does not explain the distinctive oppression women find in their situation. After all, as she notes, every group is an other for some other groups. The mere fact that, say, a group of people live on the same block leads them to define themselves in opposition to the "others" who live on other blocks. This alone does not result in oppression or restriction of the other's freedom. But the reason it does not is that, in typical cases, the opposition of consciousnesses is entirely reciprocal or symmetrical. If Americans traveling in France see the French as alien others, the French visiting the US see Americans in a parallel way. The problem for women is that, whereas they exist as the other for men, men are not in the same way the other for women. Women are defined in relation to men, but not vice versa. Rather, the male is regarded as the norm of humanity (which is why the masculine pronouns can refer to anyone at all), whereas the female is, as Aristotle and Aquinas maintained, a defective or incomplete male. Beauvoir sees her point as proved simply by the fact that it makes perfect sense to write a book such as hers about "the peculiar situation" of women, whereas there would be no point at all to a parallel book about men. "Thus humanity is male and man defines woman not in herself but as relative to him; she is not regarded as an autonomous being" (*DS*, 1: 15/xxii).

The question, of course, is why this is so. "Why is it that women do not dispute male sovereignty?" (*DS*, 1: 17/xxiv). According to Beauvoir, the reason is that women do not form a coherent community: "women lack concrete means for organizing themselves into a unit which can stand face to face with" the community of men. This in turn is because women "have no past, no history, no religion of their own" (*DS*, 1: 19/xxv). There are always men – fathers, husbands, sons – to whom they are more strongly attached than to other women. Upper-class white women identify more with similar men than they do with black or poor women. The male–female couple "is a fundamental unity", in which the female is always at least implicitly subordinated to the male and separated from unity with other women. It is, of course, true that there are ways in which men need women (as companions, as sexual partners) just as much as women need men. But this is so only in the sense that, as Hegel showed, masters need slaves. The master needs the slave perhaps even more than the slave needs the master. But the master "has in his grasp the power of satisfying this need through his own action", whereas the slave's needs are met only to the extent that this facilitates the master's satisfaction (*DS*, 1: 20/xxvi). The same is true of women in relation to men.

Beauvoir also points out that women themselves often come not only to accept but even to endorse their subordinate position. This is because "to decline to be the Other, to refuse to be a party to the deal . . . would be for women to renounce all the advantages conferred upon them by their alliance with the superior caste". Here, of course, Beauvoir is describing a classic case of Sartrean bad faith: "along with the ethical urge of each individual to affirm his subjective existence, there is also the temptation to forgo liberty and become a thing". This is a road many women take because it is an easy one: "on it one avoids the strain involved in undertaking an authentic existence". Accordingly, "When man makes of woman the *Other*, he may, then, expect her to manifest deep-seated tendencies to complicity" (*DS*, 1: 21/xxvii).

So, on a first level, the answer to the question of why women are a subordinated other, is this: men form a unified group that takes women as an other, while women are not able to reciprocate and even often come to have a bad-faith contentment with their situation. But the deeper question remains of why women have been unable to form a community of their own, why their connection to men dominates their lives in way that men's connection to women does not dominate theirs. Here, of course, the traditional answer is that women are intrinsically inferior to men.

This claim has been defended in various ways, as, for example, the will and design of God (who seems to have made Eve for the sake of Adam) or as the direct consequence of biological and psychological science (which are said to show women to be physically weaker, less intelligent, more emotional, etc.). In modern times, the rhetoric of democracy has led many men to agree that, as an abstract, general proposition, women are their equals (so that now, even more than when Beauvoir wrote, there are laws proclaiming equality of the sexes). But in fact there are countless practices and modes of thought that maintain the subordinate position of women: "It is, in point of fact, a difficult matter for a man to realize the extreme importance of social discriminations which seem outwardly insignificant but which produce in women moral and intellectual effects so profound that they seem to spring from her original nature" (*DS*, 1: 28/xxxii). As a result, even many apparently "enlightened" men still think that women as a group are different from men in ways that prevent them, with only a small number of exceptions, from reaching the highest levels of human achievement. In a similar way, men who are very strong on the principle of women's equality will often in practice regard themselves as the natural superiors of the particular women they deal with on a daily basis. In these ways, the traditional idea of intrinsic inferiority remains much stronger than we might at first think.

But is the prejudice against women mere prejudice? Does sheer biology not justify the subordination of women? There is, perhaps, no biological necessity that even advanced mammalian species reproduce sexually; "the division of a species into male and female individuals is simply an irreducible fact of observation" (*DS*, 1: 38/6). Nor is it even true that humans would be essentially different without sexual reproduction (as we would be if, for example, we did not have bodies or were not subject to death): "a mind without a body and an immortal body are strictly inconceivable, whereas we can imagine a parthenogenetic or hermaphrodite society" (*DS*, 1:

40/7). But even though sexuality is not strictly essential to humanity, it does not follow that it is not of central significance, given the way we have in fact developed. Sexual "differentiation is characteristic of [human] existents to such an extent that it belongs in any realistic definition of existence" (*DS*, I: 40/7).

Given this central, if not strictly essential, role of sexuality, it might seem that the biology of sex supports the inferiority of women. Certainly, their role in reproduction subordinates women to the species as a whole in a very striking way. As Beauvoir puts it:

Woman is of all mammalian females at once the one who is most profoundly alienated (her individuality the prey of outside forces), and the one who most violently resists this alienation; in no other is enslavement of the organism to reproduction more imperious or more unwillingly accepted. Crises of puberty and the menopause, monthly "curse", long and difficult pregnancy, painful and sometimes dangerous childbirth, illnesses, unexpected symptoms and complications – these are characteristic of the human female. (*DS*, I: 69/32)[16]

The human male, by contrast, "seems infinitely favored: his sexual life is not in opposition to his existence as a person, and biologically it runs an even course, without crises and generally without mishap" (*DS*, I:69/32).

Even apart from their role in reproduction, biology has clearly made women weaker than men: "she has less muscular strength, fewer red blood corpuscles, less lung capacity; she runs more slowly, can lift less heavy weights, can compete with man in hardly any sport; she cannot stand up to him in a fight". In sum, woman's "grasp on the world is thus more restricted; she has less firmness and less steadiness available for projects that in general she is less capable of carrying out. In other words, her individual life is less rich than man's" (*DS*, I: 73/34).

Should we conclude, then, that biology explains and justifies the subordination of women to men? No, says Beauvoir: "Certainly, these facts cannot be denied – but in themselves they have no significance" (*DS*, I: 73/34). Here Beauvoir invokes the core of her existentialist view of human existence. A mere fact has no meaning apart from that given it by consciousness. In this sense, "biology becomes an abstract science . . . once we adapt the human perspective" (*DS*, I: 73/34). Women's weakness and subordination to the

---

[16] See also Beauvoir's disconcerting portrait of pregnancy, *DS*, II: 307–8/495–6.

species have significance only in the context defined by the purposes, means, and laws that we establish. If, for example, physical mastery of nature were not a paramount human goal and violence were excluded as a source of social power, then the weakness of women would be of no significance. Similarly, "the bondage of women to the species" would be much less if society required fewer births and insisted on more care and privileges for pregnant women (*DS*, 1: 73–4/34–5). (We could, perhaps, even imagine a situation in which childbearing was regarded as a holy function, requiring the reverence and subservience of men to women.) As Beauvoir says, "the bearing of maternity upon the individual life . . . is not definitely prescribed in woman – society alone is the arbiter" (*DS*, 1: 73/35).

None of this means that we can ignore the truths of biology: "The enslavement of the female to the species and the limitations of her various powers are extremely important facts; the body of woman is one of the essential elements in her situation in the world." But biology alone tells us nothing final about the human possibilities of women. These depend on the meaning we confer on the biological facts. Accordingly, "biology is not enough" to tell us "why woman is the *Other*". Beauvoir makes the same sort of case for psychological (e.g., Freudian) and economic (e.g., Marxist) explanations. It is not the facts but the meanings we give them that are decisive. Therefore, we must "find out what humanity has made of the human female" by turning to the history, the myths, and the social practices that have constituted woman's existence (*DS*, 1: 76/37).

Beauvoir thinks the answer is apparent from humankind's earliest history, once this is understood via the categories of existential philosophy (*DS*, 1: 107/61). First, given that "conflict is the fundamental meaning of relations to the Other", it is not at all surprising that men have tried to dominate women. But why have they succeeded? According to Beauvoir, the key is in her existential categories of transcendence and immanence, categories inspired by but by no means simply taken over from Sartre. Whereas Sartre thinks of transcendence primarily in ontological terms, as the for-itself's existence outside of itself (its "not being what it is and being what it is not"), for Beauvoir it is a central ethical category. She first introduces it after laying down the basic moral and political premise of her book: "we hold that the only public good is that which assures the private good of the citizens; we shall pass judgment on institutions according to their effectiveness in giving concrete opportunities to individuals" (*DS*, 1: 30/xxxiv). But, she insists, we must not understand "private good" in terms of happiness but in terms of freedom. The "women of the harem" may be happier than women who have the right to vote and work outside the home, but the latter are better off ethically because of their greater freedom. Freedom, moreover, must be understood in terms of transcendence: "Every subject plays his part as such specifically through exploits or projects that serve as a mode of transcendence; he achieves liberty only through a continual reaching out toward other liberties. There is no justification for present existence other than its expansion into an indefinitely open future" (*DS*, 1: 31/xxxiv–v).

Transcendence, then, understood as "a continual reaching out toward" further freedom is the supreme value of human existence. Correspondingly, the supreme evil is immanence, the loss of freedom, through a relapse of consciousness into being-in-itself:

Every time transcendence falls back into immanence, stagnation, there is a degradation of existence into the "en-soi" – the brutish life of subjection to given conditions – and of liberty into constraint and contingence. This downfall represents a moral fault if the subject consents to it; if it is inflicted upon him, it spells frustration and oppression. In both cases it is absolute evil. (*DS*, 1: 31/xxxv)

Men have subordinated women by confining them to the sphere of immanence, reserving the sphere of transcendence for themselves. This subordination was made easier, though not inevitable, by women's biological role. Beauvoir's thought here is based on a tension between the biological need to preserve a species by "repeating the same Life in more individuals" and the transcendence that "creates values that deprive pure repetition of all value". Because "woman is [biologically] basically an existent who gives Life", men have been able to restrict her to the repetitive, immanent function of simply preserving the species while man "remodels the face of the earth, he creates new instruments, he invents, he shapes the future" (*DS*, 1: 112/64). From the earliest nomadic days of the race, man "furnished support of the group, not ... by a simple vital process, through biological behavior, but by means of acts that transcended his animal nature" (*DS*, 1: 110/63). The "bondage of reproduction" worked against women's joining in these transcendent acts.

By taking for themselves the morally positive, active role of transcendence and restricting women to the morally negative, passive role of immanence, men have been able to force women into the role of an inferior other and to prevent them from responding with a reciprocal categorization of men. Of course, there have been numerous changes in the status of women throughout history, and it is undeniable that, overall, their situation is now far superior to what it has often been in the past. But, Beauvoir maintains, improvements for women have typically been due to the initiatives of men more than women. "The whole of feminine history has been man-made" (*DS*, 1: 216/128). A particularly striking case is provided by societies, such as early agricultural communities, where the female, precisely because of her association with the fertility so important to those who till the soil, has been elevated to divinity. This priority of the feminine has led to speculation that early agricultural societies were matriarchies, ruled by women and by feminine values. But Beauvoir argues that this is a deep misunderstanding. First, even as a goddess, woman is still an other. It is always "*beyond* the human realm that her power was affirmed, and she was therefore outside of that realm". Within the human realm, men remain in charge: "Society has always been male, political power has always been in the hands of men" (*DS*, 1: 120/70). Moreover, "the prestige she enjoys in men's eyes is bestowed by them; they kneel before the Other, they worship the Goddess Mother. But however puissant she may thus appear, it is only through the conceptions of the male mind that she is apprehended as such" (*DS*, 1: 122–3/73).

To see that ultimate power was in male hands, we need only note that, once the technological advances of the bronze age made men less dependent on and fearful of the Nature women symbolized, the goddesses were dethroned in favor of Zeus and Yahweh and society became explicitly patriarchal. The rest of history tells the same kind of story. Christianity, for example, involves a high religious status for women through the cult of the Virgin but also the Pauline subordination of wives to husbands, and in any case Christianity is created and ruled by men. Even in our more enlightened age, "it has been the technological evolution accomplished by men that has emancipated the women of today", and "it was a transformation in masculine ethics that brought about a reduction in family size through birth control and partially freed woman from bondage to maternity" (*DS*, 1: 217/129). Similarly, we might plausibly argue that the most recent women's liberation movement, beginning in the 1960s, was itself largely due to the economic need to have women working outside the home.

Beauvoir further supports her claim about the historical dominance of men by reflecting on the relatively few cases in which women have come to prominence. There have, for example, been the great female rulers, such as Elizabeth I and Catherine the Great. But, she maintains, their achievements were possible because they were "exalted by the power of social institutions above all sexual differentiations" (*DS*, 1: 219/130) and these social institutions (absolute monarchies) were devised by and for men. Similarly, women saints such as Catherine of Siena and Teresa of Avila have attained the highest religious status, but only within the context of a Church defined as an institution by patriarchal values.

Most other women who have become famous historically have been "notable less for the importance of their acts than for the singularity of their fates". They lead lives that are interesting and even admirable but achieve little of enduring historical significance; "they are exemplary figures rather than historical agents". The life of Joan of Arc makes a good and uplifting story, but the lives of Richelieu, Danton, and Lenin transformed the world. The basic problem, Beauvoir says, is that "in order to change the face of the world, it is first necessary to be anchored in it; but the women who are firmly rooted in society are those who are in subjection to it" (*DS*, 1: 220/131). Those women who somehow evade the general subjection are "strange monsters" (*DS*, 1: 220/132), who exist at the margins of society and can have no profound effect on it.

What about the domain of culture, where women have been more successful than in science, war, or government? Women have played a special role here, but much more as subjects, inspirations, patrons, and connoisseurs than as producers. "Because of woman's marginal position in the world, men will turn to her when they strive through culture to go beyond the boundaries of their universe" (*DS*, 1: 221/132). Women have been particularly successful as writers, but even here, Beauvoir notes, "the individual contributions have in general been of less value" than those of men (*DS*, 1: 221/132). One is not born but becomes a genius, "and the feminine situation has up to the present rendered this becoming practically impossible" (*DS*, 1: 222/133).

In sum, then, women exist as the other of men because men have exploited women's biologically central role in reproduction to define them in terms of an immanence that preserves the species rather than the transcendence that takes it beyond itself and so constitutes its values.

The last part of Book 1 of *Le deuxième sexe* shows how a variety of male myths about women provide the context and justification for their definition as other. Among these, one of the most important is the myth of woman as a "mystery". This myth is perhaps the most forthright assertion that woman is other – something so alien to men that they cannot even understand it. Beyond this, the myth of mystery has a number of extremely convenient consequences. It legitimates the application to women of incompatible myths. The pure virgin and the lewd temptress, the inspiring muse and the nagging wife, the soothing comforter and the vengeful bitch – all express aspects of a femininity that can never be fully understood. Further, portraying women as essentially mysterious relieves men of the obligation of even trying to understand them and therefore of treating them in a just and consistent way. Finally, acknowledging them as a mystery can be read as an elevation to an idealized height that compensates for and covers over mundane ill-treatment.

More generally, myths allow men to ignore the actual facts about women. If a woman does not conform to a relevant myth, then she can be dismissed as "not really a woman". "The contrary facts of experience are impotent against the myth" (*DS*, 1: 383/253). In this way, women can always be treated as instances of an ideal type, never as individuals in their own right. It accordingly becomes almost impossible to convince men that there is something wrong with their portrayal of women as the other.

As an existentialist, Beauvoir does not endorse the Freudian view that anatomy (or biology) is destiny for women. Nothing human is simply the product of the external determinations of destiny. Women have been relegated to the status of other as the result of a free project of men and of their own failure to effectively oppose this project. But there is no denying that Beauvoir gives something like destiny a strong role in her account. Men's project and women's failure were both facilitated by the tendency of women's lives to be swallowed up in the reproduction of the species. The question remaining is how it might be possible to oppose this male project and allow women "to be recognized as existents by the same right as men and not to subordinate [their] existence to life, the human being to animality" (*DS*, 1: 113/65).

Although *Le deuxième sexe* never uses the term, its formulation and discussion of this question have made it a classic of *feminist* writing. It will, therefore, be useful to situate Beauvoir's question and her response to it in the context of recent debates over feminism.

It is overwhelmingly obvious that, over the centuries, women have often been treated very harshly and unfairly. Even societies espousing liberal ideals have frequently insisted that women with certain talents and aspirations not be allowed to develop them, simply because they are women. So, for example, women have been forbidden to attend universities, forbidden to be doctors, lawyers, or priests, and forbidden to own property. Feminism's first premise is that such treatment is both widespread and entirely unacceptable.

Once we agree that certain historical ways of treating women are unacceptable, the question becomes one of how best to eliminate this treatment. One view is that all we need to do is insist on equality of treatment between men and women. The thought is that all the manifest abuses of women have arisen from our treating them in ways that we do not treat men, so that the remedy is always to treat the two sexes in the same way, a view that, in a certain sense, is by now entirely noncontroversial.

But an unqualified equality-feminism remains controversial. Why, critics ask, should we assume that there are no respects in which we should treat women differently from men? There are, after all, major biological differences between the two sexes. Why think that these do not correspond to further differences in abilities and interests that should be reflected in differential treatment of men and women? A pure equality-feminism would insist that, prejudice and mistreatment aside, women have exactly the same intellectual, social, political, and moral capacities and aspirations as men. In an ideal society we should expect all differences (beyond the basic biological ones) between men and women to be eliminated. Proponents of this view will, for example, maintain that as long as there is not rough equality in the numbers of men and women in every profession, achieving and being rewarded at roughly equal rates, we will not have eliminated unjust discrimination against women.

Many, including many feminists, are uneasy with pure equality-feminism. The worry, in particular, is that it has simply accepted the values established by a male-dominated society and works to have women succeed as well as men in terms of those values. But, it might be argued, has not the mistreatment of women gone much further than just preventing them from achieving the highest human values?

Has it not also distorted the nature of human values, denying the status of values especially associated with women and asserting only those especially associated with men? This line of thought leads to what has come to be called difference-feminism, for which ending the ill-treatment of women requires allowing distinctively feminine values and virtues to flourish – for example, the values of cooperation, nurturing, and sensitivity rather than those of competition, domination, and self-expansion.

Recent discussions of women's status have often focused on the tensions between equality-feminism and difference-feminism. In practical terms, the key issue is whether feminists should be concerned with entering as equals into the world that men already occupy or with transforming in a distinctively feminine way the values defining that world. Interestingly, key elements of each viewpoint can also be the basis for supporting a subordinate role for women. There are, for example, those who agree with equality-feminists that there is a common set of values that define success for any human being but deny that women are as capable as men at achieving them. On the other hand, there are those who agree with difference-feminists that there is a distinctive set of values associated with women but maintain, in the manner of traditional patriarchies, that these values should be subordinated to masculine values.

To try to resolve these disagreements, we need to return to our initial premise that there are certain historical ways of treating women that are simply not acceptable. There is no longer any question of saying that women are not really human, exist only for the sake of men, etc. However, it is obvious that within the human species there are some individuals who have greater capacities for human achievement than others. The question is whether there are any general differences between men and women with regard to these capacities that warrant treating women as a group as the inferiors of men. Of course, even if there are such differences, we should all agree that there is no basis for refusing to allow a woman who has a capacity atypical of her sex from exercising and developing it. (Even if, for example, women are generally less good at mathematics than men, we should still admit that a woman who does have the capacity should be allowed to study advanced mathematics.) Some feminists maintain that there are no such differences. That is, they hold either that women as a group have capacities equal to those of men for achieving all human goods (equality-feminism); or they hold that men and women have different capacities that suit them for achieving different values, but that the values defining women's distinctive achievements are equal, or perhaps superior, to those defining men's distinctive achievements. By contrast, anti-feminists hold that there are differences between men and women that warrant treating women as a group as, in some respects, inferior to men. This does not mean that they think women's core human rights should be violated or that individual women with capacities at least equal to men should not be allowed to develop them. But it does mean that they think we should not expect women as a group to achieve in the same way or to as great an extent as men; and that we should take account of this in forming public policy.

How does Simone de Beauvoir stand on these issues? Specifically, what would she think about the choice between equality-feminism and difference-feminism? And how might she make the case for feminism? It might seem that, as an existentialist, she would object to both equality-feminism and difference-feminism on the grounds that they both assume an objective set of given values, equality being understood as women's and men's equal capacity to achieve a common human good and difference understood as women's capacity to achieve a distinctively feminine good at least as worthwhile as the masculine good. How could either of these views be consistent with the existentialist idea that each individual creates his or her own values? But at least for the case of equality-feminism the problem is quickly resolved. The common value posited by equality-feminism can simply be the existentialist's ultimate value of freedom; that is, of creative human activity. There is no need for equality-feminism to define the human good, equally accessible to men and women, as conformity to some preestablished substantive form of life. By contrast, there would seem to be a conflict between existentialism and difference-feminism's assertion of specific values, such as nurturing and sensitivity, that are distinctive of women. Such virtues seem to be tied to a conception of a distinctly feminine nature, independent of the choices of individuals, a conception inconsistent with the precedence of existence over essence.

It seems plausible, then, to take Beauvoir as a certain sort of equality-feminist: one who understands the fundamental human value to be creative engagement with and transformation of the world. But this interpretation faces a major difficulty. If men and women share the same value of free creativity, then, given Beauvoir's emphasis on the difficulties posed by women's "burden of reproduction", it is extremely hard to see how she can maintain that women are as capable as men at achieving this value. Admittedly, their central role in the reproduction of the species does not automatically condemn them to lives of immanence rather than transcendence. But, unless we revert to the naiveté of early existentialism, we cannot deny that women tend to immanence far more than men do. As Beauvoir continually emphasizes, their bodies and their biological role drag them down from the heights of transcendence.

We have seen how Beauvoir insists that the meaning of biological facts is determined only by the free interpretations of consciousness. But she also agrees that these interpretations can only reshape, not eliminate, the force of biological fact. Woman's reproductive role will always be in some sense a given. Moreover, it is hard to see how an interpretation that gave priority to women's reproductive role would be consistent with Beauvoir's own endorsement of transcendence over immanence, since immanence corresponds precisely to the function of reproduction or repetition rather than novel production. As Beauvoir herself puts it: "It is natural for woman to repeat, to begin again without ever inventing . . . She is occupied without ever *doing* anything, and thus she identifies herself with what she *has*. . . Her life is not directed toward ends: she is absorbed in producing or caring for things that are never more than means" (*DS*, II: 430/604). The alternative seems to be either to reject Beauvoir's fundamental value of transcendence in favor of this sort of repetitive immanence or to urge that women renounce their "natural" tendency to repetition, realizing that they will never be able to do this as completely as men.

The attempt to read Beauvoir as an equality-feminist is, then, textually plausible; but her strong emphasis on the bondage of reproduction supports the anti-feminist conclusion that women are inferior to men.[17] Given this, it is interesting that, at least toward the end of her book, Beauvoir seems to move in the direction of a kind of difference-feminism. She is adamant about the need to reject the

---

[17] Beauvoir might resist this anti-feminist talk of "inferiority" on the grounds that "all comparisons are idle which purport to show that woman is superior, inferior, or equal to man, for their situations are profoundly different". But she still admits that, "if we compare these situations rather than the people in them, we see clearly that man's is far preferable" (*DS*, II: 454/627).

old myths of femininity in order to make women genuinely free agents. She recognizes the value of the old ideal of the "charming woman" but maintains that it must be eliminated just as the joys of Southern plantation life had to be eliminated to destroy the slavery they depended on (*DS*, II: 574/729). But she also suggests that the world in which women are free need not just be a universalization of the world of male freedom. "To begin with, there will always be certain differences between men and women." For example, "her eroticism, and therefore her sexual world, have a special form of their own and therefore cannot fail to engender a sensuality, a sensitivity of a special nature" (*DS*, II:575/731). A world of feminine freedom will not, after all, just duplicate what men have achieved.

But what of the worry that the positing of uniquely feminine values just establishes women as the bearers of preserving values that are subordinated to the superior productive values of men? In particular, is not such a consequence inevitable given Beauvoir's endorsement of the priority of masculine creativity? This remains an important difficulty, but at the very end of her book Beauvoir suggests a new approach that may be able to overcome it. For the first time, she begins talking about the possibility of men and women creating new values together and suggests that the values created by free men *together with* free women will be something other than what men alone would have been able to create. She agrees that women must be emancipated from their bondage to men but, she notes, "let her have her independent existence and she will continue none the less to exist for him *also*: mutually recognizing each other as subject, each will yet remain the other for another" (*DS*, II: 575/731). Here she begins to speak of the *couple* as a unified creative agent: "when we abolish the slavery of half of humanity, together with the whole system of hypocrisy that it implies, the 'division' of humanity will find its genuine significance and *the human couple will find its true form*" (*DS*, II: 576/731, my emphasis). The suggestion, taken up, as we shall see, by later French feminists such as Luce Irigaray, is that, as they presently exist, both men and women are deprived and incomplete because of the bondage of women. Once women have moved sufficiently toward independence, the two sexes can join in a unified freedom that mutually respects the differences of each and opens up a new domain of human creativity. To achieve this, Beauvoir concludes, "it is necessary, for one thing, that by and through their natural differentiation men and women unequivocally affirm their brotherhood [*fraternité*[18]]" (*DS*, II: 577/732).

[18] Was Beauvoir consciously ironic in ending *Le deuxième sexe* with this word, which later French feminists have protested as a symbol of the Revolution's exclusion of women from the "rights of man"?

CHAPTER 7

Merleau-Ponty

> . . . like the idealist philosopher, whose body takes account of the external world in the reality of which his intellect declines to believe.
>
> (Marcel Proust, *In Search of Lost Time*, 1, 571)

Initially, Maurice Merleau-Ponty (1908–61) and Jean-Paul Sartre moved along the same path. Both studied philosophy at the École Normale (Merleau-Ponty three years behind Sartre), where they were friendly but not close, and both began teaching careers that were interrupted by the war, in which both served in the French army until its collapse. During the occupation, they worked together in the short-lived intellectual resistance group, Socialism and Liberty. This renewed and deepened their friendship, and when the war ended, they and Simone de Beauvoir founded and ran *Les temps modernes*. But whereas Sartre simply pursued his path as an independent public intellectual and writer, Merleau-Ponty combined his work at *Les temps modernes* with the traditional career of a university professor. After three years at the University of Lyon, he was called to a chair at the Sorbonne and taught there until he was elected to the Collège de France in 1952, where he remained until his unexpected death from a heart attack in 1961.

Unlike Sartre, Merleau-Ponty was a committed Catholic when he entered the École Normale[1] (Sartre mentions this as the main reason they were not close), and religion played an important role in his early intellectual formation. He wrote for *Esprit*, a Catholic journal edited by Emmanuel Mounier. *Esprit* supported Mounier's "personalist" version of French spiritualism and often published articles on the new philosophy of existence. It seems that Merleau-Ponty

---

[1] That is to say, in the odd slang of the École, he was a "tala": one who "va-**t-à la** messe" (goes to mass) on Sundays.

rejected Catholicism after a "crisis of faith" around 1935–6, but the reasons are not at all clear.[2] But throughout his life he showed much more sympathy to religion than did Sartre and Beauvoir, and he sometimes reveals an extremely sensitive and nuanced appreciation of Catholic doctrine and life.[3] It is interesting that, not long before he died, Merleau-Ponty declined to allow Sartre to identify him as an atheist in *Les temps modernes*.[4]

Merleau-Ponty did share Sartre's interest in phenomenology. He had heard Husserl's Paris lectures in 1929, and also learned about him (and Heidegger) in a course taught by Georges Gurvitch (1928–30).[5] During the 1930s Sartre and Merleau-Ponty each independently pursued their interest in Husserl and Heidegger, and when they renewed their acquaintance in 1941, they soon realized how much they had in common philosophically. As Sartre tells it: "The key words were spoken: phenomenology, existence. We discovered our real concern." He goes on to describe the mixture of comradeship and tension that colored their philosophical discussions:

Too individualist to ever pool our research, we became reciprocal while remaining separate. Alone, each of us was too easily persuaded of having understood the idea of phenomenology. Together, we were, for each other, the incarnation of its ambiguity. Each of us viewed the work being done by the other as an unexpected, and sometimes hostile, deviation from his own.[6]

These differences may well have been due to Sartre's penchant,

---

[2] "Editor's Introduction" to Jon Steward (ed.), *The Debate Between Sartre and Merleau-Ponty*, xvii. Sartre, who may or may not have known very much about the matter, says that Merleau-Ponty gave up his faith "because, as he said, 'We believe that we believe, but we don't believe'". "More specifically", he continues, "he asked that Catholicism reintegrate him in the unity of immanence, and this was precisely what it couldn't do" (Jean-Paul Sartre, "Merleau-Ponty", in *Situations*, 167).

[3] See, in particular, "Faith and Good Faith", in *Sense and Nonsense*, 172–81; and the discussion of Christianity and philosophy in "Everywhere and Nowhere", in *Signs*, 140–6. It is sometimes said that the story Merleau-Ponty tells at the beginning of the first essay (about a young man, clearly himself, who was shocked to hear priests he respected support the reactionary Dollfuss government in Austria) explains his loss of faith. But nothing in Merleau-Ponty's presentation of this anecdote supports this claim.

[4] Herbert Spiegelberg, *The Phenomenological Movement*, 754.

[5] Spiegelberg says Merleau-Ponty told him that "it was Sartre who, after his return from Germany in 1935, first acquainted him with Husserl's writings" (*The Phenomenological Movement*, 529). This does not quite fit with what we know about his earlier awareness of Husserl, or with Sartre's remark that the two had "lost sight of each other" between their school days and the war ("Merleau-Ponty", in *Situations*, 156). But there may have been an encounter with Sartre that raised the level of Merleau-Ponty's interest in Husserl.

[6] "Merleau-Ponty", in *Situations*, 159.

noted in chaper 5, for too readily mixing ontological categories with phenomenological descriptions.

Sartre and Merleau-Ponty were able to live quite happily with their philosophical differences (which have often been overemphasized). But their friendship foundered on political differences. The details are complex, but the break was ultimately over that touchstone for French intellectuals in the 1950s: support of the Communist Party. The Communists' leading role in the Resistance movement had given them a moral superiority among the French people and, especially, among intellectuals with leftist sympathies. For Sartre, Merleau-Ponty, and many others, the compelling question was why they were not members of the Party that was the vanguard against fascism and for a desperately needed social revolution. The answer, of course, always evoked the brutal and totalitarian character of Communism, especially in its dominant Soviet form. Despite often effective mechanisms of self-deception, leftist intellectuals were aware of and uneasy with such excesses as the Moscow trials and the concentration camps. The standard response was that these were accidental flaws in an essentially good enterprise and that, in any case, the incidental evils of Communism were of little weight in comparison to the intrinsic evil of capitalist oppression. In the concrete political world, the only way to work toward the elimination of absolutely unacceptable evils was to support the Communists. In 1947, Merleau-Ponty had himself argued along these lines with subtlety and passion in *Humanisme et terreur*. But by 1950, with the Korean War, Merleau-Ponty had lost faith in Communism, which he now saw as a flagrant corruption of the ideals of socialism. Unlike Camus about the same time, he was not yet willing to speak out against the evil (so as not to support the corresponding evils of capitalism) and so undertook a pointed silence. He even convinced a reluctant Sartre to accept a substantial withdrawal of *Les temps modernes* from political controversy. Things remained in this uneasy state until 1952, when Sartre, as we have seen, decided he had to give unequivocal support to the Communists.

The break with Merleau-Ponty followed quickly. The immediate cause was a dispute over Sartre's eliminating an introductory comment Merleau-Ponty had written to an article in *Les temps modernes* by a Communist intellectual.[7] Merleau-Ponty demanded

---

[7] There may well have been something more driving the issue, at least on Sartre's side, since

space in the journal to state his political position, but Sartre replied that he had no right to such space, since he had made the cowardly choice of withdrawal from political debate. Merleau-Ponty resigned from *Les temps modernes*, and their friendship was over. The break eventually led to Merleau-Ponty's strong and detailed attack on Sartre's politics in his article, "Sartre et l'ultra-bolchevisme".[8] After 1956, when even Sartre attacked the Soviet invasion of Hungary, the two had several positive contacts, and it seemed that the breach might be overcome. But Merleau-Ponty died before anything was settled. Sartre said: "There is nothing to be concluded from this except that this long friendship, neither done nor undone, obliterated when it was about to be reborn, or broken, remains inside me, an ever-open sore."[9]

Merleau-Ponty was especially stimulated by Husserl's later philosophy, particularly as it was developed in unpublished manuscripts that H. L. Van Breda saved from destruction at the beginning of the war and gathered in the Husserl Archives at Louvain.[10] He became convinced that this later philosophy, which he also found in Husserl's last book, *The Crisis of the European Sciences and Transcendental Phenomenology*, was a significant improvement on his earlier view, which Merleau-Ponty saw as too skewed toward idealism. He was particularly impressed with the idea of the *Lebenswelt* (lifeworld) as the focus of phenomenological description.

His first important publication was *La structure du comportement* (1942). This had been finished in 1938 and features, much more than phenomenology, Merleau-Ponty's intense interest in recent empirical psychology, especially Gestalt psychology.[11] *La structure du comportement* uses Gestalt psychology to construct a scientifically detailed argument against behaviorist models and then goes on to show the deficiencies of even the Gestalt account. The last chapter refers

---

in the period just before his pro-Communist crusade he had noisy breaks with several other friends and colleagues, including Camus and Claude Lefort, who was a friend and former student of Merleau-Ponty.

[8] Included in *Les aventures de la dialectique*. I discuss below aspects of this attack related to Merleau-Ponty's critique of Sartre's existentialism.

[9] "Merleau-Ponty", in *Situations*, 225–6.

[10] Merleau-Ponty was one of the first to visit the Archive, in 1938. For details on which manuscripts he consulted and when, see H. L. Van Breda, "Merleau-Ponty and the Husserl Archives at Louvain". Van Breda also tells the complex story of the establishment of a Husserl archive in Paris and of Merleau-Ponty's role in this enterprise.

[11] This interest explains why Merleau-Ponty's appointment at the Sorbonne was not as a professor of philosophy but as "Professor of Psychology and Pedagogy".

explicitly to phenomenology and suggests that it provides the standpoint for an adequate understanding of consciousness and its relation to the natural world.

Merleau-Ponty's next book, *Phénoménologie de la perception* (1945), immediately established him as a major philosopher and a leader, with Sartre, of the new movement of existential phenomenology. His later publications (mostly articles collected in *Sens et non-sens* and in *Signes*) are extensions of the fundamental position of *Phénoménologie de la perception* to topics such as language, art, and politics. However, during the last few years of his life, Merleau-Ponty began what promised to be a radical rethinking of his philosophical position. He does not seem to have envisaged a rejection of *Phénoménologie de la perception* but surely did intend to enrich and even revise his phenomenology on the basis of a deeper level of ontological thinking.

This new approach was indicated by the introduction to *Signes* (published in 1960) and sketched – although quite obscurely – in *L'oeil et l'esprit*, one of Merleau-Ponty's last completed essays (published in 1961). But these two items were just minor preliminaries to the project for a major new book, *Le visible et l'invisible*. He died just as this was getting well on its way, leaving about 160 pages of relatively finished, continuous text and a mass of working notes. The continuous text apparently would have been just the introduction to a much longer whole. The working notes – a selection of which have been published with the continuous text – are often fragmentary and generally enigmatic. These materials are useful sources for critical *aperçus* on Merleau-Ponty's earlier work and for speculations about the way his work might have gone. But enthusiastic commentators sometimes forget that, as a matter of brutal fact, there is no book titled *Le visible et l'invisible* by Merleau-Ponty (despite the published volume of that title, with his name on the cover). The very thing that makes us so interested in such a book – our conviction that Merleau-Ponty was a creative philosopher of very high order – should make us realize that we have no hope of reconstructing, from the meager materials we have, what he would have produced. The following discussion is, therefore, based on the fact that the philosophy of Merleau-Ponty is, in its core and essence, that presented in *Phénoménologie de la perception*, although I will briefly discuss the critique of Sartre in *Le visible et l'invisible* and its place in the development of Merleau-Ponty's thought.

THE PHENOMENOLOGY OF PERCEPTION

Merleau-Ponty's conception of phenomenology

Merleau-Ponty sees phenomenology as a "style of thinking" that has existed at least since Hegel and that deeply informed the work of Marx, Nietzsche, and Freud. But it is only with Husserl that phenomenology became explicitly aware of itself as a distinctive manner of doing philosophy. Husserl's message, however, was not without ambivalence. According to Merleau-Ponty, his phenomenology appears more as a set of tensions than as a single, coherent program. It is proclaimed as a realistic return to "the things themselves" but requires a transcendental "suspension" of existence claims and culminates in an idealistic science of essences. It seeks an account of the world as we are actually involved in it through our lived experience but at the same time presents itself as a rigorous, disengaged science. It seeks genetic accounts of the constitution of objects but also aspires to be a non-causal, descriptive account of what is given in our experience. Merleau-Ponty does not think that these tensions lead to contradiction but acknowledges that reconciling them requires some subordination of opposing emphases. Roughly, he sees himself as giving priority to the first side of each of the above pairs as opposed to Husserl's emphasis on the second.

As a mode of knowing our world, phenomenology is, according to Merleau-Ponty, distinct from and in crucial respects superior to both scientific explanations and to the analytical reflections of much modern philosophy, superior, therefore, to both empiricism and rationalism. In both cases, the superiority concerns the account phenomenology is able to give of our concrete engagement with the world. Science reduces this engagement to a mechanism of physical and physiological causes. Analytic reflection (characteristic of neo-Kantian idealists such as Brunschvicg – and also of Merleau-Ponty's Brunschvicgian readings of Descartes and Kant) reduces our concrete experience to a pseudo-explanatory system of intellectualized faculties (judgment, volition, etc.). The inadequacy of science and of analytic reflection is particularly apparent when we realize that each enterprise must itself be based (incoherently) on the very world of lived experience that it reduces. It is precisely this world that phenomenology aims to describe.

Merleau-Ponty's construal of phenomenology depends on his anti-idealist interpretation of Husserl's phenomenological reduction. The point of the reduction is to get beyond the common-sense prejudices associated with the "natural attitude" in which we unreflectively encounter the world. To take the reduction in an idealist sense is to see it as a return to a pre-personal transcendental subject before which the entire world appears with complete transparency. (The transparency would be due to the fact that the world is entirely constituted by transcendental consciousness from the epistemic matter – *hyle* – of sense data.) On this view, the reduction reveals the world as nothing more than meaning-for-consciousness.

Merleau-Ponty agrees that the reduction must be a withdrawal from the world as we commonly think of it, a suspension of our normal "complicity" with the world. But, contrary to the idealist construal of the reduction, he insists that the effect of this withdrawal is not a separation of the self (as transcendental ego) from the world. Rather, the withdrawal produces a more explicit awareness of the precise ways in which we are inextricably involved in the world. If the "natural attitude" is our spontaneous acceptance of ourselves as situated in the world, the phenomenological reduction is not a rejection of that attitude but a means of elucidating and appreciating the fundamental truths it embodies. The phenomenological reduction, therefore, is not the attainment of a new standpoint from which we view previously inaccessible philosophical truths but a means of sloughing off false conceptions due to, for example, the abstractions of science and ordinary language, and of returning to our original position in the midst of the world – a position that, in some sense, we can never have entirely abandoned. Phenomenological reflection does not, then, strictly separate consciousness from the world. Rather, "it slackens the intentional threads which attach us to the world and thus brings them to our notice" (*Phénoménologie de la perception* [*PP*], viii/xiii). Since these threads cannot be broken, since we always remain situated in the world, Merleau-Ponty concludes (against any idealist reading of Husserl), "the most important lesson which the reduction teaches us is the impossibility of a complete reduction" (*PP*, viii/xiv).

Husserl also speaks of an *eidetic reduction*, an extraction of the essential structures implicit in the phenomena that appear to us. Merleau-Ponty suggests that this is in fact just an integral aspect of the phenomenological reduction, so that there is really only one reduction. Specifically, the move to ideality (essential intuition) is needed because we are so tightly and unreflectively involved in the world that we cannot really know our situation unless we momentarily back away from it in its concrete facticity and describe it in terms of ideal essential structures. But such descriptions are only a means of returning to the concreteness of our true primordial relation to the world of existence. Here Merleau-Ponty distinguishes his phenomenology from the logical and linguistic analysis of the Vienna Circle, which he sees as remaining on the level of separated linguistic essences and so never returning from the meaning of words to the meaning of things (*PP*, x/xv).[12]

Merleau-Ponty also expresses his non-idealist conception of phenomenology through his interpretation of Husserl's key concept of intentionality. According to this interpretation, intentionality is not just the idea that every act of consciousness is directed toward some object, since this would be compatible with an idealist interpretation that saw subject and object as essentially correlated but with a fundamental priority residing in the subject. Merleau-Ponty sees intentionality as expressing the inextricable *unity* of world and consciousness, with neither assimilated to the other. Like Sartre, he sees the unity of "man-in-the-world" as the ultimate starting-point of phenomenology.

The domain of phenomenological inquiry is what Merleau-Ponty calls the "phenomenal field", our immediate experience as we actually live through it (as opposed to scientific, philosophical, and even common-sense reconstructions of that experience). Merleau-Ponty particularly insists on the inadequacy of both science and traditional philosophical reflection for providing an accurate and complete description of this field.

The basic problem with a scientific approach is that the deployment of its rigorously empirical and quantitative methodology requires us to regard the contents of the phenomenal field as fully determinate and totally objective (that is, in no way dependent on our experience of them). Science must conceive of its objects in a way that allows them to be understood entirely in terms of ideal mathematical constructs. This means that science understands everything, including living, feeling, and thinking bodies, as nothing more than a set of physical elements connected by causal relations.

---

[12] For further comments by Merleau-Ponty on analytic philosophy, see his discussion with Ryle and others in "Phenomenology and Analytic Philosophy", in *Texts and Dialogues*, 59–72.

As a result, even the human body becomes pure exteriority, a mere collection of parts outside of parts, interacting with one another according to scientific laws. According to this view, genuine subjectivity is eliminated, something that Merleau-Ponty regards as an obvious travesty of our experience of the phenomenal field. This is the motivation behind his dramatic statement that phenomenology's "return to the 'things themselves' . . . is from the start a rejection of science" (*PP*, ii/viii). He also thinks he can show that the purely scientific account fails systematically when it is applied to particular physiological and psychological data, when, for example, we try to understand sense perception in terms of sensations produced by the brain's interaction with the world. The general problem in all these applications is that the phenomenal field involves irreducible meanings (significations) that cannot be dealt with in objective causal terms. Science cannot, for example, explain why (to take an example from Max Scheler) "the light of a candle changes its appearance for a child when, after a burn, it stops attracting the child's hand and becomes literally repulsive" (*PP*, 64/52).

Rationalists and idealists have often opposed the scientific reduction of the phenomenal field and agreed with Merleau-Ponty that the phenomenal field is prior to the objective world of science, which represents an abstraction from it. In Merleau-Ponty's view, their mistake (and, in some texts, Husserl's) is in going on to subordinate the phenomenal field to a domain of transcendental subjectivity, a separate and entirely "inner" world accessible only via special acts of introspection or intuition. This domain is said to provide a privileged reflective standpoint from which we can, in principle, have completely explicit knowledge of the phenomenal field, by understanding how its meanings are constituted by the transcendental ego.

Despite their differences, the empiricist (scientistic) and rationalist (intellectualistic) approaches are grounded in a common desire to make our fundamental experience of the world entirely explicit and disengaged. The world must be the pure object of either an autonomous subjectivity or an autonomous scientific method. The mistake in both cases is to think that there can ever be total disengagement from the phenomenal field. Both scientific objectification and philosophical reflection are themselves rooted in and ultimately inseparable from the lived world. To overcome the mistake, we must realize that there is no going beyond the phenomenal field, neither below it via empiricist reduction nor above it by idealist constitution. We must, in other words, remain on the concrete level of existential phenomenology.

The Body

The key to avoiding empiricist and idealist errors is to maintain a proper appreciation of the central place of the *body* in our experience. The body is not an object on a par with other objects. As *my* body it is the ineradicable locus of experience, the standpoint from which I must perceive the world. This is apparent from the perspectival nature – both spatially and temporally – of perception. We experience an object situated in a surrounding world and hence as having different perspectives from different positions. In this sense, an object, far from being seen from nowhere (as empiricism and idealism would suggest), is in fact seen from *everywhere.* But among all these perspectives the one from *here* – from my perceiving body – is privileged. My gaze actually presents only those aspects of the object that are apparent from here (that is, given in a full perceptual synthesis); all other perspectives are indefinite and only presumptive.

The body is privileged with regard not only to perspective but also to all other perceived meanings, such as color or tactile sensation. How I experience, say, a pin prick, depends not only on the pin but also on the internal disposition of the body that is being pricked. "The function of the organism in receiving stimuli is, so to speak, to 'conceive' of a certain form of excitation" (*PP,* 89/75). There is a "constitution" of the objects of my experience, but it is through a pre-conceptual structuring provided by my body.

The above line of thought assumes, however, that our experience of the body cannot itself be understood in an objective, disengaged way, by either the mechanisms of empirical physiology or of introspective psychology. To exclude these possibilities – and, at the same time, to show the superiority of his account in terms of "being-in-the-world" – Merleau-Ponty discusses a paradigm case of bodily self-perception: that of the phantom limb. (For our purposes, this will also illustrate Merleau-Ponty's distinctive method of combining phenomenological description with analysis of the results of empirical scientific inquiries.)

People who have lost an arm or a leg sometimes still have

experiences that they describe as located in the no-longer-present limb; thus, "a man wounded in battle can still feel in his phantom arm the shell splinters that lacerated his real one" (*PP*, 90/76). Merleau-Ponty maintains that this phenomenon can be entirely explained neither by purely physiological nor by purely psychological considerations. Physiology alone cannot, for example, account for situations in which a mere memory of the loss of the limb evokes the phantom perception (*PP*, 91/76). But, similarly, introspective psychology cannot explain why severing the afferent nerves of the stump eliminates the phantom experience (*PP*, 91/77). From this, Merleau-Ponty concludes that to account for phantom limb experiences we need a framework that can combine both the physiological and the psychological approaches. He maintains that his viewpoint of being-in-the-world provides the needed framework.

To say that a perceiver (animal or human) exists is to say that it "has a world" (or "belongs to a world"). Having a world, however, is not a matter of having a disengaged, objective consciousness of a world. I am in-the-world in a pre-objective manner; that is, there is no sharp separation between the subjective perceiver and the objects that it perceives. There is, nonetheless, a structure (meaning) to the perceiver's situation with respect to its world. This structure defines the limits within which my engagement with the world must occur. But this defining structure is not wholly determinate; it is partially ambiguous and thus consistent with a certain range of attitudes and actions.

Applying this framework of being-in-the-world to the phantom limb case removes the need to choose between describing the phenomenon in terms of either what is strictly present (e.g., current nerve transmissions) or what is strictly not present (e.g., a remembered limb). This opens the way to regarding the limb as having what Merleau-Ponty calls an "ambivalent presence". There is, that is to say, a retention of the practical field of actions that were open to the agent before the limb was lost. This retention is apparent in a continuing perception of the world as manipulable in certain ways, even though the agent cannot in fact actually so manipulate it. The basis of this perception is the fact that certain objects (e.g., a glass an "arm's reach" from me) remain "impersonally" manipulable ("one" could reach out and take the glass) even though I cannot personally do so. Correspondingly, my body is perceived as able to manipulate the glass insofar as it is regarded impersonally as "some body or another". Thus, the limb is not present on the level of personal, first-person experience, but it is present on the level of impersonal, third-person experience. This is possible because my being-in-the-world is ambiguous between the impersonal and the personal.

Given this viewpoint, Merleau-Ponty says, we can subsume the successful aspects of both the psychological and the physiological accounts of the phantom limb. Why, for example, do memories alone evoke the phantom limb experience? Because the limb is a part of the past that remains quasi-present in the sense of continuing to have a role in the structuring of our experience. This role is normally peripheral but becomes central in certain circumstances, which are precisely those in which the phantom limb experiences emerge. To say that the phantom limb is evoked by memories is just to say that we "reopen" the past time that is still tied to the present via intentional threads such as the quasi-present limb. Similarly, the phenomenological standpoint allows us to understand why experience of the phantom limb depends on the functioning of specific nerves. The human mode of being-in-the-world involves a freedom from the momentary situation; for example, to perceive my environment I cannot be totally immersed in it (just as the eye cannot see what is flush up against it). This freedom is achieved by having a large number of functions occur in automatic ways, along pre-existing channels. In this way freedom is purchased at the price of total spontaneity. As a result, reflex actions are essential for human freedom and are, along with the physiological causal chains that underlie them, one mode of our being-in-the-world. The phenomenal field, the domain of phenomenological description, thus provides a locus for situating the truths pointed to by both traditional philosophical reflection and scientific explanation. This is why Merleau-Ponty can present phenomenology as an account that is both genuinely philosophical and receptive to scientific results. But this "synthesis" requires that we recognize the inadequacy of both traditional reflection and empirical science as autonomous accounts of our immediate experience and accept the priority of phenomenological description.

Language

As he does so often, Merleau-Ponty presents his view of language as an alternative to the inadequacies of empiricist and intellectualist accounts. Empiricism understands language use as a response, mediated through chains of association, to stimuli. Linguistic meaning is ultimately located in the external stimulus that produces an utterance (stimulus-meaning). Intellectualism (whether idealism or rationalism) sees utterances as expressions of thought, which is itself regarded as alone fundamentally meaningful. Each of these views of language has its own deficiencies. But their common failing is to deny that words in their own right have meanings. Each view, in its own way, sees words as merely derivative conveyers of meanings that in fact reside elsewhere, in stimuli or in thoughts. (In fact, Merleau-Ponty thinks that the empiricist account in the end eliminates meaning, replacing it with mere causal sequence.) According to Merleau-Ponty, "we refute both intellectualism and empiricism by simply saying that *the word has meaning*" (*PP*, 206/177). He agrees with the intellectualist, against the empiricist, that thought is a reality. But, he maintains, thought is not a private locus of meaning that is somehow expressed by language. Rather, language is itself thought as a concrete reality, just as the body is human existence.

The claim that language is thought is valid, however, only for language that Merleau-Ponty calls "first-order" or "originary" speech. A great many of our utterances do not originate meaning but merely repeat meanings articulated by previous speech. This is a practical necessity for everyday communication and lies behind our common view of language as merely expressing pre-existent thoughts. Further, originary speech need not be entirely independent of already established systems of meanings. It may originate new meanings by transformation of an already existing language.

As Merleau-Ponty sees it, linguistic expression is entirely parallel to musical expression, where there is no question of a musical meaning separate from the sounds that "express" it. We can also quite properly speak of language as a kind of gesture, like the spontaneous raising of my eyebrows that simply *is* my amazement or puzzlement at your remark.

A critic may suggest that Merleau-Ponty's view of language is not consistent with the existence of different languages, all capable of expressing what surely are the same meanings. The critic will claim that this is due to the fact that, contrary to Merleau-Ponty, the meaning is separate from the word, which expresses it merely in virtue of the conventions implicit in the particular language to which it belongs. How, for example, can "square" (in English) literally be the meaning of the geometrical entity, when this meaning is equally well expressed by "carré" (in French)?

Merleau-Ponty agrees with the critic's point for the case of merely conceptual meaning, which he understands as an abstracted core of content shared by the corresponding words of different languages. But, he maintains, the full meaning of any word cannot be separated from its concrete physicality. There are, for example, always emotional overtones and nuances, implicit in the sound or shape of a word, that form an inextricable aspect of its meaning. On this level, it is not arbitrary that French says "nuit" rather than "night". Despite a common conceptual core, there are subtle differences in the way in which French and English allow us to understand, to live, the night. On the most complete and concrete level, then, words are not conventional. "The predominance of vowels in one language, or of consonants in another, and constructional and syntactical systems, do not represent so many arbitrary conventions for the expression of one and the same idea, but several ways for the human body to sing the world's praises and in the last resort to live it" (PP, 218/187).

Merleau-Ponty's account so far has emphasized the similarity of language to other forms of bodily expressions (gesture, music, etc.). But he also insists on its distinctive character as a permanent acquisition of the human community: "alone of all expressive processes, speech is able to settle into a sediment and constitute an acquisition for use in human relations" (PP, 221/190). Here Merleau-Ponty is not referring to our ability to preserve speech by writing it down; the same, after all, can be done for music. What he has in mind is rather the reflexive character of language, the fact that there can be speech about speech (whereas there is not music about music, etc.) Because of this, present speech activity can take past speech activities as its subject and preserve them by referring to them as established givens. This, in turn, leads to the idea of a linguistic utterance that acquires a permanent status by being preserved in all subsequent speech; that is, to the idea of a truth.

Like his more general discussion of the body, Merleau-Ponty's treatment of language emphasizes the impossibility of separating consciousness from the world that is its object. In this regard, phenomenology shows the limitations of dualistic ontologies derived from the Cartesian tradition. For such ontologies, "the object is an object through and through, and consciousness is consciousness through and through. There are two senses, and two only, of the word 'exist': one exists as a thing or one exists as a consciousness." But in fact "the experience of our own body . . . reveals to us an ambiguous mode of existing" (*PP*, 231/198). The body is not merely an object and our experience of it is not merely a thought. Here, of course, Merleau-Ponty is giving not just a general critique of Cartesianism but also a pointed reminder of the limitations of the ontology of Sartre's *L'être et le néant* (but limitations, as we have seen, also quite apparent from Sartre's own phenomenological descriptions).

The Other

It might seem that Merleau-Ponty's account of language (and, more generally, his view of the body of which the account is part) would allow him to make short shrift of the traditional problem of the existence of other minds. As he says, language is a cultural object that plays "a crucial role in the perception of other people" (*PP*, 407/354). More fully, my encounter with another person depends on the fact that neither of us is a purely transparent subjectivity. Such a subjectivity "has no outside and no parts" and so cannot be part of my perceptual world. A pure subject can be directly experienced only by itself. (And Merleau-Ponty is entirely unimpressed with efforts to infer the existence of other subjectivities through arguments from analogy or to the best explanation.) But, as we have seen, my subjectivity is not pure but embodied. Further, as embodied, I am from the beginning included in a shared world with other bodies, some of which are, like me, a source of meaning. Consequently, I have always found myself in a world with meanings that are not mine but that I receive from others. The Pyramids, a can opener, my neighbor's smile are all instances of cultural or bodily meanings by which I am in direct contact with the subjectivity of other people. And language, as the primary mode of communication within this human world, would perhaps be the strongest indication that, for Merleau-Ponty, there is no problem of other minds.

But in fact Merleau-Ponty thinks there is such a problem, and understanding why reveals an important dimension of his view of human reality. The key point is that the other as encountered through its behavioral (including linguistic) expression in our shared world cannot be simply identified with the other as the lived subject of its own experience. The world I share with the other is a common domain of thought and activity, but by that very fact it is not my personal world nor the personal world of the other. On this level, "what we do in effect is to iron out the I and the Thou in an experience shared by a plurality, thus introducing the impersonal into the heart of subjectivity and eliminating the individuality of perspectives" (*PP*, 408/355-6). It is this impersonal (or pre-personal) character of the shared behavioral world that makes it inadequate as the basis for my encounter with the other in its full subjectivity. Merleau-Ponty's point here corresponds to what he thinks is an essential truth rooted in idealism (indeed, in solipsism). He has urged, against idealism, that I do not experience myself as "the constituting agent either of the natural or the cultural world: into each perception and into each judgement I bring either sensory functions or cultural settings which are not actually mine". But even so, there is another level on which I am aware of the entire content of this description of a world in which I am engaged and in which "I am outrun on all sides by my acts". My acts and their world have a meaning beyond me, but "the fact remains that I am the one by whom they are experienced, and with my first perceptions there was launched an insatiable being who appropriates everything that he meets, to whom nothing can be simply and purely given" (*PP*, 411/358). This being, this self, is not given in the shared behavioral world, although it is obviously given to itself in my fundamental experience of self-consciousness. (This would seem to be Merleau-Ponty's equivalent of Sartre's pre-reflective consciousness.) But just as I, in this sense, am not given in the world, neither is the other. Therefore, merely appealing to the body and the shared behavioral world of which it makes me a part does not show how I am aware of the existence of other persons as individual subjects.

The truth of idealism, then, is that I am more than just the self that is incarnated in my body and its world. And the truth of solipsism is that the other's self (in this sense) cannot be known in the same way that I know my self (as directly given in my experience). Nonetheless, I obviously do know other selves. I know, for example, that my friend has a first-person experience of his grief (as I do of mine), even though I can never share this experience. But how do I know this? According to Merleau-Ponty, to understand this we need to stop thinking of solitude (the self's grasp of itself) and communication (the self's grasp of others) as incompatible alternatives. We must instead think of them as two aspects of the same phenomenon.

Here he draws an analogy between my experience of others and my reflective awareness of myself. Reflection cannot occur without the nonreflective (prereflective) as its source and object. Similarly, my (solitary) experience of myself cannot occur without a non-solitary (communicative) experience of others. More fully, there is a social world (presumably not reducible to the shared behavioral world), and I am given to myself only because I am already part of this world. For me to be or to do anything is to be or do it in the social world. Therefore, my awareness of the other is not a matter of some particular perception but simply of the fact that I have my being in a social world.

Merleau-Ponty is right about the inadequacy of the world of shared behavior (the object of his earlier phenomenological descriptions) as the locus of my encounter with other people possessed, like me, of subjectivity in the full sense. But his invocation of the "social world" and its necessary role in self-awareness is, in this context, a *deus ex machina*, arbitrarily introduced to resolve an untenable situation. The problem is, first, that he has given us no account (as Sartre, on the other hand, has) of the nature of the self or of its self-awareness. Second, and more importantly, he does not tell us how, even given the context of the social world, the self is aware of other selves. In both regards, Sartre's account, with its descriptions of prereflective consciousness and of my experience of myself as the object of the other's look, offers more than Merleau-Ponty's. Moreover, by Merleau-Ponty's own showing, the common world of shared behavior is not the locus of my experience of other selves and this is precisely because here it is a question of a self that is "an insatiable being who appropriates everything that he meets". This surely lends further plausibility to Sartre's story of conflict as the origin of my awareness of the other.

The cogito and the truth of idealism

Merleau-Ponty's treatment of other minds revealed a core of truth in idealism. More generally, he thinks that there is an "element of final truth in the Cartesian return of things or ideas to the self" (*PP*, 423/ 369), despite its ultimate failure. His treatment of the cogito, the primary locus of idealist thought, is his effort to come to terms with this truth.

The evidence for realism is simply my experience of my consciousness as thrown into a world independent of it. But the idealist rightly points out that even this experience has a content dependent on the self. Objects appear as transcendent to the extent that I am ignorant of their natures and can only blindly assert that they (or certain features of them) exist. But even such a bare assertion is meaningless unless it is based on at least a "glimpse" of the nature of the object, and any such nature will have an intelligibility that depends on categories constituted by the mind. Given the fundamental role of consciousness in the constitution of any possible object of thought or experience, it follows that consciousness must be autonomous (independent of all outside influences) and timeless (outside the system of the temporal objects it constitutes). Indeed, as Merleau-Ponty sees it, consciousness must, for the idealist, be ultimately identified with absolute consciousness and therefore with God.

But idealism is mistaken and the mistake, Merleau-Ponty maintains, is its sharp (epistemic) separation of the *act* of perception from the *object* of perception. Idealists distinguish, for example, *There is a book in front of me* from *I think I see a book in front of me*, with the first being uncertain and the second certain. The certainty of the act of perception is then exploited to make the uncertain object dependent on consciousness's perceptual act. (This, for example, is the strategy of phenomenalist arguments from illusion, which maintain that material objects, because they are objects of doubt, must be constructed from the certainties of sense-data.) But, Merleau-Ponty argues, the idealists' separation of act and object is not tenable. Perception is not perception unless it attains its object: if I really see a book in front of me, there must *be* a book in front of me. Therefore, the idealist must conclude either that my perception is certain and so is its object; or that the object is uncertain and so is my perception. There is no room for the Cartesian argument (nonetheless appropriated by many idealists) that the object is uncertain but my perception of it is certain. Recognizing this undermines the case for idealism and requires us to reject the autonomy of consciousness in favor of an inextricable connection between consciousness and its objects. And, of course, it is precisely this connection that Merleau-Ponty articulates in his phenomenology of the body.

It may be suggested, however, that Merleau-Ponty's case against idealism is based only on certain peculiarities of (sense) perception. Is it likewise possible to give a non-idealist account of other domains of our experiences, in particular, introspective awareness of psychic states and exercises of pure thought such as mathematical understanding? Merleau-Ponty maintains that it is.

It may seem that in contrast to the case of sense perception, my introspective states such as anger, love, and doubt do have a certainty that is independent of the nature or even existence of their intentional objects. But in fact there can be illusion even regarding such states. Consider the case of love (*PP,* 433/378). There is such a thing as "false love", which I can mistake for true love. Beneath what I take to be love, there may be a reality quite other than love (e.g., awareness of a similarity to someone previously loved). The falseness, Merleau-Ponty says, will be indicated by the failure of my apparent love to entirely inform my consciousness, which always maintains some corner immune to it. In such a case, it is possible that I be deceived about whether or not I am in love.

But what about the case of mathematical understanding, for example, my grasp of a proof that the sum of the interior angles of a triangle is 180 degrees? Merleau-Ponty begins by noting, as did Descartes, that a grasp of such a proof requires a mental act uniting the various steps of the proof, which would otherwise remain temporally separated insights. In the case at hand, for example, I must grasp in a single act the three sides of the triangle, the three angles formed by the sides of the triangle, and the parallel through its apex. Without such a unifying act, I will be unable to see the various steps of the proof as all working to support the conclusion.

Everything depends on the nature of this unifying act. If it is the autonomous grasping of a completely transparent intellectual object, taken either idealistically as an ideal essence or positivistically as a conventional definition, then we have a counter-example to Merleau-Ponty's view of consciousness, which would, at least in this case, exist entirely independently of its objects. But Merleau-Ponty maintains that the act of mathematical understanding is an act of imaginative perception, running beyond the immanence of pure thought and itself essentially tied to a transcendent object. Consider, he says, what actually goes on when we prove a mathematical truth such the angle-sum theorem. The demonstration is not carried out by an analysis of the formal essence or definition of a triangle. We do not, for example, begin with the concept *three-sided enclosed plane figure* and discover contained in it the property *sum of interior angles equal to 180 degrees*. Rather, the property is revealed by a series of constructions (extending lines, drawing a parallel through the apex) from which the property becomes apparent. The demonstration does make explicit what is implicit in the triangle, but this is the triangle as an object in my lived space, not as a formal essence.

It may be objected that Merleau-Ponty is confusing what may well have been the psychology of the discovery of the theorem with the rigorous proof eventually given of it. Certainly, the high-school textbook presentation (based, admittedly, on Euclid's *Elements*) on which Merleau-Ponty is relying is a far cry from the proof offered in, say, Hilbert's axiomatization of geometry. Such a proof involves no appeal to our spatial imagination but proceeds entirely from an implicit definition of the triangle and its properties by the axioms of our formal system. But according to Merleau-Ponty such formalization is always a retrospective enterprise, itself presupposing an intuitive experience that it analyzes and explicates. This is especially apparent from the fact, proven by Gödel, that a formalization is always in principle incomplete. It never exhausts the richness of the intuitive imagination from which there continue to arise new insights that can only subsequently be included in our formal systems.[13]

We must, accordingly, recognize that even mathematical understanding is derived from lived perceptual experience. In the proof of the angle-sum theorem, the triangle is not an entirely ideal intellectual object. It is a pole toward which my bodily movements (as I carry out the constructions of the proof) are directed and, as such, a part of my spatial world. Since I am in this world only through my body, it follows that the body is a condition for the possibility of geometrical knowledge (which is another reason why my body cannot be regarded as just another object in space).

Merleau-Ponty further argues that the body "is the condition of possibility, not only of the geometrical synthesis, but of all expressive operations and all acquired views which constitute the cultural world" (*PP*, 445/388). The role of the body is to "throw" consciousness beyond itself toward the transcendent world. As we have seen, this role is particularly apparent in the way that language, by "embodying" thought, goes beyond what is involved in mere thought abstractly considered in itself. But Merleau-Ponty emphasizes that language has no privileged position over other, non-

---

[13] The Belgian philosopher, Jean Ladrière, later offered a thorough discussion, from a broadly phenomenological standpoint, of Gödel's theorem and related results in *Les limitations internes des formalismes*.

linguistic modes of expression (music, art) because the ideas that it expresses are cultural objects in the same sense that symphonies, churches, and paintings are.

We may object that, unlike at least some other cultural objects, ideas are indestructible. But according to Merleau-Ponty, just as a great cathedral can be destroyed by bombs, so an idea can be eliminated by the loss of the tradition in which it is embodied. We may respond that at least some ideas express eternal truths that set them off from other cultural products. After all, the Euclidean theorems are true of triangles whether anyone knows it or not. Paintings and symphonies do not express similar eternal truths that can be instantiated independently of particular cultural manifestations. For Merleau-Ponty, however, ideas can be regarded as true only to the extent that they are descriptions of real (i.e., perceived) things. Precisely as such descriptions, ideas do not have eternal validity, as we discovered when real triangles turned out not to be Euclidean.

Nonetheless, a critic will reply, Euclidean geometry remains in some sense a body of truths, even if it is not instantiated in the perceptual world. Merleau-Ponty agrees but denies that the enduring truth of Euclidean geometry requires us to think of this truth as outside time. It is eternal, if it is, only in the sense that all future formulations of geometry will somehow have to include it as a special, limiting case. (Compare this view to Bachelard's on "permanent truths" in science.) Here there is no essential distinction, such as idealism requires, between factual and rational truth. All truths are merely factual in the sense that they are formulated in categories specific to a particular historical period. If they retain any validity beyond that period, it is only because they are, as a matter of fact, able to be reformulated in the new categories of succeeding periods. So-called rational truths always retain a "coefficient of facticity" that ties them to their historical origins and makes it possible in principle that they will someday be abandoned.

Finally, Merleau-Ponty extends his view of the historicity of truth to the "self-evident" truths to which idealistic philosophy typically appeals as its ultimate foundation. According to him, every idea, every assertion of alleged truth has a "sedimentary history" extending into the indefinite past. Each idea and proposition is the product of a long series of historical usages, the accumulation of which constitutes its content at any given time. This sedimentary history not only explains how I have come to have my current thoughts (their genesis); it also determines the meaning (signification) of these thoughts. Because of this, the total evaluation of any given idea or assertion would require a complete unpacking and evaluation of every element of this history. Such a process could in principle never be complete, since it would require my stepping out of the ongoing flux of history. This is why the idea of absolutely presuppositionless truth (self-evident truth) is empty. Particular truths appear self-evident only because they define a set of conditions to which I am (perhaps only implicitly) committed as the context of my experience and thought. Self-evidence is always relative to a particular conceptual framework and reflects merely my acceptance of this framework, not the inevitable conditions of thought and experience as such (*PP*, 454/396).

Merleau-Ponty sums up his non-idealistic account of certainty and truth by saying that he is "restoring to the cogito a temporal thickness" (*PP*, 456/398). He has rejected the autonomous, eternal thinking self of the idealists. But, he notes, this does not mean that the cogito is merely another of the world's uncertain facts. As such a fact, the cogito would be opaque to me and therefore "there would no longer be either inner experience or consciousness" (*PP*, 457/399). My bodily incarnation means, of course, that I am, at each moment, a consciousness with a "sedimentary history", dependent on the world. But Merleau-Ponty thinks that I must also be a consciousness that somehow escapes from this particular history: "it is necessary that behind all our particular thoughts there should lie a retreat of not-being, a Self". The series of my historical consciousnesses "must present itself to [this] perpetual absentee". The problem, accordingly, is to understand "how subjectivity can be both dependent yet irremovable [*indéclinable*]" (*PP*, 459/400).

Merleau-Ponty's solution is to appeal to the existence of what he calls a "silent" or "tacit" cogito. Here he is starting from the fact that my involvement in the world is essentially through language (identified, as we have seen, with thought). But, he says, language does not entirely envelop and determine me. Language itself "presupposes nothing less than a consciousness of language, a silence of consciousness embracing the world of speech in which words first receive a form and meaning". This is the "tacit *cogito*, myself experienced by myself" (*PP*, 462/403). Merleau-Ponty does not regard this tacit cogito as the transcendental source of the world: "it does not constitute the world". This is apparently because its grasp of the world, although fundamental, remains generic. The particularities of our lives are founded elsewhere. "The consciousness which conditions language is merely a comprehensive and inarticulate grasp upon the world, like that of an infant at its first breath . . . though it is true that all particular knowledge is founded on this primary view, it is true also that the latter waits to be won back, fixed and made explicit by perceptual exploration and by speech. Silent consciousness grasps itself only as a generalized 'I think' in face of a confused world 'to be thought about'" (*PP*, 462/404). The compelling question is whether accepting this "tacit cogito" puts Merleau-Ponty back in the camp of the idealists. We will return to this question after we discuss his view of freedom.

Freedom

Merleau-Ponty begins his reflections on freedom with an appreciative sketch of Sartre's view of freedom as constrained by nothing beyond itself. He first notes some a priori considerations, apparently based on the very conception of freedom: that if any of my actions are free, they are all free, since there is no way for freedom to arise from unfreedom; and that the notion of attenuated freedom makes no sense: an act is either free or not, with no middle ground. He also notes that close phenomenological description eliminates what at first seem to be limitations on freedom. Allegedly "objective" determinations (being crippled, handsome, Jewish) do not really limit my freedom because they express only what I am for others; as being-for-itself my consciousness is not any of these things. Similarly, the motives that seem to determine my behavior turn out themselves to be the result of my free choices. Finally, the fact that there are certain things I cannot successfully do (be a great singer, climb a steep cliff) limits my freedom only to the extent that I have made choices that constitute certain features of the world as obstacles. In light of all these considerations, it may seem that Sartre is right to see freedom as entirely unlimited by any external factors.

But in fact, Merleau-Ponty says, Sartre must be wrong, if only because, by making all actions equally free, he in effect eliminates "free action" as a meaningful category. To see this, we need to realize that a free action is a matter of doing something, that is, of intervening in the world in a way that makes a difference. But an action that places no conditions or limitations on subsequent actions literally makes no difference. It follows that for any action to be free it must impose meaningful limitations on other actions. The existence of freedom is itself impossible if all actions are free in Sartre's sense.

What Sartre ignores is the fact that freedom can exist only in a field of possibilities that specify the probabilities, given my situation, that I will act in one way rather than another (cf. *PP*, 504–5/442). Merleau-Ponty's positive enterprise is to outline this "field-theory" of freedom.

He begins with the status of external obstacles to action, such as the steepness of a cliff I want to climb. Sartre is right that nothing appears as an obstacle except as a result of a project that I have chosen. In this sense, all obstacles are constituted by freedom itself. But, Merleau-Ponty notes, freedom constitutes obstacles only in a general way; it creates, through its project, a context in which certain things will appear as obstacles, others as aids, etc. But freedom does not determine which objects will be obstacles and which not. The particular configuration of obstacles in the field of freedom depends on the situation, not on freedom. My wanting to climb the cliff results in there being (generically) obstacles to my effort. But the particular physical structures of the cliff and of my body determine just what these obstacles will be. We can preserve Sartre's claim that all obstacles, even in their specificity, are due to the self, but only if, contrary to Sartrean ontology, we understand the self as incarnate and in the world, not as an autonomous being-for-itself.

But what about the "internal" psychic states that seem to constrain my freedom – for example, my fatigue, my inferiority complex? Sartre is, of course, correct that such states do not literally determine my behavior. I could always "explode" my fatigue or my complex and climb the cliff (or die trying). But Sartre ignores the crucial fact that, although I always *can* alter deep-rooted attitudes or patterns of reaction, it is improbable that I *will*. Probability is not merely an abstraction of mathematical thought. It is a genuine phenomenon of "weight" (or "tendency") that is given in immediate experience. Having an inferiority complex means that "I have committed myself to inferiority, that I have made it my abode". This past commitment, "though not a fate, has at least a specific weight and is not a set of events over there, at a distance from me". It is, rather, "the atmosphere of my present" that determines not how I must act but how I am likely to act, given the situation to which my freedom must "gear itself" (*PP*, 505/442).

The field theory of freedom gives us an alternative to the standard objectivist and idealist views of individuals' relation to their social and historical context. Consider, for example, social class (bourgeoisie, proletariat, etc.). In the objectivist view, this is entirely a matter of external historical facts, whereas in the idealist view it derives solely from my unfettered free choice to think of myself in a certain way. Each of these views has its specific flaws. Objectivism cannot explain, for example, why the very conditions that it posits as producing the proletariat existed for centuries before this class actually emerged. Idealism can make no sense of the fact that proletarian consciousness emerges gradually, in association with specific events, and is far more likely to develop in certain groups rather than others (e.g., workers rather than intellectuals). But more fundamentally, both objectivism and idealism assert a false dichotomy between being-in-itself and being-for-itself. Given this dichotomy, no doubt we must choose between these two categories as the fundamental source of class allegiance. But the truth is that these categories are only abstractions from the concrete reality of consciousness-in-the-world. Focusing on this reality instead of on ontological abstractions from it leads us to Merleau-Ponty's field theory of freedom.

An idealist (perhaps even a Sartrean) may object that Merleau-Ponty's view is correct but only from the point of view of the other. For others I am constrained even if not determined by my situation, but this is not so from the standpoint of my consciousness itself (the for-itself). As consciousness I am nothing. In my awareness of myself as consciousness, I am aware that my freedom has no limitations. Since my first-person viewpoint has priority over the third-person viewpoint of the other (this is the "final truth" of the cogito), we must privilege the standpoint of my being-for-itself.

But just as Merleau-Ponty rejects the sharp distinction of the for-itself and the in-itself, so too he rejects the sharp distinction of the for-itself and the for-others. If the two categories were sharply distinct, it would not be possible for me to experience the other as another self (ego): "If the other people who empirically exist are to be, for me, other people, I must have a means of recognizing them, and the structures of the For Another must, therefore, already be the dimensions of the For Oneself" (*PP*, 511/448). Here, as in his earlier discussion of the other, Merleau-Ponty invokes our primordial situation, as conscious beings, in a social world.

Given Merleau-Ponty's view of the situatedness of our freedom, we can speak of the development of meaning in human history. In a Sartrean account, history can have no meaning, since no action can depend on any other. There are, for example, no statesmen setting a course that molds the shape of the future in the light of the shape of the present. There are only adventurers who arbitrarily confer their own personal meanings on events that have no enduring significance. I may be a despot one day and an anarchist the next, with the world posing no obstacles to my random variations. As a result, there can be no meaningful connections between historical events, apart from the ephemeral ties I may create or alter from moment to moment.

By contrast, Merleau-Ponty allows for meaningful connections, independent of my choices, but without introducing determinism. In his view, we can think of ourselves as free, in our unique individuality, but only in the context of a general determination of our possibilities by our historical situation. This provides a viable sense of freedom in a situation.

We may well think that Merleau-Ponty has merely shown certain limitations in Sartre's ontology, limitations of which he was himself aware and which are balanced by his phenomenological descriptions (of the body and of situated freedom) and corrected by the social ontology of *Critique de la raison dialectique*. This, in part, was Simone de Beauvoir's reply, no doubt approved by Sartre, to the extensive critique of Sartre that Merleau-Ponty published in his *Les aventures de la dialectique*. That critique took Sartre to task for his support, in the early fifties, of the Communist Party, and tried to connect that support to the ontology of freedom developed in *L'être et le néant*. Beauvoir replied that Merleau-Ponty was attacking a "pseudo-Sartrianism" and and that he "denied coldly the whole Sartrean phenomenology of engaged freedom". She acknowledged "problems" with "the reconciliation of Sartre's ontology and phenomenology" but argued that this was no reason to ignore the one in favor of the other. She also noted that "Merleau-Ponty knows perfectly well that Sartre is preparing a work of philosophy [*Critique de la raison dialectique*] which attacks this problem directly".[14]

---

[14] Simone de Beauvoir, "Merleau-Ponty et le pseudo-sartrisme", 2122.

To this kind of defense, Merleau-Ponty seems to have two replies. The first is that in Sartre's own political thinking and action, it is the radical ontological view of freedom rather than the more nuanced phenomenological view that dominates. Discussing in *Les aventures de la dialectique* Sartre's decision (in 1952) to give decisive support to the Communist Party, while admitting grave defects in its structure and policies, he says that Sartre is working from a theory of the Party based on the "philosophy of fact, of consciousness, and . . . of time" in *L'être et le néant*. This philosophy is behind Sartre's "treating the event as ineffaceable, as a decisive test of our intentions and an instantaneous choice of the whole future and of all that we are". The revolutionary's choice of the Party cannot, according to Sartre, derive from a judicious and nuanced weighing of the relative merits of the Communists and their opponents in terms of the specifics of the present situation and its historical antecedents. "The revolutionary will of the militant . . . does not come out of what he was but out of the future, out of nonbeing . . . Because it is gratuitous, prior to any motive, and pure affirmation of value, the will additionally postulates in being what is necessary for its fulfillment."[15]

According to Merleau-Ponty, thinking about freedom in this way leads Sartre to treat contemporary political choices as matters of unconstrained choice between stark alternatives. Thus, we must either entirely support the Party or entirely support capitalist oppression. (This recalls Sartre's self-criticism of the view of freedom given in *L'être et le néant* as reflecting only the extraordinary circumstances of the war and occupation, which called for absolute commitments.) But this line of response is not convincing. The fact that Sartre may have misread (or even, as was perhaps the case with the war and occupation, correctly read) political situations in terms of his dualistic ontology says nothing about the ultimate compatibility of that ontology with a richer and more nuanced phenomenology of freedom.

Merleau-Ponty's second response to a defense of Sartre is implicit in his long critique of Sartrean ontology in the unfinished manuscript, *Le visible et l'invisible*. Here he insists that Sartre, despite his claims to the contrary, is never able to overcome his rigid separation of being and nothingness, a separation that allows no conceptual room for the concrete reality in which the two are intermingled.

[15] *Les aventures de la dialectique*, 105, 106–7.

"Nothingness and being are always absolutely other than one another, it is precisely their isolation that unites them." He acknowledges that "Sartre does indeed say that *at the end of his book* it will be permissible to move to a broader sense of Being, which contains Being and nothingness". But he insists that this never happens because for Sartre consciousness is always a disengaged spectator of human existence. As Merleau-Ponty puts it: "It cannot be otherwise if one starts with the pure negative; for it will never admit anything into itself, and even if one comes to recognize that it has need of Being, it will need Being only as a distant environment that does not adulterate it. It will dispose it about itself, as a pure spectacle or as what it has to be."[16] This attack may show that Sartre cannot ultimately reconcile the ontology of *L'être et le néant* with the phenomenology of freedom. If so, phenomenology may need an alternative ontology, perhaps of the sort that Merleau-Ponty seems to be developing in *Le visible et l'invisible*. But it does not follow that Sartre prefers his ontology to his phenomenology, a claim made particularly dubious by Sartre's development of an alternative social ontology in *Critique de la raison dialectique*.

PHENOMENOLOGY AND STRUCTURALISM

Among French existential philosophers, Merleau-Ponty provided the fullest and most acute phenomenological description of human existence. But at the same time he played a major role in the sudden fading of existential phenomenology from the French scene beginning about 1960. This role had two main dimensions. On the one hand, Merleau-Ponty pushed the effort to describe concrete human existence phenomenologically so far that he reached the limits of the project's coherence. On the other hand, he introduced into philosophical discussions Saussure's linguistics and Lévi-Strauss's anthropology, theories that were, along with psychoanalysis, the main instruments of existential phenomenology's rapid overthrow.

The strength of Merleau-Ponty's phenomenology was the extent to which, in contrast to Sartre's, it pursued the sheer complexity of our experience without introducing oversimplifying ontological categories. But at some point the ontological issue had to be faced, since his descriptions carried assumptions about just what sorts of beings

[16] *Le visible et l'invisible*, 68, 70.

the world and our consciousness of it are. We have seen, for example, how Merleau-Ponty's introduction of the "tacit cogito" suggests an implicit idealism in his description of self-awareness. More generally, as Vincent Descombes points out, phenomenology tends toward idealism precisely because, given its insistence on the primacy of "my" perception, it cannot allow a distinction between *being* and *being-for-myself*. Phenomenology becomes not just a description of the phenomena but a description based on the hypothesis that there is nothing (no meaning, no being) except in relation to my experience.[17] It is in virtue of this hypothesis that phenomenology remains, as Merleau-Ponty insists, a philosophy of the cogito.

As we have seen, however, Merleau-Ponty's cogito is ultimately "tacit", that is, not myself as this individual but a general subject, the "one" rather than the "I". It might seem that this is the key to his avoiding the collapse of being into being-for-myself. "If the 'I' harbors an impersonal subject . . . , then the same holds good for the 'we' "[18] and it is this subject common to "us" that places us in the shared world of human historical experience.

This idea of an impersonal cogito may seem no different than Brunschvicg's "universal reason", which has no concrete content of its own and serves only to deny any genuine human involvement in the actual historical world. Merleau-Ponty, however, would claim that his cogito could be distinguished from this unacceptably idealist cogito in two ways. First, it has a specific content that is expressed in the structures discovered by the new social sciences of linguistics and cultural anthropology, particularly as they have been developed by Saussure and Lévi-Strauss. Second, it is possible to develop a fundamental ontology that will show how both the subject (the phenomenological tacit cogito) and its object (the world) derive from a common "stuff" or "flesh", which sustains them as two distinct but inextricably entwined dimensions of being.

The latter response corresponds to the ontological project that Merleau-Ponty hoped to carry out in *Le visible et l'invisible*. Unfortunately, the 160 pages of fairly unified discussion he left us are primarily concerned with formulating the problem and with criticizing inadequate solutions (e.g., Sartre's). The main indications of his positive approach are sketched in twenty-five pages entitled "The

---

[17] Vincent Descombes, *Modern French Philosophy*, 66.
[18] Ibid., 71.

Intertwining, the Chiasm". These have rightly perplexed and intrigued many commentators, but they offer nothing sufficiently definite and substantial to have had much influence on future philosophical developments. By contrast, Merleau-Ponty's championing of Saussure and Lévi-Strauss (in several essays and, especially, in his lectures at the Collège de France) had an extraordinary impact and contributed to a huge upsurge of interest in the structuralist social sciences among philosophically minded students.[19] The irony, of course, is that this interest led to the undermining of existential phenomenology by structuralist and poststructuralist criticism.

The bridge from phenomenology to structuralism is apparent in the following crucial sentence from Merleau-Ponty's essay on Lévi-Strauss (derived from his presentation of Lévi-Strauss for membership in the Collège de France): "For the philosopher, the presence of structure outside of us in natural and social systems and within us as symbolic function points to a way beyond the subject–object correlation which has dominated philosophy from Descartes to Hegel" (*Signes* [*S*], 155/123). As we have seen, the positivist impulse in French philosophy split off into the scientific study of society. Durkheim was the leader of a new sociology that, as Merleau-Ponty notes, "wanted . . . to treat social facts 'as things' and no longer as 'objectified systems of ideas'" (*S*, 143/114). While positivist sociology tried to replace social meanings with causal relations among objects, French idealist philosophy continued to think of them as constituted by the intellectual activity of the mind. The one assimilated the mind to things, the other did the reverse; neither did justice to the combination of intimacy and separation that is our concrete life in the world.

According to Merleau-Ponty, Marcel Mauss, in his famous anthropological work on the gift, showed the way to a solution.[20] Mauss was sympathetic to positivist sociology (he was Durkheim's nephew and had worked with him). But he insisted that beyond the "concomitant variations and external correlations" of scientific sociology there is a "residue" that accounts for the acceptance of a given practice or institution by individuals. This residue is a domain of "social fact", not in the positivist sense of external causal factors but in the sense of "an efficacious system of symbols or a network of

---

[19] For details, see François Dosse, *History of Structuralism*, I: 37–42.
[20] Marcel Mauss, *Essai sur le don*.

symbolic values" that is "inserted into the depths of the individual" (*S*, 145/115).

Mauss, however, offered "more of an insight concerning the social than a theory about it" (*S*, 145/116). The latter task, according to Merleau-Ponty, was carried out by Lévi-Strauss, whose work parallels earlier work in linguistics by Saussure. Both Lévi-Strauss and Saussure give accounts of social realities (e.g., language, kinship relations) in terms of structures (although Saussure tends to use instead the term "systems"). These structures are meanings (that is, they "organize [their] constituent parts according to an internal principle" [*S*, 147/117]) and are therefore not reducible to causal relations among objects. At the same time, they are not the idealist's "crystallized ideas", since the subjects who live in accord with the meanings typically have no conscious grasp of them. People "make use of [structure] as a matter of course", but "rather than their having got it, it has, if we may put it this way, 'got them'" (*S*, 147/117).

Because structures are both objective realities, independent of any mind, and meanings informing the lives of individuals, they are the vehicle of the concrete unity of man-in-the-world. But we cannot limit ourselves to the study of structures alone. We also need to understand how structures enter into the lives of individuals. "The surprising logical operations attested to by the formal structures of societies must certainly be effected in some way by the populations which live these . . . systems" (for example, the kinship systems studied by Lévi-Strauss) (*S*, 149/119). Accordingly, for any given structure, we must look for "a sort of lived equivalent of that structure . . . The variables of anthropology . . . must be met with, sooner or later, on the level at which phenomena have an immediately human significance" (*S*, 150/119). In fact, Merleau-Ponty suggests, "this process of joining objective analysis to lived experience is perhaps the most proper task of anthropology, the one which distinguishes it from other social sciences such as economics and demography" (*S*, 149–50/119).

How are we to join "objective analysis to lived experience"? By "our insertion as social subjects into a whole in which the synthesis our intelligence looks for has already been effected" (*S*, 150/119). Such an "insertion" is, of course, immediately available to us in our direct experience of meanings in our ordinary life, and "we can gain some knowledge from this synthesis which is ourselves". Presumably, phenomenological description would be a main source of such knowledge. But there is also a need for "ethnological experience", which results from inserting ourselves into another culture so that we experience an "incessant testing of self through the other person and the other person through the self". Field work, in other words, is needed so that we can construct "a more comprehensive experience which becomes in principle accessible to men of a different time and country" (S, 150/120).

By understanding structure and its relation to lived experience, we come "to understand how we are in a sort of circuit with the socio-historical world" (S, 123) and thus overcome traditional philosophical mistakes of privileging the subject over the object or the object over the subject. Structuralism turns out to be just what Merleau-Ponty's phenomenological philosophy was looking for.

PART III

*Structuralism and Beyond
(1960–1990)*

CHAPTER 8

The structuralist invasion

> I liked to fix my thoughts only on what was still obscure to me, and to be able . . . thanks to the increasing but, alas, distorting and alien light of my intellect, to link to one another the fragmentary and interrupted lines of structure which at first had been almost hidden in mist.
> (Marcel Proust, *In Search of Lost Time*, v, 501)

Although Merleau-Ponty heralded structuralism as an essential complement to phenomenology and a key to solving its problem of the subject–object relation, the success of structuralism among philosophers was very soon proclaimed as the defeat of phenomenology. We need, accordingly, to look at the structuralist project and its appropriation by French intellectuals. I will begin with the two originary developments, Saussure's linguistics and Lévi-Strauss's anthropology, and then look at the work of Cavaillès, Canguilhem, and Serres, whose "philosophy of the concept" has important similarities to structuralism. Finally, I will briefly explore extensions of structuralism to social theory (Althusser), psychoanalysis (Lacan and Kristeva), and literary theory (Barthes).

SAUSSURE

From 1907 to 1911, Ferdinand de Saussure (1857–1913), a Swiss professor of linguistics, offered a course in general linguistics at the University of Geneva.[1] Although he never published anything based on this course, two of his colleagues did after his death. This book, *Cours de linguistique général*, is derived from notes taken by students the three times Saussure offered the course. Since there were very few notes made by Saussure himself and since his course was significantly

---

[1] For an excellent discussion of Saussure, see Jonathan Culler, *Ferdinand de Saussure*.

different each time he taught it, the *Cours* as published cannot be strictly regarded as an expression of Saussure's own views on linguistics. (More recent publications of the full text of Saussure's and his students' notes make it possible to go further in reconstructing what Saussure himself thought.) But it was the *Cours* as published in 1915 that so strongly influenced subsequent work in linguistics and the social sciences by putting forward the fundamental concepts of structuralism.

Saussure was convinced that despite the valuable work done on various aspects of linguistics throughout the nineteenth century, there was no clear conception of what the discipline was because there was no clear conception of what a language was. His project was to distinguish various aspects of language and to specify precisely the particular aspect that he thought should be the concern of linguistics. His main claims can be formulated in terms of a pair of distinctions he introduced, which have become fundamental in the terminology of linguistics and other structuralist studies.

The first distinction is between *parole* (speech) and *langue* (language). On the one hand, there are the actual speech acts (e.g., utterances or inscriptions of sentences) performed by people who speak a given language. On the other hand, there are the rules that govern those speech acts. The speech act "My computer crashed last night" is governed by various rules, ranging from laws of phonology to grammatical rules. If we think of language as the totality of actual speech acts, we are treating it, in Saussure's terminology, as *parole* or speech. If we think of it as the totality of rules governing speech acts, we are treating it as *langue* or language (in a technical sense). Another way to put the distinction: language is the *system* (the linguistic structure, defined by rules) that is somehow present in the mind of anyone who knows a given language; speech is the *realization* (or actualization) of this system in specific things said by a speaker. In terms later used by Noam Chomsky, language corresponds to a speaker's competence, and speech to a speaker's performance.[2]

Saussure's second key distinction is between the synchronic and the diachronic. On the one hand, a language has a specific structure

---

[2] *Langue* and *parole* apply to particular languages, not to language as a general category: *langue* is the system of rules for English or French, etc., not for language in general; *parole* is the totality of speech acts in English or French, etc. Chomsky postulated the existence of a single structure that defined generic linguistic competence, but this is not a step required by Saussure's distinction.

at any given time (e.g., right now there is a specific set of rules defining standard American English). On the other hand, every language develops over time (e.g., the transitions from Elizabethan to modern English). If we study the "instantaneous" structure of a language at a given time, we approach it *synchronically*; if we study its historical development over time, we approach it *diachronically*.

Saussure thought that the unclarity about the nature of linguistics as a discipline was largely due to confusions between language as *langue* and as *parole* and between synchronic and diachronic approaches. Some studies were historical, some structural; some focused on rules, some on acts. There was no hope of a unified discipline that tried to include all such studies. Saussure's own proposal, based on his views about what was most fundamental in language, was that linguistics should be understood as the synchronic study of linguistic systems. This did not mean that Saussure thought there was no room for studies of *parole* and of the diachronic. But he thought that linguistics as he construed it had priority over these other sorts of studies.

Given these distinctions, we can move to a discussion of Saussure's general view of language. Language (in the sense of *langue*) is not just any system but a system in which the basic elements are signs. As such, our understanding of it depends on our understanding of signs. At the heart of Saussure's linguistic theory is his distinctive (and, in many ways, counter-intuitive) account of signs.

It is perhaps easiest to understand Saussure on signs by contrasting his view with a common-sense one, which I will call "representationist". This is the view that signs are physical entities (marks or sounds) that are associated with ideas (used in the broad Cartesian sense to include concepts, feelings, perceptions, etc.) and that get their meaning from this association. On the representationist view, signs have no meanings in their own right but only from their association with ideas. So conceived, a language (a system of signs) is entirely derivative and parasitic. Meaning in the full and primary sense is in ideas ("the language of thought"), and verbal language is just an external mimicking of this primary system of meaning. Here there are two steps: first, we associate each simple idea with a single word (the concept *dog* with "dog", etc.); second, we associate relations between ideas (combinations that make for more complex ideas) with relations between words (e.g., the relation between a subject-concept – say, *dog* – and a predicate-concept – say, *barks* – is associated with the relation of juxtaposition between the words that correspond to the two concepts).

Saussure rejects the representationist view because he thinks it is based on the false assumption that ideas exist as meaningful units apart from their relation to language. According to him, thought (ideas) is not possible apart from our involvement in a linguistic system. There are, of course, mental events and states (or, at least, brain events and states) that exist independently of language. But, he maintains, such events and states have no meaning apart from their relation to linguistic systems. This is not a matter of simply reversing the representationist view and holding, implausibly, that words (the elements of language) have intrinsic meanings from which ideas derive their sense. Rather, Saussure maintains that neither words nor ideas have meanings in themselves. They come to have meaning only by being related to one another.

Saussure develops his position by introducing some crucial terminology, which became coin of the realm for structuralists. He uses "sign" to refer to the combination of a word and an idea as a related pair. (Note that, in this usage, a word is not, as we usually would say, a sign.) Further, the word as an element of a sign is called a "signifier" (*signifiant*), and the corresponding idea a "signified" (*signifié*). Thus, a sign is the union of a verbal signifier (a word) and a mental signified (an idea); and only the sign, not its components taken separately, has meaning. There is no realm of distinct thought (ideas) prior to the system that constitutes signs.

How does a sign come to have meaning? Or, perhaps better, in what does its meaning consist? Saussure's fundamental thesis here is that a sign's meaning is entirely a matter of its place in the overall system of signs and that this place is determined by the way it *differs* from each other sign. This point is best understood through a series of examples.

Consider first a non-linguistic case, the game of chess. What is a pawn? We might at first describe it in positive physical terms: a small wooden piece, narrower and round at the top, etc. But a little reflection shows that this is entirely wrong. A pawn could in fact be any sort of physical object, as we can see by thinking of substitutions we could make for a lost pawn. Realizing this, we might go on to say that what is really essential for a pawn is that it be moved in certain ways (one or two spaces forward on its first move, one thereafter, etc.). But even this can be misleading. It is not literally

The structuralist invasion

necessary that a pawn move forward; if the board were appropriately aligned, we might have to say that it moves up, down, or sideways. In fact, we could play chess in such a way that there was no literal sense at all in which the pieces moved. A "move" is nothing more than a transition from one state (position) to another. A given state could be defined by having a certain color, having clicked a certain number of times, being assigned a certain number. In sum, there is no particular set of positive characteristics that a pawn must in principle have. What is necessary is that its characteristics, whatever they are, be related to (specifically, differ from) the characteristics of the other pieces in the ways required by the rules of chess. For example, as we ordinarily play chess, a king on a far corner square can, in a single turn, move one space toward the opposite extreme square, whereas a bishop can move the entire distance. But we could play in such a way that a king could move the same as a bishop usually does, provided our board had a diagonal of sixty-four squares and a bishop was allowed to move this entire distance at once. Thus, the pawn can have any characteristic we like, provided appropriate changes are made in the characteristics of other pieces, that is, provided the differences in the characteristics are preserved.

Next consider the role of letters (and the sounds corresponding to them) in a language. We assign *b* a certain range of sounds and *d* a different range. But nothing essential would be lost if we systematically interchanged these two sound ranges – e.g., if instead of "The boy fell down" we said "The doy fell bown". Provided we maintain the systematic differences between the sounds, it doesn't matter what particular assignments are made.

Finally, consider the case of the meaning of color terms in a given language. It might seem that the meaning of a given color term is not, as Saussure maintains, simply a matter of its relation to other terms (particularly, color terms). We might in particular think that a color term's meaning essentially depends on the actual color to which it refers. (Thus, if a term means "red", then it must refer to red objects.) Suppose, however, we are trying to teach someone the meaning of "red" and do so simply by presenting a variety of red objects. Our student might never catch on, implicitly thinking perhaps that "red" refers to some other characteristic shared by all the objects presented (e.g., being smaller than the moon, being on the surface of the earth). To overcome this difficulty, we would have to present the student with objects that were exactly the same *except* for their color and tell the student that the one was red and the other blue or yellow or some other color. In this way, the student would learn all the colors at once, but precisely insofar as they *differ* from one another. Further, it would not matter at all, from the viewpoint of language competence, what actual colors the student saw, provided the system of differences were maintained. Maybe the sky is in fact blue to you but red to me (in terms of sense data or even wavelengths producing them). This does not matter as long as we both say "blue" when asked the color of the daytime sky, the sea on a clear day, etc.

To sum up: On the level of *parole* (actual speech acts), a sign (signifier plus signified) will of course always have some specific positive content. A spoken or written word (signifier) will have particular auditory or spatial qualities and will be associated with an idea (a feeling, an image – the signified) that also has particular qualities (painful, bright, etc.). But, according to Saussure, two signs with entirely different contents (signifier and signified) will have the same meaning provided the ways in which the two signs differ from other signs in their system remains the same. Linguistic meaning is, accordingly, not a matter of content but of form or structure, as defined by a system of differences. This is what is meant by saying that Saussure's linguistics is structuralist.

On Saussure's account, there are three basic levels of linguistic structure and, at each level, two fundamental types of relations among signs. The lowest level of linguistic structure is that of the phoneme (the phonological level). A phoneme is a least unit of sound (e.g., long *a*, terminal *t*), with the set of all a language's phonemes defined by the linguistically significant differences among them. (Various accents correspond to permissible ranges of differences in the same basic phonemes – i.e., to sound-differences that are not linguistically significant.) Then there is the level of the morpheme (the morphological level). Morphemes are the least units of meaning, including not only simple words but also prefixes, suffixes, and the like. Finally, there is the level of the sentence (the syntactical level). The project of linguistics is to discover the rules according to which the elements of each level combine.

At each level of linguistic structure, Saussure finds relations of two distinct types: paradigmatic (or, as he put it, associative) and syntagmatic. Paradigmatic relations obtain between terms that yield different results when substituted into a given linguistic context. Thus, at the phonological level, /s/ is partially defined by the fact that there is a phonologically significant difference between /sag/, on the one hand, and /bag/, /rag/, /tag/, etc. on the other. On the morphological level, the differences among words such as *friend, lecture, professor*, etc. are partly defined by the differences they make when combined with the suffix *-ship*. On the syntactical level, a set of expressions such as *three miles, for my health*, and *along the seashore* is differentiated from a set such as *of miles, my health*, and *the seashore* by the fact the members of the first but not the second can meaningfully follow *I ran*. In a paradigmatic relation, the related terms are opposing alternatives to one another: we get different linguistic meanings by substituting one rather than the other. Syntagmatic relations hold between terms that can be combined with one another to form more complex linguistic units. Thus, phonologically, /s/ is partly defined by the fact that, unlike other consonants, it is able to precede /p/. Morphologically, *care* can combine with *-ful, -less*, and *-ing*, but not with *-ly, -est*, or *-ness*. Syntactically, *he told* can combine with *a lie, on her*, and *what he knew*, but not with *orange, yourself*, or *into*. Terms related syntagmatically are not opposing alternatives but complementary components. Saussure maintained that every aspect of linguistic structure could be expressed in terms of these relations of contrast and combination.

LÉVI-STRAUSS

Although by his own account Claude Lévi-Strauss (b. 1908) found the initial inspiration for his structuralist approach to anthropology in geology, he soon came to see that the best model was in fact linguistics. In fact, his work is a prime example of the extension of Saussure's view of language to non-linguistic signs. (Saussure anticipated such extensions with his concept of semiology, a general science of signs of which linguistics would be just one branch.)

The basic strategy in extending structuralism to non-linguistic phenomena is to identify elements, parallel to words or other linguistic units, that can be combined to form complexes that have some sort of social "meaning". In each case, there are, first, various sets of alternative possibilities (related to each other paradigmatically) and, second, various ways of combining selections from each set to form complex expressions (defined by syntagmatic relations).

The system of fashion provides a simple example.[3] Here the paradigmatic sets of alternatives are different sorts of clothing – e.g., head coverings (hats, hoods, bonnets), leg coverings (pants, skirts, shorts), and foot coverings (shoes, sandals). The syntagmatic combinations are various total "outfits" put together by selecting one from each of the paradigmatic sets (e.g., a bonnet, pants, sandals, etc.), thereby making a fashion "statement". We can think in the same way of the dishes served at a multi-course meal, of the arrangement of furniture in a room, and of the architectural design of a building.

Lévi-Strauss takes the basic approach of structural linguistics (as developed not only by Saussure but also by others in his tradition, especially Roman Jakobson and Nicholas Troubetzkoy) and applies it to anthropological phenomena such as kinship systems and myths. In each case, appreciating what Lévi-Strauss is doing requires a clear sense of how he employs Saussure's signifier/signified distinction. Put generally, the signified is always in the domain of thought (as in Saussure, an undifferentiated mass prior to its "formation" by the relevant structure). Thus, for the case of kinship relations, the signifieds are the thoughts of a culture about family relations, for example, about degrees of relation, respect due to relationships, and incest taboos; the signifiers are the specific practices (customs, rituals, etc.) that "express" these thoughts. As in the case of Saussurean linguistics, Lévi-Strauss's approach contrasts with a representationist one. He does not see a society or culture as having certain ideas about kinship (or the gods, or animal totems) that are then implemented by practices corresponding to them, the practices being material images of the society's "self-understanding". Rather, both the ideas and the practices are specified by their shared formal structure, once again understood in terms of differences between elements within a system.

Lévi-Strauss's approach to totemism offers a useful example of his structuralist approach. Certain animals (or even natural objects such as trees or volcanoes) often play a central role in the lives of cultures. These are called "totems", and their role often seems to betray a distinctively "primitive" way of thought, characterized by absurd beliefs about the community's relation to the totems. Tribes might, for example, say that they are the children of an eagle or that their village was built by a panther. Lévi-Strauss questions our inclination

---

[3] For a more complex elaboration, see Roland Barthes' semiotics of fashion, *Système de la mode*.

to interpret such statements as naive and false. He likewise questions a standard anthropological interpretation of totems as having simply a functional value within a society (e.g., preserving a valuable resource, providing a basis for social unity, supporting the authority of the rulers). He maintains instead that totemic talk and practices should be understood as expressions of a culture's fundamental categories in concrete rather than abstract form.

Consider the following contrived and greatly oversimplified example. A given tribe says that it is descended from a Great Eagle, who nests in an inaccessible spot atop a neighboring mountain. Stories about this eagle and its relations with early members of the tribe are correlated with various tribal practices. Perhaps adolescent males are given special headdresses of eagle feathers as part of an initiation rite, it being said that they thus become eagles (or receive an eagle guardian) and so must never kill an eagle except under special, ritually controlled circumstances; pregnant women are forbidden to visit the neighboring mountain, on the grounds that the Eagle will steal the souls of the children they are carrying; clay figures of eagles are exchanged by the parents of marrying couples and said to have special healing powers.

A "primitivist" explanation would account for these practices on the basis of beliefs held by tribal members out of ignorance and confusion. Perhaps some early tribe members wore eagle head-dresses for ornament and other tribes, seeing them at a distance, mistook them for large eagles; perhaps some pregnant women had miscarriages after stumbling on the rocky terrain of the mountain. Such events, the primitivist will argue, have been transformed over time into the childish beliefs the tribe now has (helped, no doubt, by the primitives' love of the fantastic and the mysterious). A functionalist explanation would rather point out that, for example, eagle feathers are a valuable trading commodity for the tribe and the totemic status of the bird prevents overuse that might lead to extinction, that it is dangerous for pregnant women to be climbing mountains and the taboo prevents this, and so on.

By contrast with both these approaches, Lévi-Strauss would suggest that we regard the totemic Eagle as part of a categorial system whereby the tribe classifies and thus understands the objects and facts of its world. Perhaps, for example, "eagle" expresses the concept of "hunting in the mountains", which is how the tribe gets its food (whereas a neighboring tribe, that fishes in the river, might be said to be descended from a Great Salmon). More generally, Lévi-Strauss's idea is that a system of relations among natural objects becomes a complex metaphor for (or a set of categories for understanding) social practices and relations. Thus, natural facts about how eagles hunt, their relations to salmon, the nature of their mountain dwellings, etc. would all be used to express social facts about the human world of the tribe. Putting this in structuralist terms, the idea is that the natural "eagle-world" possesses the same formal structure as the tribe's social world. The totemic system is essentially a logic: a system of categories for thinking about the social world. In contrast to functionalist accounts, Lévi-Strauss's sees totems not as "good for eating" (or for other biological and social needs) but "good for thinking".

Lévi-Strauss's structuralist anthropology rejects the normative distinction between "primitive" and "advanced" societies. He agrees that thought can be either abstract or concrete but denies that there is any superiority of the latter over the former. Tribes that think via concrete categories are just doing in another way what we do with our abstractions. They are not at an earlier, less developed stage of thought.

Lévi-Strauss also asserts a universalism regarding the structures of human thought and society and insists on the priority of the unconscious in human life. He maintains that his studies provide a good inductive basis for generalizations about the structures of all human societies and also show that these structures are not typically things of which individuals are consciously aware. Our thought and behavior are informed by universal unconscious structures. Finally, the most pervasive and fundamental structure of human life is that defined by the opposition of nature and culture. The entire framework of any society's understanding of its world is developed as a response to the question of just how human beings are related to the natural (non-human) world.

STRUCTURALISM AND PHENOMENOLOGY

We have seen how Merleau-Ponty heralded structuralism as a key to solving the phenomenological problem of the relation of subject and object. The idea of cooperation between the two approaches is likewise suggested by the fact that Lévi-Strauss's *La pensée sauvage*, the major statement of the philosophical significance of his structuralist anthropology, is dedicated to the memory of Merleau-Ponty. But it is precisely in the final chapter of this book that Lévi-Strauss opposes his structuralism to phenomenology's subject-centered descriptions of human reality. He explicitly attacks Sartre's recently published *Critique de la raison dialectique*, defending "analytic reason" against what he sees as Sartre's imperialism of "dialectical reason". But his critique, if effective, clearly applies to any standpoint that takes the phenomenological subject as primary.

Lévi-Strauss's central claim is that Sartre's phenomenological (or dialectical) understanding of human beings can only be a starting-point, one that must be completed by an objective, analytic grasp of the unconscious structures underlying and common to the lived worlds of the immense variety of human communities. He does not deny that what phenomenologists describe has an irreducible validity that anthropology cannot ignore. Admittedly, he says that "the ultimate goal of the human sciences [is] not to constitute, but to dissolve man", where "man" means human beings as they concretely experience themselves. And he even goes on to speak of a "reduction" of this experience to more fundamental (eventually, physico-chemical) levels of understanding. But he also insists that for such a reduction to be legitimate "the phenomena subject to reduction must not be impoverished; one must be certain that everything contributing to their distinctive richness and originality has been collected around them" (*La pensée sauvage* [*PS*], 327/247). As a result, the reduction will not mean the elimination of the reduced level in favor of a simpler and thinner reality. Rather the reduced "superior" level will "communicate retroactively some of its richness to the inferior level to which it will have been assimilated" (*PS*, 328/248). Thus, even on the purely physical level, "when we do finally succeed in understanding life as a function of inert matter, it will be to discover that the latter has properties very different from those previously attributed to it" (*PS*, 327-8/247-8).

But even though the phenomenological level is in this sense ineliminable, it remains true that unconscious structures, not accessible to phenomenological description, are the locus of the ultimate truth about human beings. By remaining on the level of lived experience, Sartre and the other existentialists have limited themselves to the partial truths of subjectivity:

He who begins by steeping himself in the allegedly self-evident truths of introspection never emerges from them. Knowledge of men sometimes seems easier to those who allow themselves to be caught up in the snare of personal identity. But they thus shut the door on knowledge of man . . . Sartre in fact becomes the prisoner of his Cogito. (*PS*, 330/249)

And if we reply that this is not true of *Critique de la raison dialectique*, which moves from the individual to the social level, Lévi-Strauss replies that "by sociologizing the Cogito, Sartre merely exchanges one prison for another" (*PS*, 330/249). The limitation of Sartre's position is most apparent in its inability to understand the fundamental role of language, as explicated by modern linguistics: "Language, an unreflecting totalization, is human reason which has its reasons and of which man [i.e., the subject of first-person experience] knows nothing" (*PS*, 334/252).

The validity of the phenomenological standpoint is limited and local. Viewed analytically in terms of an objective and comparative anthropological account of the underlying structures of human societies, it can be only partial and misleading. Here, Lévi-Strauss maintains, Sartre has ignored the lessons of Marx and Freud. Like Sartre, they agree, as does Lévi-Strauss, "that man has meaning only on the condition that he view himself as meaningful". But they add what Sartre ignores: "that this meaning is never the right one: superstructures are faulty acts which have 'made it' socially. Hence it is vain to go to historical consciousness for the truest meaning" (*PS*, 336/253-4).

Sartre might well respond that he is entirely aware of the vast influence of pregiven, sedimented meanings, of what he himself called the "practico-inert". His only point is that we are always to at least some extent capable of constituting a meaning of our own, even if it is constrained by a given world we are not able to penetrate entirely. We are, in other words, always able to forge our own history out of the materials with which we are presented. It is this conception of humans as distinctively historical agents, that is, makers of their own existence, that is central to his position. But according to Lévi-Strauss, Sartre fails to realize that this very conception of ourselves as historical (i.e., as agents making our own history) is merely our local and contingent way of thinking about ourselves, not a fundamental truth of human reality. Whereas "primitive" societies see themselves as passive receivers of an ahistorical pattern decreed by their gods, we see ourselves as active creators of our own meanings. But there is no basis for objectively preferring our view over that of the primitives. Sartre's "position in relation to history is therefore the same as that of primitives to the eternal past: in Sartre's system, history plays exactly the role of myth" (*PS*, 336/254).

Sartre is blind to this parallel (and hence to the symmetry between the disciplines of history and anthropology) because he thinks that historical societies such as ours have the advantage of making reflectively explicit what, in primitive societies, is merely implicit in their praxis. But here he misunderstands what is going on in primitive societies. Primitive practices – for example, initiation rites, which are strikingly similar in very different societies – are not thought buried beneath blind and inarticulate customs. They are rather thought itself, organizing and making intelligible the natural and social world. The thought is concrete, in contrast to our abstract categories, but it is not for all that inferior or, more to the point, less free than ours.

Sartre's mistake, then, is to maintain that his (our) way of categorizing the world is privileged. In this, of course, he is hardly unique. "Each of the tens or hundreds or thousands of societies which have existed . . . has claimed that it contains the essence of all the meaning and dignity of which human society is capable." Sartre's claim of privilege for modern European thought differs little from the parallel claim of "a Melanesian savage". In all cases, "a good deal of egocentricity and naïvety is necessary to believe that man has taken refuge in a single one of the historical or geographical modes of his existence" (*PS*, 329/249). Accordingly, Sartre's thought is "unqualified to pass judgment on" the savage mind because it shares its fundamental characteristics. On the other hand, "to the anthropologist . . . this philosophy (like all the others) affords a first-class ethnographic document, the study of which is essential to an understanding of the mythology of our own time" (*PS*, 330n/249n).[4]

PHILOSOPHY OF THE CONCEPT: CAVAILLÈS, CANGUILHEM, AND SERRES

For all its originality, structuralism was not the first major movement in France to oppose the centrality of the subject. As Foucault, commenting on the philosophical world in which he was educated,

---

[4] In the next chapter, we will discuss Sartre's response to the structuralist challenge in the context of Foucault's *Les mots et les choses*.

pointed out, there was, well before structuralism, a basic split in French philosophy between a "philosophy of experience, of meaning, of the subject and a philosophy of knowledge [*savoir*], of rationality, and of the concept".[5] In Foucault's student days, the "philosophy of experience" was, of course, existential phenomenology (but Foucault located earlier instantiations of it in the various versions of spiritualism and in Bergson). The "philosophy of the concept" was historically tied to the French tradition, ultimately traceable to Comte, of the history and philosophy of science. In the latter half of the twentieth century, this tradition was primarily represented by Gaston Bachelard and his successor as director of the Sorbonne's Institut d'Histoire des Sciences et des Techniques, Georges Canguilhem. Although the work of Bachelard and Canguilhem was scarcely known outside of France, where French philosophy was simply identified with existential phenomenology, they were major influences on several generations of French philosophy students and their "philosophy of the concept" remained a significant alternative to existential philosophy.

Indeed, but for the contingencies of the war, there might well have been a "conceptual" appropriation of Husserl to rival Sartre's and Merleau-Ponty's "experiential" readings. Jean Cavaillès (1903–1944), writing in the 1940s, had offered a brilliant formal reading of Husserl that moved his thought away from its Heideggerian future and back toward its origins in logic and the philosophy of mathematics.[6] For example, commenting on Husserl's *Formal and Transcendental Logic*, he concluded: "It is not a philosophy of consciousness but a philosophy of the concept which can provide a theory of science."[7] Unfortunately, Cavaillès, who was one of the founders of the French Resistance to the Nazi occupation of France, was captured by the Germans and executed. His "rationalist" development of phenomenology was continued by, among others, Suzanne Bachelard (the daughter of Gaston Bachelard) and the Belgian Jean Ladrière. But the existentialized Husserl remained dominant in France.

The philosophy of the concept is also strongly represented in the

---

[5] Michel Foucault, "Life: Experience and Science", in *Essential Works of Michel Foucault, 1954–1984, Volume II: Aesthetics, Method, and Epistemology*, 466.
[6] Jean Cavaillès, *Méthode axiomatique et formalisme* and *Remarques sur la formation de la théorie abstraite des ensembles*.
[7] Jean Cavaillès, "On Logic and the Theory of Science", 409.

work of Georges Canguilhem (1904–95).[8] Although Canguilhem starts from an essentially Bachelardian view of science, the foci of his work are different from Bachelard's: philosophical history rather than historical philosophizing, the biological and medical sciences rather than physics and chemistry. Further, his results suggest a number of important modifications in Bachelard's position.

Canguilhem's most important methodological contribution is his distinction between concepts and theories. In much twentieth-century philosophy of science, concepts are functions of theories, deriving their meaning from the roles they play in theoretical accounts of phenomena. Newtonian and Einsteinian mass, for example, are regarded as fundamentally different concepts because they are embedded in fundamentally different physical theories. This subordination of concept to theory derives from the view that the interpretation of phenomena (that is, their subsumption under a given set of concepts) is a matter of explaining them on the basis of a particular theoretical framework. For Canguilhem, by contrast, there is a crucial distinction between the interpretation of phenomena (via concepts) and their theoretical explanation. According to him, a given set of concepts provides the preliminary descriptions of a phenomenon that allow the formulation of questions about how to explain it. Different theories (all, however, formulated in terms of the same set of basic concepts) will provide competing answers to these questions. Galileo, for example, introduced a new conception of the motion of falling bodies to replace the Aristotelian conception. Galileo, Descartes, and Newton all employed this new conception in their description of the motion of falling bodies and in the theories they developed to explain this motion. Although the basic concept of motion was the same, the explanatory theories were very different. This shows, according to Canguilhem, the "theoretical polyvalence" of concepts: their ability to function in the context of widely differing theories. His own historical studies (for example, of reflex movement) are typically histories of concepts that persist through a series of theoretical formulations.

Taken seriously, Canguilhem's emphasis on the history of concepts as opposed to the history of theories requires important modifications in Bachelard's view of science. Epistemological breaks, for

---

[8] For a more detailed discussion of Canguilhem, see my *Michel Foucault's Archaeology of Scientific Knowledge*, chapter 1. Translations of some of Canguilhem's important essays are available in *A Vital Rationalist: Selected Writings from Georges Canguilhem*.

example, must be construed as due to conceptual rather than theoretical innovation. Since successful conceptualizations tend to reappear in even quite diverse theories, epistemological breaks are, for Canguilhem, less frequent and, in many cases, less radical than Bachelard had suggested. The priority of concepts also requires us to rethink the notion of an epistemological obstacle. The same piece of scientific work may be an obstacle in terms of the theoretical context in which it is formulated and a creative breakthrough in terms of some of its conceptual content. Thus, the eighteenth-century chemist Joseph Black, even though he worked in the now outdated context of phlogiston theory, introduced the enduring concept of specific heat. The notion of an epistemological obstacle is more ambivalent than Bachelard suggests. Canguilhem makes particularly effective use of this ambivalence in his discussion of vitalism, so often abused as an enemy of progress in biology. Canguilhem admits that vitalistic theories have generally impeded the development of more adequate mechanistic accounts, but he maintains that the concept of vitalism, through its insistence on the uniqueness of biological phenomena, has served as a valuable protection against unfortunate reductionist tendencies of mechanistic theories.

Canguilhem's refinement of the notions of epistemological breaks and obstacles also suggests a weakening of Bachelard's sharp distinction between science and non-science. Science is what overcomes epistemological obstacles and effects epistemological breaks. To the extent that the notions of obstacle and break have become ambivalent, so has the notion of science. As a result, Canguilhem is reluctant to say more than that in a given context, a given idea or approach is "more scientific" than another (e.g., more fully integrated into current experimental procedures). Further developing this line of thought, Canguilhem (influenced here by his students, Althusser and Foucault) introduced the notion of *scientific ideology* as an intermediary between science and non-science.[9]

A scientific ideology (Herbert Spencer's philosophy of evolution is a good example) is scientific in the sense that it models itself on a successful scientific theory. It is ideological, however, because it makes claims about the world that go beyond what the science contemporary with it is able to establish; it has, in other words, pretensions that are not scientifically grounded. Such pretensions

---

[9] Georges Canguilhem, *Idéologie et rationalité*.

may very well function as obstacles to the development of science. But Canguilhem also sees a positive role for scientific ideologies: they provide an essential, if not entirely responsible, dimension of intellectual adventure, without which many scientific advances would not occur. Scientific ideologies are a prime example of the ambivalence of epistemological obstacles.

Like other anti-foundational philosophers of science, Canguilhem pays particular attention to the problem of rationality and objectivity. If there are no Cartesian certainties grounding science, if its development is a contingent historical process, what guarantee do we have that it is a reliable source of truths about the world? Bachelard tried to ground the objectivity of science through social norms. Contrary to Descartes, he holds that objectivity is not found in the individual self's intuitions (which will always remain obstacles to scientific progress) but in considerations that convince all rational minds. This move from the isolated *cogito* (I think) to the social *cogitamus* (we think), takes us, Bachelard maintains, from the subjectivity of the merely psychological to the objectivity of the epistemological.

Canguilhem offers a much more extensive treatment of norms, rooted in his analysis of biological norms.[10] He notes that whereas modern physics has rejected any distinction between normal and pathological states of its entities, biological systems (organisms) require a distinction between states that enhance their functioning and those that impede it; in other words, a distinction between health and disease. However, Canguilhem maintains, we cannot define health as simply life in accord with the relevant biological norms. In any state, even one that is clearly pathological, there will be norms specifying the proper functioning of the organism in that state. (For example, a person who has lost a kidney is in a pathological state, even though the norms for proper functioning in this state are the same as for someone with both kidneys.) The pathological must, accordingly, be understood rather as a reduction in the range of circumstances in which an organism can function properly. Correspondingly, health is a state in which an organism is not only able to survive in its current circumstances but is capable of surviving in a significant range of varying circumstances.

Canguilhem emphasizes that according to his account biological

[10] Georges Canguilhem, *On the Normal and the Pathological*.

norms are not objective in any scientific sense. Physiology can describe the states that we call "normal" or "pathological", but their normative status as such derives not from the physiological description but from the meaning of those states for the organism. Put another way, biological norms are subjective in the sense that they are constituted by the organism itself. On the other hand, this constitution is not a matter of individual idiosyncrasy but corresponds to the essential nature of the organism in question. Biological norms are not objective in the sense of being derived from value-neutral scientific inquiry, but they are rooted in the biological reality of the organisms that they regulate.

Turning to the question of social norms, such as those Bachelard sees as governing scientific practice, Canguilhem notes that there are important ways in which societies are similar to organisms and that social norms can have the same sort of necessary force that biological norms do. The biological analogy works, however, only for so-called "traditional" societies, where there is a set of norms that defines, once and for all, the essential nature and purpose of the society. Modern societies have no such "intrinsic finality", since the question of what should be their fundamental direction is contested in principle. A distinguishing feature of a modern society such as ours is dissent regarding basic norms. Canguilhem does not conclude, however, that a consensus, no matter how formed, would legitimately establish norms in a modern society. He criticizes, for example, Thomas Kuhn's account of scientific norms because, in his view, it derives them from a contingent, merely psychological agreement that has no genuine regulative force. Canguilhem makes a similar criticism of Bachelard, who, he suggests, poses but does not solve the problem of finding a middle ground between grounding scientific norms in the illusion of Cartesian foundations and reducing them to the merely descriptive realm of empirical psychology. Unfortunately, Canguilhem himself never provides a solution to this problem and, after all the subtlety of his analysis of norms, they are still left without a philosophical basis. Canguilhem's treatment of normativity provides the context for Foucault's discussions, especially in *Surveiller et punir* and volume 1 of *Histoire de la sexualité*, of norms as an instrument of societal power.

The work of Michel Serres (b. 1930) not only continues the tradition of the philosophy of the concept; it also converges with structuralism. Vincent Descombes, in fact, says that, strictly speaking, Serres is the only structuralist philosopher.[11] Although he is by no means a disciple of Bachelard and Canguilhem, there are important ways in which Serres's work is a continuation and transformation of theirs. Like Bachelard, Serres emphasizes the dispersed, regional character of scientific work. Each domain is like a Leibnizian monad, with a life and intelligibility of its own. (The comparison to Leibniz is far from superficial. Serres wrote his thesis on the Leibnizian system and his subsequent work can be very fruitfully read as a twentieth-century reformulation of Leibniz's philosophy.) But here, unlike Bachelard but like Foucault, Serres sees a structural unity that connects independent scientific domains. He explicates this unity in terms of the concept of communication, which he expresses through both the metaphor of the Greek god Hermes and the formalism of modern communication theory.[12]

Serres also questions Bachelard's sharp demarcation of science from non-science. Here one of his motives is ethical: he thinks that science separated from the humanities compels us to the terminal violence represented by nuclear weapons.[13] But Serres also offers interpretations designed to show how domains conventionally regarded as non-scientific, such as art and literature, share the structures of scientific disciplines and must be regarded as their epistemic peers. So, for example, he claims that Emile Zola expressed thermodynamics in his novels before it was explicitly formulated by physicists, tries to show the structural identity of Descartes' *Méditations* and La Fontaine's fables, argues that "Turner translates Carnot", and presents Lucretius' *De Rerum Natura* as a contribution to twentieth-century physical theory.

Similarly, Serres's own writings are a stimulating, if often disconcerting mixture of the mathematical, the philosophical, and the artistic. His style combines close technical analysis with poetic evocation, and casual readers may be in doubt as to whether they have picked up a philosophical treatise or a prose poem. Serres would, of course, maintain that such apparent incongruities simply

---

[11] Vincent Descombes, *Modern French Philosophy*, 85, 87. The structuralism derives, however, not from structuralist social science but from mathematics (especially abstract algebra and topology), which Serres studied at an advanced level. See Michel Serres and Bruno Latour, *Conversations on Science, Culture, and Time*, 10.

[12] *Hermès*, in fact, is the general title of the five volumes of essays that make up the bulk of Serres's publications from 1968 to 1980.

[13] Serres says he has been strongly influenced in this by Simone Weil's reflections on violence (Serres and Latour, *Conversations on Science, Culture, and Time*, 18).

reflect the limitations of conventional intellectual categories and that the pursuit of truth requires the transgression of artificial disciplinary boundaries.

Serres's more recent work has moved from historical commentaries to the construction of a poetico-philosophical cosmology that can be thought of as expressing the metaphysics implicit in his earlier writings. The cosmology is one of flux and relations, a "philosophy of prepositions", not of substantives, that bears a broad resemblance to Deleuze's. Here Serres's preferred mathematical structures are chaos theory and fractal geometry, and the image of Hermes is replaced by that of a multitude of angels, embodiments of the chaotic multiplicity of messages that constitute reality.[14]

The continuing tradition of philosophy of the concept provided an alternative to Sartre and Merleau-Ponty even in the heyday of existential phenomenology and was an important factor in the positive reception of structuralism in the 1960s. It was particularly significant, as we shall see in discussing Michel Foucault, for its ability to sustain an approach to the history of thought that did not assume the centrality of subjectivity. Moreover, after the decline of structuralism, it helped sustain poststructuralist decenterings of the subject and its experience.

THE HIGH TIDE OF STRUCTURALISM

In the 1960s, structuralism spread quickly to philosophy from its base in linguistics and anthropology and particularly gained force from its association with a second wave of French interest in German-language thinkers.[15] Whereas the 1930s had seen appropriations of Hegel, Husserl, and Heidegger, now similar attention was directed to, as Ricoeur famously put it, the three "masters of suspicion": Marx, Freud, and Nietzsche. Interest in Nietzsche was primarily tied to later, poststructuralist developments, but Marx and Freud were the focus of the structuralist projects of Althusser and

---

[14] See *Le tiers-instruit*, *Le contrat naturel*, and *La légende des anges*, all of which have been academic best-sellers in France.

[15] One of the requirements for a *licence* in philosophy was a certificate in some scientific area. Since most philosophy students had little background in the "hard" sciences, they frequently chose to fulfill the requirement in the social sciences. This helps explain the rapidity with which philosophers became aware of new developments in the social sciences. See Michel Serres's comments on this point in Michel Serres and Bruno Latour, *Conversations on Science, Culture, and Time*, 35.

Marx and Althusser

French philosophical disdain for scientistic positivism, combined with the overwhelming social and political dominance of the bourgeoisie, stifled any serious interest in Marx before the 1930s. But the "existential" readings of Hegel by Wahl and, especially, by Kojève led to similar approaches to Marx. This "new Marx" found a ready audience among the young philosophers of existence. The interest increased enormously after the war. On the political side, this was due to the existentialists' commitment to "engaged thinking" and the moral high ground the French Communist Party held because of its central role in the Resistance during the war. Intellectually, there was the increasing availability of Marx's early and much more "humanistic" writings[16] and the engagement with them (focusing on the concept of alienation) by a wide range of intellectuals, from Communists such as Henri Lefebvre to Catholics such as Jean Calvez.[17] We have already seen Sartre's stormy political relation to Communism and his intellectual synthesis of Marxism and existentialism in *Critique de la raison dialectique*.

French Communist Party intellectuals, mainly occupied with the dubious business of justifying Stalinist policies, themselves took quite a while coming to terms with the new Marx. However, with the ideological and political thaw that followed Khrushchev's denunciation of Stalin in February 1956, Party philosophers, led by Roger Garaudy, joined in the Marxist humanist parade. They began discussing topics such as alienation and, in line with the new Soviet policy of "peaceful coexistence", initiated dialogues with non-Marxist existentialists and even Christians.

Louis Althusser (1918–90), a young philosopher and Communist Party member, opposed the humanistic interpretation of Marx with

---

[16] Translations of the early writings began appearing in 1927, although even by 1937 there was only a partial and defective translation of the important Paris manuscripts of 1844 (translated as *Économie politique et philosophie*). For details on the early history of Marxism in France, see chapter 2 of Mark Poster, *Existential Marxism in Postwar France*.

[17] These French discussions were also influenced by earlier developments of a humanistic Marxism by the "Central European Marxists", especially Georg Lukács, whose thought was introduced into France by his disciple, Lucien Goldman.

his structuralist-inspired "theoretical anti-humanism". Althusser taught at the École Normale, where he was charged with preparing students for the *agrégation*[18] and developed an enthusiastic circle of young Marxist disciples, including Pierre Macherey and Étienne Balibar.[19] Like Lévi-Strauss, Althusser held that the experience given primacy by phenomenology and existentialism represented nothing more than subjectivist mythology. In Marxist terms, individual experience is just a form of ideological distortion that cannot function as the basis of an objective theory of society. Althusser did not deny that Marx's earlier work, inspired by Hegel, had the subjectivist cast of the humanist interpretations. But he maintained that Marx broke with this approach around 1845 (with his *German Ideology* and *Theses on Feuerbach*) and that his mature theory in *Capital* fits the structuralist ideal of objective science.

In opposition to the phenomenologists' claim that lived experience is epistemically primary and provides the basis for a philosophical foundation of science, Althusser adopted Bachelard's view that we must begin from an undisputed scientific achievement and develop our philosophical view of the world and of science by reflection on that achievement.[20] What Newton and Einstein had provided for the physical world, Marx's *Capital* had provided for the social world. Following standard Marxist lines, Althusser distinguished between *historical materialism*, understood as Marx's achievement of an objective scientific account of the social world, and *dialectical materialism*, understood as a philosophical grasp of the nature and significance of Marx's scientific work. In Althusser's view, Marx's writings establish the science of historical materialism but do not fully carry out the philosophical conceptualization of this achievement through dialectical materialism.

Again deploying Bachelardian concepts, Althusser reads Marx's historical materialism as effecting a twofold "epistemic break": first with the existential subjectivism present in his early writings, and second with scientific models that reduce the social to a nexus of mechanical causes and effects. According to Althusser, Marx's path

---

[18] This was the position known in the slang of the École Normale as *caïman* (alligator).
[19] For the views of a student with a strongly negative assessment of Althusser's influence, see Jacques Bouveresse, *Le philosophe et le réel*, 91–4.
[20] For a detailed and critically perceptive account of Althusser's relation to Bachelard, see Peter Dews, "Althusser, Structuralism, and the French Epistemological Tradition", in Gregory Elliott (ed.), *Althusser: a Critical Reader*, 104–41.

between these two "epistemic obstacles" is precisely that of structural analysis. Marx understood any society ("social formation") as made up of a "base" of economic forces ("forces of production") and a "superstructure" of political, cultural, and intellectual objects and institutions. On naive scientific accounts, any element of the superstructure (say, the outcome of a given election or the writing of a given novel) is viewed as directly caused by specific features of the economic base. Althusser sees Marx as rejecting such accounts and instead explaining social phenomena by appealing to the joint operation of a variety of levels of structures, including not only the economic but also, among others, the political and the ideological. Rather than reductively explaining in terms of only economic forces, Marx explains via a structuralist principle of "overdetermination" (in the Freudian sense), according to which each level of social structure makes an irreducible contribution to the outcome. At the same time, since the various levels of social structure operate independently of individual consciousnesses, Marx also avoids subjectivism.

The principle of overdetermination guarantees the relative autonomy of the social superstructure, but it is nonetheless consistent with Marx's fundamental insistence on the ultimate priority of the economic base. This is because the overall structure of a society and the mode of interaction of its various structural levels is determined "in the last instance" by economic factors. In any given explanation, all structural levels will be involved and the economic may even be of relatively minor significance. (In some social formations, in fact, a non-economic level may typically dominate; for example, according to Althusser, the primary mode for explaining features of feudal society is political.) But if we persist in seeking deeper and deeper levels of explanation (for example, if we ask why political structures dominate feudal society), the ultimate answer will have to be in economic terms. In this way, Althusser's Marx can avoid naive postulations of immediate economic causes of everything that happens without giving up his insight into the final social priority of the economic.[21]

Since humanist Marxists were strong critics of Stalinist repression, Althusser's anti-humanism tended to be seen as a defense of Stalin-

---

[21] In a similar way, theologians have been able to maintain the autonomous action of created "secondary causes" while still recognizing God as the sole "primary cause". This comparison would not have been entirely foreign to Althusser, who in his youth had been a devout Catholic.

ism. But although like many other Party members Althusser often remained silent in the face of Soviet outrages, there is no need to read his Marxist theorizing as an endorsement of terror. Seeing the experiences of individuals as having no effective role in the development of society does not entail having no concern for human suffering. Moreover, Althusser saw his view as providing a Marxist response to the Stalinist claim that political events and institutions such as the Moscow trials and the concentration camps were justified as inevitable superstructural features of a clearly desirable socialist economic base. Given the relative autonomy of the superstructure, Althusser could maintain that Stalin's terror was the product of superstructural factors not necessitated by a socialist economic base.

The work of Althusser and his students in the 1960s quickly eclipsed that of existential Marxists such as Sartre. In particular, their theorization of Marxism provided the basis, during the late 60s, for the support of the French Communist Party by *Tel quel*, the leading avant-garde literary journal. Although Althusser, like the Party itself, had little role in the student and worker revolts of May–June 1968, he did become especially prominent during the wave of political interest that followed *les événements de mai*. His influence declined with the turn away from Marxism in the 1970s. In 1980 Althusser strangled his wife, but he escaped prosecution on the grounds of mental instability. (He had been under psychiatric care for depression on and off for over thirty years.) He spent the last ten years of his life in and out of mental hospitals.[22]

Freud, Lacan, and Kristeva

French interest in Freud came late. An official psychoanalytic organization was founded in France only in 1926, and it remained a small and marginal group until well after World War II. During the 1950s the dominance of existentialism, with its rejection of the unconscious, made Freudianism a non-starter. But the structuralist assault on existentialism was a natural opening for a theory based on mental realities outside of our lived phenomenological consciousness, and Jacques Lacan's reformulation of psychoanalysis in explicitly structuralist terms was a prime candidate for exploiting this

---

[22] Althusser's only significant writing after 1980 was a memoir published posthumously, *L'avenir dure longtemps*.

opening. A key development occurred in 1963, when Lacan accepted Althusser's invitation to offer a seminar at the École Normale. Althusser had concluded that Lacan's structuralist approach overcame the orthodox Marxist objection that psychoanalysis gave improper primacy to the individual subject, and Althusser's theory of overdetermination allowed psychoanalytic structures relative autonomy from determination by the economic base.

Jacques Lacan (1901–81) was a practicing Freudian psychoanalyst who insisted that his theorizing was simply a matter of getting back to the real meaning of Freud's text. In his view, this meant restoring Freud's meaning in opposition to the standard interpretations accepted by his followers. (It also meant correcting some parts of Freud's text in the light of others.) Lacan's story up to 1963 was one of complex theoretical and clinical evolution and stormy, Byzantine relations with the French psychoanalytic community. But what is significant for our purposes is the mature interpretation of Freud that he began presenting to an increasingly fascinated philosophical audience in 1963.

Lacan's main challenge to the Freudians concerned the privileged place they assigned the ego. On the standard picture, the psyche is made up of three domains. Two of these are entirely unconscious: the id, which is the locus of raw drives for immediate satisfaction, and the superego, which lays down inflexible commands, usually contrary to the id's desires, for conformity to societal norms. The third domain, primarily conscious, is that of the ego, which has the task of dealing with the real world and seeing that the demands of the id and the superego are sufficiently controlled to allow a person to lead a "normal" life. Mental illness (neurosis or psychosis) occurs when the ego is overwhelmed by unconscious desires and commands and so cannot function as a stable, coherent whole in the world. The point of psychoanalytic therapy is to restore the integrity of the ego (to bring it to its true identity) and so make it capable of functioning in the real world.

Lacan, however, maintains that the ideal of an integral and stable ego that is my true identity is always a deception, a false identification of my reality with some image outside myself. His point, moreover, is not that my true identity lies elsewhere, outside the domain of the ego, but rather that the very idea of "true identity" is a falsification of the human situation. The ego and any other notions of true identity are constructs in the realm of what Lacan will call *the Imaginary*.

What does have priority in human existence for Lacan is the domain of the unconscious. The question, however, is how to understand this domain. Freud himself sometimes thought of it as ultimately reducible to a physical energy system, taking literally his metaphors of repression, displacement, etc. Lacan rejected this reductionist model from the beginning. His discovery of what he regarded as the correct model of the unconscious derived from his encounter with structuralist linguistics (due, in all probability, to his friendship with Lévi-Strauss). This enabled him to formulate in a fruitful way the idea that the unconscious is structured like a language, that it is, specifically, a system of signs in Saussure's sense. So understood, the unconscious belongs to the realm of what Lacan calls *the Symbolic*. He maintains that this insight is implicit in Freud, who was unable to articulate it properly because he had no knowledge of Saussure's linguistics.

Some of Lacan's earliest important theoretical work concerned what he called the "mirror stage" in psychological development. He maintained that, somewhere between six and eighteen months, each infant comes to have an image of itself as a stable self (ego, *moi*) that is the author of its actions. Specifically, the infant, guided by its elders, identifies with something outside itself – perhaps literally its image in a mirror, perhaps with a sibling or a playmate – and thus begins to think of itself as a distinct and autonomous being. Lacan's point is not that this initial identification is in itself decisive. Rather, it is the beginning of a series of identifications that represent a persistent and developing project of making oneself into a stable ego. Thus, at later stages, I may find my identity in my role as devoted son, successful physician, star athlete, and so on.

As we have seen, Lacan does not see any such identifications as the proper culmination of psychological development (the emergence of maturity or some such). They are not normative goals but self-deceptive misunderstandings. The point, of course, is that in some basic sense, I am not the ego (image) with which I identify. But what then am I? We already know that Lacan rejects this question if it is taken to imply that I have some other stable identity. He does, however, introduce a crucial distinction between the *moi* (ego) and the *je* (subject, I). It is my fundamental reality as a subject that is ignored or misrepresented by an imaginary identification with an ego. The question, of course, is how we are to understand the subject. Lacan's answer merges with his account of the unconscious in terms of language and takes us into his domain of the Symbolic.

First of all, the subject must be contrasted with the ego: it is not a structured stable whole, but an unstable, divided flux. As Lacan puts it, "The I is an other" (evoking Rimbaud's "Je est un autre"); that is, the subject is non-self-identical, other than itself.[23] Thus, Lacan puts division, dissolution, and alienation at the heart of human reality. So far, it might seem that Lacan's subject is no different than Sartre's consciousness. But his view is in fact quite opposed to Sartre's. For one thing, Lacan's subject depends on the unconscious (a notion the existentialist Sartre rejects), the realm of desires that are excluded from the conscious existence of the ego. Even more important, unlike Sartrean consciousness, Lacan's subject has a structure, even though it is not the self-identical structure of the ego. This structure is that of a language as understood by Saussure, and Lacan accordingly calls the unconscious the domain of the Symbolic.

There is an immediate oddity in the claim that the unconscious is a language in Saussure's sense. For Saussure a sign is a combination of a signifier and a signified, with the former being a mark or sound and the latter a mental reality correlated with the mark or sound. Non-linguistic semiology (for example, Lévi-Strauss's anthropology) has practices and the like as signifiers, but still maintains mental items as signifieds. But if we treat a mental domain such as the unconscious as a Saussurean sign system, how do we get both signs and signifiers? We can take thoughts themselves as signs, perhaps, but then what do they signify? (What signifieds correspond to them?) According to Lacan, the signified is "the diachronic set of concretely pronounced discourses".[24] So it seems that Lacan has introduced *parole* itself as the signified of the unconscious.

We can understand this by thinking it through in the context of psychoanalytic therapy. Lacan emphasizes that the analytic situation involves nothing but language: the patient (analysand) speaking to the analyst. Through techniques such as free association and the recounting of dreams, the analysand puts forth a narrative of his or her life and its significance – e.g., recollections of a set of events in a given sequence. The premise of psychoanalysis is that this sequence does not have meaning in its own right. (The analysand may assign

[23] *Écrits*, 517. [24] *Écrits*, 126.

it a certain meaning – i.e., make it a certain sort of self-identity – but this is based on misunderstanding and belongs to the realm of the Imaginary.) The sequence is in fact meaningful only in relation to the code defined by the system of signifiers that is the unconscious. In this sense, the diachronic sequences spoken by the analysand (i.e., the analysand's actual speech acts – *paroles*) are the signifieds correlated with the unconscious subject's signifiers.[25]

The unconscious so conceived is "other" in two senses. First, it is metaphysically separate from the conscious ego; it exists as a separate domain. Second, its structure (or "logic") is radically different from that of ordinary conscious thought and talk (the conscious thought and speech of the ego). This has been apparent since Freud's work on dream interpretation and slips of the tongue.

The Real is Lacan's term for the unattainable and inexpressible limit of language. As we have seen, the heart of Lacan's formulation of psychoanalysis is his claim that the unconscious mind has the structure of a language in Saussure's sense of a system of signs whose meanings are entirely defined by their roles in the system. The fundamental Freudian processes of condensation and displacement, often misunderstood as analogous with transformations of energy, become instances of, respectively, metaphor and metonymy. As a self-enclosed linguistic system, the unconscious has no essential connections to external objects, and its desires fail to reach beyond the semiological system from which they receive their meaning. Lacan does speak of an ultimate object of desire, calling it the *object a (l'objet petit a)*, but the *a* denotes *autre* (other), and the *object a* corresponds to whatever, in a given psychoanalytic context, is the unattainable object of desire.

Lacan's construal of the Oedipal complex provides a good example of how his interpretation differs from standard Freudianism. In the usual account, male sexuality is initially defined by the little boy's love of his mother, which eventually takes the form of a desire to possess the mother sexually. Here the boy finds that he is a rival to his father. Knowing that the penis is the instrument for sexual possession of the mother and that the mother lacks a penis,

---

[25] An oddity remains, however, since Lacan also says that the unconscious system, which we are treating as just the signifiers, is the parallel of *langue*. But *langue* is the combination of signifiers and signifieds. This perhaps reflects the fact that, on the level of the unconscious, there is no real role for thoughts (the signified), and we can effectively reduce the sign to the signifier.

the boy comes to fear that his father will take away his penis (castrate him) to eliminate him as a rival. Because he sees the father as all-powerful, the boy represses his desire for his mother. Adult character derives from the specific nature and effectiveness of this repression. Lacan's account replaces the penis (as physical organ) with the phallus, understood as symbolic signifier. The crux of the complex, then, is not the separation of penis from body but the separation of signifier (phallus) from signified. What the little boy must ultimately come to terms with is not so much the possible loss of his penis as the loss of the unattainable object of the signifier that constitutes his desire. (But, presumably, in a given case the physical penis could come to stand for the phallus-signifier.)

Lacan's reading of Freud also has major consequences for psychoanalytic therapy. Standard psychoanalysis regards the mature conscious ego and the "objective" adult world to which it adapts itself as the realities to which the fantasies of unconscious desires must be subordinated. The point of analysis, therefore, is to give the ego control over the unconscious so that it can relate in a stable way to reality. The standard means of achieving this is transference, whereby the analysand attains stability by identifying with the mature ego of the analyst. But Lacan, as we have seen, places this ego and its world in the domain of the Imaginary and insists on its subordination to the Symbolic, the unconscious as an autonomous sign system. Consequently, the point of analysis must be to destroy the illusion that the ego and its objective world are realities and replace it with an acceptance of the autonomy of the unconscious realm of signifiers. Transference is a threat, not a means, to effective therapy. To prevent transference and, therefore, the analysand's fall into stability, Lacan introduced disruptive techniques such as abruptly terminating analytic sessions or even refusing to meet with the analysand. These techniques, which were said to have produced catastrophic relapses and even suicides, were a focus of Lacan's disputes with official psychoanalytic organizations.

Another fertile combination of structural linguistics and psychoanalysis was Julia Kristeva's work on what she came to call "semanalysis". Kristeva (b. 1941) arrived in Paris from Bulgaria as a student in 1966, and the following year married Philippe Sollers, the avant-garde writer and editor of *Tel quel*. She studied linguistics in Roland Barthes' seminar and later trained as a Lacanian psychoanalyst, before receiving a chair in linguistics at the Vincennes branch of the University of Paris. In her doctoral thesis, *La révolution du langage poétique* (1974), she introduced a fundamental distinction between the *semiotic* and the *symbolic*. The symbolic is language in the standard sense of a rule-governed system employed by a community of speakers to refer to their shared world. The semiotic is a pre-discursive articulation, in the chaotic space of bodily functions, of unconscious drives, and it emerges even before the Oedipal phase. It does not itself signify (have meaning), but it provides the conditions (biological and social) of possibility for the significance of the symbolic. Kristeva employs Plato's terminology of the *chora* (literally, place or space) to express the semiotic's role as the matrix of linguistic meaning. In psychological terms, the semiotic is the locus of the unconscious drives from which the self is generated, but which also threaten its stability. The symbolic corresponds to the social world in which a stable self is created from semiotic "matter". Kristeva's semanalysis provides a basis for her influential work as a literary analyst. Literature, especially certain sorts of poetry, is a mode of expression in which the semiotic component of language dominates, and where, accordingly, the pre-Oedipal drives ordinarily repressed by the symbolic structures of adult "normality" break through the fabric of language. Kristeva's literary criticism subtly tracks the semiotic and its complex interrelations with the symbolic.

Barthes

Roland Barthes (1915–80) provides some of the best examples of a structuralist approach to literary criticism as well as a clear indication of the limits of structuralism. This is not the place for a comprehensive account of Barthes' work,[26] and our discussion will be limited to two particularly instructive examples of his use of structuralist concepts: his cultural treatment of what he called *mythologies*, and the method of structuralist literary analysis presented in *S/Z*.

Mythology is Barthes' term for a use of language (or other signs) to express a second-level meaning, one beyond the meaning primarily expressed by the sign. However, this formal characterization ignores the flavor of Barthes' analyses of mythologies, which are almost always aimed at revealing the special interest of a particular

---

[26] For an excellent overview, see Jonathan Culler, *Roland Barthes*.

social class (usually the bourgeoisie) behind an expression of second-level meaning. The mythological use of language is, for Barthes, roughly equivalent to propaganda.

It is, however, simplest to begin with a pure (non-propagandistic) example. The student of Latin opens a grammar book and, in a section on agreement of subject and verb, reads: *quia ego nominor leo* ("because I am named lion"). On the first level of meaning this is a sentence from a Latin fable. (A lion is asked to share its prey with others and says no on the grounds that it is a lion.) But in the present context this first-level meaning is subordinated to another meaning – i.e., "this is an example of noun–verb agreement". The first-level meaning (about a lion and its status) is there in the text, but it is employed to express another meaning (about Latin grammar).

A more complex and typical example is Barthes' famous discussion of a *Paris-Match* cover photo of a black soldier saluting (presumably the French flag). Here the first-level meaning of the photo is something like "here is a black soldier in the French army giving a salute". But in the context of the cover of a mainstream French magazine, this meaning itself expresses a further meaning – something like, "You see, the French army is open to the black race, and blacks are good patriotic soldiers, just like anyone else" (a meaning which directly responds to discussions of racial prejudice, the ethno-centrism of the French nation, exploitation of native peoples by the French Empire, etc.).

Using these sorts of examples, Barthes proposed a general structuralist analysis of mythology.[27] Following Saussure, he regards a sign as composed of a signifier and a signified, although he generalizes to include non-linguistic signs. Thus, a rose signifies a lover's passion for a beloved: the rose is a signifier, the passion is a signified. But Barthes goes on to note that this sign (signifier + signified) can itself be the signifier in another sign. In such a case, the sign as a meaningful whole signifies a new signified. For example, someone may point to the rose given to the beloved as a typical example of middle-aged sentimentality (or of marital fidelity). Here a sign that has meaning on one level (rose-signifying-passion) is also involved in a second level of meaning. On this second level, what is a sign on the first level is, on the second level, a signifier in another sign (in our example, the rose-signifying-passion signifies

---

[27] See "Myth Today", the concluding essay in *Mythologies*.

sentimentality or fidelity). We can schematize this "mythological" situation as follows:

Level I (the linguistic system): signifier + signified = sign
Level II (the mythological system): sign [= SIGNIFIER] + SIGNIFIED = SIGN,

where terms in lower case operate at level I and terms in upper case operate at level II. The connection between the levels is made through the identity, sign = SIGNIFIER. Barthes calls the (linguistic-level) sign a *meaning* and the (mythological level) SIGNIFIER a *form*. What on the linguistic level is a sign, hence a unit of meaning, is, on the mythological level, "reduced" to the empty form of a signifier that needs completion by a signified to have meaning in the full sense.

It might seem that a myth can never be effective in convincing people of its message. For there seem to be only two possibilities: the reader of the myth is aware of only its form or the reader is aware of both its form and its meaning. In the first case, the reader does not get beyond the merely linguistic meaning of the myth's signifier, seeing, for example, only the soldier saluting and making nothing else of it; to such a reader, the signification of the myth is not even conveyed. In the second case, it would seem that the reader would see through the myth, being aware of the mythological meaning to which the form is being connected. But what in fact happens when a myth is effective is this: the reader is aware of the mythological meaning but regards it not as merely a meaning (just someone's interpretation) but as part of nature (a simple fact). If I recognize that the myth's evocation of the French nation (as an embodiment of liberty, equality, fraternity) is merely a way of thinking that the journalist is trying to get me to accept when looking at the picture (the form or mythological signifier), then I will not be taken in. I will perceive the meaning as an interested motive behind the presentation of the form. But when the myth is effective I will see the idealized French nation as a reality, a reality that causes the action portrayed by the picture, as the black soldier recognizes and salutes the liberty, equality, and fraternity France has provided him. Correspondingly, the form (the picture) will not be seen as the contrivance of an interested motive but as evidence for the reality of the idealized French nation. In sum, Barthes says, when myth is effective, what is actually just a system of signs (a semiological system) is taken to be a system of facts.

Language is susceptible to mythologization because of two of its typical characteristics. First, we ordinarily expect language to express something beyond the sheer literal meaning conveyed by its signs, since it rarely exists at the "zero-degree" of a sign that has no second-level meaning; and, second, the meaning of a sign is typically incomplete (not fully determined) and so is open to further interpretation. Myth is particularly effective among us because our capitalist society has so thoroughly taken on the mask of the natural; it has convincingly presented itself not just as a contingent historical development but as the way human beings naturally are.

Barthes makes many and diverse uses of what can be called "structuralist" approaches to literary texts, but the most extensive and important use is in his book *S/Z*, a detailed analysis of Balzac's short story "Sarrasine" (the analysis is six or seven times as long as the story).[28] His approach is through what he calls the *codes* on which the meaning of Balzac's text depends. In the most general terms, a code is simply a sign system, i.e., a set of (paradigmatically related) elements that can be combined (syntagmatically) in various ways. Specifically, Barthes here has in mind codes already established in previous writings and practices of a culture that govern a literary work and with which a reader must be familiar to understand the work. A trivial example: you could not understand a novel built around a baseball game unless you understood the code (the rules) that defines baseball.

Barthes analyzes "Sarrasine" in terms of five basic codes. He divides the text of the story (about thirty pages in printed form) into 561 brief segments (called *lexias*: units of reading) and discusses each in terms of the codes relevant to it. The hermeneutic code governs language that is used to pose questions or problems and to give clues to the answers. The proairetic code (from Aristotle's term for the ability to determine rationally the result of an action) provides typical patterns of action in terms of which we can anticipate and make sense of a plot's development. The semic code provides connections between behavior, situation, social position, etc., and various character traits, enabling us to determine the nature of the characters from the events and descriptions of the story. The symbolic code specifies the ways, within a given text, that specific

---

[28] The title *S/Z* derives from the initials of the two main characters, Sarrasine and Zambinella – with a lot of complicated semantic play involved.

details are able to be seen as having symbolic significance. The referential (or cultural) code is a set of sub-codes, each expressing a body of accepted "knowledge" (science, conventional wisdom, etc.) that the text takes for granted.

Barthes' emphasis is on the way the five codes are interwoven with one another throughout the text. All five occur before the end of the story's first sentence, and each lexia typically involves elements of more than one code. The result, Barthes argues, is that the text does not have any single overall structure; it is rather an irreducible complex of alternative, sometimes conflicting, sometimes intermeshing structures. In contrast to what we might expect of a structuralist analysis, Barthes explodes the text rather than unifying it.

More specifically, Barthes' analysis transforms what seems to be a preeminently *readable* (*lisible*) text into a *writable* (*scriptible*) text. A readable text, in Barthes' sense, is one that is easily accessible to the reader because it follows expected patterns (fits conventional codes). A writable text, by contrast, in one that confounds our expectations and so is difficult to read. Whereas reading a readable text is a basically passive experience, reading a writable text requires our active engagement. In a sense, the reader must be involved in the writing of the text, constructing its meanings from scratch out of what the author has produced. Barthes makes entirely clear his preference for writable texts.

Classic literature (such as Balzac) would seem to be a model of readable writing. The readability comes from the role of familiar codes in the text. This, however, presupposes that the codes work together, supplement one another to produce a unified, self-contained text. What Barthes does through his tracing of the codes of "Sarrasine" is to reveal a writable text beneath the surface readability. He shows how the various codes collide and intertwine with one another to complicate Balzac's text in a way that undermines any easy, comfortable reading. The codes do not combine to suggest a unifying meaning but rather push the text in opposing directions. Barthes, however, insists that we should not make the traditional mistake of ascribing the complexity of "Sarrasine" to the explicit intentions of Balzac as an author. The complexity is rather the result of Balzac's mostly unconscious immersion in the codes embedded in the story. Balzac's own intentions (e.g., his aesthetics of realism, his moral viewpoint) explain only the most superficial aspects of the story. In the deepest sense, "Sarrasine" is "written" more by the codes underlying its production and the readers who decipher the codes. We see, then, how Barthes' approach reveals what he called "the death of the author".

Although S/Z is Barthes' fullest employment of structuralist techniques, it in effect undermines the structuralist project by failing to discover a unique structure controlling the text.[29] Structural analysis appears as an excellent way of generating new levels of textual interpretation, particularly ones that do not refer all meaning back to authorial intention. But the irreducible variety of conflicting structures is inconsistent with the idea that structuralism is a scientific method leading to the fundamental truth of a text. This becomes particularly apparent when we widen our perspective to include Barthes' other work and the work of other literary critics employing structuralist techniques. There is no scientific convergence to a unique or unified structure for any given text but rather a proliferation of diverging interpretations. Moreover, it rapidly becomes clear that this proliferation, although somehow rooted in the text, is also greatly dependent on the creative ability of individual critics to constitute new interpretations. As a result, the structuralist elimination of the authorial subject is balanced by the emergence of the reader (particularly the literary critic) as a subject constituting not *the* meaning of the text but an endless succession of meanings.[30]

POSTSTRUCTURALISM

It was along such lines that the project of a structuralist science of literary texts was transformed into a poststructuralist deconstruction of the very idea of texts as fixed structures capable of scientific investigation. Similar transformations occurred in virtually all the domains structuralism had so quickly captured during the 1960s. Behind the change was structuralism's failure to sustain its claim to provide objective, scientific knowledge of the human domain. The failure derived from a crucial confusion in the conception of science implicit in structuralist projects. The assumption was that an analysis was scientific as long as it assumed an objectivist stance (eliminating

---

[29] Since S/Z appeared in 1970, it may well have been influenced by Derrida's early works.
[30] The role of the reader becomes particularly apparent in Barthes' later emphasis on the priority of the reader's enjoyment of literature, in *Le plaisir du texte*.

the perspective of the subject), employed a refined technical vocabulary, and applied complex formal schemata in a logically rigorous way. There was no attention paid to the crucial attribute of empirical adequacy. Althusser's treatment of Marx is a striking example. He assumed that *Capital* could be assigned the same sort of cognitive authority as Newton's *Principia* or Darwin's *Origin* and treated, in the manner of Bachelard, as an epistemically privileged object of philosophical reflection. This was an illegitimate assumption because, despite its trappings of objectivity and rigor, Marx's account has never passed the test of careful empirical testing. Therefore, the most that can be claimed for it is that it provides a self-consistent (and perhaps theoretically stimulating) interpretation of a given body of data. But there are alternatives equally consistent (and stimulating), and, given the lack of empirical tests, there is no scientific way of deciding between them and Marxism. The same is true of Lacan's psychoanalysis and even Lévi-Strauss's anthropology. They have their strengths as interpretations of the data but lack the genuinely scientific status of an empirically confirmed theory. The brief prestige of structuralist accounts rested on a confusion of the formal trappings of science with science itself.

Although the scientific claims of structuralism soon collapsed (and were never taken seriously by most social scientists), the movement had a continuing impact on literary and, more broadly, cultural studies as well as philosophy. This impact corresponds to what has, rather uninformatively, come to be termed "poststructuralism". Poststructuralism combines the structuralist *style* of objective, technical, and even formal discourse about the human world with a rejection of the structuralist *claim* that there is any deep or final truth that such discourse can uncover. The poststructuralist project need not be self-contradictory, but it is inevitably ironic, since it sees its methods of analysis as both necessary and, given traditional goals, doomed to failure. French poststructuralist philosophy continued the structuralist attack on phenomenology and developed structuralist-style methods (Foucault's archaeology, Derrida's grammatology, Deleuze's logic of multiplicities) to replace that of phenomenology. But at the same time it tried to undermine the structuralist assumption – shared, moreover, by the Western philosophical tradition – that there is an objective body of ultimate truth that can be known by such methods.

What has come to be called poststructuralism, then, is by no means merely a continuation of or reaction against the epiphenomenon of structuralism. It is, rather, a fundamental challenge to the defining intellectual ideal of philosophy since Plato: the possibility of attaining knowledge about the ultimate nature and meaning of human existence. More locally, this ideal had defined French philosophy since Descartes and had, during the twentieth century, been pursued through the varieties of spiritualism, critical idealism, and finally phenomenology. Positivism, which maintained that final truth was scientific truth, challenged not the ideal of ultimate truth but the claim that philosophy rather than science was the means to the ideal. Perennially, the only other alternative seemed to be a skeptical denial of all serious truth claims.

As the 1960s began in France, the traditional claims of philosophy were represented by phenomenology and the perennial positivist challenge by structuralism. As we have seen, after Merleau-Ponty the major issue seemed to be that of complementing the subject-centered standpoint of phenomenology with the objectivist stance of scientific structuralism and somehow basing the synthesis on an ontology more adequate than Sartre's. But the new generation of thinkers, led by Foucault and Derrida, had a far more radical project. They questioned the ideal of ultimate knowledge that defined not only phenomenology and structuralism but the very enterprise of philosophy. This questioning, however, was not based on the poverty of a skeptical denial of knowledge as such. The idea was not merely to undermine the old ideal but to replace it with a new mode of philosophizing, one that did not seek ultimate truth but could claim to be the legitimate successor to the tradition that had.

It was not, accordingly, structuralism that undermined existential phenomenology. The claim that it did was an illusion due to an indefensible reading of structuralism as the final scientific truth that would replace subjectivist phenomenology. Once this pretension collapsed, it would have been entirely feasible to return to Merleau-Ponty's project of synthesizing phenomenological description with structuralist interpretation. That this never happened was due to the poststucturalist questioning of the assumption, shared by phenomenology and structuralism alike, that we could attain deep truths about the human situation. Phenomenology fell not to an external scientific critique but to an internal metaphilosophical revolution.

One way in which the poststructuralists still resembled their immediate philosophical ancestors was in their demand for the concrete. As much as Sartre, Merleau-Ponty, and Beauvoir they sought a connection to directly lived experience. But they rejected phenomenology's version of such experience because, they maintained, it was based on an untenable centrality of the individual subject that came to be called "humanism". Here "humanism" referred to the family of modern philosophical conceptions, from Descartes' cogito through Kant's transcendental ego to Sartre's being-for-itself, that made individual subjects the ultimate sources of meaning and truth. The term had become current when Sartre, in his famous lecture in 1946, proclaimed against Catholic and Marxist critics that "existentialism is a humanism" and Heidegger, in his "Letter on Humanism" to a French disciple, Jean Beaufret, argued that this was precisely its failing, since humanism presupposed the very sort of traditional metaphysics that Heidegger's fundamental ontology had overcome.

The poststructuralists found the concrete without humanism in literature, though not, of course, the standard fare of realist novels or romantic poetry, which (apart from the sort of deconstruction Barthes carried out on Balzac) they saw as merely explorations or celebrations of humanist consciousness. They turned instead to avant-garde writers such as Bataille and Blanchot, who delineate the collapse of the concepts that structure our conscious life and, as Derrida put it, "make the limits of our language tremble". Such literature provides "the non-place [*non-lieu*] which would be the 'other' of philosophy"[31] as it has been traditionally understood, and shows the way to new, non-humanist modes of thought.

Foucault, for example, was particularly fascinated by Bataille's concept of transgression,[32] which he applied to the act of writing, understood as implying "an action that is always . . . transgressing and reversing an order that it accepts and manipulates". As a result, he saw writing as "a question of creating a space into which the writing subject constantly disappears".[33] Similarly, Foucault was impressed with Blanchot's conception of a "literary space" in which authorial identity is dissolved.[34] For Foucault, Blanchot's writings

[31] "Dialogue with Jacques Derrida", in Richard Kearney (ed.), *Dialogues with Contemporary Continental Thinkers*, 112.
[32] See his "A Preface to Transgression", *Essential Works of Michel Foucault, 1954–1984, Volume II: Aesthetics, Method, and Epistemology,* 69–87.
[33] Michel Foucault, "What Is an Author?", in *Essential Works, Volume II*, 206.
[34] Maurice Blanchot, *L'espace littéraire*, 1955. For a perceptive study of Blanchot's literary and philosophical significance, see Gerald Bruns, *Maurice Blanchot*.

"lay bare what precedes all speech, what underlies all silence: the continuous streaming of language. A language spoken by no one: any subject it may have is no more than a grammatical fold." With Blanchot, "we now know that the being of language is the visible effacement of the one who speaks".[35]

Derrida paid special attention to Bataille's "notion of expenditure",[36] the idea that any apparently coherent system (a "restricted economy" in Bataille's terminology) produces an excess that makes no sense in terms of the system and in so doing subordinates the restricted economy to a "general economy" in which its concepts lose their coherence.[37] Blanchot attracts Derrida both for the self-reference of his texts, which lead not to the clarity of self-understanding but to fundamental structural instability, and for his expression of the paradoxical status of language as a border that limits us even as we cross it (as in Blanchot's title, *Le pas au-delà*, which means both "the step (*pas*) beyond" and "the not (*pas*) beyond").[38]

A main locus of poststructuralist literary interests was the journal *Tel quel*, founded in 1960 and particularly associated with Philippe Sollers and Julia Kristeva.[39] In addition to its regular articles, the journal published books (in its "Collection *tel quel*") and sponsored conferences. It promoted — with varying emphases over its twenty-two years of publication — avant-garde writing, literary theory, and leftist political action. *Tel quel* was a major venue for Sollers' avant-garde writing and for Kristeva's literary theorizing. Barthes and Derrida were also frequent contributors. Shortly after the May '68 student and workers revolt, the journal became increasingly interested in politics and, during the 1970s, adopted a strongly Maoist orientation, culminating in 1974 in a visit of members of the editorial board (including Sollers, Kristeva, and Barthes) to China. In its later years, *Tel quel* reflected Sollers' eventual disillusion with Marxism and his new interests in sexuality and theology. In 1982, a switch to a

---

[35] Michel Foucault, "The Thought of the Outside", in *Essential Works, Volume II*, 166.
[36] Georges Bataille, "The Notion of Expenditure", in *Visions of Excess*.
[37] Jacques Derrida, "From Restricted Economy to General Economy: a Hegelianism without Reserve", in *Writing and Difference*.
[38] Jacques Derrida, "La loi du genre" and "Pas", both in *Parages*.
[39] The journal's title (meaning literally "such as" or "just as") evokes the (identical) title of a book by Paul Valéry and, especially, Nietzsche's proclamation that we should "affirm this world *just as* it is".

new publisher and a name change (to *L'infini*) amounted to its effective demise.[40]

The poststructuralists also made their own appropriation of German philosophy, finding particularly fruitful reflection on Hegel, Nietzsche, and, of course, Heidegger.[41] Hegel's techniques of dialectical argument were attractive because of their capacity for showing the incoherence of specific concepts, but more than anything the philosopher of absolute spirit was a warning of how easily the critique of philosophy could itself become just the most recent pretender to supreme cognitive authority. Foucault spoke of how "we have to determine the extent to which our anti-Hegelianism is possibly one of his tricks directed against us, at the end of which he stands, motionless, waiting for us".[42] Derrida says that his key notion, *différance*, "must sign the point at which one breaks with the system of the *Aufhebung* and with speculative dialectics".[43] But like Foucault, Derrida is extremely wary of the Hegelian temptation, and in *Glas* (1974) he went to extreme lengths of artifice and obscurity to confront Hegel without falling victim to the System's uncanny power to assimilate its critics. He split his text into two columns on each page, the left providing an analysis of Hegel on the family and the right an analysis of Jean Genet's novels. By making the final import of his text reside in the never expressed relations between the two columns, Derrida eludes Hegel by placing himself outside his own discussion of him.[44]

Before the 1960s, French interest in Nietzsche was more literary than philosophical. It arose first around the turn of the century, in writers such as Valéry and Gide. Beginning in the 1930s, Bataille and, later, Blanchot were at the center of another wave of interest.[45]

---

[40] For background on *Tel quel* and a selection of articles from it, see Patrick ffrench and Roland-François Lack (eds.), *The Tel Quel Reader*. Julia Kristeva's novel, *Samouraïs*, contains fictionalized versions of many of the personalities and events connected with *Tel quel*.

[41] Derrida explains his preference for German (and Greek) philosophy over French: "I have a profound respect for the great French thinkers, but I have always had the impression that a certain kind of rigorous analysis could render their texts accessible and exhaustible. Before a Platonic or Heideggerian text, by contrast, I feel that I am confronting an abyss, a bottomless pit in which I could lose myself" (Richard Kearney [ed.], *Dialogues with Contemporary Continental Thinkers*, 113).

[42] Michel Foucault, "The Discourse on Language", in *The Archaeology of Knowledge*, 235.

[43] *Positions*, 44.

[44] As Christina Howells notes, Derrida's treatment of Genet is also a (generally implicit) critique of Sartre and the latter's biography of *Genet* (see *Derrida: Deconstruction from Phenomenology to Ethics*, 85).

[45] See, for example, Georges Bataille, *Sur Nietzsche*.

The structuralist invasion 255

Nietzsche finally became a major influence in French philosophy through philosophers' interest in Bataille and Blanchot. Foucault, for example, says it was they who led him to read Nietzsche.[46] The poststructuralists became excited about Nietzsche mainly because he philosophized in opposition to the traditional ideal of absolute philosophical truth. As Deleuze, who in 1962 published a very influential study of Nietzsche, put it, he was most important for his "radical transformation of the image of thought that we create for ourselves. Nietzsche snatches thought from the element of truth and falsity. He turns it into an interpretation and an evaluation, interpretation of forces, evaluation of power."[47]

To Foucault, this renunciation of truth first meant the rejection of "man" as the locus of claims to absolute knowledge, a rejection he connected to the death of God. "Rather than the death of God – or, rather, in the wake of that death and in profound correlation with it – what Nietzsche's thought heralds is the end of his murderer."[48] Later, Foucault was especially taken with Nietzsche's replacement of philosophical systems with meticulous historical genealogies: "If I wanted to be pretentious, I would use 'the genealogy of morals' as the general title of what I am doing."[49] Derrida was fascinated by Nietzsche's notion of play, which he not only discussed but also often exemplified in the punning rococo of his literary style, including his dazzling and frustrating monograph, *Éperons: les styles de Nietzsche*. Later, Derrida worked through the vexed question of the Nazi appropriation of Nietzsche's thought in *Otobiographies: L'enseignement de Nietzsche et la politique du nom propre*.

Heidegger's postwar influence in France owed much to the interest of literary figures such as Blanchot and the poet René Char. Char, along with Heidegger's main French disciple, Jean Beaufret, organized an important conference on his work at Cerisy-la-Salle in 1955, and at Char's invitation Heidegger gave three seminars in Avignon during the later 1960s. Poststructuralist appropriations of Heidegger rejected the existentialists' "humanist" reading, which presented him as a philosopher of consciousness and freedom, and,

---

[46] "I read [Nietzsche] because of Bataille, and Bataille because of Blanchot" ("Structuralism and Poststructuralism", interview with Gérard Raulet, in *Essential Works, Volume II*, 439). His interest in Nietzsche probably also derives from his reading of Heidegger, another source of the French turn to Nietzsche.
[47] Gilles Deleuze, "Preface to the English Translation", in *Nietzsche and Philosophy*, xiii.
[48] *The Order of Things*, 385.   [49] *Power/Knowledge*, 53.

consistent with Heidegger's self-interpretation in his "Letter on Humanism", saw him as a critic of subject-centered philosophy.[50]

Heidegger's influence on Derrida is particularly strong and explicit. His key notion of *différance* has obvious connections to Heidegger's ontological difference (the difference between beings and their Being). It is not surprising that Derrida once told an interviewer: "Nothing that I have tried to do would have been possible without the opening of Heideggerian questions . . . without the attention to what Heidegger calls the difference between Being and being, the ontic-ontological difference as it remains unthought in a certain fashion by philosophy."[51] Derrida's Heideggerian pedigree is also apparent in his penchant for detailed commentaries on the history of philosophy, using a technique that he calls "deconstruction", a term he introduced to translate Heidegger's *Destruktion*. Further, the primary result of Derrida's deconstructions, a critique of "metaphysical presence", is very similar to Heidegger's criticism of representationalist metaphysics. But Derrida remains very suspicious of what he sees as Heidegger's "nostalgia" for pre-Socratic unveilings of Being, which he regards as a lapse back into the metaphysics of presence, and eventually acknowledged a substantive tie between Heidegger's philosophy and his Nazi politics.[52]

Hubert Dreyfus has especially emphasized the importance of Heidegger for Foucault,[53] a claim Foucault confirms.[54] At first, however, Foucault took Heidegger as an existentialist thinker and was particularly impressed with Ludwig Binswanger's *Daseinanalysis*, a Heideggerian version of existential psychology.[55] But from the beginning Foucault expressed reservations about this Heideggerian existentialism, and *Les mots et les choses* (published in 1966), with its hope for an imminent "death of man", is clearly influenced by

---

[50] See, for example, Jacques Derrida, "The Ends of Man", in *Writing and Difference*.
[51] *Positions*, 18.
[52] See *De l'esprit* and *Psyché: inventions de l'autre*.
[53] Hubert Dreyfus, "On the Ordering of Things: Being and Power in Heidegger and Foucault", in T. J. Armstrong (ed.), *Michel Foucault: Philosopher*, 80–95.
[54] "My entire philosophical development was determined by my reading of Heidegger." But Foucault continues, "I nevertheless recognize that Nietzsche outweighed him", and a little later says, "I am simply Nietzschean" ("The Return of Morality", in Michel Foucault, *Politics, Philosophy, Culture*, 250, 251).
[55] Foucault's first significant publication, in 1954, was a long introduction to a French translation of Binswanger's article "Traum und Existenz" (translated as M. Foucault and L. Binswanger, *Dream and Existence*). There are also clear traces of the existential Heidegger in Foucault's *Histoire de la folie à l'âge classique* (1961).

Heideggerian anti-humanism. This is particularly apparent in the treatment of language, which is also much indebted to Blanchot. Foucault's conception of power, central in his writings of the 1970s, does, as Dreyfus shows, have some important affinities to Heidegger's notion of Being, but Foucault is far more interested in detailed genealogical studies of how power is embodied in specific institutions and practices than in its ontological roots. Further, as Paul Rabinow has suggested, it is difficult to give a Heideggerian reading of Foucault's central concern, at least during the 1980s, with subjectivity and ethics.[56]

[56] Paul Rabinow, "Modern and Countermodern: Ethos and Epoch in Heidegger and Foucault", in Gary Gutting (ed.), *The Cambridge Companion to Foucault*, 199.

CHAPTER 9

Foucault

> You remember that book of philosophy we read together at Balbec, the richness of the world of possibilities compared with the real world.
> (Marcel Proust, *In Search of Lost Time*, III, 148)

Michel Foucault (1926–84) was born in Poitiers, where his father was a prominent physician. In 1945 he studied under Jean Hyppolite at the Lycée Henri IV in preparation for the entrance examination for the École Normale Supérieure, where he began studies in 1946. He received *licences* in both philosophy and psychology, working with, among others, Maurice Merleau-Ponty. Dissatisfied with French culture and society, Foucault was able to avoid the usual "purgatory" of lycée teaching and instead took various temporary academic posts in Sweden, Poland, and Germany from 1955 to 1960, while he completed his doctoral thesis (on madness in the Classical Age). During the 1960s Foucault held a series of positions in French universities, and in 1969 he was elected Hyppolite's successor in the Collège de France, where he chose the title "Professor of the History of Systems of Thought". From the 1970s on, Foucault was very active politically, helping found the *Groupe d'information sur les prisons* and supporting protests on behalf of homosexuals and other marginalized groups. He also frequently lectured outside France, particularly in the United States, and in 1983 agreed to teach annually at the University of Caifornia at Berkeley. One of the first prominent victims of AIDS, Foucault died in Paris on June 25, 1984.

Contrary to common views of authorship as self-expression, Foucault said that he wrote to escape from any fixed identity: "I am no doubt not the only one who writes in order to have no face."[1] Correspondingly, there is no methodological or theoretical unity of

[1] *The Archaeology of Knowledge*, 17.

Foucault's thought that will support any single comprehensive interpretation. His writings instead fall into several main groups, each characterized by a distinctive problematic and method of approach. It is fruitful to follow certain themes through some or all of these groups, but the core of his effort at any point is defined by what is specific to the problems then engaging him.[2]

In all his various projects, Foucault, like Sartre and Merleau-Ponty, sought a manner of thinking that was based in the concrete reality of human existence and oriented toward human liberation. Sartre and Merleau-Ponty sought concreteness in phenomenology and liberation through Marxism; and Foucault, pursuing a philosophical education in a France dominated by their work, initially found himself with the same orientation. "I belong to that generation who as students had before their eyes, and were limited by, a horizon consisting of Marxism, phenomenology, and existentialism."[3] Particularly because of the influence of Althusser at the École Normale, Foucault's early intellectual attachment to Marxism was strong, as his 1954 book, *Maladie mentale et personnalité*, makes clear. He characterizes non-Marxist approaches, including the existential, as providing only "mythical explanations", and maintains that mental illnesses arise ultimately from "contradictions" determined by "present economic conditions in the form of conflict, exploitation, imperialist wars, and class struggle".[4] Foucault was even for a time a member of the French Communist Party. But he was very soon disillusioned with both the theory and the practice of Marxism. He quit the Party after only "a few months or a little more",[5] and in the second edition of his book on mental illness (retitled *Maladie mentale et psychologie*) in 1962, he eliminated almost all Marxist elements, including his entire concluding chapter. From then on, Foucault maintained a leftist but distinctively non-Marxist politics.

The ties to existential phenomenology were much stronger, but there is no doubt that Foucault rather soon rejected the subjective standpoint of phenomenological description. He shared a general

---

[2] For further development of this line of thought, see my essay, "Michel Foucault: a User's Manual", in Gary Gutting, *The Cambridge Companion to Foucault*.
[3] "An Interview with Michel Foucault" (with Charles Ruas), "Postscript" to Michel Foucault, *Death and the Labyrinth: the World of Raymond Roussel*, 174.
[4] *Maladie mentale et personnalité*, 86.
[5] "Michel Foucault répond à Sartre", 21.

sense that, especially given the work of Saussure, Lévi-Strauss, and Lacan, phenomenology could not give adequate accounts of language, the unconscious, and social structures.[6] A more distinctive and personal challenge came from Foucault's passion for literature, particularly avant-garde writers such as Roussel, Beckett, Robbe-Grillet, and Butor, whose rejection of the traditional psychological novel provided an alternative to phenomenology and existentialism.[7] As we have seen, Foucault found the same sort of questioning in Bataille and Blanchot.[8]

But Foucault's break with existential phenomenology occurred primarily on the field of history. Sartre, as we have seen, realized the importance of history and was quite prepared to revise his abstract ontology to take account of the historical situatedness of consciousness. But he always insisted, against structuralist critics, that the meaning of history derives from the free subject. By rejecting this subject, Sartre claimed, the structuralists (and here he included Foucault) rejected history. According to Foucault, however, Sartre was ignoring the most successful historiography of his time, the *Annales* school, particularly associated with Ferdinand Braudel. Braudel and his colleagues obtained extremely interesting results (especially in social history) by giving up the perspective of individual experience (history as the acts of kings, generals, diplomats, revolutionaries) and assuming the much broader standpoint of long-term factors such as geography, climate, and natural resources. Without taking over any of Braudel's specific results or methods, Foucault tried to effect a parallel change of perspective in the history of thought: a move away from the standpoint of the individual thinker and toward the standpoint of broader but more fundamental categories and structures.

More directly influential were Bachelard's and Canguilhem's histories of science, which were centered not on subjective experience but objective concepts. Much of Foucault's historical work (especially *Les mots et les choses*) is an extension to the social sciences of

---

[6] "Structuralism and Poststructuralism", interview with Gérard Raulet, in *Essential Works of Michel Foucault, 1954–1984, Volume II: Aesthetics, Method, and Epistemology*, 436–7.
[7] "An Interview with Michel Foucault" (with Charles Ruas), 174. See Foucault's *Raymond Roussel* (1963), and various literary essays from the same period reprinted in Michel Foucault, *Essential Works, Volume II*.
[8] The influence of Blanchot, especially early on, was particularly strong. Speaking of the early 1950s, Foucault once told his close friend, the historian Paul Veyne, "At the time, I dreamed of being Blanchot" (Didier Eribon, *Michel Foucault*, 133).

the kind of studies Bachelard had done for the physical sciences and Canguilhem for the biological sciences.[9] Foucault also took for granted many of the key claims of Bachelard's and Canguilhem's philosophy of science. These included the essentially historical character of science and the central role of epistemological breaks or discontinuities. On a deeper level, Bachelard's notion of epistemological obstacle foreshadows Foucault's project of showing the historical, contingent nature of concepts and practices that present themselves as ahistorical necessities. Just as Bachelard spoke of a psychoanalysis of knowledge, Foucault characterized his own work as an effort to discover the unconscious of our knowledge.

Canguilhem's strongest methodological influence on Foucault was through his emphasis on the history of concepts as opposed to the history of theories. On Foucault's appropriation of Canguilhem, experiencing subjects (individual scientists) are primarily sources of new theories, which, however, employ concepts that derive from linguistic structures prior to the subject's experience. Accordingly, Canguilhemian histories of concepts extend the structuralist decentering of the subject to the history of science.

Beyond his rejection of the priority of the phenomenological subject, Foucault's enterprise differs from Sartre's in two major respects. First, he does not see his role to be the construction of universally valid theories. He will develop theories (for example, of language, of social power, of the ethical subject) but only to elucidate a specific regional issue such as madness, punishment, or sexuality. Despite occasional bending to temptation, he eschews theoretical generalization for its own sake. This instrumental approach to philosophical theory keeps Foucault from the construction of systematic monuments such as *L'être et le néant* and *Critique de la raison dialectique*. His alternative is to write critical histories of concepts that have embodied limitations on thought and action that appear necessary but are in fact contingent. In a late essay, Foucault characterized this project as a positive inversion of Kant's critical philosophy:

If the Kantian question was that of knowing [*savoir*] what limits knowledge [*connaissance*] must renounce exceeding, it seems to me that the critical question today must be turned back into a positive one: In what is given to

---

[9] Foucault's historical work is also influenced by the proto-structuralist studies of Georges Dumézil on the comparative study of Indo-European religions.

us as universal, necessary, obligatory, what place is occupied by whatever is singular, contingent, and the product of arbitrary constraints? The point, in brief, is to transform the critique conducted in the form of necessary limitation into a practical critique that takes the form of a possible crossing-over [*franchissement*].[10]

In accord with this understanding of his project, Foucault's historical methodology depended more on a sensitivity to the particularities of historical events and structures than on fundamental views about knowledge and reality. On the other hand, he was not a "pure" historian, simply displaying neutral truths about the past. His histories originate from specific experiences and concerns about contemporary society: a concrete awareness that something is wrong with our treatment of mental patients or prisoners, with our sexual attitudes and practices. He says, for example, that he undertook a historical study of psychiatry (in *Folie et déraison*) "because I had had a certain amount of practical experience in psychiatric hospitals and was aware of the combats, the lines of force, tensions and points of collision which existed there. My historical work was undertaken only as a function of those conflicts" (*Power/Knowledge* [*PK*], 64).

It is this origin in contemporary experience that led Foucault to characterize his work as a "history of the present".[11] But this origin does not mean that Foucault thought his histories provided expert solutions to our social and political problems. His history of madness, although taken up by Laing and others in the anti-psychiatry movement, was not intended as a call to abolish asylums or for any other specific reforms in society's treatment of the mad. In Foucault's view, decisions about how to deal with political and social problems are the province of those immediately involved in and familiar with them. Disengaged intellectual analysis is important but only as a background suggesting possibilities, not as a normative summons to action. "The project, tactics and goals to be adopted are a matter for those who do the fighting. What the intellectual can do is to provide instruments of analysis, and at present this is the historian's essential role . . . [The historian provides] a topological and geological survey of the battlefield. . . . But as for saying, 'Here is what you must do!', certainly not" (*PK*, 62).

---

[10] "What Is Enlightenment?", in Michel Foucault, *Essential Works of Michel Foucault, 1954–1984, Volume I: Ethics: Subjectivity and Truth*, 315.

[11] *Discipline and Punish*, 30–1.

On the other hand, Foucault does think there is a sort of intellectual who has the right to recommend particular policies and tactics. This is the "specific intellectual", who "has at his disposal, whether in the service of the State or against it, powers which can benefit or irrevocably destroy life" (*PK*, 129). Included under this rubric are all those experts (teachers, engineers, doctors, consultants) who develop and deploy domains of knowledge within the power structures of society. Foucault distinguishes the specific intellectual from the "universal intellectual", a free spirit, "the spokesman of the universal", "speaking in the capacity of master of truth and justice" (*PK*, 126). He suggests that such autonomous intellectuals – Voltaire and Sartre are no doubt premier examples – once played an important role. But today the relation between theory and practice has changed, and we can no longer expect universal systems of morality to provide effective responses to social and political domination. We need, rather, specific responses formulated by those concretely involved in the problems. Foucault's "specific intellectuals" are of course not the only ones so involved; there are also the direct objects of society's power structures (e.g., prisoners, asylum inmates, students), as well as a network of nonintellectual functionaries (prison guards, office workers). But specific intellectuals' specialized knowledge and reflective capacities make their efforts particularly important.

The intellectual role Foucault sees for himself does not seem to be that of either the specific or the universal intellectual. His work is grounded neither in the latter's general moral principles nor in the former's specific responsibilities within society's power structures. We might (though Foucault does not use the term) call him rather a "critical intellectual". Critical intellectuals do not speak with the authority of universal principles or of specific social or political responsibilities but simply on the basis of their historical erudition and analytic skills. Neither "the rhapsodist of the eternal" nor "the strategist of life and death" (*PK*, 129), the critical intellectual provides the intellectual tools – awarenesses of strategic and tactical possibilities – needed to combat arbitrary constraints on human freedom.

Although critical intellectuals' social and political concerns explain their choices of particular historical phenomena for analysis, they do not account for the historical methods employed or for the results these methods yield. Foucault, for example, chose to study the historical origins of certain disciplines and institutions because he regarded them as particularly dangerous contemporary threats to freedom. But his studies themselves were intended to help generate reliable strategies for combatting these threats. Consequently, they had to be designed to yield accurate historical accounts, not ideological caricatures. Foucault was committed to struggles for freedom in the manner of an intelligence analyst, not a propagandist. Consequently, he always aimed at a reliable understanding of the historical phenomena he was investigating. He sought, as he said, "a discourse which would be both true and strategically effective . . . a truth which could have a political effect" (*PK*, 64).

MADNESS

The first example of this approach is Foucault's critique of mental illness in his *Folie et déraison* (1961).[12] His earlier work on madness (*Maladie mentale et personnalité*) took for granted the concept of mental illness as an objective, essentially nonhistorical given. *Folie et déraison* moves to an entirely new level by seeing our notion of mental illness as merely a contingent historical construct. Philosophically, it represents the beginning of Foucault's gradual move away from the influence of existential phenomenology (although the book still often speaks of the "experience of madness") and toward a non-subject-centered approach. Historically, it shows him groping for a new method of analysis: amid a good deal of standard historical description and explanation, there is also the germ of his archaeological method.

The book, especially in its preface (dropped in the second edition) and conclusion, also shows Foucault's inclination to a romantic irrationalism that sees art and literature, via its association with madness (in such figures as van Gogh, Artaud, Roussel, Neval, and, especially, Nietzsche) as having special access to a deep truth about human reality. However, this emphasis does not pervade the entire book, which on the whole remains a history of psychiatry, not a history of madness in itself.

Foucault sees the history of madness in Europe as characterized by

---

[12] The English version of *Folie et déraison*, *Madness and Civilization*, is a translation of only just over half of Foucault's text. For a discussion of the status of Foucault's work on madness as history, see my "Foucault and the History of Madness", in G. Gutting (ed.), *The Cambridge Companion to Foucault*.

two major "breaks": one in the mid-seventeenth century which sharply separates "Classical" (that is, seventeenth- and eighteenth-century) views of madness from those of the Middle Ages and Renaissance; another at the end of the eighteenth century that inaugurates the modern view of madness. His treatment of pre-Classical (medieval and Renaissance) madness is cursory. But he does make one claim crucial for his argument: prior to the Classical Age, madness was seen as an integrally human phenomenon. Madness was opposed to reason, but as an alternative mode of human existence, not a simple rejection of it. Consequently, madness, even if disdained or abhorred, was a meaningful challenge to reason. It could engage in ironic dialogue with reason (as in Erasmus) or claim a domain of human experience and insight not available to reason (as in medieval painting or Renaissance tragedy).

In contrast to the medieval and Renaissance views, the Classical Age saw madness as merely the negation of the essential human attribute of reason. It was regarded as unreason (*déraison*), a plunge into an animality that had no human significance. There was, accordingly, a *conceptual exclusion* of the mad from human society. (Here Foucault cites as a prime example Descartes' rejection in the First Meditation of the possibility of his own madness as a grounds of doubt.) Correlative to this conceptual exclusion, there was a physical exclusion of the mad effected by their confinement in institutions that isolated them from ordinary human life. This was most strikingly signaled in France by the "Great Confinement" of 1656, when, within a period of just a few months, over 1 percent of the population of Paris was compelled to move into one or another division of the Hôpital Général. Foucault notes that similar confinements occurred throughout Europe.

The conceptual and physical exclusion of the mad reflected a moral condemnation. The moral fault, however, was not the ordinary sort, whereby a member of the human community violates one of its basic norms. Rather, madness corresponded to a radical choice that rejected humanity and the human community in toto in favor of a life of sheer (nonhuman) animality. In the Classical view, the animality of the mad was expressed in their domination by passions, a domination that led them to a delirium in which they mistook the unreal for the real. Passionate delirium thus resulted in a fundamental blindness that cut the mad off from the light of reason. So construed, Classical madness is an affliction of the mind–body composite, not something distinctly psychological or somatic. Specifically, it is not conceived as a "mental illness".

With the modern age (roughly, from the nineteenth century on), the mad are once again regarded as being within the human community, not as animals beyond the pale of humanity. But within the human community they are now seen as moral offenders, violators of specific social norms, who should feel guilt at their condition and who need reform of their attitudes and behavior. Corresponding to this new conception of madness is the characteristic modern mode of treating the mad: not merely isolating them but making them the objects of a moral therapy that subjects them to social norms. This is the move from the merely custodial confinement of the Classical Age to the modern therapeutic asylum, founded by Samuel Tuke in England and by Philippe Pinel in France. Although this institution was widely regarded as an unquestionable advance in humanitarianism, Foucault sees it as merely a more subtle and thorough method for controlling the mad. Rather than a true liberation of the mad, it is a "gigantic moral imprisonment".

The most striking feature of the moral domination of the asylum was what Foucault calls "the apotheosis of the medical personage".[13] To us, it seems natural that the doctors should rule the mad, since we see the latter as "mentally ill". But Foucault claims that in the asylum the rule is not really so much by medical as by moral authority. Doctors have authority not because they have the knowledge to cure (this is haphazard at best) but because they represent the moral demands of society. This is evident today in psychiatric practices such as psychoanalysis. The practice is accompanied by the trappings of medical science, but the key to therapy remains the personal moral authority of the therapist, who serves as an instrument of social values.

We readily see that for Foucault the identification of madness as mental illness was not an objective scientific discovery. Rather, it was introduced as a means of legitimating the authority of physicians in the asylum once the idea of a distinctively moral therapy was abandoned. More fully, the fact that physicians came to be in charge of asylums initially had little to do with their medical expertise. The moral treatment recommended by Tuke and Pinel was not essentially medical and could be carried out by any person with moral

[13] *Madness and Civilization*, 278, 269.

authority. However, as the nineteenth century developed, medicine became dominated by the ideal of objective, value-free knowledge, which left no room for value-laden moral therapies. The idea of a distinctively mental sort of illness was introduced primarily to justify the continuing authority of doctors over the mad, not because of its scientific truth or curative success.

In the conclusion of *Folie et déraison*, Foucault turns from a historical analysis of how different periods have conceived madness to an effort to evoke the viewpoint of the mad themselves. Here he sees art (literature and painting) as particularly important. The idea is not that madness expresses itself in art (rather, "madness is precisely the absence of the work of art").[14] But Foucault thinks that some of the best art has been produced by artists who, having experienced madness, were trying to come to terms with it in the face of society's opposing violence. His suggestion is that there is a deep truth about human reality that we reject in rejecting madness and that art can help lead us back to this truth. This romantic idea lingers in Foucault's thought for a surprisingly long time – even into *L'archéologie du savoir*. However, it remains a separable element on which his historical analyses do not essentially depend (although it does have a deleterious effect on his prose style, which suffers from purple efforts to evoke these mysterious depths).

ORDER

Like Foucault's other books, *Les mots et les choses* (1966) tries to understand a contemporary cognitive enterprise through its historical antecedents, the ultimate goal being our liberation from unnecessary constraints associated with the enterprise. Here, however, the topic is of immense scope: the entire body of the modern human sciences ("the sciences of man"). Foucault's specific claim is that the human sciences, as they originated at the turn of the nineteenth century, are based on a distinctive concept which he calls the concept of man; and that this concept, far from being the inevitable essence of humanity, is a lately emerging, entirely contingent, and not even clearly coherent notion. It is, moreover, Foucault says hopefully, one that may well be vanishing.

Les mots et les choses covers roughly the same chronological periods

---

[14] *Madness and Civilization*, 287.

as *Folie et déraison*: the Renaissance, the Classical Age, and the modern age. For each period, Foucault sketches the general epistemic structure (the episteme) underlying its thought and then shows how the disciplines that are the counterparts of today's human sciences can be understood in terms of this basic epistemic structure. This, he maintains, shows that these earlier disciplines are not halting anticipations of the modern human sciences but autonomous alternative ways of construing human reality. From this he will argue for the contingency and replaceability of the human sciences.

Methodologically, *Les mots et les choses* is the full fruition of the archaeological method toward which Foucault was groping in *Folie et déraison* (and also *Naissance de la clinique*, his 1963 study of modern clinical medicine).[15] Archaeology emerges as a method of analysis that reveals the intellectual structures that underlie and make possible the entire range of diverse (and often conflicting) concepts, methods, and theories characterizing the thought of a given period. Concepts, methods, and theories belong to the conscious life of individual subjects. By reading texts to discover not the intentions of their authors but the deep structure of the language itself, Foucault's archaeology goes beneath conscious life to reveal the epistemic "unconscious" that defines and makes possible individuals' knowledge. As Foucault explains in his subsequent methodological treatise, *L'archéologie du savoir*, archaeology is similar to logic and grammar in that it discovers rules governing our discursive behavior of which we may well not be aware. Grammar formulates the rules defining the domain of sheer meaningfulness and logic the rules of sheer consistency. But it is obvious that there are many grammatically and logically acceptable statements that are never uttered in a given domain of discourse. We may be inclined to attribute this simply to the fact that no individuals happen to want to make these statements. But Foucault maintains that, in addition to the rules of grammar and logic, there are further underlying rules limiting the range of permissible statements. (For example, the rules of classical discourse about madness did not permit the statement: "Madness is simply a disease of the mind.") Foucault's archaeology, the archaeology of knowledge, is the historical method that uncovers such rules.

[15] For fuller discussions of Foucault's "archaeological" works, see my *Michel Foucault's Archaeology of Scientific Reason*.

Foucault's project is to sketch the *epistemes* of various periods of intellectual history. His use of this term often suggests that he is thinking globally, comprehensively characterizing the fundamental categories of any and all thinking in a given age. Certainly most readers have taken him to be doing this (and with good textual basis), and criticisms by historians have frequently insisted on counter-examples to his generalizations. Foucault, however, explicitly denied any global intent, and the logic of his project requires an accurate characterization of only the modern human sciences and their antecedents. We should admit, against Foucault, that there are grand speculations about the general structure of Renaissance, Classical, and modern thought in *Les mots et les choses*, but also realize that such speculations are not essential to the argument of the book.

Foucault's characterizations of the epistemes of the Renaissance, the Classical Age, and the modern age are formulated in terms of, first, an episteme's fundamental manner of ordering the objects of thought and experience (its "order of things"[16]); second, the consequences of this ordering for the nature of signs (especially linguistic signs); and third, the consequences of the episteme's view of order and of signs for its conception of knowledge.

The fundamental way in which things are related for Renaissance thought is *resemblance*. The basic relation between any two objects will not depend on (as will be the case for later periods) the essential properties that they share or fail to share or on the causal functions they do or do not have in common. The relation is rather due to the similarities (e.g., analogies) in virtue of which they resemble one another. For example, Renaissance thought regarded the plant aconite and the human eye as closely related because the seeds of the plant look very much like little eyes. Likewise, there is an important connection between the human head and the planetary system because the number of orifices in the head (seven) is equal to the number of planets. Resemblance is also the relation between signs and the things they signify. Words, for example, are not conventional representations of their referents but rather have a fundamental

---

[16] This title for the English translation of *Les mots et les choses* apparently had Foucault's sanction. According to the "Publisher's Note" to the translation, a new title was sought because there were two other English books entitled *Words and Things*, and "the publisher . . . agreed with the author on the alternative title *The Order of Things*, which was, in fact, M. Foucault's original preference" (*The Order of Things*, viii).

similarity to them, though to see the resemblance fully we may have to trace a word's roots back to the primal language before Babel.

The Classical Age replaced the vague and amorphous Renaissance notion of resemblance with the much more precise notions of identity (sameness) and difference. The essential relations among things are determined not by the varying degrees to which they are similar to one another but by the precise properties that they do or do not have in common. Thus, Descartes will maintain that we must penetrate beyond the resemblances evident to the senses and reach a precise (clear and distinct) intellectual analysis of the simple natures that define things in their true reality. Foucault emphasizes, however, contrary to a common view among historians, that Classical order does not necessarily mean thinking of nature in quantitative mathematical terms. Purely qualitative properties can be the basis of strict identities and differences. The Classical Age was not merely the age of mathematicized mechanisms.

The Classical conception of signs and language likewise abandons the vagueness of resemblance in favor of the more exact notion of representation. A sign is now not just another thing in the world, related to its referent in the way all things are related (although now by identity and difference). Since a sign must exactly represent a thing, it would, if it were part of the world, simply be the thing itself. Therefore, Classical signs must be placed in an entirely different order from that of reality. This, of course, is the realm of ideas, so central in seventeenth- and eighteenth-century philosophy. Idea-signs have no content of their own – no ontological "thickness" – but are entirely transparent expressions of what they represent. Moreover (and very importantly), for the Classical Age thinking is entirely identified with representing. Thought is of its very nature representative. This does not, of course, mean that every idea is true; what it represents may not in fact exist. But there is no questioning – as there was later for Kant and the modern age – of how or whether a given idea is able to represent its (real or unreal) object.

Given this view of order and signs, Classical knowledge will be a matter of constructing a system of signs that accurately represents the identities and differences that exist among a given domain of objects. Such systems of knowledge are formulated in the great Classical tables, such as those of genera and species in natural history. In contrast to Renaissance knowledge, which was in principle incomplete (since there is no end to the chain of resemblances),

Classical knowledge could aspire to the ideal of complete knowledge. Such knowledge would be formulable in an exhaustive set of tables that displayed precisely how each thing differed from every other thing.

The Classical ordering of things is based on the sameness and difference of properties; it is essentially ahistorical and continuous, each thing filling one slot in the chain of being defined by all possible combinations of presence and absence of basic properties. By contrast, modern order derives from similarities and differences in *function*. An entity is understood and related to other things in virtue of the role it plays not in an ideal table of possibilities but in a real, historically developing environment. As such, modern (functional) order is essentially historical and discontinuous. The discontinuity derives from the impossibility of defining function in terms of the combination of a set of basic properties; the same function can be achieved by quite different combinations of properties, as in the case of lungs and gills.

With regard to signs and language, the key feature of the modern episteme is what Foucault calls "the decline of representation". This does not mean that representation is no longer an important category. But it does mean that representation is no longer regarded as identical with thought itself; thought is no longer seen as by its very nature representative. This is because representation is an analytic procedure in which simple mental units (ideas) are combined in a way that exactly matches the combination of properties in the thing being analyzed (and hence represented). Within the modern episteme, we can still undertake such analyses, but there is no guarantee that they will adequately catch the concrete reality of the thing analyzed, since this reality is expressed in the thing's historical function, not its ahistorical properties. Analysis can discover only the ahistorical (logically or conceptually necessary) features, not those that are historical and contingent.

This decline of representation has, according to Foucault, resulted in the fragmentation of modern knowledge. This is apparent first in the division we have just been discussing between analytic knowledge of logical and conceptual truths and synthetic knowledge of contingent facts. This division leads, in turn, to the distinction between formal (a priori) and empirical (a posteriori) disciplines. There is, further, a division between the formal and the empirical disciplines, on the one hand, and philosophy, on the other. This arises because representation maintains an important role even in the modern empirical sciences. Even though thought does not by its very nature represent the world, it obviously does represent it (and accurately so) in many cases. This poses the question of how thought is able to represent reality and of what limits there might be to this ability. Answering this question is precisely the (critical) task of philosophy as it has been understood from Kant on.

At the center of the modern episteme is the concept of man. By "man" Foucault obviously does not mean simply human beings as members of a biological and social species. Rather, "man" refers to certain aspects of the human capacity for forming representations of the world. Foucault maintains that the concept of man is distinctive of the modern age, that "man" did not exist in, for example, the Classical Age. This is not to say that people in the Classical Age were not capable of representing the world or that they were not aware of themselves as having this capacity. Foucault's point is rather that only in the modern age has this representational capacity become available as an explicit object of knowledge. In Classical terms, representation could be an object of knowledge only through an expression of its sameness and difference with respect to other forms of thought. It would, in other words, have to be presented as one species within the genus of thought. But this was not possible because, for the Classical Age, thought was identical with representation. In other words, representation was too fundamental a Classical category to possess the status of an ordinary object of knowledge. For the same reason, man – defined by the capacity for representation – could not be an object of knowledge. Or in Foucault's melodramatic phrase, "Man did not exist" (*Les mots et les choses* [*MC*], 319/308). After Kant, however, the question of man's status becomes unavoidable: the fact that thought is no longer conceived as inevitably representational allows and requires us to ask how human thought (man) is able to represent reality.

The question of "man" is particularly difficult because man is understood as simultaneously the source of representations (a subject) and an object of representation. Because of this, the question of how representation is possible becomes the question of how there can be a being that is both the ultimate subject of representation and a represented object. Developing a coherent conception of man in this sense has been the fundamental project of philosophy within the modern episteme (i.e., philosophy since Kant).

Foucault discusses this project in what is perhaps the most difficult section of *Les mots et les choses*, "Man and His Doubles". He distinguishes three different modern ways of formulating the distinction of man as subject and man as object. First, there is the division, especially associated with Kant, between a *transcendental* subject that establishes the conditions of the possibility of knowledge, and an *empirical* object of scientific knowledge. Second, there is a division, especially associated with Husserl, between the thinking *cogito* and the *unthought* encountered as the object and limit of thought. Third, there is the division, especially associated with Heidegger, between a recapturing of the historical meaning of human existence through a *return* to its origin and the perpetual *retreat* of this origin into an inaccessible past. These three divisions arise from the construal of human objectivity in terms of, respectively, science, the lifeworld, and history.

Of particular interest from our viewpoint is Foucault's assessment of phenomenology as a path to resolving the dual status of man. Here a first possibility is the Husserlian project (e.g., in the *Cartesian Meditations*) of deriving all objective meaning from the constituting activity of the transcendental ego. If this project could actually be carried out, it would, Foucault acknowledges, resolve the problem of man, since man as object would be reduced to man as constituting subject. However, Foucault agrees with his teacher, Merleau-Ponty, that transcendental subjectivity is, through the body, itself in the world of objects, so that the separation of subject and object required for Husserlian reduction and constitution is impossible. This might suggest that Foucault would be open to Merleau-Ponty's version of existential phenomenology, which gives primacy to embodied consciousness ("man-in-the-world"). He does, in fact, applaud existential phenomenology's "analysis of actual experience" (*MC*, 332/321) for its opposition to reductions of man to either the empirical or the transcendental component. It has, he agrees, tried to provide "a discourse whose tension would keep separate the empirical and the transcendental, while being directed at both" (*MC*, 331/320). But, Foucault maintains, existential phenomenology's analysis of actual experience cannot in the end escape its own reduction of the transcendental to the empirical.

This analysis seeks to articulate the possible objectivity of a knowledge of nature upon the original experience of which the body provides an outline; and to articulate the possible objectivity of a culture upon the semantic density which is both hidden and revealed in actual experience [*l'expérience vécu*]. It is doing no more, then, than fulfilling with greater care the hasty demands laid down when the attempt was made [e.g., by Comte and Marx] to make the empirical, in man, stand for the transcendental. (*MC*, 332/321)

This is not a very satisfactory critique, since Foucault gives no reason for his claim that the world of lived experience is simply the empirical world. Here he seems to be ignoring his own recognition, before the statement of this criticism, of the irreducible ambiguity of lived experience, which he describes as "a specific yet ambiguous stratum, concrete enough for it to be possible to apply to it a meticulous and descriptive language, yet sufficiently removed from the positivity of things for it to be possible, from that starting-point, to escape from that naïveté, to contest it and seek foundations for it" (*MC*, 332/321). Why, we wonder, if lived experience in fact has this "mixed" nature, does Foucault insist that phenomenological description is always "empirical despite itself" (*MC*, 337/326)?

Perhaps his point is just that existential phenomenology provides no satisfactory account of how lived experience can have the ambiguous status its descriptions reveal. But what, then, are the grounds for Foucault's apparent insistence that the viability of a concept requires an adequate philosophical (or other theoretical) explication of it? Suppose we grant him that there are no coherent, non-reductive theories of just how human consciousness can be both a constituting subject and a constituted object. It still does not follow that there is not a genuine, irreducible phenomenon corresponding to this duality.

In any case, we are now in a position to discuss Foucault's assessment of the human sciences. As he uses the term, "human sciences" refers to disciplines that are built around the modern concept of man. These he distinguishes from the modern empirical sciences that deal with human beings – biology, economics, and philology, concerned respectively with life, labor, and language. Whereas the empirical sciences treat human beings as part of nature (and therefore simply as objects of knowledge), the human sciences (sciences of man) also treat humans as subjects, capable of representing the world and themselves. So understood, the primary modern human sciences are psychology, sociology, and literary analysis. (However, Foucault links each human science to a corresponding empirical science by arguing that biology, economics, and philology each provide models for, respectively, psychology, sociology, and literary analysis.) Foucault also gives history a distinctive place as a human science that provides a temporal dimension to disciplines that in themselves treat man only in terms of a set of "synchronous patternings" (*MC*, 382/370).

Although it might seem that the failure of philosophy to formulate an adequate account of man undermines the human sciences, Foucault would not agree with this inference. This is because, in his view, the human sciences themselves have been more successful than philosophy in developing a coherent concept of man. They have, in particular, posited unconscious functions, conflicts, and meanings that explain how man is able to represent the fundamental realities of his world. (Presumably, philosophy is not able to do this because it treats the problem of representation entirely on the level of consciousness.)

However, this introduction of the unconscious itself eventually undermines the concept of man. The human sciences posit the unconscious, but they do not have the resources to give a positive account of its nature and capacities. For this, we need to develop more fundamental accounts that provide conditions of possibility for man himself – and, particularly, for his powers of representation. Such accounts are available in the new structuralist disciplines: Lacan's psychoanalysis provides the conditions of possibility for representations on the level of individual psychology, Lévi-Strauss's ethnology on the level of society. Foucault also anticipates a special, not-yet-realized version of linguistics that would unite the levels of psychoanalysis and ethnology into a single account of the unity of individuals and their cultures. The problem, however, is that these new disciplines, which Foucault calls *countersciences*, are based on systems of structures that are not themselves constituted by human representations but rather underlie and constrain these representations. In this fundamental intellectual sense, these countersciences entail the "death of man"; that is, the elimination of man as a basic category for understanding ourselves.

None of this means that Foucault thinks that there is no truth available from the human sciences. It is just that whatever truth there may be concerns a content that can (and ultimately must) be formulated without the use of the category of man. (Here Foucault might invoke Bachelard's view that permanent scientific truths can be formulated in frameworks that are later discredited.) Foucault also admits that he cannot be sure that it is the structuralist countersciences that will replace the sciences of man or even that the cultural elimination of man will in fact be carried out. His concluding comment is merely that "if some event of which we can at the moment do no more than sense the possibility" should in fact fundamentally alter our episteme, "then one can certainly wager that man would be erased, like a face drawn in sand at the edge of the sea" (*MC*, 398/387). But what he does claim to have established is the historical contingency of the modern episteme and its peculiar conception of human reality, man.

Although *Les mots et les choses* was directed against the entire modern episteme from Kant on, its immediate target was the orthodoxy of existential phenomenology, already under strong attack from Lévi-Strauss's structural anthropology. Sartre himself launched a counterattack in an interview that appeared in October 1966, right after the publication of *Les mots et les choses* (which sold 8000 copies in six weeks after publication).[17] He argued that Foucault's method should not be compared to archaeology but to geology (recall that Lévi-Strauss had found his initial inspiration in geology). Archaeology, Sartre noted, tries to reconstruct a structure ("style" is Sartre's term) that has the appearance of a "natural situation". But in fact the ruins to be reconstructed are "the result of a *praxis*"; they were "conceived and built by human beings". Foucault, however, merely presents us with a series of "layers", each defining "the conditions of possibility of a certain type of thought that triumphed during a certain period". He has no interest in "how each thought is constructed on the basis of these conditions nor how humans pass from one thought to another". To ask these questions – and, according to Sartre, they are the really interesting ones – Foucault would have to deal with praxis and hence with history, which is "precisely what he refuses to do". Sartre admits that there is a sense in which Foucault's perspective is historical: "he distinguishes epochs, a before and an after" ("Jean-Paul Sartre répond" [SR], 87). But he presents merely instantaneous "stills" of the past, with no sense of the movement of history (which, in Sartre's view, is provided by human subjectivity).

Sartre goes on to say that he has nothing against this and other

---

[17] Sartre was responding not only to *Les mots et les choses* but also to an interview Foucault had given in connection with its publication in which he dismissed Sartre's *Critique de la raison dialectique* as "The magnificent and pathetic effort of a man of the nineteenth century to think the twentieth century" ("L'homme est-il mort?").

structuralist approaches, provided "structuralism remains aware of the limits of its method" (SR, 88). In this regard, he distinguishes two levels of analysis of any human phenomenon, taking as an example the very phenomenon of language on which Foucault and his cohort place such emphasis. On one level, language is "an autonomous system, reflecting a social unification . . . The linguist takes this totality of relations as an object of study and is right to do so since it is already constituted. This is the moment of structure" (SR, 89). But, Sartre says, it is nonetheless true that this structure itself has been "worked by man and bears the trace of man". Language exists only because it has been *spoken* by men. Therefore, a full understanding of language requires a second level of analysis, one that reintroduces praxis to show how the structures of language have been made.

Sartre agrees that "man is . . . the product of structure". He "receives structures – and in that sense we can say that they make him". But Sartre also maintains that man "receives structures insofar as he is himself engaged in history" and engaged in such a way that he must destroy these structures and "constitute new ones that, in turn, serve as conditions" for other men (SR, 91).

It is hard to see how Foucault could consistently disagree with Sartre's claims here. His entire archaeological project, after all, is directed ultimately toward human liberation, which surely requires just the sort of praxis in the face of structures that Sartre emphasizes. Moreover, the critique developed in *Les mots et les choses* is not directed against the notion of individual human beings as free agents but against a particular philosophical conception of human beings. Sartre's ontology may or may not be an instance of that conception. But, as I argued above, there is no basis for Foucault's claim that the embodied consciousness of Sartre's and Merleau-Ponty's phenomenological descriptions is such an instance. There is even less basis for thinking that the ethical and political subject, the concern of both Sartre's and Foucault's liberationist activism, is reducible to "man". In this fundamental sense, Sartre is surely right about the limitations of Foucault's structuralist history.

Finally, it is striking that Foucault never connects his critique of the human sciences in *Les mots et les choses* to the issue of human liberation. Thinking in terms of "man" may well be a cognitive limitation, but how is it a significant impingement on human freedom in any moral sense? His later, "genealogical" histories do (as did *Folie et déraison*) discuss the evils that arise from making humans the objects of the human sciences and further show how our own self-awareness as subjects can be a tool of control. But even here there is no indication of how such developments could be related to the specifically philosophical view of man that is the focus of *Les mots et les choses*. As a result, *Les mots et les choses*, for all its intrinsic interest as intellectual history, remains oddly marginal to Foucault's fundamental project. This marginality corresponds to the ultimate irrelevancy, noted in chapter 8, of structuralism to the collapse of existential phenomenology.

DISCIPLINE

With *Surveiller et punir*, Foucault's work returns to the explicitly ethical motivations of *Folie et déraison*, but now with a firm sense of how to incorporate causal accounts of changes in knowledge systems. His particular focus is the emergence of the modern discipline of criminology and other related social scientific disciplines. With a bow to Nietzsche, he characterizes his new approach as genealogical. The general idea is hardly original: that shifts in the power structures of a society produce changes in epistemic formations. What is new is his understanding of the nature of power and of the precise way in which power and knowledge are related. I will here comment briefly on the latter point but defer the former to our discussion of *Histoire de la sexualité*.

Genealogy deals with the connection between nondiscursive practices and systems of discourse (bodies of knowledge). In this regard, Foucault's central claim is that there is an inextricable interrelation of knowledge (discourse) and power (expressed in nondiscursive practices, in particular, the control of bodies). This is why an understanding of his genealogical approach requires an understanding of his view of the relation of knowledge and power.

Negatively, Foucault does not have in mind the standard Baconian idea, which sees knowledge first existing as an autonomous achievement which is then used as an instrument of action (e.g., pure science vs. technology). He maintains that knowledge simply does not exist in complete independence of power, that the deployment of knowledge and the deployment of power are simultaneous from the beginning.

On the other hand, Foucault does not go so far as to identify knowledge with power, to make knowledge nothing more than an expression of social or political control. As he said, "The very fact that I pose the question of their relation proves clearly that I do not *identify* them."[18] His positive view is that systems of knowledge, although expressing objective (and perhaps even universally valid) truth in their own right, are nonetheless always more or less closely tied to the regimes of power that exist within a given society. Conversely, regimes of power necessarily give rise to bodies of knowledge about the objects they control, but this knowledge may – in its objectivity – go beyond and even ultimately threaten the project of domination from which it arises. Foucault pretty clearly intends this interconnection of knowledge/power as a general thesis, but he defends and is specifically committed to it only with respect to particular modern disciplines.

In *Surveiller et punir* Foucault treats knowledge/power with respect to the connection between the disciplinary practices used to control human bodies in the modern period and modern social scientific disciplines. His primary example is the practice of imprisonment as a way of punishing criminals in its relation to criminology and related social scientific disciplines. But he discusses imprisonment in the context of modern disciplinary practices in general (as employed in schools, factories, the military, etc.), and he shows how the prison served as a model and center of diffusion for this whole range of disciplinary practices.

As always, Foucault begins by contrasting the modern age with the Classical Age immediately preceding. He notes that the most striking and essential difference between the two periods was the violent and flamboyantly public nature of the punishment of criminals of the premodern period in contrast to the physically much milder and "low profile" modern punishment of imprisonment. Whereas standard accounts have attributed this difference primarily to a more humane and compassionate modern attitude (based on new philosophical ideas and a scientific understanding of criminality), Foucault's power/knowledge hypothesis suggests that there is something else going on, although he agrees humaneness may be a secondary factor. Specifically, he explores the idea that punishment becomes milder not simply for the sake of mildness but for the sake of new, more effective and more extensive forms of control. As he puts it, the point was not so much to punish less as to punish better.

[18] *Politics, Philosophy, Culture*, 43.

In Foucault's account, modern discipline is distinctive in three ways. First, its object of control is not primarily the mind (thoughts, feelings, etc.) but the body itself. Second, its scale of operation is not a general control of the body as a whole but a control in detail exercised on specific corporeal mechanisms. Third, its modality of control is to focus not simply on the results of bodily activity (by seeing that, one way or another, people do what is desired) but to maintain a constant supervision and control of the processes of bodily activity. The result is a "docile body": i.e., one that not only does what one wishes but does it as one wishes.

Modern discipline is, moreover, implemented through three distinctive techniques. The basic technique is *hierarchical observation*, careful monitoring by observers who are not themselves observed. Such observation lays the groundwork for *normalizing judgment*: an assessment of the deficiencies of those disciplined that is directed not toward punishment for the sake of revenge, as in the premodern age, but to reform of deviant behavior. Premodern judicial punishment was concerned merely with whether actions were in accord with a given law. Modern reformist judgment further situates individuals in a system of evaluation that pronounces them normal or abnormal. Thus, the Normal takes its distinctive place in modern society alongside the standard forms of power such as Law and Tradition. Indeed, normalization becomes a primary instrument of modern power. An example of normalizing judgment is the *examination*, a "normalizing gaze" whereby individuals are differentiated and judged, for example by tests in schools, medical examinations, job evaluations. Foucault also cites Bentham's "panopticon" prison design as an ideal model of how modern disciplinary power controls through its normalizing gaze.

Although modern disciplinary practices originated in isolated, enclosed institutions such as prisons and asylums, they rapidly spread throughout society, to schools, factories, medical clinics, welfare agencies, etc. In this expansion, these practices became positive as well as negative, not just preventing disapproved behavior but increasing production and knowledge. Detached from particular institutions, the practices also fell under the control of the nation-state and exerted their influence on society as a whole. The general result was the transformation of society from one of violent spectacle to one of insidious surveillance.

Foucault concludes *Surveiller et punir* with a discussion of the consequences of the extension of the prison model of knowledge/ power to society as a whole, the development of what he calls the carceral society or the carceral archipelago. A first result has been the establishment of a single continuum on which is located every form of improper behavior, from felonies to minor infractions of family or school rules. This continuum reflects the fact that in the modern age all improper behavior is regarded as of the same basic nature: a deviation from the norm. A serial murderer and an unruly schoolchild are both "deviants", and the behavior of the one is merely a ramification or an anticipation of the behavior of the other. Given this continuum of deviancy, we no longer think of a special set of "outlaws", who exist beyond or at the border of society. Rather, the class of deviants (delinquents) exists within the bosom of society, where it is cultivated, monitored, and controlled.

With the development of the carceral archipelago, the notion of law in the traditional sense of legislative acts and judicial interpretations of these acts becomes subordinated to the new law of the norm. Norms are not determined by senators or judges but by psychiatrists, criminologists, social workers, and teachers. These, accordingly, become the de facto authorities in society. Their authority, of course, itself derives from the authority of the social sciences of which they are the trained representatives. The carceral system of modern power is symbiotically related to the system of social-scientific knowledge. The power system's techniques of observation and documentation are essential conditions for the development of the knowledge system, and the knowledge system provides legitimation for the power system's exercise of authority.

This relation of power and knowledge is the basis of Foucault's genealogical account of the transition from one episteme to another:

I am not saying that the human sciences emerged from the prison. But, if they have been able to be formed and to produce so many profound changes in the episteme, it is because they have been conveyed by a specific and new modality of power: a certain policy of the body, a certain way of rendering the group of men docile and useful.[19]

It is, however, striking that the above text is the only mention of epistemes in *Surveiller et punir*. This suggests that, though Foucault is not rejecting the archaeological results of *Les mots et les choses*, he has not found those results particularly relevant to the concerns of *Surveiller et

---

[19] *Discipline and Punish*, 305.

punir. In accord with my previous remarks, I take this as an indication that the "subjects" and "objects" of disciplinary power and knowledge are quite different from the modern epistemological sense of those terms at work in *Les mots et les choses*. Certainly, there is no suggestion in *Surveiller et punir* that the threats of modern disciplinary power are on the verge of evaporating in the wake of the "death of man". In fact, Foucault's brief discussion of factors that might undermine carceral power cite new national and international systems of illegality that escape the disciplinary network (arms and drug sales, international business transactions) and the take-over of the prison system itself by autonomously operating medical and educational systems. These are obviously social trends that will continue to exist independent of epistemological conceptions of the self.

SEX

Foucault's history of sexuality began as a fairly straightforward extension of the genealogical approach of *Surveiller et punir* to the topic of sexuality. His idea was that the various modern bodies of knowledge about sexuality (various "sciences of sexuality", including psychoanalysis) have an intimate association with the power structures of modern society and so are prime candidates for genealogical analysis. Volume I, *La volonté de savoir* (1976), was intended as the introduction to a series of studies on particular aspects of modern sexuality (children, women, perverts, population control). It outlines the project of the overall history, explaining the basic viewpoint and the methods to be used.

A main theme of *La volonté de savoir* is that our standard view of the history of sexuality is distorted by our acceptance of the "repressive hypothesis", according to which the primary attitude of modern society toward sex (beginning in the eighteenth century, reaching a peak in the Victorian age, and still exerting strong influence today) was that, except for the closely delimited sphere of monogamous marriage, it was to be opposed, silenced, and, as far as possible, eliminated.

In order to understand the repressive hypothesis, Foucault argues, we must see it in relation to the fact that the last three centuries have produced a "veritable discursive explosion" regarding sex.[20]

[20] *History of Sexuality*, volume I, 17.

The explosion begins in the religious realm, with the Counter-Reformation's development of rules for confessions. These rules emphasized the need for penitents to examine themselves and articulate to their confessors not just all their sinful sexual actions but all the thoughts, desires, and inclinations behind these actions, there being nothing too small to be worthy of concern. The distinctive modern turn, however, is the secularization of this concern with knowing and expressing the truth about sex. This appears in a wide range of contexts: confessional literature, the political and economic problem of population (size and quality), infantile sexuality (extraordinary efforts to control masturbation and homosexuality in boarding schools), and beliefs about the sexual origin of physical and mental illness.

It might seem that all this talk about sex is nonetheless designed to repress sexual activity (prevent masturbation, reduce illegitimacy, discourage homosexuality). However, on analogy with his conclusion in *Surveiller et punir*, Foucault suggests that a much more plausible reading is that modern discourse about sexuality in fact constitutes various categories of sexual deviation, not to eliminate them but to exercise control over those who fall into them. Thus, the obsession with masturbation did not stop the activity, but it did establish unprecedented mechanisms for controlling the thoughts and behavior of adolescents. Similarly, homosexuality was by no means eliminated (or decreased), but homosexuals were much more closely enclosed in the net of social control.

Modern control of sexuality also parallels modern control of criminality by making sex, like crime, an object of allegedly scientific disciplines, which simultaneously offer knowledge and domination of their objects. However, it becomes apparent that there is a further dimension of the power associated with the sciences of sexuality. Not only is there control exercised via others' knowledge of individuals; there is also control via individuals' knowledge of themselves. Individuals internalize the norms laid down by the sciences of sexuality and monitor themselves in an effort to conform to these norms. Thus, they are controlled not only as *objects* of disciplines but also as self-scrutinizing and self-forming *subjects*.

This is the reason Foucault sees our apparently liberating focus on our sexuality as just a reinforcement of the mechanisms of social control. In trying to discover our deep sexual nature through self-scrutiny and to express this nature by overcoming various hang-ups and neuroses, we are merely shaping ourselves according to the norms and values implicit in modern sciences of sexuality. We may break with certain social conventions and constraints, but we do so only by putting ourselves just as firmly in the control of another system of constraints.

In accord with his critique of the repressive hypothesis, Foucault maintains his view, already developed in *Surveiller et punir*, that power is not purely negative but is a positive, creative force in society, producing both new forms of knowledge and new social categories and structures (along with the constraints corresponding to these). A further point – also developed in *Surveiller et punir* – is that power cannot be understood in terms of the action of any single central point of control. A society contains numerous centers of power (a "microphysics of power") that interact in complex ways. Power is dispersed and does not flow from one (or just a few) centers that are the key to seizing it.

In *La volonté de savoir* Foucault emphasizes the Christian background to the history of modern sexuality in practices such as confession. In his outline of the entire six-volume effort, he projects the next volume as a discussion of the antecedents of modern sexuality in the Christian notion of the flesh. This was to be followed by volumes on "The Children's Crusade" (about efforts to eliminate childhood masturbation), "The Hysterical Woman", "Perverts", and "The Malthusian Couple" (on population control). But although Foucault wrote the volume on Christianity, *Les avoux de la chair*, he never published it, and the others were never written.

What seems to have stopped Foucault was his realization that the true topic of his history of sexuality was the development of the modern conception of the self as a reflective subject. He was, of course, also still dealing with the topic of knowledge/power and with the development of the modern concept of sexuality. But his focus became the question of how, in its thought about sexuality, the modern age has constituted a unique idea of what it is to be a self (the modern notion of a subject), which is itself a major instrument of modern disciplinary control. (Perhaps there is an implicit recognition of the point I made about *Les mots et les choses*: that its central notion, the modern concept of *man*, had little connection with techniques of social control.) Given this understanding of his project, Foucault decided that it would not be sufficient to give a relatively brief sketch of the Christian antecedents of the modern concept of the self. Rather, he felt he needed to obtain a fuller understanding of these antecedents by following the process whereby the Christian notion of the self developed out of ancient (Greek and Roman) notions. Consequently, Foucault expanded his inquiry so that it would begin with two volumes on ancient sexuality – volume II (*L'usage des plaisirs*) on the fifth and fourth centuries BC, and volume III (*Le souci de soi*) on the second and first centuries BC – before turning to Christianity and, finally, the modern period.[21]

In the introduction to *L'usage des plaisirs* Foucault offers a very helpful overview of his final understanding of his basic project as a historian and of how his methods fit into this project. On the broadest level, he says, the work he has done is a contribution to a "history of truth". He conceives this history as having three main aspects: an analysis of "games of truth" (i.e., various systems of discourse developed to produce truth), both in their own right and in relation to one another; an analysis of the relation of these "games of truth" to power relations; and an analysis of the relation of "games of truth" to the self.

It seems clear that the first aspect, the analysis of games of truth, corresponds to Foucault's archaeological method – an analysis of systems of discourse in their own right. Similarly, the study of discourse in its relation to power is the domain of his genealogical method, as deployed in *Surveiller et punir*. The third aspect, the relation to the self, corresponds to his realization, in *La volonté de savoir*, that there is a distinction between power that operates by constituting us as objects and power that operates by constituting us as subjects. Both are the concern of genealogical analysis, but we need to distinguish a genealogy of an object from a genealogy of a subject. It is the latter that is the concern of Foucault's history of sexuality.

In principle, then, Foucault's work in the last two volumes of *Histoire de la sexualité* does not represent a radical break with his previous work, either in archaeology or genealogy. These remain his distinctive methods, even though they are employed in a very new context. However, Foucault does point out that in this later work he

---

[21] Foucault died before he could publish any of his recast project beyond the two volumes on the ancients. He did, however, continue reflecting on modern power – in lectures at the Collège de France and in seminars at Berkeley – with particular focus on the "governmental rationality" (or "governmentality") of modern societies. This line of thought has been taken up by his associates, François Ewald and Daniel Defert. See the essays by Foucault, Ewald, Defert, and others collected in Graham Burchell, et al. (eds.), *The Foucault Effect*.

has been able to enrich his conceptions of archaeology and genealogy. First, archaeology is now seen as concerned with human beings' "problematizations" of themselves, their world, and their actions. In other words, archaeological analyses of the structure of discourses are now seen as especially important because they reveal the fundamental issues and problems in terms of which individuals confront their existence. Further, genealogy is now seen as concerned with the "arts of existence"; that is, "those intentional and voluntary actions by which men not only set themselves rules of conduct, but also seek to make their life an *oeuvre* that carries certain aesthetic values and meets certain stylistic criteria".[22]

This focus of archaeology and genealogy on problematizations and practices represents a very important new emphasis of Foucault's work. He has in the end returned to a focus on the viewpoint of the individuals trying to understand and live in their world. He has not renounced his earlier position on the highly derivative and ephemeral status of the individual. Our history is still, to a very great extent, structured by discursive and nondiscursive practices that operate at much deeper levels than that of human consciousness. But this does not mean that we (as conscious subjects) are not real or that our concerns have no significance. In his final work, Foucault turned to this level of the individual self – what he calls "ethics".

L'usage des plaisirs is a good example of this new turn. Foucault begins with what is readily recognizable as an archaeology of ancient pleasures, designed to compare the ancient pagan view of sexuality with that of Christianity. He notes that there are very strong similarities at the level of moral codes (i.e., of rules of conduct and actual patterns of behavior determined by these rules). But there are fundamental differences at the level of the formation of an ethical subject; that is, in the way individual selves are formed by the ethical code. Foucault distinguishes four aspects of this formation (the four "forms of subjectification"): ethical substance (the basic conception of the sort of acts sexual ethics is concerned with); mode of subjection (the manner of – and the basis for – an individual's subordination to an ethical code, e.g., social convention, religious duty, means of self-fulfillment); forms of elaboration (that is, different modes of making oneself an ethical subject, such as the meticulous following of rules vs. a sudden change of life); and the telos of the

---

[22] *The Use of Pleasure*, 10–11.

ethical subject (the ultimate goal of ethical practices – e.g., self-mastery, purification for immortality).

Foucault's archaeology of ancient Greek sexuality consists of an analysis of its view on each of these four topics. The ethical substance of Greek sexuality was *ta aphrodisia*, the vaguely defined range of sexual acts. The key point, in contrast with early Christian views, is that *ta aphrodisia* were not regarded as evil in their own right (and hence morally problematic intrinsically and inevitably). They were rather regarded as natural and necessary. Nonetheless, the Greeks did see sexual acts as objects of moral concern because of their natural inferiority (they were, for example, shared with animals) and their great intensity. This led to a particular concern with the dangers of these actions not in themselves, as for the Christians, but because of excesses to which they could lead. Consistent with this, the Greek mode of subjection to the code of sexual ethics was not the Christian one of absolute exclusion or restriction to strictly specified circumstances. Rather, it was a matter of the proper use (*chresis*) of pleasures. It was not a matter of avoiding certain actions that were strictly forbidden (because essentially evil) but of engaging in the full range of sexual activities (heterosexual, homosexual, in marriage, out of marriage) with proper moderation. The way in which the Greeks constituted themselves as ethical subjects was through self-mastery (*enkrateia*). This was a matter of struggling with oneself for control over one's desires. The key to winning this struggle was training (*askesis*) through exercises of self-control. By contrast, Christian subjectivity was achieved primarily through self-renunciation. Finally, the telos of Greek ethics was moderation (*sophrosyne*), understood as a form of freedom – both negative (from one's passions) and positive (as mastery over others). Foucault also discusses how freedom in these two senses was essentially tied to truth, showing the distinctively Greek concern with an "aesthetics of existence" in contrast to the Christian "hermeneutics of the self".

The preceding archaeology shows the general way the ancient Greeks problematized sexuality. Foucault next turns to the presumably genealogical analysis of issues this problematization raised in specific domains of life and of the practices in which these issues were dealt with. He discusses the relation of sex to the Greek obsession with health, the role of pleasure in marriage, and, especially, the problems of homoerotic relations.

It is easy to see Foucault's analysis of the four forms of subjectification as an archaeological account of the ancient Greek view of sex, and as such it is very effective in presenting us with a striking contrast with our own view of sex. But it is much less easy to see the book as developing a genealogy, since there is almost no discussion of the factors whereby ancient sexual knowledge is causally tied to the power structures of a society. Admittedly, any genealogy Foucault is offering would be a genealogy of the subject (self), not of the object of a body of knowledge. Such an analysis would have to distinguish between authentic self-formation and self-formation coopted by an external power network, and to analyze the latter by showing the tie between a set of "techniques of the self" and an external power network (as was done in *La volonté de savoir*). *L'usage des plaisirs* offers little or nothing along these lines. There is no account of an ancient Greek regime for making individuals objects of social power, no demonstration of how techniques of self-formation are tied to this regime.

Moreover, it is easy to see why Foucault does not especially need to carry out this genealogical analysis. He is not concerned with the arbitrary constraints that may have been acting on the ancient Greeks but with the light Greek views can shed on Christian (and ultimately modern) techniques of self-formation. As always, he is writing a history of the present. Consequently, it is no surprise that Foucault pays little or no attention to questions of power that are not relevant to our current situation. But saying this is to admit, contrary to Foucault's own suggestions, that *L'usage des plaisirs* (and *Le souci de soi*) is primarily archaeological, not genealogical – at least as he understood these notions in the 1970s.

The archaeology of *L'usage des plaisirs* is, however, an effective vehicle for Foucault's critical history of the present; it provides fruitful alternatives to our present understanding of sexuality, thereby suggesting ways of transgressing its boundaries. Foucault insists that there is no question of "going back to the Greeks". But there is reason to think that – much more than in any of his other works – he does find inspiration in ancient history for a new view of sexuality (especially the notion of an "aesthetics of existence"). Here more than anywhere else, we get some idea of what might be involved in a positive Foucaultian view of sexuality and, more generally, a Foucaultian ethics.

CHAPTER 10

Derrida

> We feel in one world, we think, we give names to things in another; between the two we can establish a certain correspondence, but not bridge the gap.
> (Marcel Proust, *In Search of Lost Time*, III, 56)

Foucault and Derrida both reject the traditional project of philosophy, although they also propose alternative employments for its intellectual legacy. (They seek not a continuation of philosophy by other means but a continuation of philosophy's means for other ends.) But where Foucault is centrifugal in relation to philosophy, moving away from its traditional aporiae toward successor projects of archaeology and genealogy, Derrida is centripetal, relentlessly dissecting the body of failed philosophical knowledge. In this important sense, Derrida remains closer to the traditional vocation of the philosopher, a fact for which there are reasons both in his education and in his philosophical position. Both Foucault and Derrida were *normaliens*,[1] and Derrida, four years younger, attended a lecture course that Foucault, at Althusser's invitation, gave at the École Normale in the early 1950s. But whereas Foucault was from early on as interested in psychology and history as in philosophy, Derrida pursued an exclusively philosophical training and first made his name as a Husserl scholar.[2] Further, while Foucault had little

---

[1] Derrida was born and raised in Algeria and entered the École Normale after three years of preparation at the Lycée Louis-le-Grand in Paris.

[2] In particular, Derrida's translation of Husserl's "Origin of Geometry" (*Introduction à "L'origine de la géometrie" de Husserl*), with its long introductory essay, and *La voix et le phénomène*, a close study of Husserl's theory of signs, were applauded by the French university establishment. But Derrida's later works were much less well received, and he has remained at the margins of the power centers of French academic philosophy, never having held a university professorship. From 1964 to 1984 he taught at the École Normale (as *maître-assistant*). In 1983 he became a director of studies at the École des Hautes Études en Sciences Sociales and also was chosen as the first director of the Collège International de philosophie, a teaching and

interest in traditional modes of philosophical thought (except when, as in *Les mots et les choses*, they formed part of his historical subject-matter), Derrida maintained that although traditional philosophical issues are undecidable in principle, they are also ineliminable from our thought and in some sense require our constant attention. As a result, Derrida's writings, unlike Foucault's, are a constant and explicit probing of traditional philosophical concepts.[3]

Derrida presents himself, however, not as a practitioner of traditional philosophy but as its most assiduous reader. And he is, indeed, above all a remarkable reader with a distinctive talent for close, subtle, and imaginative scrutiny of texts. Nor is his reading limited to philosophers. Along with his studies of Plato, Rousseau, Condillac, Hegel, Marx, Husserl, Heidegger, and Levinas, there are essays on literary figures such as Kafka, Valéry, Mallarmé, Joyce, Artaud, and Blanchot and on major contributors to the human sciences (e.g., Freud, Saussure, Lévi-Strauss). More than any important philosopher since the Middle Ages, Derrida has devoted himself to reading and commenting on the writings of others.

Reading Derrida himself is frequently an intimidating and frustrating project. To say the least, his texts are much closer to the "writerly" than to the "readerly" end of Roland Barthes' spectrum. This has particularly irritated Anglo-American analytic philosophers such as John Searle, and there are circles in which Derrida is regarded as an obscurantist charlatan. I would hope that our discussion here will refute the noun, but there is something to the adjective.

The fault is not entirely Derrida's. He discusses difficult thinkers, generally at a very high level of sophistication, so that readers who are not fully up to the level of his discussion will of course have problems. More importantly, Derrida deploys a variety of writing styles, most of which have little to do with the analytic philosopher's efforts to clarify and refine our common-sense intuitions. He will, for

---

research center he helped to found. He has also regularly held visiting appointments at American universities (although typically in literature rather than philosophy departments), first at Johns Hopkins and later at Yale and then the University of California at Irvine.

[3] The one direct confrontation between Derrida and Foucault arose from Derrida's critique (first presented at a meeting of Jean Wahl's Collège de Philosophie) of Foucault's treatment of Descartes in *Folie et déraison*. See Derrida's "Cogito et histoire de la folie", in *L'écriture et la différence* and Foucault's response, "My Body, This Paper, This Fire". See also Derrida's later discussion of Foucault in "'To Do Justice to Freud': The History of Madness in the Age of Psychoanalysis".

example, play with language through puns, bizarre associations, or perverse self-referentiality, simply to effect a disorientation of our ordinary conceptual categories. (The final section, on signatures, of "Signature événement contexte" is a good brief example, as is the opening of his extraordinary response to John Searle in *Limited Inc*. The whole of *Glas* is a much longer and more aggravating instance.) He will also strain or break conventional categories in order to introduce new vocabularies, as in his famous essay, "La différance".[4] One key to appreciating Derrida is to realize that such negative and positive pyrotechnics have their own distinctive functions and are not failed efforts to analyze concepts or construct arguments. At the same time, it is often hard to avoid the conclusion that there is little purpose to the immense length and complexity of many of these displays.

But many of Derrida's efforts do require conceptual explication and logical argument of a broadly analytic sort. This is frequently called for in his deconstruction via close reading of a text's fundamental dichotomies. *La voix et le phénomène* shows Derrida at his best in this mode. It is a very "responsible" study, the difficulties of which derive primarily from the closeness of the argument and the thorniness of the Husserlian texts being analyzed. Unfortunately, in other cases, Derrida falls considerably short of the clarity and rigor his discussion requires. This happens, for example, in the essay on Austin, "Signature événement contexte", which drew Searle's criticism. Searle undoubtedly misreads Derrida, but the syntactic complexity and conceptual confusions of Derrida's text (including, despite his protests, a muddling of the use/mention distinction) give ample opportunity for misunderstanding. But even Derrida's most difficult texts offer significant rewards to the persistent reader, and it is hard to believe that those denouncing him as an intellectual fraud have made a serious effort to come to terms with his thought.

DECONSTRUCTION

Why should a philosopher, particularly one at Derrida's historical site, be so obsessed with what others have written? Because, as Derrida sees it, writing reveals the essential peculiarities and limitations of human thought. A written text will always escape total

---

[4] Included in *Marges de la philosophie*.

clarification. There will always be textual ambivalences that remain unresolvable and prevent us from understanding fully "what the author really means". We may think, as Plato sometimes suggests, that the problem is due simply to the medium of writing. If we could directly speak to the author, our perception of intonations and gestural nuances – along with the possibility of follow-up questions – would eliminate all ambivalence, all undecidability. But of course even face-to-face speaking will not convey a message perfectly. The inevitable differences (in past experience, in expectations, in idiolect) between speaker and hearer maintain permanent possibilities of misunderstanding. Suppose, then, that to eliminate these differences, I consider just the case of my own internal formulation of my thoughts. Even here, Derrida maintains, the linguistic formulation will not be totally adequate. The generality of any linguistic expression will make it a less than perfect expression of the precise details of my thought or the exact nuances of my feelings. It would seem that perfect adequacy is achieved only in the immediate, pre-linguistic presence of my thought to itself. But Derrida argues that there is no such pure presence of thoughts to the self. All thought is mediated through language and can never attain such total clarity. There is always a difference between what is thought (or experienced or said or written) and the ideal of pure, self-identical meaning.

The above line of argument is a prototype of Derrida's repeated demonstrations, in different contexts and terms, that the apparently contingent and remediable defects of writing are in fact inevitable features of all thought, all expression, all reality. Derrida's philosophical project is an unending extrapolation of the reader's inability to master a text.

In search of total clarity, philosophers (and others) since Plato have repeatedly insisted on a sharp distinction between speech and writing. As Derrida presents it, the basic contrast of the dichotomy is always between speech as the primary and immediate expression of thought and writing as a secondary and derivative expression of thought. When I hear someone speak, the source of the thought (the speaker) is immediately present to me, so there is minimal possibility of misunderstanding. When I read what someone has written, the source is absent, and there are many more possibilities for misinterpretation. Derrida shows how thinkers from Plato to Rousseau and Saussure have derogated writing in comparison to speech and associated the division between the two with all the standard philosophical dichotomies.[5] Speech involves presence, reality, truth, certainty, purity; writing involves absence, appearance, falsehood, doubt, impurity.

At the same time, Derrida points out, the very texts in which Plato, Rousseau, and Saussure celebrate speech over writing undermine or reverse the distinction. Plato, for example, defines thought (of which speech is supposed to be the pure expression) as a kind of "writing inscribed in the soul". (This leads Derrida to speak of a more fundamental form of writing – *archi-writing* – of which speech itself is an instance.) Further, writing, for all its dangers, is in the end the only way that speech, which itself exists only in the fleeting moment, can be preserved. This is why Plato refers to writing as a *pharmakon*, which means both poison and remedy. Similarly, Rousseau, while denouncing the deceptions of writing, admits that it, rather than speech, is the only way in which he can express his true self. And Saussure, although he makes the standard points about the derivative nature of writing, eventually uses it as his primary model for the way in which the meanings of signs are specified by differences. Derrida refers to the project of studying the role of writing in Western thought, including both its denigrations and surreptitious returns, as the discipline of *grammatology*, from the Greek for letters or writing (although he later tends to speak of his efforts here as just one example of deconstruction).

Despite our relentless failure to attain perfect meaning and truth, all our philosophical thought and language is based on the assumption of and drive for such perfection. This assumption and drive can be formulated by three principles that are central in the Western philosophical tradition. (Derrida himself never states the principles in these terms, but they catch what he has in mind by "logocentric" thinking.) First, the basic elements of thought and language are pairs of opposing concepts, such as presence/absence, truth/falsity, being/nothingness, same/other, one/many, male/female, hot/cold. This we can call the principle of opposition. Next, the opposing pairs are regarded as exclusive logical alternatives, governed by the principles of identity (A = A) and non-contradiction (nothing is both A and not-A). This we can call the principle of logical exclusion. For example, being present excludes being absent; the present is simply

---

[5] On Plato, see "La pharmacie de Platon", in *La dissémination*. On Rousseau, see *De la grammatologie*, part II; on Saussure, part I, chapter 2.

what it is (present) and is in no way what it is not (absent). Finally, each fundamental pair is asymmetrical in the sense that one term has in some crucial sense priority over the other (e.g., is more fundamental, more real, morally better than the other). This is the principle of priority.

A typical Derridean reading will reveal the extent to which a given text does not fit the model of a logical system as defined by the above three principles. Specifically, it will show that the binary oppositions on which the text is based are not sustained, that the alleged relations of logical exclusion and priority cannot be coherently formulated and are implicitly denied by the very text that formulates them. Derrida calls this technique *deconstruction*. Deconstruction shows how texts based on binary oppositions themselves violate both the principle of exclusion and the principle of priority. Thus, a deconstructive reading of a text reveals points at which it introduces one of the opposing terms into the definition of the other or reverses the order of priority between the two terms.

Derrida characterizes in various ways the views put into question by deconstructive analysis. The general project of deconstructing the fundamental dichotomies built into thought yields a critique of *logocentrism*. The dominant terms of the standard polar oppositions always correspond to some sort of presence, a reality that is positive, complete, simple, independent, and fundamental (Plato's forms, Aristotle's substances, Aquinas's God, Hegel's absolute). This presence is always understood as the polar opposite of something that is negative, incomplete, complex, dependent, and derivative (matter, creatures, appearance, etc.). Derrida's deconstructive analyses show, however, that the purity and priority of presence is never sustained in the texts of the great metaphysicians. For example, Plato discovers that the forms participate in non-being, Christians think of God as somehow humanly incarnate, and so on. The result is a critique of *metaphysical presence*.[6]

The epistemological parallel to doctrines of metaphysical presence are the various forms of *epistemological foundationalism*. These express efforts to ground all knowledge in some fundamental certainty such as intellectual insight (various rationalisms, from Plato through

---

[6] Here, as elsewhere, the point of deconstruction is not to reverse the standard bifurcation and give, for example, priority to absence over presence, a reversal that would merely continue logocentrism in another key. See, for example, Derrida's critique of absence in "Violence et métaphysique" (in *L'écriture et la différence*).

Descartes) or sense experience (various empiricisms, from Aristotle through Hume). Foundationalists assert something present and immediate (to the mind, in experience) that opposes and overcomes what is absent and derivative, for example, opinions received from others, unjustified inferences, interpretations that go beyond the given facts. Deconstruction, however, shows that the foundational elements themselves are "tainted" by the very epistemological limitations they are designed to overcome. Thus, entirely clear and hence infallible intellectual insights are found to contain questionable hidden assumptions, allegedly pure sense data turn out to embody culturally relative interpretative frameworks, and so on.

In the domain of ethics, deconstructive analysis reveals that values asserted as eternal verities are in fact simply reflections of the historically developed and contingent practices of a particular culture. This effects a critique of *ethnocentrism*. Derrida and, especially, some of his followers have focused on the specific version of ethnocentrism that privileges male over female. This is *phallocentrism*, which presents distinctively "masculine" traits as obviously superior to distinctively "feminine" traits (e.g., domination over sympathy, clarity over depth) and concludes that the social and political subordination of women to men is entirely natural and appropriate. (Derrida sees phallocentrism as derivative from logocentrism and so speaks of *phallogocentrism*.)[7]

At the very least, Derrida is a philosopher in the traditional sense of continuing the Socratic project of questioning our assumptions. His questioning is distinctly radical in its probing of philosophy's own presuppositions about itself. We have already noted his questioning of the basic concepts in terms of which philosophers construct their views of reality. But Derrida also questions the very form of philosophy, raising objections to the idea of "a philosophy" as a unified body of philosophical work and even problematizing the distinction between philosophy and its ancient Platonic rival, literature.

His point applies, in the first instance, to his own writings: "In what you call my books, what is first of all put in question is the unity of the book and the unity 'book' considered as a perfect totality." We think of a book as a self-contained unity, perhaps part of a larger whole, but still a unit intelligible in its own terms. (Or, if there is

---

[7] See also the comments on Derrida and feminism in my discussion of Irigaray in chapter 11.

reason to think that this is not so, then we expect to be able to read the material in question as part of a text that does form a self-contained unity.) Derrida says his books "do not conform to this ideal unity of a book". Moreover, they are written to show that other "books" also lack this unity. All so-called books are "entirely consumed by the reading of other texts"[8]: a text can be understood only by relating it to other texts, from which it draws its problems, concepts, vocabulary. "Other texts" also includes other parts of the given text. Understanding what I say here requires understanding what I have just said and what I will say twenty pages on. A text has an infinite openness to other texts that makes impossible the reduction to the strict unity that we fantasize when speaking of it as a "book". This is explicit in Derrida's own writing, which almost always takes the form of close commentary on the writing of others and, at the same time, wraps the reader in an endless spiral of self-references. Similarly, his commentaries on the texts of others show how what at first seem to be coherent wholes split, on scrutiny of the external and internal relations that constitute them, into divergent and incommensurable multi-dimensionalities. Derrida's books, both those he writes and those he reads, are not really books because they can never be closed.

Derrida sums up his perspective as writer and reader through a metaphor of infinite complexity borrowed, ironically, from Husserl, who in his *Ideas I* imagines a situation in which:

> A name on being mentioned reminds us of the Dresden gallery . . . We wander through the rooms . . . A painting by Teniers . . . represents a gallery of paintings . . . The paintings of this gallery would represent in their turn paintings, which on their part exhibited readable inscriptions and so forth.[9]

Here one thing always leads to another with a growth that can never be caught in any principle of pattern or progression. In such a case – and this is, for Derrida, the case with everything we call a book or the work of an author – there can be no ultimate unity or coherence.

The above line of thought might lead us to revise our thinking about the unity of philosophical (and other) writings. But it does not of itself mean that we cannot still define philosophy as a distinct genre, clearly separated from other sorts of writing, particularly

---

[8] *Positions*, 3.
[9] *Ideas I*, no. 100, as cited in *Speech and Phenomena*, 104.

literature. Of course, there are various ways of understanding a philosophy/literature distinction: in terms of truth/fiction, reason/emotion, general/concrete, etc. But Derrida's view is best approached in terms of a putative distinction between philosophy as a mode of expression for which all that matters is the pure essential conceptual content of language and literature as a mode of expression devoted to making effective use of the contingent features of the specific language employed. Thus, philosophers, unlike poets, will not care whether they have achieved mellifluous rhythm or ironic rhyme, as long as they have conveyed their "basic ideas". The point is particularly vivid for the central literary trope of metaphor, which will for the philosopher at best be an aesthetic or pedagogical enhancement of what could be well enough said without it, but will be the very heart of what the poet says. In other words, philosophical metaphors will always be translatable into literal language without loss of philosophical content, whereas a literal paraphrase always loses the poetry.

Derrida insists that his texts "belong neither to the 'philosophical' register nor to the 'literary' register".[10] But, even more, he tries to show us that no text, not even the clearest, most literal and transparent logical discourse, can avoid an essential reliance on literary devices. Indeed, as Derrida points out, the very clarity that pure philosophy would contrast with the obscurities of literary metaphor is itself a metaphor: "the appeal to criteria of clarity and obscurity would suffice to confirm . . . that this whole philosophical delimitation of metaphor already lends itself to being constructed and worked by 'metaphors'. How could a piece of knowledge or language be properly clear or obscure?"[11]

None of this means that Derrida denies the existence of philosophy as a distinguishable aspect of intellectual history, even one associated with distinctive cognitive skills and habits of mind. But he does reject the claim that the contingent historical phenomenon we call philosophy corresponds to an epistemically privileged mode of fundamental cognition.

---

[10] *Positions*, 71. Nonetheless, some of his writings, such as the closely argued critique of Husserl in *La voix et le phénomène*, are much closer to the philosophical end of the continuum and others, such as *La carte postale*, which includes something close to an epistolary novel, are much closer to the literary end. There are also texts such as *Glas* that deliberately aim to blur the line between the literary and the philosophical.

[11] "White Mythology", *Margins of Philosophy*, 252.

DIFFERANCE

Derrida's deconstructive readings are complemented by a more positive and, in some ways, even systematic philosophical project. This is carried out through his repeated efforts to introduce vocabularies that attempt to adumbrate the level – which we might call ontological or even preontological – where dichotomies dissolve and their oppositions reverse and slide into one another. This project is systematic both in the comprehensive applicability of each of the vocabularies and in the complex interconnections that bind together terms from different vocabularies. We will discuss first the vocabulary of *differance*, the one Derrida has most fully developed and most often deploys, and then, more briefly, the vocabularies of *supplement* and of *trace*.

"Differance", a transliteration of the French neologism *différance*, is meant to evoke the instability of the binary oppositions fundamental to logical systems. Derrida designed the term to have two basic connotations: difference and deferral. (The French verb from which it derives, *différer*, means both *to differ* and *to defer*.) The first connotation corresponds to the way in which any pair of binary opposites always fails to match exactly the domain to which it is supposed to apply. There are always irreducible differences between the structure of the actual phenomenon (a historical event, a text, a personality) and the binary divisions required by a logical system. For example, Rousseau's actual use of the concepts *speech* and *writing* does not correspond to the sharp division he claims to make between them.

Further, efforts to impose the sharp distinction required by binary oppositions must always be "put off" (deferred) in the face of the recalcitrance of the phenomenon. For example, when we see that Plato has violated the speech/writing dichotomy by defining the thought expressed by speech as a writing in the soul, we may try to fall back to a distinction between "good writing" – which is like speech – and "bad writing". The idea is that, even if the distinction fails at one level, it can be revived at another level (we merely "defer" drawing it). But, Derrida maintains, further analysis will show that even the "fall-back" distinction can be undermined and that a truly sharp distinction will remain elusive, will have to be indefinitely deferred.

We see, then, Derrida's point in forming a noun from *différer*. But why does he introduce the "misspelling" *différance* instead of the standard *différence*? First, although he wants his term to recall the standard one, he also wants to emphasize the difference between his use of the term and its use by other thinkers (Hegel, Saussure, Heidegger). Further, the *a* in the final syllable follows the pattern in French for forming verbal nouns (gerunds), so that *différance* maintains a pointed ambivalence between an action (a making different) and the state resulting from this action (a difference). In this way, Derrida's term suggests a reality not caught by such standard metaphysical dichotomies as active/passive, event/state, action/passion. Finally, the fact that there is a *written* but no *spoken* difference between *différance* and *différence* evokes Derrida's discussion of the speech/writing dichotomy, and gives a priority to writing (which alone can express Derrida's meaning) that subverts the force of the standard distinction.

Having seen Derrida's general strategy for deploying his new word, we can now explore its role as an "alternative" ("replacement" or "supplement") to standard philosophical terminologies. Derrida often characterizes differance in the language of movement and causality. For example: "differance refers to the (active *and* passive) movement that consists in deferring". Further, this movement "is the production of . . . differences" between basic philosophical oppositions such as "sensible/intelligible, intuition/signification, nature/culture, etc.".[12] However, Derrida also emphasizes that we cannot literally conceive of differance in terms of the standard categories of movement and causality (cf. *Marges de la philosophie* [*MP*], 12–13/12). They too are terms of philosophical dichotomies (rest/movement, cause/effect) and so must themselves be the "products" of differance. Eventually, Derrida says, he must deconstruct the meanings even of movement and cause (but he "defers" the deconstruction to another occasion).

The above way of talking about differance is neither incoherent nor merely cute. It reflects rather Derrida's conviction that despite the intrinsic limitations of the standard dichotomies – signaled in their "production" by a differance that eludes them – we have no way of thinking apart from them. There is no standpoint outside of the dichotomies from which we can overlook and master them. Differance is not, like Hegel's absolute, a synthesis of all opposites

---

[12] *Positions*, 8, 9.

into a fully intelligible whole. It is itself caught in the endless play of differences, neither controlling nor controlled, always generating new paradoxes. We can use "differance" to indicate the limitations of our concepts and language but not to overcome them. Derrida's questioning of the distinctions on which thinking is based is not undertaken in the name of a new set of definitive answers (i.e., a new set of dichotomized concepts) but in the name of the perpetual need to be aware of the limits of any answers.

The philosophical significance of differance is most readily approached through the question of language, the system of signs through which meanings are expressed. Here we can begin with Saussure, who saw the arbitrary and the differential character of signs as their fundamental and inseparable features. Signs are arbitrary because "the system of signs is constituted by the differences in the terms, and not by their plenitude". The principle of difference as the basis of signs "affects the *totality* of the sign, that is, the sign as both signified and signifier" (*MP*, 11/10). The key point, as Saussure says, is that although "a difference generally implies positive terms between which the difference is set up . . . in language there are only differences *without positive terms*".[13] From this, Derrida says, it follows "that the signified concept is never present in and of itself . . . Every concept is inscribed in a chain or in a system within which it refers to . . . other concepts, by means of the systematic play of differences." Differance is precisely this sort of play, which is why it is not a concept "but rather the possibility of conceptuality, of a conceptual system and process in general". Similarly, differance is not a word: it is not "the calm, present, self-referential unity of concept and phonic material" (*MP*, 12/11).

Within a language as a system there are only differences, but "these differences are themselves effects". Differance is "the playing movement that 'produces' – by means of something that is not simply an activity – these differences, these effects of difference . . . Differance is the non-full, non-simple structured and differing 'origin' of differences" (*MP*, 12/11). If, as classical thought has it, a cause had to be a presence (subject or substance), we would here soon be led to speak of effects without causes, and therefore we

---

[13] Ferdinand de Saussure, *Course in General Linguistics*, 120 (cited by Derrida in *Margins of Philosophy*, 11).

would shortly stop speaking even of effects. (As we shall see, Derrida tries to fill this conceptual gap with the notion of a *trace*.)

Derrida cites Saussure's claim that language (*langue*) is needed for speech (*parole*) to be intelligible, while speech is necessary for language to be established historically, and suggests extending the thought to signs in general. Thinking this way, we can define différance as "the movement according to which language, or any code, any system of referral in general, is constituted 'historically' as a weave of differences". Derrida notes that he uses terms such as "constituted", "historically", etc. only "for their strategic convenience" and in preparation for "their deconstruction at the currently most decisive point". He further insists that différance, even though he has described it in terms of the genesis of a structure "is no more static than it is genetic, no more structural than historical. Or is no less so . . . . Such oppositions have not the least pertinence to différance, which makes the thinking of it uneasy and uncomfortable" (*MP*, 13/12).

We may, however, object that it will not be so easy to extend différance beyond the realm of language. There is, for example, the experience that our language (both verbal signifiers and signified concepts) is ultimately about. Surely, we may claim, this has a fixed content that escapes the endless play of linguistic differences.

Derrida's response to this challenge is most fully developed in his reflections in *La voix et le phénomène* on Husserl's phenomenology, which accords to experience just the sort of privileged role that Derrida questions. Without trying to follow all the twists and turns of this close discussion, let me try to formulate the central thrust of Derrida's critique. We can put Husserl's challenge in this way: on the purely linguistic level, there is, as we saw in our discussion of Saussure, no reason why someone could not completely master a certain part of our language (say, the language of colors) without any actual experience of the objects the language is used to refer to. So, for example, a blind person, even though never having seen a color, could speak quite exactly about colors, shades, tones, and intensities solely on the basis of a knowledge of the way these terms play against one another (the "differences" among them). To this extent, Derrida's story about différance as the "source" of all meaning is correct. But, we want to argue, something further is available for those who have experienced colors. They have seen the color as a directly perceived presence, not just referred to it as the trace of a system of signs. Surely this means that they know something more about the color than the blind person. (A parallel example is Diderot's blind mathematician, who may know much more about geometrical shapes than I do but does not know *how they look*.)

Derrida cannot plausibly deny that those who see have access to something that the blind do not. But his question would be whether this access is itself independent of the linguistic system (system of differences). Is not our very capacity to see colors, tones, and shades itself a function of the linguistic system in which we operate? Without language, in other words, would we in fact have experience in anything other than a brute physiological sense? Derrida's view suggests that the answer is no, so that we never achieve any knowledge or meaning apart from the play of differences that constitutes language.[14] This is what Derrida means by his famous assertion, "There never was any 'perception'."[15]

Finally, a few words about *supplement* and *trace*. Derrida is attracted to the term "supplement" (which he encounters in his readings of Rousseau and Condillac on language) because of its dual meaning. On the one hand, a supplement can be an inessential extra (e.g., an advertising supplement to a newspaper). On the other hand, it can be an essential addition, remedying a crucial incompleteness in that to which it is added (e.g., a vitamin supplement required to remedy a deficiency in a patient's diet). In the binary oppositions of Western thought, the second term is treated as a supplement, in the inessential sense, to the first term. Thus, reality (e.g., Plato's forms) is complete in itself, and appearance (the material world) is just an unnecessary and imperfect imitation. Likewise, speech expresses the fullness of meaning, while writing is just an inessential reflection of speech. Deconstructive analysis, however, shows ways in which the supplement is in fact essential, ways in which it remedies an incompleteness in the first term. Thus, it may turn out that appearance is the only way that the eternal can be realized in time or (as Derrida's analysis of Saussure shows) that writing is the model for understanding speech as a meaningful system. So, like differance, supplement refers to aspects of the realities with which we deal (whether they be texts, lives, or whatever) that escape and undermine the divisions and subordinations that binary oppositions try to impose.

---

[14] Here, of course, Derrida is very close to analytic philosophers such as Sellars and Quine, who have criticized the "myth of the given".

[15] *Speech and Phenomena*, 103.

Derrida particularly develops the notion of supplement in his discussion of Rousseau in *De la grammatologie*. A first example concerns the speech/writing dichotomy. Rousseau frequently emphasizes that the living presence of speech is far superior to writing, which is a mere inferior supplement to the spoken word. Nonetheless, in a striking passage cited by Derrida, Rousseau says: "I would love society as others do if I were not sure of showing myself not just at a disadvantage but as completely different from what I am. The decision I have taken to write and to hide myself is precisely the one that suits me. If I were present people would never have known what I was worth."[16] So the unnecessary, inferior supplement becomes the essential means of expressing the truth.

Similarly, Rousseau famously glorifies human beings in their natural state, maintaining that our entire good is there and is only corrupted by the artificialities of society and civilization. On this reading, education, to which Rousseau pays so much attention, would be a mere supplement to nature. But in fact his discussions of education makes it clear that our natural goodness is always only implicit and that education is in fact necessary to allow it to emerge full-blown.

Finally, Rousseau refers disdainfully to masturbation – which clearly obsessed him – as "that dangerous supplement", which he presents as an inferior and unnecessary substitute for "normal" sexual relations with a partner. But his own experiences showed that even so-called normal sex involves strong elements of fantasy and self-focus that it shares with masturbation.

"Trace" is a term that emerges from reflection on the way that what traditional philosophy presents as solid, unproblematic presence always dissolves in the face of deconstructive analysis. It is as though presence itself is a derived phenomenon, something we can at best catch a glimpse of amidst the play of differences. It is not that there is literally nothing there, but that what is there appears only indirectly, obliquely; we might say it is present through its absence. Derrida uses "trace" to refer to this phenomenon. The notion of "trace" is implicit in Saussure's view of language. Traditional views would locate the meaning of a sign in the thought it signifies, with the thought taken to be the meaning itself, fully and positively present to the mind. But, as we have seen, for Saussure the meaning

---

[16] Jean-Jacques Rousseau, *Confessions* (cited in *Of Grammatology*, 142).

of a sign corresponds not to a presence but to a system of differences that distinguish one sign from all the others. The meaning, we might say, exists in a given sign but only as a set of traces of all the other signs from which the sign differs. I think of *dog* and understand its meaning. But this meaning is not something I read out of a present concept. It is rather something I discern from my awareness of the ways that *dog* differs from other signs such as *cat, animal,* and *bark.*

Zeno's old paradox of the arrow provides a simple but helpful example of thinking in terms of the trace.[17] Regarding the arrow in motion as a mere succession of self-contained presences fails to yield the concrete phenomenon of a *moving* arrow. To avoid paradox, we must insinuate into each "point" of motion essential reference to past and future points that are not present but somehow leave their traces.[18]

IS DERRIDA A SKEPTIC?

Derrida's deconstructions challenge both the philosophical pretensions of phenomenology and the scientific pretensions of structuralism. But critics suggest that it further rejects *any* project of rational thought by denying the "logocentric" assumption that reality can be grasped through concepts the meaning and application of which are precisely defined by the laws of logic (identity and non-contradiction). This is the position of those who think Derrida falls into the trap of a self-refuting radical skepticism. We need therefore to look at the possibilities for a skeptical interpretation of Derrida's philosophy.

The most radical possibility would be to read Derrida as denying or seriously questioning the laws of logic, denying, for example, that there is any meaningful distinction between a truth and its false denial. If so, it would seem that his thought refutes itself. For, as Aristotle long ago pointed out, those who truly question, say, the law of non-contradiction destroy any possibility of coherently expressing their position. If I say that both *p* and not-*p* can (in exactly the same sense) be simultaneously true, then my saying *this* conveys no information, since it is entirely compatible with its denial. There is, however, nothing in Derrida that suggests this incoherent view. He

---

[17] See Jonathan Culler, *On Deconstruction,* 94–5.
[18] This is a theme we have seen in Bergson and will encounter again in Deleuze.

accepts the logic of non-contradiction as a necessary condition on thought and discourse, and surely means all of his assertions to entail the denial of their contradictions.

Derrida makes this perfectly clear in his response to the objection that

since the deconstructionist (which is to say, isn't it, the skeptic-relativist-nihilist!) is supposed not to believe in truth, stability, or the unity of meaning, ... how can he demand that his own text be interpreted correctly? How can he accuse anyone else of having misunderstood, simplified, deformed it, etc.?

Derrida says the response is simple:

this definition of the deconstructionist is *false* (that's right: false, not true) and feeble .... The value of truth (and of all those values associated with it) is never contested or destroyed in my writings, but only reinscribed in more powerful, larger, more stratified contexts. (*Limited Inc.* (*LI*), 270/146).[19]

Perhaps, however, Derrida admits that the laws of logic necessarily govern our thought and communication but denies that they are true of the world about which we think and speak. If so, his skepticism would still seem indefensible. For he would be either simply denying the reality of a world outside of our thought and language or he would be accepting that reality but allowing for the truth of contradictory statements about it. Either alternative is surely absurd.

Derrida is often said to hold the first alternative, mainly on the basis of his famous, "Il n'y a pas de hors texte" ("There is nothing outside the text").[20] However, the point of this assertion is not that there are no things, only words. It is rather meant to convey that at every level – both that of reality itself and that of our language and thought about reality – there are no simply present facts or meanings but only the unending play of differences that Saussure has shown to characterize language. There is nothing outside the text (language) only in the sense that both language and reality are systems of differences and nothing else, and that the metaphysics of presence applies to neither. Once again, Derrida himself makes the point quite clearly:

"there is nothing outside the text" ... does not mean that all referents are suspended, denied, or enclosed in a book .... But it does mean that every

---

[19] The French edition of *Limited Inc.* (to which the first page number refers) is a direct translation of the English edition, in which Derrida's text first appeared.
[20] *De la grammatologie*, 227/158.

referent, all reality has the structure of a differential trace, and that one cannot refer to this "real" except in an interpretive experience. The latter neither yields meaning nor assumes it except in a movement of differential referring. That's all. (*LI*, 273/148)

It may seem, nevertheless, that Derrida at least allows for the truth of contradictory statements about reality. He does, after all, maintain that the binary oppositions of logic do not apply to reality, so that, for example, what is present is also absent and what is also is not. But what we need to understand here is that the paradoxical assertions sprinkled throughout Derrida's texts are expressions of the limitations of our logical systems, not descriptions of the nature of reality. He is not saying, for example, that some aspect of reality is itself simultaneously and in the same sense both present and absent. He is rather pointing out that if we insist on applying to reality the precisely defined categories *present* and *absent*, we will inevitably say such contradictory things.

Consider some simple examples. If I insist on describing the world of colors with only the two predicates "red" and "not-red", I may well be obliged to say that certain intermediate shades are both red and not-red; or, if I am forced to describe a football game in the language of baseball, I will find myself saying things that violate defining principles of baseball – for example, the pitcher (quarterback) struck out three times (threw three incomplete passes) and then hit a home run (threw a touchdown pass). Or, to cite a more significant case, if we must use the language of classical physics to describe quantum phenomena, we are forced to make claims that violate categorical truths regarding space, time, and causality. Derrida is noting the limits of all our logical schema for talking about reality on a fundamental level, not making absurd statements about reality.

The next possibility is that Derrida is an epistemological skeptic; that is, even if he accepts the laws of logic and does not deny the existence or logical consistency of reality, it may seem that he at least denies the possibility of our having any significant knowledge of reality, of our being epistemically justified in preferring one interpretation of it to another. But although Derrida is skeptical of any philosophical claims to have uncovered a deep, univocal meaning of reality, this questioning of fundamental philosophical claims need not entail a rejection of the everyday, common-sense knowledge that is the basis of any inquiry about our world.

Derrida's attitude here is indicated by his views on the special case of textual interpretation, where he has often been accused of the skeptical view that no interpretation is superior to any other. In contrast to this characterization, he says in *De la grammatologie*, for example, that there is a need for a "doubling commentary", a kind of "literal" statement of the text's meaning that provides an "indispensable guardrail" without which "critical production would risk developing in any direction at all and authorize itself to say almost anything".[21] Twenty years later, responding to Gerald Graff's citation of this passage, Derrida expresses some dissatisfaction with the term "doubling commentary", which he says is "perhaps clumsily" put. This expression should not, he says, be taken to mean that there is "a moment of simply reflexive recording that would transcribe the originary and true layer of a text's intentional meaning, a meaning that is univocal and self-identical" (*LI*, 265/143). But he still insists that interpretation must begin with a grasp of a text's language and context that provides an understanding of "what interpretations are probabilistically dominant and conventionally acknowledged to grant access to what [the author] thought he meant and to what readers for the most part thought they could understand" (*LI*, 267/144). There is, in other words, a "'minimal' deciphering of the 'first' pertinent or competent access to structures that are relatively stable (and hence destabilizable!) and from which the most venturesome questions and interpretations have to start" (*LI*, 268/145). Without such a starting-point, he says, "one could indeed say just anything at all and I have never accepted saying, or encouraging others to say, just anything at all" (*LI*, 267/144–5). None of this, however, means that Derrida thinks there is some absolute, univocal truth about the meaning of a given text.

More generally, there is no reason to think that Derrida is skeptical about our common-sense knowledge from which we must begin any inquiry about the world, even though he is skeptical about philosophical claims to have determined the essential nature of reality. He questions such claims on the grounds that the fundamental categories (expressed in binary oppositions) they propose for understanding the world collapse from the internal tensions revealed by deconstructive analysis. But this does not mean that he denies the viability of such categories for everyday life.

[21] *Of Grammatology*, 158.

It might be maintained, however, that it is not possible to doubt the philosophical foundations of our common-sense and scientific knowledge without calling into question that knowledge itself. This corresponds to Descartes' point that without a firm philosophical justification for its principles, neither science nor common sense has any defense against skeptical questioning. But to this Derrida will surely respond (as have contemporary philosophers from the later Wittgenstein to Rorty) that the demand for a philosophical foundation of non-philosophical knowledge is misplaced. In any case, he can surely consistently maintain that the demand for such foundations is a philosophical one that has no more claim on us than the rest of the traditional philosophical enterprise (which deconstruction has called into question).

The final possibility is that Derrida is a moral skeptic, denying that we have any genuine knowledge of values; or perhaps a moral relativist, holding that moral truths are valid only for given cultures or individuals and have no absolute status. Up until about 1980, Derrida had little to say about specifically ethical issues, and, in contrast to Sartre and Foucault, for example, he did not tie his philosophical reflections to political activity. But subsequently he has made ethics (and religion) a major theme. Some attention to this development will both provide a response to the question of moral skepticism and serve as an introduction to Derrida's more recent writings.

ETHICS

Ethics concerns our treatment of others and is therefore tightly linked to the notion of community.[22] Derrida readily admits to feelings of unease regarding community:

I don't much like the word community, I am not even sure I like the thing.

If by community one implies, as is often the case, a harmonious group, consensus, and fundamental agreement beneath the phenomenon of discord or war, then I don't believe in it very much and I sense in it as much a threat as promise.

I have always had trouble vibrating in unison.[23]

---

[22] For Derrida's recent treatments of ethical topics, see, for example, *De l'esprit*, *Spectres de Marx*, and *Politiques de l'amitié*.

[23] *Points*, 355, 348.

Derrida's doubts about community can be connected to a tension apparent in the word's etymology, which refers to a fortified city (cum=common, munis=defense, as in "munitions"). The problem, etymology aside, is that community simultaneously implies sharing and exclusion (sharing with a circumscribed group and exclusion of everyone else). A moral commitment to a specific community requires cutting oneself off from a whole range of other people, something Derrida finds is in tension with an ethical concern for the other as such.

A similar tension shows up if we reflect on another term that initially has very positive ethical connotations: hospitality. In fact, at first glance, hospitality might seem to offer a solution to the problem of the exclusionary undertones of community. For, even if I do have a special commitment to one community (my family, my church, my country), surely there can and should be an attitude of welcoming strangers, those who don't belong to the community. Hospitality does not make strangers belong to my community, but, short of this, it does provide a special mode of acceptance.

But even here there are tensions, once again signaled by the etymology. For "hospitality" derives, first, from "hospes" (guest), which itself derives from "hostis", which originally means "stranger" but comes to mean "enemy". Moreover, the second part of the word derives from "potes", meaning "power". So there is an etymological sense in which welcoming a guest means having power over (or, perhaps, giving power to) an enemy.

We can notice this tension on a practical level in the commonplace expression, "Make yourself at home." Hosts can say this only because they in fact own their homes, that is, they are in control of the space that the guest is entering. Also, guests have no right to literally make themselves at home – and a host would be shocked and outraged if a guest did so. There is clearly a limit to the welcome and a subordination of the guest to the power of the host. But at the same time the essence of hospitality is to move beyond this limit and this subordination. Good hosts continually act to put themselves entirely at the disposition of their guests, but the good guest will never fully accept what is so unconditionally offered. At the ideal limit, the perfect host would offer all he has to the guest – and sincerely so. But, if the guest accepted this, the host would no longer be in possession of his home and so would no longer be able to be the host. In this sense, hospitality is what we might call a "self-exceeding" concept. In moving toward realizing it, we also move to destroying the conditions of its application. This self-excess is the source of the tension between host and guest that accounts for the etymological trace we discovered of the guest as enemy.

The same self-exceeding character shows up in another key ethical concept, that of the gift. Surely, giving to others is the essence of ethical behavior. But what actually happens when I give a gift – say a birthday present to a friend? First of all, I, the giver, am established as someone who has done the right thing, maybe more than the right thing, if the gift exceeds the minimum that would have been expected. This "moral" gain may offset any expense of money or time the gift may have cost me. Thus, all things considered, I am better off than I was before I gave the gift. At the same time, the recipient of the gift is now indebted to the giver to reciprocate. In fact, the obligation goes beyond that. Recipients cannot just literally reciprocate, by, for example, just giving back the same gift. They have to seek out something roughly equal in value but clearly different, to show that they have not just mechanically responded but have made, as we say, a "thoughtful" gift. Moreover, they cannot immediately relieve themselves of the obligation (e.g., by taking the giver to dinner that evening). They must live with the burden of owing a gift until an appropriate time for reciprocation occurs (e.g., the giver's own birthday). It follows that the final result of the gift giving is that the recipient is worse off. This, then, is the paradox of the gift: on the deepest level, it is the giver who receives and the recipient who winds up in debt.

So in all three of these key ethical concepts – community, hospitality, the gift – we encounter the same thing: an understanding of the way we should relate to other people that is revealed as internally incoherent once we push it far enough. This, of course, is an example of what Derrida means by "deconstruction". It might seem that the point of such a deconstruction is to produce skepticism about ethics, to show that there is no sense or point to ethical behavior, because the ideas on which it is based collapse upon analysis. This, however, is emphatically not Derrida's point. We can best see this by realizing that, in each case, his deconstruction is in the name of and for the sake of something that he recognizes as *not* deconstructible. What is this? It is precisely the reality of community, of hospitality, of gift-giving in our lives. Despite the inadequacies of our concepts to these realities, we know that they exist and have an undeniable value. Deconstruction is not meant to assail the lived reality that our concepts are trying to catch. It is rather directed against our complacency in thinking that the understanding these concepts provide of the reality is adequate, that they can in effect replace – without leaving a trace unaccounted for – the reality.

Here Derrida's language of "trace" expresses the fact that reality (the truth) always somehow eludes our thought and even our experience (which itself is impossible without a conceptualization of what we experience). We have access to it only as a trace, present only indirectly as what our thought and experience somehow points to but cannot express. The point can likewise be expressed in other Derridean terms. The "trace-reality" corresponds to the *differance* between reality and what we think and experience, and it is the necessary *supplement* to this thought and experience.

Derrida's point, then, is not that there is no ethical reality but that every direct access we have to ethical reality is inadequate to its object. At the same time, he is not saying that the truth of ethics lies in some mystical, inaccessible beyond. The only way the truth is or could come to us is as differance, as trace, as supplement. In this sense, then, Derrida does acknowledge a truth beyond deconstruction that defines the domain of the ethical.

All the above issues come to a head in Derrida's treatment of the central ethical concept of justice.[24] Here he once again begins from an essential tension: justice is in one sense nothing other than the rule of law; but in fact the mere, literal application of the law is generally unjust. The point is not merely the traditional one that there is a distinction between any positive law (legislated by some particular human society) and the absolute standards defined by, say, divine command, the Form of Justice, or human nature. Derrida's claim is much stronger: that any system of laws – human, natural, divine – will never be able in itself to specify adequately the conduct that is just in a given situation.

Accordingly, any system of laws is subject to deconstruction. No matter how stable, consistent, and coherent it may be in its own terms, there will be points of application where it becomes incoherent. Consider, for example, the case of murders by children below the legal age of responsibility. It makes perfect sense, when setting up laws, to have some age limit on various sorts of responsi-

---

[24] See, for example, *Du droit à la philosophie* and *Force de loi: le "fondement mystique de l'autorité"*.

bility. But such laws are confounded when children behave like vicious adults. At such critical points of application, we see the tension between law and justice.

Derrida does not, however, mean to suggest that we have access to justice through anything other than law. There is, as always, no question of some special access, through a privileged experience or insight, to what lies beyond the law. Just as we can never get beyond our concepts, we cannot get beyond our laws, which are only conceptualizations of ethical obligations. Rather, we move toward justice simply by remaining ever sensitive to possible limitations of laws, by being always ready to deconstruct laws that are working against justice. This is one reason why Derrida can suggest that "deconstruction is justice".[25] Or, as he says in a less lapidary explanation:

The law as such can be deconstructed and has to be deconstructed. That is the condition of historicity, revolution, morals, ethics, and progress. But justice is not the law. Justice is what gives us the impulse, the drive, or the movement to improve the law, that is, to deconstruct the law. Without a call for justice we would not have any interest in deconstructing the law.[26]

This deconstruction is not a skeptical rejection of the law but a clearing of the ground for a new judgment of how we should behave. This new judgment (decision) does not itself draw authority from any system of law – how could it, when it presupposes a deconstruction of previous systems? But neither does it draw authority from some privileged insight beyond the law (say a Platonic intuition of Justice). The judgment is a leap, a taking of a stand when there is no adequate justification for taking a stand. In this regard, Derrida cites Kierkegaard: "The instant of decision is a madness"; it is the movement of the individual beyond the universal. But this leap does not take us beyond the realm of law as such. It moves beyond previous formulations of law but must in turn justify itself by constructing a new, more adequate system of law that will, of course, itself be subject to deconstruction. In contrast to dangerous irrationalisms (e.g., fascism, religious fanaticism) that leave reason behind in a flood of mere will or emotion, Derrida's deconstructive approach always subjects our "leaps" beyond one system of rational thought

---

[25] "Force of Law: The 'Mystical Foundation of Authority'", in D. Cornell, et al. (eds.), *Deconstruction and the Possibility of Justice*.
[26] "Villanova Roundtable", in John Caputo (ed.), *Deconstruction in a Nutshell*, 16.

to the constraint of constructing a new system of rational thought. In this way, he balances reason and a sense of its limitations against one another in a constant play of tensions.

Perhaps the best way to sum up Derrida's deconstructive view of ethics is to say that it is at root *an openness to the other*. This first of all expresses a traditional ethical concern for the welfare of others. It further corresponds to the strong contemporary ethical valuation of alternative viewpoints ("diversity", "multiculturalism"). But, most of all, it expresses Derrida's belief that our convictions always have dangerous limitations that may lead us away from justice unless we continually try to think beyond them. Such thought keeps us moving, as we must, toward an other that will always lie beyond our current horizon.

RELIGION

This formulation, "an other that will always lie beyond our current horizon", evokes the transcendence associated with God, and Derrida's reflections on ethics thus easily take on a religious tone (a tone also anticipated by his ethical emphasis on the gift, which of course evokes divine grace). The religious theme becomes explicit in, for example, the last two chapters of Derrida's book *Donner la mort*, where he reflects – following Kierkegaard – on the story of Abraham's sacrifice of Isaac.[27]

This story, from the book of Genesis, is taken by Kierkegaard (in *Fear and Trembling*) to present Abraham as the "father of faith", the first and greatest example of faith. Kierkegaard reads the story as illustrating the difference between the ethical and the religious viewpoints; that is, between a universal law that we can articulate and understand and an individual relation to God that we can neither grasp nor express. He sees this difference especially in the silence of Abraham, who never explains to Isaac or to his wife the real purpose of his journey to the mountain. Even when he does speak – e.g., to answer Isaac's question about where they will find a lamb to sacrifice – he replies (saying that God will provide one)

---

[27] Derrida's turn to religious topics correlates with his interest in his own Jewish origins. See, in particular, "Circumfession", his running response to Geoffrey Bennington's exposition ("Derridabase") of his thought, in G. Bennington and J. Derrida, *Jacques Derrida*. For a thorough and stimulating discussion of Derrida on religion, see John Caputo, *The Prayers and Tears of Jacques Derrida*.

in a way that, although not a lie, does not convey what he takes to be the truth of the situation. (Although, as Derrida points out, it does convey what is in fact the truth of the situation.) For Kierkegaard, this silence contrasts with the panoply of explanations and justifications that are available to those who are acting ethically. They can appeal to chapter and verse of the law to clarify just what they are doing and why they are doing it. This, of course, is because the law is something formulated in human concepts and so totally accessible to our understanding. But Abraham's obedience to God is an obligation of faith, not of ethics. It arises from an entirely mysterious communication from God that can make no ethical sense to Abraham and which provides no justification for his action.

It is not just that what Abraham does makes no sense ethically, that it lies outside the domain of ethics. Rather, his actions go directly against his ethical responsibility. He is proposing to murder his son. Anyone who did this we would condemn out of hand, no matter what he or she might try to say about divine commands or religious duty. As Kierkegaard presents it, the Abraham story shows the conflict between ethical and religious responsibility. Faith, the act by which we enter the religious sphere, involves our acting against our fundamental ethical responsibilities. This is apparent in such strong language as that of Luke 14:26: "If anyone comes to me and does not hate his own father and mother and his wife and children and brothers and sisters, yes, and even his own life, he cannot be my disciple."

There are two obvious ways of reacting to Kierkegaard's reading of the Abraham story. On the one hand, we might try to tone down the radical view of religion and say that Abraham's behavior does not really outrage ethical norms, that religion does not really require a choice between God and morality. On the other hand, we might accept Kierkegaard's view of religion but claim that this is precisely why religious faith is not an option for a sensible person: anything that requires subordinating morality to some alleged divine revelation is simply unacceptable. Another approach, common among religious believers, is not to reflect on the story's implications but just point to it as an example of the total mysteriousness of faith and consequent lack of any need to think it through at a fundamental level. This, however, is entirely contrary to Kierkegaard's point in meditating on the story.

Derrida, however, does not take any of these routes. Instead, he suggests that the story might be telling us something about the nature of ethical responsibility itself, rather than distinguishing ethical from religious responsibility. Is there, he asks, really something so distinctive and different about Abraham's situation? Is it not rather the situation of everyone, everyday? In Kierkegaard's reading of the Abraham story, "God" is the name for an other to whom Abraham has an absolute responsibility, one that overrides his duty to anyone else. But, Derrida suggests, this is precisely the situation of any of us when we find ourselves ethically responsible to another person. If I am truly responsible, here and now, for my spouse, my children, my friend, my country – then this responsibility overrides other duties I might have elsewhere. For example, if I am responsible for watching my children this morning, I cannot take care of my ailing father, or help improve education in the inner city, or work for the relief of world hunger. In accepting one responsibility, I must, like Abraham, renounce all the others.

We may respond that clear ethical thinking will enable us to rank our various responsibilities so that we have a firm basis for saying which take precedence over others. But a little (Sartrean) reflection should make it clear that there are no ethical rules specific enough to tell us whether we should, for example, spend more time with our family or more time working at a homeless shelter. Our ethical principles can provide some values relevant to such a decision, but it is up to us to decide just how to weight the values. No matter how fully informed and reflective we are, our decision will simply be our own, not the consequence of compelling rational considerations. As Derrida puts it: "At the instant of every decision and through the relation to every other... every one else asks us at every moment to behave like knights of faith."

Clearly Derrida has found the Abraham story and Kierkegaard's reflections on it valuable for expressing his deconstructivist view of ethics. But what about the specifically religious dimensions of the story? Derrida is aware that his use of the story differs from Kierkegaard's. The key difference is that for Derrida the "other" to whom we are obligated is anyone to whom we have an ethical obligation – that is, everyone without exception. For Kierkegaard (and surely for a religious interpretation in general) the "other" who calls Abraham is distinctively and uniquely God. As Derrida himself puts it, in an amazing understatement, his reading "perhaps . . .

displaces a certain emphasis of Kierkegaard's discourse: the absolute uniqueness of Yahweh doesn't tolerate analogy".[28]

We may be tempted to go even further and say that Derrida's reading represents a rejection of a religious viewpoint in favor of a purely human ethics. After all, religion is a response to a call from God, not from other human beings. Human others no doubt have their own mystery and inaccessibility and, as we have seen, establish a limit to the application of our ethical laws. But to substitute such human, mundane mystery for the God who transcends everything human would seem to be precisely what it means to renounce religion.

But there is religion and there is religion; or, as Derrida has put it, there is religion and there is faith.[29] Faith, in this terminology, is simply the acceptance of the "call" of the other as we have seen it in Derrida's interpretation of the Abraham story. Its object is "merely human" in the sense that it does not posit any "presences" (entities, substances) beyond the human world. But the object of Derrida's faith is certainly not humanity and its values as we encounter them. It is, rather, ethical value as the inaccessible limit of any possible human thought or experience. Put this way, it is not so outrageous to say that Derrida in some sense accepts the divine. Religion, by contrast, is what we get when we interpret the "other" of Abraham's call as the God of one of the historical religions, a God who is no longer the nondeconstructible limit of all our thought and experience but a being who has been revealed to (some of) us as having specific characteristics: performing certain actions, having certain desires, issuing certain commands. For religion, the divine as other is a presence, something "here", to which we have positive access, even if "through a glass darkly".

Derrida is very uneasy with the further move to religion. His worry is that religion absolutizes all-too-human categories by *identifying* the other with one particular conceptual formulation. This gives a God who is categorical rather than transcendent, a God who is of the Jews or of the Catholics or of the Muslims – in short, a God who is a reflection rather than an unreachable limit of thought and experience. Derrida suggests that religion in this sense is the ultimate form of idolatry.

[28] *The Gift of Death*, 79.
[29] "Villanova Roundtable", in John Caputo (ed.), *Deconstruction in a Nutshell*; see also Caputo's commentary, 164–8.

The point can also be made in terms of Derrida's reflections on the religious notion of the messiah – the savior who is to come. Derrida has no problem with this notion provided the messiah is *always* yet to come. This would correspond to what he calls the idea of the messianic – the perpetual "beyond", the other that is always imminent (casting its shadow over us) but never actually here, that which makes us constantly aware of the limits and surpassability of our conceptions and experiences (e.g., our systems of ethical law). But religion gives us, instead of the messianic (or messianicity), what Derrida calls messianism: a messiah who has already come (or will someday actually come). For messianism, the coming of the messiah is a specific historical reality occurring in real time and therefore colored and limited by the features of that particular historical period. Derrida's worry is that in accepting such a messiah we falsely privilege the thought and experience of one particular historical period, and that, in particular, we accept as absolutes values that are in fact just the expression of a limited culture, a culture that itself needs deconstruction. Derrida's messianic view is expressed in Blanchot's vignette: one day on the outskirts of Rome, I meet a man in rags who is, in fact, the Messiah. What should I say to him? I should ask him: "When will you come?".[30] Even if the Messiah were somehow here, we should still think of him as he who is yet to come.

In sum, Derrida's deconstruction is open to religion in the sense that its focus on the other can be plausibly read as a reference to the divine as the absolute transcendent that is the enlightening and enlivening limit of our thought and experience. But it is not consistent with religion that presents itself as a special means of access to a divine reality that somehow becomes a positive, presently grasped truth for us. This is the traditional self-understanding of religious institutions (churches), but it is no part of the faith of Jacques Derrida.

---

[30] Maurice Blanchot, *The Writing of the Disaster*, 141–2. Cited by Derrida, *Politiques de l'amitié*, 55n.

CHAPTER 11

Philosophies of difference

> As for the truths which the intellectual faculty – even that of the greatest minds – gathers in the open, the truths that lie in its path in full daylight, their value may be very great, but they are like drawings with a hard outline and no perspective; they have no depth because no depths had to be traversed in order to reach them, because they have not been re-created.
> (Marcel Proust, *In Search of Lost Time*, vi, 303)

Although Derrida's talk of *différance* is tinged with his own peculiar coyness and taste for paradox, the general theme of difference is fundamental for all poststructuralists, who are in principle wary of thought that reduces diverse elements to the sameness of unifying concepts or theories. Moreover, even though Derrida is most strongly associated with the notion, he offers a focused discussion of it in only one essay ("La différance"). By contrast, Lyotard, Deleuze, and Irigaray provide extensive developments of what they call, respectively, the differend, difference, and sexual difference.

LYOTARD

Even before his book-length treatment of difference in *Le différend*, Jean-François Lyotard (1924–98) insistently and powerfully developed the theme of a reality somehow beyond and different from intelligible structure. He did this in a variety of keys, speaking of desire in the context of psychoanalysis, of line in the context of art, and, in a wide range of contexts, of figure, event, and singularity.

A good initial example is his critique of Lacan's structuralist account of desire. As we have seen, Lacan claims that the unconscious mind has the structure of a language, understood as a system of signs whose meanings are entirely defined by their roles in the system. The unconscious is entirely a function of this linguistic system. In opposition to Lacan, Lyotard asserts the autonomy and primacy of desire as a non-linguistic force (Freud's "primary process"). So understood, desire is not merely the lack or limit of the unconscious as a symbolic system. It is a dynamic process, a sheer undifferentiated energy that fuels the life of the unconscious. Lyotard compares the case of desire to that of immediate perceptual experience. Even though the perceptual object is not "simply given" to the mind in an experience unformed by any linguistic categories, it does not follow that the content of experience is exhausted by language. "We can say that the tree is green, but this does not put the color into the sentence."[1] A similar argument can be made for desire. Just as perception is fulfilled by an object with an intrinsic content that cannot be reduced to the linguistic structures of consciousness, so too desire can be fulfilled by an object irreducible to the linguistic structures of the unconscious. In this way, desire takes us beyond the boundaries of a purely structuralist understanding of the unconscious.

Lyotard makes a similar point in aesthetic contexts through his distinction between *letter* and *line*. By "letter" he means a linguistic sign as understood by Saussure: an element in a system that has significance solely in virtue of its differences from other elements in a system. If, for example, a Magritte painting contains the written message, "This is not a pipe", the letters used can have any physical shape at all (so long as those shapes allow us to distinguish a *t* from a *p*, etc.) and still convey the message. But, as *lines* in the painting, the precise shapes of the *p*, *t*, etc. are crucial. A thick red script will convey one aesthetic meaning, a thin green another. For the *p* and *t* as *letters*, pre-linguistic content is irrelevant, but for them as *lines* it is crucial. For "This is not a pipe" as *read*, there is no content irreducible to the linguistic system; but for "This is not a pipe" as *seen*, there is.

In a parallel but more fundamental way, Lyotard distinguishes between *discourse* and *figure*. Discourse is the system of conceptual structures whereby we represent the world. It is, accordingly, the domain of meaning and rationality, of that which can be explicitly formulated in language (and hence translated from one language to another). Figure, by contrast, is what remains unassimilable to discourse – what cannot be represented or formulated in our language,

---

[1] *Discours, figure*, 52.

what defines the limits of meaning and rationality. It is, for example, what remains of the poem after we have completely paraphrased and explicated it in prose (or what remains of an experience after our concepts have exhaustively described it). Figure is not outside of or in opposition to discourse. That would be to say that the real poetry is outside the poem or that the singular feel of the experience is outside the experience. Figure is better regarded as an essential inverse of discourse, whereby discourse is always entangled with something it cannot master.

For many years before his main philosophical works, Lyotard was a political intellectual, an instigator of protests at Nanterre just before May '68 and a member of the activist group Socialisme ou Barbarie, where he specialized in the Algerian problem.[2] It is, accordingly, not surprising that his work has consequences for social and political thought or even that, as Geoffrey Bennington has asserted, "his thought is fundamentally political".[3] So, for example, Lyotard claims that psychological desire and political power must be thought of as necessary counterparts. Desire is precisely that which power constrains, and that which struggles against power. It made sense, therefore, for Lyotard to develop a "libidinal politics": a theoretical and practical standpoint based on the fundamental value of the flourishing of a plurality of diverse desires. This he did in his 1974 book, *Économie libidinale*. Lyotard, like Foucault, saw knowledge and power as essentially connected, and maintained that "totalizing" theories (e.g., Marxism) claiming universal validity are sources of totalitarian social structures that destroy the plurality of desires.[4]

Lyotard pays particular attention to what he sees as the inevitable conflict between justice and truth. We continually – and properly – make judgments that particular situations or actions are unjust. But we are also inclined to think that these judgments themselves require

---

[2] Socialisme ou Barbarie and the journal of the same name were founded in 1949 by Cornelius Castoriadis and Claude Lefort, themselves both important political thinkers. The group was radically leftist but extremely critical of Stalinism and other versions of Marxist totalitarianism.

[3] *Lyotard: Writing the Event*, 175. Lyotard combined his political activism with an academic career. After failing to win a place at the École Normale, he studied philosophy at the Sorbonne. He taught for ten years in lycées and held various university positions, ending with his appointment as Professor of Philosophy at the University of Paris VII (located first at Vincennes and later at St. Denis). He was also active, along with Derrida, in the Collège Internationale de la Philosophie and taught regularly in the United States.

[4] For an excellent discussion of Lyotard, Lacan, and Foucault on issues at the intersection of desire and politics, see Peter Dews, *Logics of Disintegration*.

justification through derivation from a general account of the nature of human society. We think, that is, that particular prescriptions regarding justice must be justified by the truth of general theoretical descriptions. Lyotard, however, maintains that this appeal to general truth is itself an instance of injustice. The general description presents a total picture of society that excludes all alternative views as false and rejects as unacceptable desires based on these views. But according to Lyotard such an exclusion is inconsistent with the fundamental value of maintaining a plurality of desires.

Despite the importance of this earlier work, I will focus rather on Lyotard's later book, *Le différend* (1983), which provides the most explicit and comprehensive exposition of his philosophy of difference.[5] This book is also of special interest because, although it presents views generally similar to those of *Discours, figure* and *Économie libidinale*, the formulation is strikingly different, both stylistically and conceptually. The writing eschews the baroque intensity and complexity of the earlier books in favor of a deliberately "zero-degree" style often reminiscent of analytic philosophy. The book's organization, however, is closer to the notebook jottings of the later Wittgenstein than to that of a standard analytic treatment. Lyotard's position is developed around the linguistic notion of the phrase, thus giving, at least methodologically, the leading role to discourse rather than figure (although, as we shall see, the claims of figure – differently named – eventually assert themselves).

Le différend begins by describing a situation in which I cannot prove the existence of gas chambers in Nazi Germany because I am arguing before a tribunal that requires that any proof be from an eye witness who died in a gas chamber (and so cannot testify). In such a situation making my case requires arguing in conformity with "establish[ed] procedures defined by a unanimously agreed-upon protocol" (*Le différend* [D]17/4), but, by the nature of my claim, it cannot be established using these procedures. It is not just that there does not happen to be evidence for my claim but that, given the standards of evidence, there could not be evidence for it. In Lyotard's terminology, such a situation is a *différend* (which, in ordinary French, means simply "conflict"). Differends involve wrongs (*torts*), that is, damages "accompanied by the loss of the means to prove the

---

[5] I am also ignoring Lyotard's studies, published the year he died, of spiritual and even religious themes in *Chambre sourde* and *La confession d'Augustin*.

damage" (*D*, 18/5). Or, as Lyotard also puts it: "I would like to call a differend the case where the plaintiff is divested of the means to argue and becomes for that reason a victim" (*D*, 24/9). The logic of the differend mirrors the logic of various ancient paradoxes, especially that of the law suit between Protagoras and his pupil.[6]

Lyotard's examples of differends are most often ethical or political, but they can also arise in other contexts such as science, where Lyotard's differend would seem to be illustrated by Kuhnian incommensurability. (However, as we shall see later, there is a sense in which for Lyotard all differends are political.) Lyotard also emphasizes that a differend will always obtain for "Ideas" in the Kantian sense of concepts of such scope or absoluteness that there are no procedures available for establishing the reality of their referents.

The fundamental structure of a differend can be specified linguistically, in terms of what Lyotard calls "phrases". A phrase is, roughly, a unit of linguistic meaning. It is often a sentence (the standard meaning of "phrase" in French), but can also be an intelligible fragment of a sentence ("phrase" in the ordinary English sense) or something with a non-linguistic meaning such as a gesture or even a silence. The phrase presents four elements or, in Lyotard's terminology, "instances": the addressor (the one speaking), the addressee (the one spoken to), the sense (*sens*) of the claim being made, and the alleged referent of this sense. In a differend, the victims' inability to make their case can be understood in terms of the elements of the phrase: they cannot show that the referent of their claim exists because the relevant procedures do not authorize the addressor (the victim) to speak; or they do not require the addressee to listen; or they render the evidence put forward senseless (*D*, 22–3/8).

The "procedures" and "requirements" governing phrases and their elements are expressed in two kinds of fundamental linguistic rules. One is the *phrase regimen*, the set of rules that "constitutes" a phrase, in the sense of defining the linguistic function that it performs. Phrases that provide descriptions, give orders, ask questions,

---

[6] Protagoras had trained a student to argue in the law courts and had agreed to postpone receiving his fee until the student won his first case. After several years, the student had not even tried a single case, and Protagoras sued for the fee. He argued that, if the court found in favor of the student, he would have won a case and so would owe the fee in virtue of their agreement; and that, if the court found against the student, he would by that very fact owe the fee.

recount events, express logical inferences, or point out objects all belong to distinct phrase regimens (*D*, 10/xii). Given a number of phrases, in general from different phrase regimens, a second set of rules becomes relevant. These define the *genre of discourse* and are rules for linking phrases together, that is, for moving from the utterance of one phrase to the utterance of another. A genre is distinguished by the distinctive goal that lies behind its linking of phrases. As examples of goals, Lyotard cites "to know, to teach, to be just, to seduce, to justify, to evaluate, to rouse emotion, to oversee" (*D*, 10/xii). A differend arises when the rules of regimen and of genre exclude certain people from the discussion.

Lyotard in effect distinguishes two conceptually different forms of differend. In the first, the victims (those who cannot plead their case) simply lack a language in which to do so. There are no phrases available to articulate their situation and interests (e.g., the pain or affront that they feel). In such a case, the victims are treated unjustly simply because their judges wrongly presuppose that the victims possess a message that they can communicate to the judges. Understood in this way, "the differend is the unstable state and instant of language wherein something which must be able to be put into phrases cannot yet be" (*D*, 29/13). Lyotard notes that for such cases we typically say there is a "feeling" that cannot be put into words. Such a situation calls for efforts to "find new rules for forming and linking phrases that are able to express the differend disclosed by the feeling". According to Lyotard, "what is at stake in a literature, in a philosophy, in a politics perhaps, is to bear witness to differends by finding idioms for them" (*D*, 30/13).

But Lyotard also speaks of a differend arising between two already established modes of expression. This second case occurs when "phrases belonging to different regimens or genres . . . encounter each other to the point of giving rise to differends" (*D*, 50/28, no. 39). Such encounters do not imply a common "universe" of meaning in which they occur, since such a universe is always relative to a specific family of phrases. When there is this sort of shared meaning and when, therefore, there are shared rules for resolving disputes, Lyotard will speak of "litigation" rather than "differend". It is not possible to avoid encounters leading to a differend, since even remaining silent constitutes a phrase that responds to another phrase. So, for example, when a native of Martinique, a French colony, says "I protest the fact that I am required to be a French citizen", even the judge who remains silent (because there is literally nothing that can be said in a French court to such a claim) has responded to the claim. This illustrates Lyotard's view that "it is necessary to link" (to respond to any phrase with another phrase), even though "the mode of linkage is never necessary" (*D*, 52/29, no. 41). A differend arises from the availability of two or more different genres for linking phrases.

Lyotard insists that phrases (and therefore differends) should not be understood in terms of the intentional meanings of subjects. The addressor and the addressee, for example, are, quite apart from their mental states, entirely defined by their roles of following (or not following) the procedural rules that govern the disputed issue. Also, the reality of the referent is not established because it is "'given' to this or that 'subject'"; rather it is justified by "establish[ed] procedures defined by a unanimously agreed-upon protocol, and from the possibility offered to anyone to recommence the effectuation as often as he or she wants" (*D*, 17/4). Similarly, the meaning of the claim depends on the rules governing the use of the phrase.

It might seem that our analysis of a differend must at least take account of the competence and "good faith" of the individual subjects involved in it. But Lyotard maintains that the rules themselves are sufficient to determine that the participants in a dispute are competent and of good will. So, for example, "one 'plays the game' permitted by these rules; and the addressee's rejoinder shows that he or she does not observe them" (*D*, 38/19). And, if a participant tries to simulate conformity to the rules by, say, fabricating evidence that seems to meet the standards of proof, then this charade can itself be discovered by challenges based on the rules of the discussion. (Lyotard cites the case of the Dreyfus affair.)

The existence of phrases and corresponding differends presuppposes a set of rules by which we can evaluate the participants in a dispute. But what about the initial setting up of the rules? "What about those who establish these rules, aren't they prejudging their competence to establish them? How, indeed, could they not prejudge it as long as the rules have not been established and as long as they therefore lack the criteria by which to distinguish competence?" (*D*, 38/19). Indeed, to identify a differend is to challenge the authority of the rules that make it impossible for victims to plead their cases.

It might be claimed that the idea of such a challenge is incoherent and that, therefore, genuine differends do not exist. One might, for example, argue that if there is no established cognitive basis for someone's claim, then there can be no reason to take the claim seriously. But, Lyotard says, this argument confuses the referents established by a particular phrase-regimen with reality itself. Nothing says that these particular referents are real, as is clear from the fact that "in many phrase families [presumably, phrases belonging to the same phrase regimen], the referent is not at all presented as real" (*D*, 50/28). (Lyotard cites examples of poetic, mathematical, and aesthetic discourse, among others.) The assumption that all disputes are about reality and therefore resolvable through the cognitive genre of discourse is a pervasive false assumption of modern thought.

We cannot, therefore, avoid the problem of the authority of our rules. Nor can we solve the problem by appeal to some ultimate, totally privileged linguistic system; for example, a discourse on the rights of man or a Hegelian "tribunal of the world" (*D*, 54/31, nos. 44, 45). For any such tribunal would itself be just another phrase family and genre of discourse (*D*, 54/31, no. 45). The ultimate validation of a phrase comes not from the rules of its regimen or genre but from its reception. Consider, for example, the order "Stop singing" and the appraisal "What a beautiful aria!". According to Lyotard, "the validation of the order would seem to be for the addressee to stop singing, and the validation of the appraisal for the addressee to partake in the addressor's emotion" (*D*, 54–5/31, no. 45). We will return below to the question of validation when we discuss Lyotard's account of judgment.

Lyotard pays special attention to the referent that is "presented" (along with the addressor, the addressee, and the sense) by a phrase. He is particularly concerned to show, against phenomenology and idealism, that the reality of the referent does not depend on (is not "constituted" by) the experiencing subject.[7] He argues that establishing the reality of a referent has three distinct aspects; one is descriptive, one nominative, and one ostensive. For example, to establish the reality of Paris, we must: (1) describe it (as, for example, "the capital of France"); (2) name it ("Paris"); (3) point it out with a deictic or ostensive phase ("This is it", "Here it is"). The phenomenologist claims that reality is established simply by the referent's being

---

[7] Here Lyotard is coming to terms with his own early attachment to phenomenology, especially in Merleau-Ponty's formulations. See his *La phénoménologie* (1954).

given in experience, and that, therefore, reality is established by description (1) and ostension (3) alone. But according to Lyotard this claim is refuted by a classic dilemma (*D*, 70/42, no. 64). The referent is either merely what is given in experience or it is not. If the referent is merely what is given, then it may be merely an appearance (just the way things seem to us) and so not real. If the referent is not just what is given, then there is no decisive evidence for the reality of the referent (since, on the phenomenological assumption, givenness in experience is the only such evidence); therefore, once more, the referent may not be real. To avoid the force of this argument, we need to recognize the role of naming (2) as a "linchpin" between description and ostension (givenness).

Lyotard understands names as, in Kripke's phrase, rigid designators. That is, a name refers to its referent in all possible worlds (in which the referent exists) and it does not of itself entail any particular description of the referent. As such, the name depends neither on how the referent appears to us nor on any particular description under which we may know it. This is why it is able to act as an independent connector between ostension and description.

Lyotard's account of the reality of the referent supports his view of the differend. There is no "absolute eyewitness" (*D*, 86/53, no. 88) – no Cartesian self, no Hegelian absolute – that can determine once and for all the truth of the referent. Therefore, at any moment the referent remains the possible subject of an indefinite number of senses. We can assign the referent a definition, but future events may place it in phrase regimens and genres of discourse that are incommensurate with our definition. The fact that referents are never definitively constituted by a unifying subjectivity makes differends permanent possibilities.

It may seem that, with all this emphasis on language, Lyotard has reversed his earlier view and given priority to discourse. Where, in this philosophy of the phrase, is there room for his former themes of desire and figure? The answer is, first of all, in the differend. Differends arise precisely because of the inadequacy of phrase regimens and genres of discourse to formulate a victim's plea. Lyotard even says that a differend is a state "signaled by what one ordinarily calls a feeling: 'One cannot find the words,' etc. A lot of searching must be done to find new rules for forming and linking phrases that are able to express the differend disclosed by the feeling" (*D*, 29/13, no. 22).

But Lyotard's old theme is present even in his view of phrases themselves. A phrase is, after all, an event (a linguistic token, not a type), an occurrence with its own singular reality. It is, as Lyotard puts it, an "It happens" (or even, an "Is it happening?", where the interrogative presumably corresponds to the conceptual elusiveness of events). Lyotard emphasizes that "it happens" is to be distinguished from "what happens": "*It happens* is not what happens, in that sense that *quod* is not *quid*", where "quod" refers to an intelligible nature and "quid" to sheer "thereness" apart from any nature. A phrase "is", but there need not be any thing (essence) that it is. "*Is* doesn't signify anything, it would designate the occurrence 'before' the signification (the content) of the occurrence" (*D*, 120/79, no. 131).

Admittedly, the phrase presents a situation, that is instances (addressor, addressee, sense, referent) related to one another. But the phrase as presentation is not the situation presented. It possesses its own singularity and thus provides the figure of its own discourse. Because of this, no phrase is ever intrinsically wedded to any particular genre of discourse. The utterance of a phrase always poses the question of how we will link into it; that is, under which genre of discourse we will subsume it. The context of previous linkages may exert strong pressure: in standard contexts, a "Thank you" calls for a "You're welcome". But linkages are never determined; "to link is necessary, but a particular linkage is not" (*D*, 122/80, no. 136). There is no genre of discourse that has the ultimate power to determine what phrase is to follow any given phrase. It follows that every phrase poses its own differend: the question, unresolvable by any genre of discourse, of what should follow it. This is why Lyotard says that "no matter what its regimen, every phrase is in principle what is at stake in a differend between genres of discourse. This differend proceeds from the question, which accompanies any phrase, of how to link on to it" (*D*, 199–200/137–8, no. 188). The differends posed by phrases are thus a direct connection of phrases to the unarticulated "feeling" that will lead to the utterance of the next phrase.

This continuity of *La différend* with Lyotard's earlier works becomes entirely explicit in the book's treatment of the ethical and the political. Here his discussion begins with a distinction between normative and prescriptive phrases. A prescriptive phrase has the form: *X is obliged to do A*. According to the rules of the prescriptive phrase regimen, such a pronouncement calls for a response from its addressee, which may range from immediate compliance to direct refusal. By contrast, a normative phrase has the form: *It is a norm for Y that X is obliged to do A*. This is a performative statement, in itself putting a norm into place and so calling for no response to confirm its normative status.

Of course, not just any utterance in normative form actually sets up a norm. The effectiveness of the performative requires a social context in which it is recognized as valid. Consider some examples. A norm might be formulated in an entirely self-focused way: *I set up as a norm that I am obliged to do A*. But this has no ethical authority, since it may simply express my idiosyncratic intention regarding how I should behave. On the other hand, a norm might be formulated in an entirely external way: *Y sets up as a norm that X is obliged to do A*. Here Y's decrees may have no authority for X. Ethical authority requires an appropriate union between the addressor of the normative phrase and the addressee of the prescriptive phrase (which is embedded in the normative phrase). This is the function of the "we" in ethical discourse. Thus, a typical ethical norm will be: *We set up as a norm that we are obliged to do A*, from which would follow more specific norms such as *We set up as a norm that I (a member of the normative "we") am obliged to do A*.

But according to Lyotard the ethical "we" is problematic. Historically, there have been two ways of understanding it. The first is a premodern understanding, for which "we" is a particular tribe, nation, or culture, privileged over against everyone else as the sole addressors of normative claims. The "Aryan" morality of Nazism, which made non-Aryans the addressees but not the addressors of its racist norms, was a tragic reversion to premodernity. The second is a modern understanding, for which "we" embraces all mankind or even, as in Kant, all rational agents. Whereas a premodern "we" is unacceptable because of its arbitrary exclusions (and consequent differends, since those excluded have no ethical voice), the modern "we" is unjustifiable. On the one hand, it cannot claim to represent the de facto state of ethical discourse, and so cannot appeal to a "this language-game is played" defense. On the other hand, attempts to provide it with a theoretical justification – say through Kantian philosophy or Christian theology – have collapsed with the postmodern failure of the "grand narratives" (comprehensive accounts of human nature and history, as opposed to the "little narratives" of premodern societies) characteristic of modernity.[8]

Lyotard also suggests that modern efforts to justify ethics conflict with the nature of moral obligation. Such efforts amount to an application of the cognitive genre of discourse, with its goal of knowledge, to normative phrases expressing obligations. This genre asks for a justification of the authority of the addresser of an ethically normative phrase. This leads to a dilemma. If the justification is given, then the authority of the justifying reason replaces that of moral obligation. (Here Lyotard refers to Levinas, who, as we will see, emphasizes the utterly unconditional, underived nature of the other's ethical demand for recognition.) But if no justification is forthcoming, then the authority is judged to be arbitrary and so without force. As Lyotard puts it: "In the idiom of cognition, either the law is reasonable, and it does not obligate, since it convinces; or else, it is not reasonable, and it does not obligate, since it constrains" (*D*, 172/117, no. 176).

Our discussion so far has merely defined the limits within which the ethical must be understood. One boundary is set by the fact that ethical prescriptions cannot be derived from knowledge of non-ethical truths (e.g., of the essence of humanity, the nature of society, the will of God). There are, in other words, no independent criteria on the basis of which we can judge ethical prescriptions to be valid or not. In Kant's terminology, ethics is not ruled by *determinate judgments*. On the other hand, ethics is not a matter of the uncritical assertion of a given individual's or group's will (as in the case of Nazism). Ethical prescriptions must derive from critical reflection and hence from judgment. Since this cannot be determinate judgment, based on criteria, it must be what Kant called *regulative judgment*: judgment not derived from criteria and therefore not reducible to the arguments of the cognitive genre of discourse.

The absence of determinate judgment means, of course, that ethical decision lies in the realm of desire, figure, the event, the differend. Lyotard identifies this as the realm of politics: "Politics, however, is the threat of the differend. It is not a genre. It is the multiplicity of genres, the diversity of ends, and par excellence the

---

[8] This theme is developed in Lyotard's most widely read book, *La condition postmoderne*. See also his discussion of narrative as a genre of discourse in *La différend*, nos. 219ff.

question of linkage" (*D*, 200/138, no. 190). Politics is not a genre of discourse because then it would be just another one of the genres competing to determine the linkage of phrases. As the locus of the regulative judgments that decide among genres, it must lie outside all genres. Politics has a privileged role, but it is not that of "the genre that contains all the genres" (*D*, 201/139, no. 192). There is often confusion about this point because we tend to think that the ancient Greeks "invented" politics when what they actually did was subordinate all political decisions to the dialectical and the rhetorical genres. Other cultures have given hegemony to other genres (e.g., the Industrial Revolution led to the dominance of the technical genre). But the decision to let one genre, rather than any other, resolve all differends is itself a political act, and one that cannot be validated by the rules of a particular genre.

Lyotard concludes that "everything is politics" in the sense that "politics is the possibility of the differend on the occasion of the slightest linkage" (*D*, 201/139, no. 192). It might seem that this is far too broad a conception of politics, since it makes political any decision about which genre of discourse to apply. Why, for example, should a choice between a chemical and a biological explanation of a physical phenomenon (i.e., the decision to link "Why do salmon spawn?" with phrases about organic molecules rather than phrases about evolutionary niches) be political? Lyotard's answer is that "the universe presented by a phrase is immediately 'social'" in the sense that "an addressor [and] an addressee . . . are situated together within it" (*D*, 201–2/139, no. 193). To the extent that decisions about social relations are political, every resolution of a differend is political.

Lyotard resists the Platonic and Aristotelian view that politics is the science (or art) of the good. This is because decisions about differends always exclude certain ways of linking with phrases (that is, of going on with our social life) and, as such, involve evil. This is so because "by evil, I understand, and one can only understand, the incessant interdiction of possible phrases". Such interdiction, which is an essential component of political decisions, is "a defiance of the occurrence [event], the contempt for Being". Given Lyotard's understanding of politics and of evil, "politicians cannot have the good at stake, but they ought to have the lesser evil". Or, putting it another way, "the lesser evil ought to be the political good" (*D*, 203–4/140, no. 197). Given this, it is impossible to take entirely seriously the law established by political sovereignty, since it will always create victims, those whose voices are silenced by the laws. Lyotard sees humor as the locus of opposition to the inadequacies of the law: "The law should always be respected with humor because it cannot be completely respected." The people must always to some extent laugh at the law: "The 'people' is not the sovereign, it is the defender of the differend against the sovereign. It is full of laughter. Politics is tragedy for the authorities, comedy for the people" (*D*, 209/144, no. 208).

DELEUZE

While Lyotard develops the notion of difference far more extensively than Derrida, the notion has much the same role for both of them. Differance and the differend alike evoke the limits of thought, limits that make it impossible for us to ground or even fully explicate our central practices (aesthetic, ethical, and political) through conceptual formulations. For both Derrida and Lyotard, difference represents the insurpassable boundary of thought and, therefore, the inadequacy of traditional philosophizing. Philosophy may still survive as an essential critical or disruptive dimension of our thought, but the grand pretensions of, say, systematic metaphysics must be pronounced dead.

Gilles Deleuze (1925–95) ignores proclamations of the death of philosophy and even expresses support for systematic metaphysics.[9] He remains a poststructuralist in rejecting the unifying devices of mainstream philosophy (subject, object, representation, cause, etc.), and his sympathy with projects of systematic philosophy is based on their construal not as searches for truth in the traditional sense of representation but as creations of new concepts.[10] The fact remains that past philosophers – the Stoics, Lucretius, Hume, Bergson, Nietzsche, and even arch-systematists such as Spinoza and Kant – provide much of the materials Deleuze employs to construct his intellectual vision of reality as a flux of irreducible plurality. Among

---

[9] "I've never been worried about going beyond metaphysics or any death of philosophy" (*Negotiations*, 136); "I believe in philosophy as systematic" (Deleuze's preface to Jean-Clet Martin, *Variations: la philosophie de Gilles Deleuze*).

[10] "Philosophy is always a matter of inventing concepts" (*Negotiations*, 136). Note also the comment of Deleuze and Guattari in *What Is Philosophy?*: "Thought as such produces something *interesting* when it accedes to the infinite movement that frees it from truth as supposed paradigm and reconquers an immanent power of creation" (140).

the poststructuralists, Deleuze is most impressive for his effort to work out of rather than against the tradition of systematic metaphysics.[11]

For Deleuze, however, systems must be open, not closed. A closed system assimilates everything it encounters to the pre-established identities that define its essential structure. An open system always recognizes the possibility of connecting with new, heterogeneous elements that will transform the system rather than assimilate to it. A system is "an open system when the concepts relate to circumstances rather than to essences".[12] As a result, "the logic of someone's thought is the whole set of crises through which it passes; it's more like a volcanic chain than a stable system close to equilibrium".[13]

Deleuze's thought develops out of two fundamental "intuitions", one of being, the other of the thinking whereby being is grasped. The first intuition is that being is radically diverse, the second that, correspondingly, thought is a recognition of ontological diversity, not a reduction to unity. We can get a purchase on Deleuze's work, as it develops through his central texts, by following the ontological and the epistemological threads that correspond to these two intuitions, explicating his understanding of being via his notions of *multiplicity*, *difference*, and *event* and his view of thinking by his notions of the *concept* and the *idea*.

Deleuzian multiplicity emerges from the series of historical studies that were his initial publications, from 1953 to 1966.[14] These studies (on Hume, Nietzsche, Kant, Bergson, and Spinoza) are easily read as historical expositions, but, particularly in retrospect, they show Deleuze adumbrating his own standpoint by rethinking classical themes. His approach was distinctive because he generally focused

---

[11] This may have some connection with Deleuze's philosophical formation, which did not occur at the École Normale but at the Sorbonne, where he studied especially with Hippolyte and Canguilhem. After teaching at lycées from 1948 to 1964, Deleuze taught at the University of Lyon until 1968, when he was appointed Professor at the new University of Paris at Vincennes (on the recommendation of Foucault, who was head of the philosophy department). Deleuze remained at this post until he retired because of ill-health (severe respiratory problems) in 1987. His health continued to deteriorate and seems to have led to his suicide in 1995.
[12] *Negotiations*, 32.
[13] Ibid., 84.
[14] The volume on Hume appeared in 1953. There followed a period of nine years during which Deleuze published almost nothing, but from 1962 to 1966 he published a book each year.

on thinkers who were not, at the time, particularly fashionable in France, and because he seems scarcely concerned with the dominant Germans, Husserl and Heidegger.

Deleuze sees multiplicity as central to Bergson's thought, since his key distinction of space and time (duration) is between two different sorts of multiplicities (groups of diverse elements): that which is organized quantitatively and that which is organized qualitatively. Deleuze is particularly interested in the fact that Bergson puts this distinction in place of the traditional metaphysical distinction between the one and the many, a distinction that Deleuze thinks always leads to the primacy of unity, either by deriving, in Platonic fashion, the many as an imitation of or emanation from the one or by combining the one and the many, in Hegelian fashion, in a dialectical synthesis. By refusing any irreducible principle of unity, Bergson is true to Deleuze's intuition of the basic diversity of being.

Further, Deleuze maintains that unity must itself be understood in terms of multiplicity. Unity involves an affirmation of multiplicity, something Deleuze finds originally in Heraclitus, when he asserted that becoming (the flux) is the sole reality. But the point is most fully developed in Nietzsche, in the doctrine of the eternal return. Deleuze gives particular weight to the image of the dicethrow in *Thus Spake Zarathustra* (Part III, "The Seven Seals"). The throw of the dice, the moment of pure chance, corresponds to multiplicity as sheer diversity. The "fall back" of the dice, with its fixing of a specific number as the throw's result, is, of course, itself entirely a chance result. But this result takes on the character of necessity when we affirm it by joyfully accepting an existence in which it will recur to infinity, that is, by accepting a world in which there is nothing more than the mundane events of our human history. Deleuze does not see Nietzsche's eternal return as a metaphysical assertion of literal recurrence; the point is rather that, by affirming such a recurrence, we express our total acceptance of this world, independent of any relation to a grounding and saving transcendence. This affirmation provides, on the level of values, the unity sought by Platonic and Hegelian metaphysicians but without their ontological reduction of multiplicity to the one.

While Bergson's duration helps articulate a Deleuzian ontology of multiplicity, and Nietzsche's eternal return a Deleuzian ethics of multiplicity, Spinoza provides a formulation of a Deleuzian politics of multiplicity.[15] The key here is the notion of power, a metaphysical category that Spinoza uses to redefine the ancient conception of natural rights: each individual has a right to maximize its power (that is, its capacity for positive action) in relation to all other individuals. The result is a multiplicity of individuals in conflict with one another, and the Spinozist (and Deleuzian) problem of politics is to organize this multiplicity into a stable, coherent group that still allows all individuals to assert their power. Further, the organization must not subordinate the multiplicity to an external authority, such as a transcendent God who guarantees individual rights. This means that the organization of the social multiplicity must derive solely from interactions among the individuals that are its elements. In the terminology of Spinoza's *Political Treatise*, the multiplicity must be transformed into a multiple, a multiplicity in which individuals as such are empowered by their union. Since this empowerment is impossible without the common consent of those achieving it, the multiple must take the form of a democracy.

At the end of the 1960s, in *Différence et répétition* and *Logique du sens*, Deleuze turned from historical adumbrations to full-blown expositions of his philosophy in its own terms. Although Deleuze does not entirely abandon the language of multiplicity in these books, two parallel terms, *difference* (in *Différence et répétition*) and *event* (in *Logique du sens*), assume a dominant role. Deleuze's "difference" is the key to his radical reformulation of the classical problem of the one and the many. One standard source of this problem is our experience of the different individuals that are examples (instances) of the same sort of thing. There are many trees in the forest, many human beings on the earth. How is this possible? How, that is, can many things all be what would seem to be just one thing? Traditional metaphysics responds by distinguishing between (1) a general structure (or form), consisting of the essential characteristics that define a kind to which each individual belongs and (2) an unstructured stuff (or matter) that, when appropriately related to the general structure, becomes a concrete individual of the given kind. Classic metaphysical debates concern the precise ontological status of this form and matter and the precise nature of the relation between the two. Do, for example,

---

[15] Deleuze's overall reading of Spinoza also shows how the ontological and the ethical conceptions of multiplicity are formulable in Spinozist terms. See Michael Hardt, *Gilles Deleuze: an Apprenticeship in Philosophy*, for enlightening discussion of this point as well as of Deleuze's appropriations of Bergson and Nietzsche.

forms exist independently, as Plato thought, with individuals arising only through matter's "imitation of" or "participation in" the forms? Or is it rather, as Aristotle held, that forms themselves exist not separately but as principles of structure for the matter of a given individual?

Deleuze objects to the assumption of these debates: that there must be principles of unity (forms, whatever their ontological status) that constitute the essential nature of concrete realities. Traditional metaphysics privileges the unity of forms by making it the basis and explanation of all differences. Differences in kind occur because one kind includes forms that another does not. Within a given kind, differences between individuals are due to the fact that the individuals belong to different sub-kinds. In either case, what differentiates something (kind or individual) from something else is entirely a matter of the forms that determine its reality. Difference is always derived from unified metaphysical structures (forms) that, therefore, constitute the reality of everything there is.

Traditional metaphysics, accordingly, denies Deleuze's intuition that the fundamental principle of reality (being) is not unity but difference, that at root to be is not to be one but to be diverse. This denial is not always as straightforward as the (roughly, Leibnizian) metaphysics of forms sketched above. Traditional metaphysics does often recognize the irreducibility of the many (difference) to the one (form) by introducing a special principle corresponding to the many, such as the non-being of Plato's *Sophist* or Aristotle's prime matter. But any such principle is explicitly outside the principles of unity and subordinated to them; it functions merely as an unintelligible surd element on which forms are somehow impressed. Hegel's dialectic may seem to offer more, since it makes non-being (negation) the creative principle of metaphysical development. But for Hegel, even more than for Plato and Aristotle, non-being is external to the being that it contradicts. A being is different only because it is negated by everything external to it. As Deleuze puts it in an early article on Bergson: "In Hegel, the thing differs with itself because it differs with everything that it is not." Deleuze, like Bergson, insists that "the thing differs with itself *first, immediately*".[16]

Deleuze's positive ontological project is to develop concepts and language that express this view that "the thing differs with itself",

---

[16] "La conception de la différence chez Bergson", 96.

that to be is to be different. In *Différence et répétition* he does this by recasting the standard distinction between difference and repetition. In the standard view, for which the being of concrete realities is understood in terms of forms, two concrete things differ by expressing different forms or they repeat one another by expressing the same form. Difference and repetition are, therefore, on this understanding, exclusive alternatives. Deleuze, however, asks us to think that to repeat is to differ. In one sense, of course, standard metaphysics allows this. Every repetition (instance) of a form will differ, in some non-essential way, from other repetitions of the form, by, for example, having a different spatial or temporal location. Deleuze's thought, however, is that a repetition is essentially different from what it repeats. This will, of course, seem absurd in terms of our standard understanding, for which to be is to be the same (that is, to be this sort of thing rather than any other). But if to be is to be different, what could repetition be other than an expression of a being's difference with itself?

We must not, however, think that identifying being with difference gives ontological priority to negation. Deleuzian difference is affirmation not denial, since denial presupposes something *else* that is negated and thus leads to precisely what Deleuze is trying to avoid: a relativization of difference to sameness. Difference must be understood as a matter of what a being is in itself, not of how it is related to other things. A being, simply as a being, is a locus of the heterogeneity (novelty, creativity) that is difference. The repetition of a being – for example, its continued existence through time or a new instantiation of it – can only be an expression of this heterogeneity.

Deleuze's ontology further requires a radical revision of our epistemological concepts, that is, our conception of what it is to think about beings. The epistemic counterpart of traditional metaphysics is representationalism, which thinks of knowledge as the accurate reproduction in the mind of the forms that define an entity. The basis of such knowledge is the concept regarded as an expression of the unity (the form) common to a multiplicity of instances. Truth is a matter of formulating concepts that accurately represent the individuals falling under them. Deleuze has no use for such an understanding of concepts, since, according to him, being is not defined by the structural identities (forms) that concepts are supposed to represent. A Deleuzian concept is not a meaning (comprehension) under which instances (extension) fall. It is rather a continuum of variations in several dimensions, embracing numerous relations among the varying elements but providing no overall sense or order to them. On a Deleuzian reading, for example, the concept of the cogito is not, as Descartes thought, that of a (finite) thinking substance.[17] It is, rather, a melange of at least three ranges of "intensive variations": thinking (a variable ranging over feeling, imagining, conceiving, etc.), doubting (ranging over doubt that is scientific, neurotic, metaphysical, etc.), and being (ranging over the infinite, the finite, the extended, the thinking, etc.). The concept of the cogito is the complex set (multiplicity, Deleuze will say)[18] of connections among all these variations, including, for example, the facts that to doubt is to think, to think is to be, to doubt is to be finite. The concept has unity only in the sense that there is a continuous path through all the variations and relations that it comprises. There is no extrinsic unity provided by transcendental subjectivity or any other totalizing grasp. Further, concepts, like the world of which they formulate knowledge, are dynamic, open to continual novelty and development. In fact, Deleuze denies any sharp distinction between concepts and beings, thereby excluding the dualism of subject and object that is at the heart of representationalism.

Deleuze's position, particularly as he formulates it in *Différence et répétition*, appears as a parodic inversion of Kant's critical philosophy.[19] According to Kant, knowledge occurs only within the epistemic interval between the extremes of pure sensations and pure ideas. This interval, in which the categories of the understanding simultaneously structure sheer sensory immediacy and restrict sheer intellectual speculation, is, for Kant, the sole domain of legitimate representative knowledge. Outside of this domain, there is only the unintelligible sensible continuum, which is less than knowledge, and the realm of transcendental illusions, which pretends to an intellectual intuition beyond the limits of our knowledge. Deleuzian knowledge, however, derives precisely from the extremes outside the Kantian interval, unmediated by the categories of representational understanding. The intensities of pure sensation and the paradoxes of pure ideas combine to produce an anti-Kantian "synthesis" of

---

[17] For this example, see G. Deleuze and F. Guattari, *What Is Philosophy?*, 24–9.
[18] Deleuze also speaks of a concept as a "plateau" and as a "rhizome" (the latter being a plant, such as an iris, with a root structure that is not unified in a central core).
[19] For Deleuze's analysis of Kant, see his *La philosophie critique de Kant*.

non-representational knowledge. We must not, however, think of ideas and sensations as separate principles that need to be brought together to constitute knowledge. Such a separation would risk leading us back to an ontological dualism (an opposition of two fundamental identities) that would deny the primacy of difference. Rather, sensory intensity is an aspect of an idea, specifically, that aspect whereby its virtuality as an abstract schema transforms the idea into an actuality. Acccordingly, Deleuze says that his view is a "transcendental empiricism" rather than a transcendental idealism.[20]

For Kant, the categories can constitute objects only when they are expressed ("schematized", as he says) in the temporal form taken by our lived experience. Similarly, Deleuze requires that ideas be expressed temporally, although not, of course, according to the common-sense notion of time Kant takes for granted, which assumes the spatialization of time criticized by Bergson. Instead, Deleuze develops in *Différence et répétition* an elaborate account of three "temporal syntheses", the first corresponding to Husserl's conception of the present as incorporating retentions of the past and protentions of the future, the second to the past as understood in terms of Bergson's pure memory (and Proust's involuntary memory), and the third to the future as seen by Nietzsche's myth of the eternal return.

Deleuze also develops his metaphysics of time through his notion of the event, which plays a central role in *Logique du sens*. Given the affinity for process metaphysics implicit in the priority Deleuze gives to difference, it is not surprising that he assigns events a major place. But he does not merely invert the Platonic priority of forms over flux, a move that would retain ontological dualism. Rather, he appropriates the anti-Platonic Stoic distinction of bodies and events, according to which events are the locus of incorporeal meanings that do not exist in a separate Platonic realm but instead "float" on the surfaces of substantial bodies, of which they are the epiphenomenal effects. (At the same time, Deleuze construes the existential concreteness of bodies along the lines of Bergsonian duration rather than of Democritean atoms or Aristotelian substances.) Understanding events in this way, *Logique du sens* continues, in another key, the metaphysics of intensities and ideas developed in *Différence et répétition*.

[20] See his late article, "L'immanence: une vie...", *Philosophie* 47 (1995), 3–7.

Philosophies of difference

The above survey of key Deleuzian ideas gives at best only a rough general understanding of his metaphysics of difference. Consistent with his intuition of the diversity of reality, Deleuze presents multiple versions of his philosophical vision, appropriating, among others, the philosophical vocabularies of Humean empiricism and Foucaultian archaeology,[21] the mathematical vocabularies of set theory and of differential geometry, and aesthetic vocabularies derived from reflection on Proust's novels and Francis Bacon's paintings. Of special importance, for scope and detail and, above all, for the development of Deleuze's ethical and political thought, are his two major collaborative works with Félix Guattari, *L'anti-oedipe* (1972) and *Mille plateaux* (1980), presented as the two parts of an overall project entitled *Capitalisme et schizophrénie*. The focus on social and political issues corresponds to Deleuze's turn to militant political activism, particularly in Foucault's Groupe d'Information Prison and in support of Palestinian rights.

Capitalisme et schizophrénie has, as Manfred Frank puts it, a "consciously dadaist and carnivalesque style"[22] that purposely eludes systematic analysis.[23] The overall goal seems to be a Nietzschean synthesis of psychoanalysis and Marxism, a synthesis that also combines Deleuze's metaphysics with Guattari's psycho-social theorizing.[24] The leading notion is that of desire, which can be construed as a psycho-social expression of Deleuzian difference, since desire is precisely the impetus for becoming other (differing).

Traditionally, however, from Plato through Freud, desire has been subordinated to the lack that it is construed as striving to fulfill. This contradicts Deleuze's intuition of the primacy of difference by deriving it from an anterior need. Deleuze and Guattari instead propose a view of desire that, like Nietzschean will to power, is a

---

[21] His *Foucault* is an impressive analysis but one that sheds more light on Deleuze himself than on Foucault.

[22] Manfred Frank, *What Is Neostructuralism?*, 316. Frank's characterization is particularly apt for *L'anti-oedipe*. *Mille plateaux* is less exuberant but prodigiously – and deliberately – unorganized.

[23] A good introductory guide is provided by Eugene Holland, *Deleuze and Guattari's Anti-Oedipus: Introduction to Schizoanalysis*.

[24] Félix Guattari (1930–92) was a Lacanian psychoanalyst and political activist. Before his collaboration with Deleuze his theoretical work combined a Freudian and a Marxist viewpoint by emphasizing the social nature of individual consciousness and distinguishing the subjected group (*groupe assujetti*), which allows itself to be determined by fantasies imposed from outside, from the group-subject (*groupe-sujet*), which creates and transcends its own fantasies. See the essays collected in his *Psychoanalyse et transversalité*.

pure affirmation of difference for its own sake. Such desire is "deterritorialized", that is, not rooted in any pregiven nature or institution. So construed, desire corresponds to modern capitalism's model of individuals as autonomous choosers of goods valued only because they are desired, not in virtue of any intrinsic worth (e.g., ethical, religious, cultural). Deleuze and Guattari have no problem with this model; their criticism of capitalism is rather that it goes on to accord general (public) value to desires only on the basis of their market value, relegating any non-economic modes of valuation to the private sphere.

They agree with Marxism's call for a critique (and revolutionary overthrow) of this capitalist alienation of desire but in turn criticize Marxism for its own reduction of values to those of economic production (labor), a reduction that eliminates desire as an irreducibly psychological category. Here they see the need to correct Marxism in the light of psychoanalysis. But they also think that psychoanalysis as formulated to date (even by Lacan), has been in complicity with capitalism. This occurs particularly through the theory of the Oedipal complex, which sees all desires as ultimately restricted to the family (in particular, to love or hatred of the mother or the father), thereby legitimating the capitalist relegation of non-economic desire to the private sphere. The project of *L'anti-oedipe* is to reformulate psychoanalysis and Marxism in ways that avoid the above deficiencies and, combining with a Deleuzian (Nietzschean) theory of desire, will be able to launch an effective critique of capitalism.

In the terminology of Deleuze and Guattari, "schizophrenia" refers to the deterritorialized desire that is generated by capitalism and endorsed by Deleuzian philosophy of difference. They see schizophrenia in this sense not as an illness to be cured but as a value to be nurtured. The problem is that capitalism restricts schizophrenic desire to either its economized (public) or its Oedipal (private) form. Those who try to live out non-economized desires in the public realm are violently repressed and lead the lives of terror and frustration that define what is generally termed "schizophrenia". The horror of such lives is real, but it is a product of the capitalist system, not an inevitable feature of deterritorialized desire. Deleuze and Guattari offer a "schizoanalysis" of capitalism designed to expose and help eliminate the arbitrariness of its constraints, thereby freeing the creative power of "schizophrenia".

The positive basis of Deleuze and Guattari's project is their fundamental characterization of human beings in terms of *desiring-machines*. They speak of "machines" not to endorse any sort of mechanism or determinism but to emphasize the productive nature of desire (what Deleuze and Guattari call "desiring-production", their equivalent of Nietzsche's will-to-power). In their terminology, a "machine" is a productive (creative) entity, and to say that we are desiring-machines (or, rather, aggregates of desiring-machines) is to say that the desires constituting our existence are creative achievements in their own rights, not responses to lacks determined by factors (the world, human nature) outside of our desires. The notion of a desiring-machine is Deleuze and Guattari's synthesis of Freudian desire with Marxist production, a synthesis that simultaneously makes desire part of the Marxist infrastructure and gives socio-economic significance to Freudian desire (libido). They employ the notion – along with a dizzying panoply of related concepts – to criticize standard formulations of Marxism and psychoanalysis, to argue that such formulations simultaneously support systems of philosophical representationalism and of socio-economic capitalism, and to construct their own alternative of creative schizophrenia.

IRIGARAY

The difference that concerns Luce Irigaray (b. 1930) is sexual difference. She approaches sexual difference in philosophical, linguistic, and pyschoanalytic terms, interests corresponding to her own academic training: a doctorate in philosophy (1955) from the University of Louvain in Belgium, where she was born, a degree in psychopathology (1962) from the Institut de Psychologie in Paris, a doctorate in linguistics from the University of Vincennes (1968), and a French state doctorate in philosophy (1974). She has held teaching positions (e.g., at the University of Vincennes) as well as research positions (e.g., at the Centre National de Recherche Scientifique), and is also a practicing psychoanalyst.

Irigaray sees sexual difference as "one of the major philosophical issues, if not the issue, of our age". She thinks it is also "probably the issue in our time which could be our 'salvation' if we thought it through" (*Éthique de la différence sexuelle* [EDS], 13/5). On the one hand, Irigaray evokes utopian consequences of developing an adequate grasp of the differences between men and women: "Sexual difference [properly understood] would constitute the horizon of worlds more fecund than any known to date – at least in the West . . . For loving partners this would be a fecundity of birth and regeneration, but also the production of a new age of thought, art, poetry and language: the creation of a new *poetics*." On the other hand, Irigaray has a profound sense of the difficulty facing the effort to understand sexual difference. Contemporary sexism is not only rooted in social and economic practices; it derives from our fundamental linguistic and ontological frameworks. "We need to reinterpret everything concerning the relations between the subject and discourse, the subject and the world, the subject and the cosmic, the microcosmic and the macrocosmic" (*EDS*, 14/6).

For Irigaray, then, male dominance cannot, ultimately, be effectively addressed by political or social reform or even revolution, although she agrees that actions at these levels are still called for. In the end what is required is a philosophical revolution in the fundamental categories through which we think our world and our place in it. This is because "man [in the sense of the masculine sex, contrary to claims that the term is neutral and universal and so includes women] has been the subject of discourse, whether in theory, morality, or politics. And the gender of God, the guardian of every subject and every discourse, is always *masculine and paternal*, in the West" (*EDS*, 14/6–7).

Philosophy is Irigaray's main focus "inasmuch as this discourse sets forth the law for all others, inasmuch as it constitutes the discourse on discourse" (*Ce sexe qui n'en est pas un* [*CS*], 72/74). Philosophy carries out this meta-linguistic domination (reminiscent of the Barthesian motto: "meta-language is terrorism") through "its power to reduce all others to the economy of the Same", that is, to reduce all experience, all reality to a fixed set of fundamental categories. And, as we have seen, Irigaray maintains that one fundamental consequence of this reduction is "to *eradicate the difference between the sexes* in systems that are self-representative of a 'masculine subject'" (*CS*, 72/74).

Irigaray's primary tool for exposing the implicit sexism of philosophical discourse is psychoanalysis, which reveals the "sexual indifference [refusal to recognize the difference of the sexes] that underlies the truth of any science, the logic of every discourse" (*CS*, 67/69, italics omitted). Her assumption seems to be that psychoanalysis shows how all human cultural achievements express the resolution of the tensions surrounding childhood sexuality (particularly, the response to the Oedipal complex) and that, accordingly, the fundamental philosophical framework of culture will embody this resolution. Freud's essential contribution is to show that our childhood tensions are resolved by the reduction of feminine sexuality to masculine sexuality. "Female sexuality . . . is never defined with respect to any sex but the masculine . . . The 'feminine' is always described in terms of deficiency or atrophy, as the other side of the sex that alone holds a monopoly on virtue: the male sex" (*CS*, 67–8/69). Thus, we have the all too familiar story of "penis-envy" as the key to female sexuality and fear of losing the penis as the key to male sexuality. The feminine is understood entirely as the lack of what defines male sexuality.

In Freudian terms, the turning point in the development of male sexuality is the little boy's repression, from fear of castration by his father, of desire for his mother. Given the unconscious nature of this desire, it can express itself as a desire for anything that the unconscious sees as the symbolic equivalent of the mother. Renouncing the mother therefore means devaluing all of these symbolic equivalents. This includes anything viewed as passive, receptive, soft, lacking, enclosing – any of the attributes of women as recipients of the penis and bearers of children. At the same time, the opposites of these attributes, particularly the distinctively masculine (penile) powers of action, penetration, hardness, are particularly valued. The result is a way of thinking that sharply separates "female" qualities from their "male" opposites, leading to dichotomies between the active form and the passive matter it molds, between advancing time and receptive space, between solid objects and the places that contain them. On another level, the female is associated with matter and the material world in general, because of both its passivity and its role in our nurture and support. This leads to sharp distinctions between mind and body, intellect and sense, action and passion, with, in each case, the first term corresponding to a male value and the second to a female disvalue. Along the same lines, vision, being more active and disembodied, is valued over the other senses.

Female sexuality develops in distinctive ways but with the same ultimate "philosophical" effects. Like the little boy, the little girl desires her mother sexually. The girl, however, soon learns that her desire cannot be fulfilled because she has no penis. This leads the girl to hate her mother for not providing her with this essential organ and, more generally, to value women negatively for being "castrated". Correspondingly, she comes to love the father and regards the mother as a rival for his affection. But, unlike the boy, the girl (having no penis) cannot fully identify with the father. This leaves her with no way of identifying herself except by the unfulfillable desire of being a man. She is thus led to disvalue her femininity and to see her worth as dependent on male approval. Thus, girls come to accept the same asymmetrical dichotomies as boys do, although their psychological route to this acceptance is quite different.

It might be objected that Freud's account is itself the product of a sexist view determined to give priority to the male and that, therefore, a feminist should pay no attention to it. Irigaray agrees that Freud's own work is pervaded by sexism (see her critique of Freud in *Speculum de l'autre femme*). But, she maintains, this does not mean that his description of human sexuality is incorrect: "Freud is describing an actual state of affairs"; the feminine is indeed understood entirely in terms of the masculine (*CS*, 68/70). Freud's failing (and also Lacan's) is to accept this description as an unquestioned norm and so endorse the contingent historical fact as an inevitable constraint on human existence. We rightly object to Freud's acceptance of the phallocentric order, "but that order is indeed the one that lays down the law today" (*CS*, 71/73).

Irigaray does not, however, simply argue from the general descriptive truth of psychoanalysis to the masculine dominance of philosophical discourse. She also analyzes philosophical texts to show precisely how they embody this dominance. One of her most important analyses is of Plato's myth of the cave, carried out in the long concluding essay of *Speculum de l'autre femme*.

Exposing the masculine bias of philosophy is merely the preliminary stage of Irigaray's project. She also proposes to find a way to express female sexuality in its own terms, without subordinating it to masculinity. This requires her to "solve the problem of the articulation of the female sex in discourse". This is particularly difficult since, on Irigaray's own account, our thought and language is, at the most fundamental level, dependent on the system of "masculine logic". "How can we introduce ourselves into such a tightly-woven systematicity?" (*CS*, 73/76). It would seem that women must choose between not speaking at all or speaking in terms of categories that subordinate their sexuality to that of men.

Irigaray agrees that any sort of direct assault on masculine logic would mean "demanding to speak as a (masculine) 'subject'" and so would "postulate a relation to the intelligible that would maintain sexual indifference" (*CS*, 74/76). Her positive project is to develop a distinctive feminine identity, not as it is defined by masculinist thought but as it can be constructed from feminine "residues" that elude masculine domination (alternatively, from the feminine "matter" that is never entirely assimilated by the masculine "form"). Such an identity emerges, we might say, from the interstices of the masculinist system and does not mirror the male conception of women. At the same time, it constitutes a basis for women to assume a parity with men that does not simply turn them into men.

Irigaray's indirect approach to constructing a feminine identity emphasizes what she calls "mimicry". Mimicry is a traditional role of the female, tied both to her function of biological reproduction (providing men with their images in her children) and to her status as inferior reflection of male qualities. But Irigaray's thought is that this role can be turned against male dominance to reveal "by an effect of playful repetition, what was supposed to remain invisible: the cover-up of a possible operation of the feminine in language" (*CS*, 74/76).

Specifically, she suggests that women can develop their own distinctive femininity by taking on, in their own way, stereotypically feminine attributes. Her idea can be understood in terms of the traditional identification of woman with matter, determined by the organizing force of (masculine) form. (Consider, for example, long-established views about the relation of passive ovum to active sperm.) Construed in these terms, woman is viewed as the epistemic matter structured by the conceptual forms of male rationality. But, as we have seen, Irigaray suggests that there always persists a material residue, something never fully assimilated to or controlled by form. Deliberately assuming and "playing" roles defined for them by masculine concepts may allow women to unearth and develop this residue. Such a procedure might, then, provide a foothold for autonomous female speech and destroy the male monopoly on discourse. As a result, "the masculine would no longer be 'everything'", and "the right to define every value . . . would no longer belong to it" (*CS*, 77/80).

Irigaray does not, however, propose to develop a "new theory of which woman would be the *subject* or the *object*". Such a theory would be merely women's effort to rival men in masculine terms by constructing a "logic of the feminine". Rather, Irigaray speaks, adapting Lacan's terminology, of constructing a feminine "Imaginary" to replace the dominant images of women derived from the male unconscious. Her goal is "jamming the theoretical machinery itself" by evoking a positive feminine "disruptive *excess*" where in the past masculine theory has assigned women only the negativities of lack and deficiency (*CS*, 76/78). This jamming of male theory will, at the same time, initiate distinctively feminine discourses.

One of the prime loci of Irigaray's positive construction of feminine identity is her rethinking of the traditional categories of natural philosophy. "The transition to a new age [in which sexual difference would be properly recognized] requires a change in our perception and conception of *space-time*, the *inhabiting of places*, and of *containers* or *envelopes of identity*" (*EDS*, 15/7). It also requires new ways of thinking about the matter and form that constitute objects in space-time and about the intervals between these objects.

Here one key problem is that women are understood simply as places for men: the wombs in which they grow, the homes in which they are sheltered. This leaves the woman with no place of her own – a problem recalling Aristotle's aporia: how can a place itself have a place? Irigaray notes, however, that women are also associated with the intervals ("empty" spaces) between things and the thresholds through which they enter and exit (prototypically, the vagina). She evokes the beauty and worth of woman as an intermediate, mediating place that connects and unifies the world. Women as creative "intervals" are, she suggests, like angels, the messengers between heaven and earth. "These messengers who never remain enclosed in a place, who are also never immobile . . . circulate as mediators of that which has not yet happened, of what is still going to happen, of what is on the horizon. Endlessly reopening the enclosure of the universe, of universes, identities, the unfolding of actions, of history" (*EDS*, 22/15). She also evokes women's lips (facial and genital), always partly open, partly closed and so "strangers to dichotomy and opposition", as images of the feminine (*EDS*, 24/18).

Irigaray further develops the theme of woman as interval by showing how, in the *Symposium*, Diotima, whose words are reported by Socrates, proposes an alternative to Plato's dialectic (and all the subsequent dialectics in the history of philosophy). Instead of moving from term to term in a way that requires the abandoning or destruction of earlier terms, "she establishes an intermediary that will never be abandoned as a means or a path" (*EDS*, 27/20). Diotima's dialectic moves from "here" to a "beyond", but "a beyond that never abolishes the here". Moreover, its means, its intermediary, is love, a love that we "do not have to give up . . . in order to become wise or learned" (*EDS*, 28/21). This conception of dialectic would allow for a knowledge of the intelligible that did not require a renunciation of the sensible, a grasp of the eternal that would not have to take place outside of time. Unfortunately, this conception of dialectic is abandoned in the second half of Diotima's speech – perhaps Socrates as a male could not keep the message unmuddled? But it remains as a basis for a feminine antidote to the relentless dichotomies of male thought.

Irigaray also develops a poetry of the fluids whose lack of substance and definition have marginalized them in masculine thought – a point she supports by citing the lagging development of fluid mechanics in the history of science (*CS*, 103/106). Here she speaks of the red blood (*sang rouge*) with which women nourish children in the womb, in contrast to the (re)semblance (homophonically, *sang blanc*, white blood) of male representationalist epistemology; and of the mucus that lubricates tissues and, especially, facilitates sexual union. These liquids evoke both the feminine themes of inclusive becoming (opposed to exclusive dialectics of being and non-being) and of connection and nourishment.

The project of articulating female sexuality is not the final goal of Irigaray's philosophy. This project is pursued as an essential precondition of a viable ethics. For Irigaray, because our conceptions of sexual difference are fundamental to all thought and action, ethics must take the form of sexual ethics. This does not mean that all ethical questions are explicitly about sex; Irigaray emphasizes, for example, the ethical importance of environmental and technological issues. But questions of sexuality are ethically central and implicit in virtually all moral concerns. (For example, Irigaray regards environmental and technological problems as due to the limitations of our masculinist conception of science.)

The concern of Irigaray's sexual ethics is the fruitful interaction of men and women. At present, there are no alternatives to the subordination of women to men, since women have no distinctive sexual identity. They can be thought of only as inferior men and therefore as mere instruments for social relations among men. In this regard, Irigaray speaks of our society as "hom(m)osexual": there are relations of equality only among members of the same (*homos*, in Greek) sex, namely men (*hommes*, in French). In such a society, women can only be "servants of the phallic cult, or the objects of use and exchange between men, rival objects on the market". But ethics must not be limited to creating an identity for women. As Irigaray sees it, men too need to develop an identity beyond that provided by masculinist thought. Just as we need to avoid "subordinating women to destiny without allowing them any access to mind, or consciousness of self and for self", so too we must avoid "closing man away in a consciousness of self and for self that leaves no space for the gods" (*EDS*, 121/126).

We have already seen how Irigaray tries to develop an alternative vision of the feminine through a transformation of fundamental vocabulary and hence of ontological categories. To be ethically effective, this transformation must also be realized in women's relations to one another and, specifically, to one another's bodies. There must, in other words, be the possibility of genuine homoerotic relations among women: "What we have to do . . . is to discover our sexual identity, that is, the singularity of our auto-eroticism, of our narcissism, the singularity of our homosexuality."[25] Irigaray is not claiming, as some radical feminists do, that the only appropriate sexual relations for women are lesbian. Her point is rather that one concrete consequence of an independent female sexual identity must be the capacity of women to overcome Oedipal hatred of the feminine and to love one another. Such love would be quite different from female homosexuality understood, as in Freudian theory, simply as a mimicking of masculine desire.

But Irigaray seems to regard female homosexuality as itself only a step to the ultimate goal of productive male–female relations. Only women capable of loving one another for their own sakes have the autonomous identity needed to love men as "equals". Here, of course, "equals" does not imply that men and women share an identical nature. Rather, Irigaray's idea is that men and women must develop their own independent identities as male and female, identities that provide the basis for truly creative, nonexploitative interaction between the sexes.

The emotional and intellectual force behind such interactions is

---

[25] *Le corps-à-corps avec la mère*, 30–1.

wonder, "this first passion . . . indispensable not only to life but also or still to the creation of an ethics". Given his or her own distinctive sexual identity, "this other, male or female, should *surprise* us again and again, appear to us as *new, very different* from what we knew or what we thought he or she should be". Wonder precedes a relation that does not involve reduction or assimilation of the other. "Wonder goes beyond that which is or is not suitable for us . . . We would in some way have reduced the other to ourselves if he or she suited us completely." We wonder at the excess of the other, that is, at "the other's existence and becoming as a place that permits union and/through resistance to assimilation or reduction to sameness" (*EDS*, 77/74). Irigaray suggests that wonder before the other would lead us to a "second birth", namely a birth into "a transcendence, that of the other". As transcendent, the birth would be spiritual, but it would also be "physical and carnal", and so would overcome the spirit/matter bifurcation subtended by the masculinist distinction of male and female. We would have reached a "place of incidence and junction of body and spirit" (*EDS*, 84/82), the locus of the "sensible transcendental" (*EDS*, 124/129).

Irigaray's language of "wonder" and "transcendence" has obvious religious connotations, connotations she is willing to endorse and develop. Her descriptions of the experience of sexual encounter deploy the traditional religious terms of infinity and ineffability, speaking, for example, of "an embrace that transcends all limits" and in which "each one discovers the self in that experience which is inexpressible yet forms the supple grounding of life and language". Irigaray's next comment becomes explicitly religious: "For this, 'God' is necessary, or a love so attentive that it is divine." This is because "love always postpones its transcendence beyond the here and now, except in certain experiences of God" (*EDS*, 25/19). This cannot, of course, be the God of traditional ontology and religion, which is simply the ultimate expression of masculine dominance. But since "it seems we are unable to eliminate or suppress the phenomenon of religion", it is "crucial that we rethink religion, and especially religious categories, initiations, rules, and utopias, all of which have been masculine for centuries".[26]

This rethinking must, according to Irigaray, include first of all a development of female religious genealogies (scarcely existent in the

---

[26] *Sexes and Genealogies*, 75.

West, except for some isolated Greek cases), which will allow women to have their own religious identity. It also requires symbolic alternatives to sacrifice, a notion too closely tied to the male penchant for bifurcation and elimination. Finally, Irigaray calls for the spiritualization of sexual relations, which in turn will make them, as we have seen, the site of our experience of the divine.[27]

Of course, this new God, like the female identity and the new realm of sexual relations so closely linked to it, is still to come (although, unlike Derrida, Irigaray seems to hope for an actual coming of the divine). Irigaray even cites Heidegger's (and Hölderlin's) "Only a god can save us now" (*EDS*, 123/128). But unlike Heidegger she sees the advent of the divine as requiring our own creative efforts. As she says at the end of the title essay of *Éthique de la différence sexuelle*, in a passage that also sums up her project of creating a female sexual identity: "Not only in mourning for the dead God of Nietzsche, not waiting passively for the god to come, but by conjuring him up among us, within us, as resurrection and transfiguration of blood, of flesh, through a language and an ethics that is ours" (*EDS*, 123/128).

Irigaray's critiques of philosophical thought have obvious strong affinities to the work of other philosophers of difference such as Lyotard and, especially, Derrida. The most obvious connection is her effort to undermine the "metaphysics of the same" whereby Western thought has excluded the "others" (prototypically women) that correspond to the devalued terms of its asymmetrical dichotomies. Like Lyotard and Derrida, she offers, for example, a critique of representationism, the understanding of knowledge as a reflection in the mind (as in a mirror) of the same object that exists in reality. Irigaray points out that in such a view of knowledge objects are knowable only to the extent that they resemble the reflecting mirror (the male mind). A profoundly different object, such as a woman, can appear only as a defective man – as a flat mirror image will show the female genitals as simply an absence of a penis.[28] (She also suggests that woman corresponds instead to the materials from which the mirror is made – e.g., the tain (thin tin plate) behind the reflecting surface (*CS*, 147/151); and that knowledge of female sexuality requires – both literally and metaphorically – a curved

---

[27] For a fuller discussion of Irigaray's religious thought, see Margaret Whitford, *Luce Irigaray: Philosophy in the Feminine*, 140–7.
[28] *Speculum of the Other Woman*, 89.

mirror, e.g., a speculum.) Irigaray's affinity with deconstruction is all the stronger given Derrida's own singling out of the male/female dichotomy as a target of deconstructive analysis and his resulting critique of phallogocentrism.

There is, nonetheless, an apparent tension between Derrida's and Irigaray's deconstructive projects, as is particularly clear from Derrida's rejection of feminism.[29] As he put it in a 1985 interview:

> For me deconstruction is certainly not feminist. At least as I have tried to practice it. I believe it naturally supposes a radical deconstruction of phallogocentrism, and certainly an absolutely other and new interest in women's questions. But if there is one thing it must not come to, it's feminism. So I would say that deconstruction is deconstruction of feminism, from the start, insofar as feminism is a form – no doubt necessary at a certain moment – but a form of phallogocentrism among others.[30]

Derrida's rejection makes sense if we think feminism must be either the mere demand that women be treated just as men are or else an effort to reverse the valuation of the male/female dichotomy, making the female the superior term. (These options, of course, correspond to the standard distinction between equality-feminism and difference-feminism.) In either option, feminism is a reassertion of the traditional dichotomy that Derrida wants to deconstruct. It would be an attempt to "improve the lot" of women without addressing the metaphysical basis of male dominance, and Derrida would no doubt predict that such an attempt will lead only to the triumph of phallogocentrism in some other form.

Irigaray, however, has a different understanding of feminism. She explicitly rejects the equality and the difference options, the first because it has women seeking to be *man's equal*, hence reducing them to "potential men", and the second because it embraces a "femininity" that "is a role, an image, a value, imposed upon women by male values of representation" (*CS*, 80/84). Her own feminism can be thought of as aiming at goals similar to those of equality-feminism and difference-feminism, but without their phallogocentric presuppositions.

Irigaray's vision (at least in its utopian limit) is of a world in which women and men have their own equal but distinctive identities that allow them to interact with a fecundity impossible in today's

---

[29] For a fuller discussion of Derrida and Irigaray on feminism, see Margaret Whitford, *Luce Irigaray: Philosophy in the Feminine*, 126–35.

[30] J. Creech et al., "Deconstruction in America: An Interview With Jacques Derrida", 30–1.

world.[31] As she says: "To remember that we must go on living and creating worlds is our task. But it can be accomplished only through the combined efforts of the two halves of the world: the masculine and the feminine" (*EDS*, 122/127). Such a conception of feminism may or may not be possible or realistic, but it does not reduce to feminism in either of the senses in which Derrida rejects it. There is, then, no inconsistency between Irigaray's feminism and the project of deconstructing the categories of traditional metaphysics and epistemology.

[31] This vision recalls Beauvoir's conception of the couple, sketched at the end of *Le deuxième sexe*.

CHAPTER 12

Fin-de-siècle again: "le temps retrouvé"?

> The power to make me rediscover days that were long past, the Time that was Lost.
> (Marcel Proust, *In Search of Lost Time*, VI, 263)

The last twenty years of French philosophy have been more a matter of assessing and reviving the past than of breaking out in new directions. A particularly striking illustration is the fact that the two most prominent figures during the period have been philosophers who were contemporaries of Sartre and Merleau-Ponty: Emmanuel Levinas and Paul Ricoeur. Indeed, both Levinas and Ricoeur were important figures in the history of existential phenomenology. But they were also, though in quite different ways, outsiders to the Parisian mainstream dominated by Sartre and Merleau-Ponty and eventually went considerably beyond their existential origins. Their recent popularity reflects not only a renewed interest in the subject-centered philosophy of the 1940s and 1950s but also a rehabilitation of themes and emphases that had been long repressed in French thought. After discussing these two major voices from the past, I will conclude with a brief overview of other recent currents.

LEVINAS

Emmanuel Levinas (1906–95) was literally an outsider; born in Lithuania, he lived there and in the Ukraine before moving to France in 1923, where he received his philosophical training at the University of Strasbourg. After a year of study in Freiburg with Husserl and Heidegger, he lived in Paris without a university position, teaching at and eventually heading the École Normale Israélite Orientale. It was only in 1961, after the publication of *Totalité et infini*, that Levinas became a professor at a French university, in Poitiers. He subsequently held positions at the University of Paris-Nanterre and at the Sorbonne.

Levinas was not only geographically and institutionally outside the mainstream of Parisian existential phenomenology; he was also separated by his religious interests and commitments. Levinas was raised in an orthodox Jewish family and, particularly after World War II, was very active as a distinctively Jewish thinker, writing numerous essays on religious topics, including a number of Talmudic commentaries. His coolness to Marxism – as a child he had lived through the Soviet Revolution in the Ukraine – put him at a further remove from Parisian intellectual life, although he was a good friend of Maurice Blanchot. Levinas knew both Sartre, whom he had met at Gabriel Marcel's Friday discussion sessions, and Merleau-Ponty, whom he frequently saw at Jean Wahl's Collège de Philosophie;[1] and he occasionally published in *Les temps modernes*. Further, as we have seen, Levinas's was the first book Sartre read about Husserl. But Sartre and his circle did not welcome religious believers with no interest in Marxist politics.

We have already encountered Levinas for his seminal work in introducing Husserl (and Heidegger, through whose lens he read Husserl) to France. Through the 1950s, his publications were primarily critical commentaries on Husserl and Heidegger, with his own distinctive philosophy only gradually and partially emerging. But in 1961 he published *Totalité et infini*, which immediately established him as an important independent thinker, although one scarcely in tune with the developing turn to structuralism.[2] The book's grounding in careful experiential descriptions – for example, of the enjoyment the self takes in "living off of" (*vivre de*) the natural goods of the world, and of the experience of the other with its call to an absolute ethical obligation – show the author's phenomenological roots. But Levinas had come to see Husserl and even Heidegger as involved in a fundamental mistake that has tainted all of Western philosophy: the subordination of the other to *the same*.

What Levinas means by the same is perhaps best expressed in his

[1] The Collège de Philosophie, which Wahl founded in 1946 and directed until 1966, was an important forum, through its weekly meeting, for discussing new philosophical ideas. It has recently been revived by Luc Ferry and Alain Renaut.
[2] Levinas's second major book, *Autrement qu'être*, is to an important extent a reformulation of *Totalité et infini* in a new vocabulary, one designed to eliminate what he came to see as the earlier work's dependence on terms too closely tied to the philosophies of the same that have dominated philosophical thought. Here he seems to have been in part motivated by Derrida's sympathetic but forceful critique of *Totalité et infini* in "Violence et metaphysique" (in *L'écriture et la différence*). With a few exceptions, I limit my discussion to the more influential and, for all its formidable difficulties, more accessible *Totalité et infini*.

notion of totality, an encompassing whole in which each part has intelligibility solely through its place within the whole. To belong to a totality and therefore to be completely understood as part of a whole is to be "reduced to the Same". The project of Western philosophy has been one of reduction to the same because it has always insisted on understanding everything in relation to some self-intelligible whole, whether it be Platonic forms, Aristotelian substance, the divine pure act of the medievals, or Hegel's absolute. Philosophers have acknowledged loci of "otherness" that lie outside the totality but have always wound up understanding them only in their relation to the totality. So Plato's non-being is relative to the forms, Aristotle's primary matter can exist only as part of a substance, finite beings require a divine creator, and Hegelian negations are always subsumed in a subsequent synthesis. Levinas's fundamental claim is that no totality truly encompasses all reality, that there always remains an other independent of any relation to the totality.

Taking account of the other requires thinking in terms not of totality but of what Levinas calls *infinity*: a whole, but one encountering an other that it cannot include. Here Levinas evokes Descartes' argument in the "Third Meditation" for the existence of God, based on his claim that we have an idea of infinite substance that we are, nonetheless, unable to comprehend. This infinity, once we detach it from Descartes' substance ontology and his vain effort to prove the existence of the utterly other, well expresses the "transcendence" of the other: "a relation with a reality infinitely distant from my own reality, yet without this distance destroying this relation and without this relation destroying this distance" (*Totalité et infini* [*TI*], 12/41). Levinas also characterizes the other in terms of its *exteriority*, that is, its separation from the immanence of totality.

It will be no surprise, given his insistence on the irreducible other, that Levinas rejects Husserlian phenomenology because of its relativization of everything to the transcendental ego. Here he readily invokes Heidegger's critique of the transcendental subject, with its claim, echoed in Merleau-Ponty's philosophy of ambiguity, that talk of such a subject is an abstraction from the concrete reality of "being-in-the-world". But Levinas thinks that Heidegger himself falls into a philosophy of totality.[3] It may seem that Heidegger's

---

[3] Levinas limits his discussion of Heidegger almost entirely to *Being and Time*, regarding it as

Being, so sharply distinguished from the totality of beings (the things that are), is just what Levinas has in mind in insisting on an other outside any totality. But Levinas maintains that *Dasein* (Heidegger's expression for human-reality-in-the-world) functions as a totalizing center. Admittedly, *Dasein* is presented as "thrown" into the world, a contingent "being-for-death" that lacks the agency and autonomy of Husserl's transcendental ego and that can only await Being's self-revelation. But Levinas maintains that *Dasein* remains the center of a "panoramic disclosure" (*TI*, 248/270) of Being, a center without which there would be no truth. (In another vein, Levinas sometimes suggests that Heideggerian Being itself, as the horizon of all existents, functions as an ontological totality.)[4]

Levinas does not, however, limit his discussion of the other to the above high level of ontological abstraction. The other is not merely a principle or entity separate from any totality we might encounter or envision. Rather, the other is the *other person* as an absolute ethical demand, unconditionally, non-negotiably requiring my respect and responsibility. The ontological ideal of a totality is overturned by the ethical imperative of the other. Levinas rejects, therefore, the standard idea that metaphysics is "first philosophy" and that, therefore, ethics must be somehow derived from it. On the contrary, "morality is not a branch of philosophy, rather, it is first philosophy" (*TI*, 281/304, translation modified).

In *Totalité et infini* Levinas precedes his treatment of our encounter with the other with a detailed description of human existence apart from this encounter. Such a description is, of course, an abstraction from concrete reality, which always involves the other. But it catches the way in which we often like to think of our lives and provides a useful background for focusing the effect of the other on our existence.

The standpoint of Levinas's descriptions is the self or ego regarded as in full possession of its world, as the source and focus of all meanings. As Levinas sees it, this is the standpoint of standard phenomenology, including both Husserl and the Heidegger of *Being and Time*, and he characterizes it as the standpoint of *interiority* (as opposed to the exteriority introduced by the other). The standpoint

---

one of the greatest philosophical books ever written but seeing much less value in Heidegger's later philosophy.

[4] For more on the complex issues of Levinas's critique of Heidegger, see Adriaan Peperzak, *To the Other*.

can also be thought of as expressing how things would look if the traditional viewpoint of totality (the same) were sufficient. The attention Levinas gives to this description reflects the fact that, although he rejects the ultimate truth of totality, he recognizes it as one crucial dimension of human existence.

The life of interiority does not ignore external objects, but it appropriates them for the enjoyment of the self. We "live off of" (*vivre de*) the things of our world (*TI*, 82/110), using them not only as means to ends but as satisfactions in their own right. The satisfaction consists in the pleasure we experience by incorporating external objects into our domain of control, by taking them "home" (*chez nous*).[5] Levinas's model here is eating, a process admittedly necessary as a means to sustain life, but also one we enjoy for its own sake as an assimilation of the other to the self. Levinas insists that life is not a matter of Heideggerian care (*Sorge*) but of enjoyment (*jouissance*), which "is not a psychological state among others . . . but the very pulsation of the I" (*TI*, 85/113). Enjoyment is not the goal of our life's activity but the very condition of its existence. To live is to be happy. "The I is, to be sure, happiness, presence at home with itself" (*TI*, 116/143).

The enjoyment of interiority is not unreal, but it is only one dimension of human existence and a dimension that could not exist without the exteriority of the other. Enjoyment presupposes a self that has the freedom to appropriate and assimilate its world in accord with its taste. But how does there come to be a free self? According to Levinas, the self is free not for the sake of its enjoyment but for the sake of the other. This is why his description of the life of interiority ultimately makes sense only in the context of the exteriority of the other.

The encounter with the other is most fully described in a crucial section of *Totalité et infini* entitled "Ethics and the Face". According to Levinas, I encounter the other through its face (*visage*) and through its speech (*parole*).[6] I see the face of the other, but not as an object contained in my world (my interiority), available for my enjoyment. Rather, "the face is present in its refusal to be con-

---

[5] This tie of the life of interiority to the domestic explains Levinas's characterizing it in terms of "economy", with its etymology of "household [*oikos* in Greek] management".

[6] Of course, I need not literally see the face or hear the cry of the other; the encounter may be effected by other means. But seeing a face and hearing a cry are typical forms of the encounter to which alternatives (touching the arm, feeling the pulse) are equivalent.

tained", as something that I cannot "comprehend" or "encompass" (*TI*, 168/194). The face is not an object that I can perceive but an epiphany, a revelation (*TI*, 168/194).

The content of this revelation – and here we move naturally to the speech of the other – is the simple injunction: *Do not kill me*. This is neither a threat (*If you try to kill me, I will try to kill you* or *If you kill me, society will punish you*) nor an application of a general principle (*Killing is wrong, so don't do it to me*). It is not, in other words, an expression of either a utilitarian or a deontological ethics. It is, rather, a simple assertion of the inviolability of this person before me, of my absolute responsibility to respect this person's presence, to refrain from trying to make it just another element of the domain in which I hold sway.[7] According to Levinas this responsibility is both infinite and asymmetrical. It is infinite in that there are no considerations, not even that of my own death, that can in any way limit my obligation to the other. "To expose myself to the vulnerability of the face is to put my ontological right to exist into question."[8] The responsibility is asymmetrical because, unlike Kant's categorical imperative, it does not logically require a reciprocal obligation to me on the part of the other. No doubt other people have their own experiences of the other (perhaps even of me) that confront them with their own infinite responsibility. The point, however, is that the responsibility can arise only from their own experiences, not from some sort of generalization of or inference from mine. Given my experience – and this is all I am given – I am in no position to assert any obligation of the other.

The incursion of the other jolts the world of interiority in which I reign as master of my enjoyment and transforms it into one in which I am constantly challenged by the reality of the other. To this extent, Levinas's treatment recalls that of Sartre in *L'être et le néant*, where the other is likewise experienced as disrupting the world that I have constituted for myself. It is tempting to say that there is a fundamental difference in that Sartre's account is merely ontological, with no ethical significance. But although this is certainly what Sartre intends, he could not deny that, to some extent at least, the conflict

---

[7] Presumably, then, the injunction is not merely that I not kill the other, as though any violation short of that would be permitted. But killing is the paradigm case of violation, and any claim of a right to treat the other as an object of my enjoyment – which I legitimately make of the rest of the world – would ultimately imply the right to kill the other.

[8] Richard Kearney (ed.), *Dialogues with Contemporary Continental Thinkers*, 60.

between two consciousnesses concerns the values implicit in the meanings each confers on the other. Pride and shame, Sartre's paradigm modes of experiencing the other, inevitably have moral connotations. Similarly, we might cite the fact that, for Sartre, the encounter with the other is entirely symmetrical. I can always respond to the other's look with my own reciprocal gaze, making the other an object for me in turn. This seems in fundamental contradiction with Levinas's experience of an obligation imposed by the other that I am not able to impose on the other. But Levinas's asymmetry reflects the fact that, although I experience myself as responsible for the other, I am not able to impose a reciprocal experience on the other. A similar asymmetry holds for Sartre: given that I experience shame or pride before the other, nothing I can do will guarantee a parallel experience in the other, since this depends on what the other makes of, for example, my look of disdain.

Rather, the fundamental difference between Sartre and Levinas concerns freedom. According to Sartre, the experience of the other requires the antecedent freedom of both myself and the other; being-for-others is the being *of* a free consciousness *for* a free consciousness. For Levinas, the self becomes free only in face of the other, since freedom is nothing but my reaction to the other's demand for respect. Sartre might respond that even the self in Levinas's state of pure interior enjoyment is free, because it chooses how and when to appropriate objects for its pleasure. But Levinas maintains that, insofar as it is genuine, this freedom itself derives from the encounter with the other. Mere (Sartrean) spontaneity is not freedom. Freedom does not consist in an arbitrary choice that creates the very value of what it chooses. It is rather the opportunity to choose for or against a value that exists independently of our choice.[9] As Levinas says in a passage obviously directed against Sartre:

Existence is not in reality condemned to freedom, but is *invested* as freedom. Freedom is not bare. To philosophize is to trace freedom back to what lies before it, to disclose the investitude that liberates freedom from the arbitrary. (*TI*, 57/84–5)

---

[9] Levinas further argues that there is not even a world of objects, available for our choice, apart from our encounter with the other. Apart from the other, I would be entirely immersed in my enjoyment of the world and would lack the distance needed to constitute it as a domain of distinguishable objects. This distance arises only when I come to experience my world as also available to the other and therefore as a locus of intersubjective meaning and reality. See *TI*, 142–9/168–74 and Peperzak, *To the Other*, 165–6.

It is, for Levinas, the other that "invests" me with freedom by presenting me with an ethical value not constituted as such by my choice. The difference between Levinas and Sartre lies, then, in their fundamentally opposed conceptions of freedom.

Levinas's depiction of the other in terms of its radical alterity and absolute demands often evokes the language of religion, particularly as it has been deployed by Kierkegaard and others set on opposing the subordination of religious experience to totalizing philosophical conceptions. This is no accident, and Levinas, although the theme is muted in *Totalité et infini*, is quite willing to develop his philosophy of the other in a religious direction. He does not, however, identify the other of our ethical experience with God. "God is not simply the 'first other', or 'other par excellence' or the 'absolutely other', but other than the other, other otherwise, and other with an alterity prior to the alterity of the other, prior to the ethical obligation to the other."[10] Thus, Levinas rejects Buber's I–Thou relation (and Marcel's similar view) as a model for our relation to God on the grounds that it destroys the utter alterity of the divine.[11] At the same time, our only access to God is through the other. Our "responsibility for the Other" is a "responsibility prior to the Law", and this responsibility "is God's revelation".[12] Somehow, God's "absolute remoteness, his transcendence, turns into my responsibility . . . for the other".[13]

Levinas is nearly obsessive in his caution regarding any efforts to speak of God. In his foreword to the collection of essays that contain some of his most important discussions of God, he "wonders whether it is possible to speak legitimately of God without striking a blow against the absoluteness [*absoluité*] that his word seems to signify".[14] He is even dubious of the standard trope – which he nonetheless often employs – of negative theology. His worry, presumably, is that even to deny an attribute A of God is to suggest that he at least falls within the conceptual domain defined by A and its negation (as, for example, saying that something is not blue suggests that it falls within the domain of color). Levinas tries to avoid such problems by introducing neologisms such as "illeity" (an abstract

---

[10] "God and Philosophy", in *Of God Who Comes to Mind*, 69.
[11] *Otherwise than Being*, 12–13, and "Dialogue", in *Of God Who Comes to Mind*, 137–51.
[12] *Ethics and Infinity* (interviews with Philippe Nemo), 113.
[13] "God and Philosophy", 69.
[14] *Of God Who Comes to Mind*, xii.

noun based on the French third-person masculine pronoun), which is designed to prevent us from thinking of God as accessible via a direct, personal encounter. Another move, perhaps more successful, is to substitute *à-Dieu* for *Dieu*, with the striking double meaning of "towards (*à*) God", suggesting that we can never actually reach the divine, and "farewell" (*adieu*), suggesting both that we are going beyond standard categories and that we encounter God only as he is leaving.[15]

Levinas's philosophical discussions of God are not developed within the context of any particular claim to religious revelation and could presumably be appropriated by anyone committed to the idea that there is a transcendent deity that reveals itself to us. He allows that his philosophy may well be rooted in his Judaism, but nonetheless insists on a clear distinction between what he calls his "philosophical and confessional texts", on the grounds that they employ "separate languages" and distinct methods of justification.[16] At the same time, there is considerable overlap in terminology and ideas between Levinas's philosophical writings and his explicitly Jewish "confessional works", and each group of texts sheds considerable light on the other.[17]

Whereas Levinas's ethics of the other is readily extended to the transcendent religious realm, there remain serious questions about its applicability or even relevance to the humdrum world of everyday moral problems. Given that I recognize my absolute responsibility for the other, just what consequences does this have for my daily actions? Does it require a radical pacifism or a life of total self-sacrifice? Or is it somehow consistent with standard principles of individual morality and social justice? Levinas acknowledges the difficulty, noting that the suggestion that, as Richard Kearney puts it, "the ethical relation is entirely utopian and unrealistic" is "the great objection to my thought". Levinas's immediate response to Kearney was simply that the ethical relation's "being utopian does not prevent it from investing our everyday actions of generosity or

---

[15] See, for example, "The Bad Conscience and the Inexorable", in *Of God Who Comes to Mind*, 176–7. Levinas also speaks of the "trace" of God to express the elusive divine "presence through absence", a term with roots in Husserl and Freud that, as we have seen, is also central for Derrida.

[16] See "Dialogue with Emmanuel Levinas", in Richard Kearney (ed.), *Dialogues with Contemporary Continental Thinkers*, 53–5.

[17] See the helpful discussion of this topic in Colin Davis, *Levinas: an Introduction*, 100–19. A good selection of Levinas's "Jewish writings" is collected in *Difficile liberté*.

goodwill toward the other".[18] But this hardly suffices to show how this might happen and, especially, what specific moral guidelines might result.

To move his ethics of the other at least in the direction of practical morality, Levinas introduces his notion of *the third party (le tiers)*.[19] This seems to be based on a recognition that "everyday morality", even if ultimately grounded in an asymmetrical absolute responsibility for the other, requires at some level principles of symmetry and reciprocity that constitute a community of moral peers. The response to specific moral issues cannot be merely my total subordination to the other; there must be some way in which all moral agents, including myself, can be recognized as having moral standing. The third party is another person, in addition to myself and the other, whose reality Levinas finds somehow implicit in my encounter with the other. One suggestion he makes is that the third party enters the picture because the other is not other in virtue of some special personal traits or situation but only in virtue of being vulnerable to harm. Therefore, there may well be other others of whom I must also take account. He also suggests that I may become aware that the other to whom I am responsible is itself responsible to an other, who is thus also included in my responsibility. In either case, my ethical situation becomes complicated by the need to assume responsibility for two or more others, whose needs may conflict in ways that make it impossible for me to entirely satisfy them both. Such a situation requires precisely the sorts of arrangements (compromises and prioritizations) that characterize ordinary human societies. The principle of these arrangements is the equal distribution of limited resources to those in need of them, a principle that introduces the equality of persons essential to ordinary systems of morality. Once such a system of universal equality is established, consistency requires that even I, despite the asymmetry of my basic obligation to the other, be included in it.[20]

Appearing in 1961, just when the structuralist critique of all subject-centered thinking was beginning to command the field, *Totalité et infini*

[18] Richard Kearney (ed.), *Dialogues with Contemporary Continental Thinkers*, 68.
[19] "The third party" is briefly introduced in *TI*, 187–90/212–4, and somewhat more fully developed in *Otherwise than Being*, 157–62. For a thorough and lucid critical discussion of this frustratingly opaque material, see Peperzak, *To the Other*, 167–84.
[20] Levinas nonetheless seeks to maintain something of the asymmetry, often citing the perplexing but moving line from *The Brothers Karamazov*: "We are all responsible for everything and everyone in the face of everybody, and I more than the others."

was respected for its subtlety and originality, but was met with few serious discussions and even fewer supporters. The poststructuralist philosophers of difference were quite sympathetic to Levinas's critique of the same and his emphasis on radical alterity. But they remained very uneasy with the central place he gives to subjectivity and, especially, to a religiously oriented ethics.[21] It was only with the "return of the subject" and of ethics in the 1980s that Levinas's work became a center of intense philosophical interest in France.[22]

RICOEUR

Paul Ricoeur (b. 1913) failed the exam for the École Normale ("a failure", he said, "that marked me for a long time"[23]) and so received his philosophical education through the master's degree at the provincial university of Rennes. He spent just one year (1934–5) studying in Paris, in preparation for the *agrégation*, after which he taught in provincial lycées until the war. Shortly after the war, Ricoeur became professor of philosophy at Strasbourg, where he remained until called to the Sorbonne in 1957.

Ricoeur comes from a strongly religious family and has always been active in liberal Protestant groups. During his youthful year in Paris, he was introduced to Marcel's Friday circle. He was very impressed by Marcel, who remained an important influence on his work.[24] In the years before the war, Ricoeur was very active in Christian socialist and pacifist circles and particularly associated with Emmanuel Mounier and his journal *Esprit*. When the war began, he was called up as an officer in the French army and spent five years in German prisoner-of-war camps, where he was, however, able to carry out intense studies of Karl Jaspers (on whom he later

---

[21] So, for example, Descombes's 1979 survey of the contemporary scene has only two passing references to Levinas – both incidental to a discussion of Derrida (*Modern French Philosophy*, 139–40). Feminists such as Beauvoir and Luce Irigaray have criticized Levinas's portrayal of femininity (in his description of enjoyment and of the erotic) as based on a demeaning conception of women as mere negations of men (Beauvoir, *The Second Sex*, xxii n. 3; Irigaray, "Questions to Emmanuel Levinas: On the Dignity of Love", in R. Bernasconi and S. Critchley (eds.), *Re-Reading Levinas*; "The Fecundity of the Caress: A Reading of Levinas, Totality and Infinity, 'Phenomenology of Eros'", in *An Ethics of Sexual Difference*.

[22] An early sign of this interest was the collection edited by François Laruelle, *Textes pour Emmanuel Levinas*, which contains essays by, among others, Derrida, Blanchot, Lyotard, and Ricoeur.

[23] Paul Ricoeur, "Intellectual Autobiography", in Lewis Hahn (ed.), *The Philosophy of Paul Ricoeur*, 6.

[24] See Ricoeur's early book, *Gabriel Marcel et Karl Jaspers: philosophie du mystère et philosophie du paradoxe*.

co-authored a book with a fellow prisoner, Mikel Dufrenne), begin his translation of Husserl's *Ideas*,[25] and start work on what eventually became the first volume of his *Philosophie de la volonté*. After the war, as Ricoeur developed his own philosophical position, his affinities with existential phenomenology were clear. As he put it, his project was to apply Husserl's method of eidetic analysis to Marcel's problematic of the embodied self.[26] This project was obviously very close to that of Merleau-Ponty, and Ricoeur, very excited by the appearance of *Phénoménologie de la perception*, sought him out. They had some contacts, but no real connection was formed.[27] Although Merleau-Ponty's pre-war background was rather similar to Ricoeur's, it would seem that a Christian and a politically moderate socialist was simply not the sort of thinker that Sartre's co-editor at *Les temps modernes* could take seriously.[28] Sartre himself is said to have spoken of Ricoeur as "a kind of parson [*curé*] who was interested in [*s'occupait de*] phenomenology".[29]

Ricoeur has always been a devout Protestant, and much of his philosophical work – for example, the seminal concern with evil and with the interpretation of texts – has religious motivations. Moreover, he has ventured into distinctly theological areas such as Biblical exegesis, and both his philosophical and theological works have been very influential in departments of theology and of religious studies.[30] However, like Levinas, he has insisted on a strict separation between philosophy and faith. Specifically, he insists that whatever religious origin his interests or ideas may have, he always supports his conclusions with arguments that do not presuppose premises accepted on religious authority.[31] Nonetheless, even strictly as a philosopher, he has, like Levinas, taken religious themes and commitments seriously in a way unheard of among other major French philoso-

---

[25] This translation was published in 1950. Along with Ricoeur's accompanying introduction and commentary, it has long had a major influence on Husserl scholarship.
[26] "Intellectual Autobiography", 12.
[27] Acccording to Roger Mehl, a long-time friend of Ricoeur, "Merleau-Ponty always avoided contact. He didn't even answer his letters" (François Dosse, *Paul Ricoeur: les sens d'une vie*, 134 [author's interview with Mehl]).
[28] Ricoeur was, however, quite capable of taking difficult political stands. For example, in 1961 he was seriously harassed by the French police for his outspoken support of Algerian independence.
[29] Dosse, *Paul Ricoeur: les sens d'une vie*, 134 (author's interview with Marc Richir).
[30] Ricoeur's primary appointment at the University of Chicago was in the Divinity School, where he succeeded to the chair held by Paul Tillich.
[31] See, for example, his comments in an interview in Charles Reagan, *Paul Ricoeur: His Life and Work*, 125–6.

phers after Marcel and before the later Derrida. There is no doubt that this religious orientation is a significant part of the explanation for the long period of neglect of his work in France.

In later years, despite Ricoeur's distinguished publications and immense popularity as a lecturer at the Sorbonne, he remained outside the group of lionized Parisian intellectual "stars". Eventually, his situation in France became untenable. His 1965 book on Freud was viciously attacked by Lacanians outraged at what they wrongly regarded as his unacknowledged borrowings from their master. Then, as Dean of the Faculty of Letters at Nanterre in 1969, he suffered humiliating confrontations with student militants and an embarrassing police invasion of his campus. After the debacle at Nanterre, Ricoeur took a three-year leave from the University of Paris, during which he effectively moved his center of activities away from France, first to Belgium (at the University of Louvain) and later to the United States (at the University of Chicago). For the fifteen years from 1970 to 1985 he became increasingly distant from French intellectual life, so much so that most of his articles were published in other countries. It was only in the mid-1980s, with the publication of the three volumes of *Temps et récit*, that Ricoeur became once again a major figure in France.

Ricoeur's initial project was to apply phenomenological method to the description of the affective dimension of human existence, particularly phenomena connected with volition. In *Le volontaire et l'involontaire*, he presented a Husserlian "eidetic analysis" which he hoped would do for the sphere of practice what Merleau-Ponty had done for perception. At the same time, by showing how involuntary factors, from the body and its environment to emotion and character, are essential correlates of voluntary action, he offered an implicit critique of Sartre's radical existentialist ontology of freedom.

From the beginning, however, Ricoeur had emphasized that a phenomenology of the essential structures of volition could not explicate the contingent but – especially for a Christian – crucial phenomenon of the evil will. Since there is nothing in the nature of the will that compels it to evil, this aspect of human existence would require another mode of philosophical reflection. Such reflection was a concern of the next stage of Ricoeur's *Philosophie de la volonté*. Under the general title *Finitude et culpabilité* he published in 1960 two volumes, *L'homme fallible* and *La symbolique du mal*. The first volume remained within the domain of necessary truths, although it is as

Kantian as it is Husserlian, seeking the conditions of the possibility of evil within the essential structures of the will. Ricoeur finds these conditions in what he calls, evoking Pascal, an "ontology of disproportion". The disproportion, which he uncovers at the three levels of knowledge, practice, and feeling, is always between a tendency to the finite and a tendency to the infinite. In knowledge, for example, the limitations of perception to a specific profile of its object is in tension with the understanding's drive to think in terms of general categories. Similarly, on the practical level of morality, there is tension between limits that define my character and my desire for unlimited happiness; and, on the level of feeling, between my contentment with a familiar situation and my openness to the total range of affective experiences. Human frailty consists in our precarious balance at the mid-points between the extremes defining these tensions, and evil corresponds to the possibility of our suppressing one extreme in favor of the other.

In *La symbolique du mal*, Ricoeur finally turns to the contingent fact of willed evil. We have already seen that the contingency of an evil will places it outside the domain of phenomenological description. Positively, Ricoeur maintains that an account of evil has to be given in hermeneutic terms, specifically through the interpretation of the great religious and cultural symbols and myths of evil. The hermeneutic turn is required by our tendency to hide our evil, to deny it or to distort its nature. This makes direct self-reflection (phenomenological or otherwise) an inappropriate vehicle for exploring it. But artistic and religious traditions contain our implicit understanding of our evil. Ricoeur's turn to hermeneutics in *La symbolique du mal* does not, however, derive simply from the peculiar features of his topic. It also reflects his conclusion that, quite generally, there is an opaqueness in consciousness that limits all phenomenological projects of self-knowledge and requires the "detour" of hermeneutic interpretation of cultural symbols and myths.[32] Ricoeur did not deny the validity of phenomenology in its limited domain, nor did he reject – as many French philosophers would soon do – the central role of subjectivity in human existence. But from *La symbolique du mal* on he has insisted on the need for the philosophical study of human reality to combine phenomenological description with hermeneutic interpretation.

[32] See Ricoeur's essays on Husserl collected in *À l'école de la phénoménologie*.

Ricoeur's hermeneutic turn provided him with an excellent vantage point for evaluating and appropriating the structuralist critique of the subject that swept the French philosophical world in the 1960s. A major focus of his confrontation with structuralism was his book *De l'interprétation: essai sur Freud* (1965). He was initially led to Freud by an interest in the phenomenon of guilt, and had been reading him systematically since 1960. At the same time, Freud was becoming of great interest to structuralist critics of phenomenology, who thought his account of the unconscious undermined the primacy of the conscious subject. Ricoeur agreed that a strictly phenomenological view – limited to the analysis of meanings – could not do justice to the Freudian unconscious, which required description via a mixture of the language of meaning and the language of force. The unconscious is precisely the intersection of language and desire, involving both intentional categories such as wish, distortion, and fulfillment, and physical categories such as drive, displacement, and repression. Psychoanalysis provides a method of interpreting unconscious meanings in their relation to physical expressions of desire. It is, therefore, a hermeneutic discipline dedicated to unearthing meanings that are inaccessible to phenomenological reflection because of their entanglement with desires. But it does not support the structuralist claim to eliminate the center of subjective meanings that is consciousness.

Ricoeur's presentation of psychoanalysis as hermeneutic required, however, an expansion of his conception of hermeneutics. Previously (in *La symbolique du mal*) he had recognized only interpretation that revealed a meaning worthy of incorporation into our self-understanding (for example, of ourselves as guilty before God). His study of Freud revealed that, besides this sort of progressive (or ampliative) interpretation, there was another sort, uncovered by psychoanalysis, that discovers archaic or infantile meanings that we need to overcome rather than incorporate (for example, incestuous or murderous desires). Ricoeur was thus led to distinguish between a teleological hermeneutics that enriches human experience and an archaeological hermeneutics, the "hermeneutics of suspicion", that purifies it.[33] He now held that a full understanding of human

---

[33] In his "Intellectual Autobiography", Ricoeur cites Gadamer as having recently "renovated" teleological hermeneutics and associates this enterprise with phenomenology (as "enriched by Merleau-Ponty") and "the tradition of reflexive philosophy illustrated by Jean Nabert". All these are opposed to the "masters of suspicion", who include not only Freud

existence required a dialectical "conflict of interpretations" that recognized both the separate validity and the mutual opposition of the archaeological and the teleological moments.

Ricoeur's direct reactions to structuralism combined an appreciation of its value as a specialized method for addressing certain issues, with criticism of the extrapolation of its viewpoint into a universal theory of human reality, an extrapolation that he characterized as a "Kantianism without a transcendental subject".[34] He argued, for example, that Lévi-Strauss's structuralist analyses of myths required supplementation by a hermeneutic study of the historical traditions that transmitted the myths from one generation to another. He also opposed the structuralist claim, derived from Saussure, that linguistic meaning was entirely a matter of differential relations among signs. According to Ricoeur, this ignored the central linguistic role of the sentence as the vehicle of linguistic expression. Once we recognize this role (as does, for example, Benveniste's system of linguistics), we must understand language (discourse, in Benveniste's terminology) as requiring not only structural rules but also someone who uses these rules to say something to someone. So understood, language requires essential reference both to a world of objects and to speaking and listening subjects.

Following his work on Freud and structuralism, Ricoeur was in a position to formulate his own hermeneutical theory in a systematic way.[35] Typical of Ricoeur, this theory continues the classical tradition of hermeneutics while also incorporating the more recent standpoints of structuralism and poststructuralism. The classical subject-centered standpoint is recognized through Ricoeur's insistence that meaning is rooted in the communicative function of language: a sentence is addressed by someone to someone. But he also emphasizes that language is often sufficiently distant from its

---

but also Feuerbach, Marx, and Nietzsche ("Intellectual Autobiography", 22). "Reflexive philosophy" is Ricoeur's term for the French spiritualist tradition. Jean Nabert's 1924 thesis, *L'expérience intérieure de la liberté* (reissued with additional essays and a preface by Paul Ricoeur, 1994) established him as one of the last leading figures in this tradition, which was soon swamped by existentialism. He also published an important study of ethics, *Eléments pour une éthique*. A later work on evil and religion, *Essai sur le mal*, particularly impressed Ricoeur and was an important influence on his *Finitude et culpabilité*. More generally, Ricoeur has always shown a strong appreciation for the spiritualist tradition, beginning with his master's thesis (1934) on Lachelier and Lagneau on the problem of God.

[34] "Structure and Hermeneutics", in *The Conflict of Interpretations*.
[35] See his brief exposition, *Interpretation Theory*, and his essays collected in *Le conflit des interprétations*.

subjective origin that it can be fruitfully analyzed as an abstract system, so that structuralist explanation can be integrated into classical hermeneutic understanding. Ricoeur goes even further to argue that understanding itself requires a distancing of language from its production in speech, so that the object of hermeneutics must be the *text* in the sense of written discourse. In this way he enriches his hermeneutics with Derrida's poststructuralist critique of logocentrism.[36]

Ricoeur complemented his hermeneutics with a series of studies on the creative resources of language, paying special attention to metaphor and narrative.[37] The standard Aristotelian theory of metaphor deflates it into a simple attribution of a property generally associated with one thing to another, similar thing. So I say, "Man is a wolf", meaning that although we do not typically think of it, human beings have some of the more unpleasant properties ordinarily assigned to wolves. But, Ricoeur points out, metaphor can be creative far beyond such minimalist extensions of our vocabulary. It may set up so strong a tension between two terms – by connecting them in a way so outside our standard usage – that we can make sense of the metaphor only by construing the entire semantic field defining the terms' meanings. This is what happens, for example, when we try to understand Shakespeare's comparison of time to a beggar with a wallet on his back (*Troilus and Cressida*, III, iii, 145–50). Ricoeur defines metaphor in terms of its power to thus transform our system of meaning (and the more mundane sorts of metaphor readily fit in as "infinitesimal" transformations). He further maintains that a deeply effective metaphor may transform not just meanings but also our grasp of reality. We may be able to make sense of a sufficiently radical change in our system of meanings only by revising our understanding of the world this system describes. Accordingly, poetry, so often regarded as a mere gloss on literal truths or, with more sophistication, as an isolated game played entirely for its own sake, actually has the creative power of redescribing our world.

Ricoeur later expanded this creative view of literary language from metaphor to narrative. Like a metaphor, a (fictional) narrative may vary only minimally from the true stories by which we recount

---

[36] Derrida was the teaching assistant in Ricoeur's seminar on phenomenology at the Sorbonne in the early 1960s and, despite deep philosophical differences, the two maintained a cordial if often distant relationship.

[37] See *La métaphore vive* and the three volumes of *Temps et récit*.

the events of our lives. But understanding a more deeply creative narrative may require a radical reconceptualization of the possibilities of a life-story, and such a reconceptualization may lead to a new understanding of our historical lives. Such transformations have deep connections with how we think of time: new conceptions of time will generate new modes of narrative, and vice versa. Ricoeur's *Temps et récit* explores thoroughly and subtly the complexities of these connections.

Ricoeur's initial philosophical project was the understanding of the practical and affective world of human volition. The necessary hermeneutic detour from his original direct phenomenological approach to this topic led him through many years of second-order discussions of the language by which we must understand ourselves. But since, as Aristotle long ago emphasized, narrative is an imitation (*mimesis*) of action, Ricoeur's development of a sophisticated account of narrative provided a natural vehicle for returning to his original project.[38] He further develops Aristotle's insight by showing how actions can, for analytic purposes, be treated as texts, since agents are distanced from what they do in the same way that authors are distanced from what they write. This tie between action and language also provided Ricoeur with a natural opportunity to integrate his hermeneutic approach with approaches of analytic philosophy such as Searle's speech-act theory and Davidson's action theory.[39] Parallel to his earlier integration of structuralist explanations and hermeneutic understanding of texts, Ricoeur attempts to dissolve the alleged dichotomy, often emphasized in analytic discussions, between the causal explanation of actions and the hermeneutic understanding of their meaning. His work on action also naturally led Ricoeur into the areas of ethics and political theory.[40]

Ricoeur's later work also brings him back to his roots in phenomenology.[41] He does not reject his earlier criticisms of phenomenology but notes that they apply only to the foundationalist version of the

---

[38] Ricoeur notes ("Intellectual Autobiography", 32) that this reentry via action, in comparison with his original approach through will, leads him to emphasize results rather than intentions and the social rather than the solitary.

[39] See, for example, the essays in Paul Ricoeur, *Soi-même comme une autre*.

[40] Ricoeur's ethical writings have shown a particular interest in the work of Levinas. See, for example, "Emmanuel Levinas, penseur du témoignage", in J.-C. Aeschliman (ed.), *Répondre d'autrui: Emmanuel Levinas*, 17–40.

[41] See "Phenomenology and Hermeneutics", in Paul Ricoeur, *Hermeneutics and the Human Sciences*.

method that Husserl puts forward, for example in his *Cartesian Meditations*. It is the demand that phenomenology provide rigorous foundations for all knowledge, which in turn leads to demands for total self-reflective transparency and apodictic certainty, that is undermined by structuralism and hermeneutics. However, hermeneutics, like phenomenology, seeks the meanings implicit in human existence and must, as we have seen, accept the phenomenological claim that these meanings are ultimately rooted in subjective consciousness. We need, therefore, only separate the phenomenological search for subject-centered meaning from the Cartesian demand for foundational certainty. Ricoeur notes that this separation is already present in Husserl's early formulation of phenomenology in the *Logical Investigations*, which Ricoeur sees as a model for the hermeneutic deployment of phenomenology. In this sense, he is ready to assert that "phenomenology remains the unsurpassable presupposition of hermeneutics".[42]

RECENT DIRECTIONS

The interest in Levinas and Ricoeur, beginning around 1980, corresponded to a new generation of French philosophers who were ready to cast a cold eye on poststructuralism. Critiques typically centered on the perceived connection between fashionable philosophers such as Althusser, Foucault, Deleuze, and Derrida, and the student revolts of 1968. Not that the revolts were inspired by the philosophers, who on the contrary seem, in strictly political terms, to have been themselves radicalized by the *événements de mai*. But many of the founding texts of poststructuralism were nearly simultaneous with the revolts – for example, Foucault's *Les mots et les choses* (1966), Derrida's *De la grammatologie* (1967), Deleuze's *Différence et répétition* (1968) – and it was tempting to see their philosophical radicalism as somehow of a piece with the students' political radicalism.

As early as the mid-1970s, there had been the noisy but philosophically inconsequential assault of the "new philosophers". These were former student radicals – especially Bernard-Henri Lévy and André Glucksmann – who briefly dominated the media with impassioned proclamations of their disillusion with Marxism, which they belatedly recognized as responsible for such horrors as the Soviet

---

[42] "Intellectual Autobiography", 34.

Gulags. The tone is apparent in the opening sentence of Lévy's *La barbarie à visage humain*: "I am the bastard child of an unholy union between fascism and Stalinism."[43] Of course, except for Althusser, none of the poststructuralists were Marxists, but Lévy and Glucksmann raised the not obviously illegitimate issue of possible connections between philosophical anti-humanism and ethical outrages against humanity. Their discussions, however, offered more political polemic than philosophical insight.

In similarly polemical vein, but with much more nuance and substance, was Luc Ferry and Alain Renaut's *La pensée 68* (1985). Ferry and Renaut characterize the poststructuralist "thought of '68" as a critique of modernist humanism, derived from Marx and Heidegger (via Nietzsche). The primary object of this critique was the modern notion of the subject as the epistemological, metaphysical, and ethical center of existence. Poststructuralists rejected the metaphysical (and epistemological) primacy of the subject on the basis of Heidegger's deconstruction of Western philosophy. Although they did not accept Marxism, which for them was in its harder materialist form too positivist and in its softer existential form too humanist, they were, as leftist intellectuals, sympathetic to its critique of bourgeois morality and politics. But they did read Heidegger's critique of metaphysics as undermining the ethical primacy of the subject, a result that destroyed the intellectual basis of bourgeois morality and politics. In this way, poststructuralism achieved Marxist ends by Heideggerian means.

Ferry and Renaut are largely sympathetic to the Heideggerian critique of metaphysics but deny that it undermines the ethical primacy of the subject. The critique effectively attacks the idea of a "self-transparent subject that lays claim to the mastery of everything that exists", a subject with its own absolute existence that constitutes the world.[44] But this does not eliminate a unified consciousness, finite, temporal, and essentially dependent on the world and society, as the core of each person's identity and moral status. In fact, Ferry and Renaut maintain, the *Dasein* of *Being and Time* is just such a subject. Indeed, they argue that Heidegger's *Dasein* is equivalent to Kant's transcendental subject, once that subject's concepts have been made applicable to the temporal world through what Kant

---

[43] Bernard-Henri Lévy, *Barbarism with a Human Face*, ix.
[44] Luc Ferry and Alain Renaut, *French Philosophy of the Sixties*, 213–14.

calls "schematization". They further argue that such a subject can be established as the bearer of moral rights and responsibilities, thus providing a non-metaphysical basis for ethics.

Ferry and Renaut also maintain that the moral primacy of the subject is required to make sense of the poststructuralists' own political commitments to individual freedom and to resisting totalitarian oppression. If the Heideggerian critique of the subject is allowed to extend to the ethical and political spheres, then there is no way to oppose Heidegger's own disdain for democracy. The poststructuralists in effect tried to escape this conclusion by substituting the *individual* for the *subject*. Both the subject and the individual are free. But the (poststructuralist) individual is nothing other than this freedom, and the individual's good consists simply in the unrestricted exercise of its free creativity, in the manner of Deleuze and Guattari's desiring-machines. A subject, by contrast, exercises freedom not for its own sake but for the sake of an objective good recognized as the appropriate end of a rational will. The freedom of a subject is *autonomy* in Kant's sense, which is "perfectly compatible with the idea of persons submitting to laws or norms as long as these are freely accepted" . The freedom of an individual is *independence*, understood as an ideal that "can no longer tolerate such a limitation of the self; on the contrary, it aims at the pure and simple affirmation of the self as a value".[45] For Ferry and Renaut, the self has an inviolable ethical value, but this does not derive from pure self-assertion but from a consensus among rational minds as to the objective truth of this inviolability. This objective truth, however, is grounded not in dogmatic knowledge of the subject's transcendent metaphysical nature; rather, it expresses a critical grasp, in the Kantian sense, of the conditions required for coherent moral action.[46]

The work of Ferry and Renaut is a central example of the striking emergence of liberal political theory in France, a development that represents a move to the center in both content and method.[47] The dominant thinkers of postwar France saw no middle ground between

---

[45] Alain Renaut, *The Era of the Individual*, 19.
[46] Renaut and Ferry have also drawn their non-metaphysical approach to subjectivity from reflections on Kant's *Critique of Judgment* and on Fichte's early writings. See (on Kant) Luc Ferry, *Homo aestheticus* and (on Fichte) Alain Renaut, *Le système du droit*.
[47] For an excellent survey and analysis of recent French political theory, see the editor's introduction to Mark Lilla (ed.), *New French Political Philosophy*.

revolutionary radicalism and reactionary conservatism. Sartre, for example, saw the respect of Raymond Aron (an old friend from the École Normale) for American democracy and the moral hesitations of Albert Camus regarding revolutionary violence as nothing less than abandonments of the struggle against oppression. With the 1980s, however, Aron and Camus gained the respect of a new generation that had drawn its own conclusions from the postwar history of the Soviet bloc and saw traditional liberalism as an attractive basis for thinking about politics. This generation also found a methodological middle ground between the highest level of philosophical theorizing and engagement in concrete political causes. Whereas both Sartre and, especially, the poststructuralists alternated between abstract ontological constructions or deconstructions and dramatic political gestures, the new generation's taste was for middle-level theories that lack the ambitions of those promulgated by the "master thinkers" but connect far more directly and, they hope, fruitfully with the practical problems of democratic politics.

While philosophers such as Renaut and Ferry see ways around the poststructuralist proclamations of the "end of philosophy", others have continued the Derridean project of philosophy as deconstruction of its past. To cite the most prominent example, Jean-Luc Nancy (b. 1940) accepts Derrida's view that the logocentrism defining the philosophical tradition is both impossible and unavoidable, and sets out to understand the human condition through its confrontation with this paradoxical situation. For all its modern humanist connotations, the existentialist expression "human condition" is appropriate here because Nancy explicitly undertakes a poststructuralist meditation on the classic Sartrean themes of existence, freedom, and the other.[48] According to Nancy, however, Sartre's insistence on the priority of existence over essence is insufficiently radical.

Nancy argues that we must, rather, think simply in terms of existence, with no reference at all to essence, even in a subordinate

---

[48] Nancy and Renaut seem to agree that Sartre's was the last major effort to philosophize in the traditional grand manner, though they differ on the lessons that follow from the failure of that effort. See Alain Renaut, *Sartre, le dernier philosophe*. Seeing Sartre as even a significant part of the philosophical past is a distinct advance on the almost total eclipse his reputation suffered in France during the 1970s and 80s. For another example of renewed interest in Sartre, see the recent biography by Bernard-Henri Lévy, *Le siècle de Sartre*.

ontological role. Our reality is not a matter of our existence constructing an essence through its free choices; it is entirely encompassed by existence itself. Sartre's picture is of human beings (consciousnesses) defining themselves (giving themselves essences) by choices made within a world with its "coefficient of adversity", corresponding to the causal nexus against which freedom acts. But for Nancy "freedom . . . does not designate a force opposed to or combined with other forces of nature". On the contrary, freedom "designates that from which there can rise relations of force as such, between human beings and nature and between human beings themselves. It is the force of force in general, or the very resistance of the thing's existence."[49] Whereas Sartre's ontology distinguishes the passive materiality of the world (being-in-itself) from the active actuality of consciousness (being-for-itself), Nancy sees existence as combining within its own non-self-identical reality the passivity of matter and the agency of consciousness. "Accordingly, [freedom] is a transcendental force, but one that is a material actuality . . . Prior to every determination of matter, this materiality of existence, which sets down the fact of freedom, is no less endowed with the material properties of exteriority and resistance."[50]

Nancy's ontological eradication of essence corresponds to his project of confronting us with the consequences of the end of philosophy. But this confrontation, he maintains, also opens the way to a fruitful treatment of community and the political that escaped existentialism. The opening derives from the fact that we are all defined not by each constituting a distinct essence but by our shared lack of any essence at all. We are all together, not because of any common essence but precisely because of our shared lack of any such essence. This is Nancy's starting point for a deconstructionist account of community. This account argues for a sense of "the political" that is not reducible to "politics". Politics, in this sense, is the effort to define and achieve the shared essence that we lack. But this project – no doubt at the heart of Renaut and Ferry's political theorizing – is precisely a denial of what Nancy calls "the political": the living of our shared lack of essence.[51] Indeed, Nancy identifies "wickedness" (in Kant's sense of "radical evil") as the destruction of the political by politics.[52]

[49] *The Experience of Freedom*, 102.   [50] *The Experience of Freedom*, 102, 103.
[51] Nancy's major treatment of the political is in *Communauté désoeuvrée*.
[52] *The Experience of Freedom*, chapter 12.

Although Derrideans such as Nancy do not share Ferry and Renaut's negative assessment of Heidegger's influence on French philosophy, their turn to the political required a serious rethinking of Heidegger's own loyalty to the Nazi cause, particularly given the intense controversy over Heidegger's political activities that followed the publication in France of the sharply critical biographies by Victor Farias (1987) and Hugo Ott (1990). Here the work of Nancy's colleague and collaborator, Philippe Lacoue-Labarthe (b. 1940), is crucial. Lacoue-Labarthe is concerned above all with the distinction, at the very origins of Western philosophy, between philosophy as a search for the truth of reality and art (especially literature) as a mere "imitation" (mimesis) of reality. On his reading, philosophy uniformly insisted on this distinction until the late eighteenth century, when early German romantics began questioning the sharp separation of truth from mimesis.[53] Lacoue-Labarthe reads Heidegger's deconstruction of metaphysics as the most important continuation of this questioning, but one that implicitly retains the old distinction through a picture of Being as the "type" of which beings are the inadequate "traces". This residue of the mimetic makes Heidegger's thought susceptible to a political aestheticism that regards the community as a "work of art" imitating the model laid down by its leader, an aestheticism that is at the heart of Nazi ideology.[54] Lacoue-Labarthe tries to construct a new conception of mimesis that gives it parity with truth, thereby avoiding the classic dichotomy that made Heidegger susceptible to Nazism.

The Derridean focus on historical studies, particularly of Husserl and Heidegger, has flourished among recent French thinkers, even those not entirely comfortable with Derrida's placement of phenomenology at the "end of philosophy". Jean-Luc Marion, Michel Henry,[55] and Jean-François Courtine,[56] in particular, while attentive and often sympathetic to the Derridean standpoint, have developed strategies for continuing the phenomenological projects of Husserl and Heidegger. Marion (b. 1946), for example, thinks that phenomenology requires a third "reduction", understood as an access to what is experientially given. Via Husserl's transcendental reduction we are given objects, the meanings of which are constituted by their

[53] Lacoue-Labarthe and Nancy document this development in *Absolu littéraire*.
[54] See Lacoue-Labarthe and Nancy, "The Nazi Myth".
[55] See his *L'essence de la manifestation*.
[56] See his *Heidegger et la phénoménologie*.

Fin-de-siècle again: "le temps retrouvé"?

relation to transcendental consciousness. Via Heidegger's "existential reduction" beings are given to *Dasein*, the being through which Being itself is revealed. According to Marion, each of these reductions corresponds to merely one limited aspect of what is given (the given as meaningful, the given as existing). Marion's third reduction purports to give nothing other than givenness (or the gift) itself. The "object" of the reduction is beyond meaning, even beyond being, a sheer givenness that is nothing but a call for us to respond to its givenness: "the pure form of the call". Correspondingly, the "subject" of this third reduction is neither an ego nor a being-in-the-world (*Dasein*) but "the pure and simple figure [of] an auditor preceded and instituted by the call".[57] Marion, who is also an important figure in Catholic theology, is prepared to take his construal of phenomenology in a religious direction, ultimately identifying the call of givenness with the offered gift of a God who, although he exists, is "without being".[58] Marion has also developed his thought through close and imaginative studies of Descartes.[59]

An increasingly important current in French thought is one that allies itself with the international movement of analytic philosophy. Here the main representative is Jacques Bouveresse, who is often seen as the quintessential outsider of French philosophy – a position neatly accepted in the title of his article "Why I Am So Very UnFrench", denouncing poststructuralist obscurantism and lauding the virtues of clarity and argumentative rigor.[60] But he has also become an important French intellectual figure, as is apparent in his recent (1995) election to the Collège de France. Nor is Bouveresse entirely without predecessors. His own intellectual lineage is traceable through G.-G. Granger (b. 1920) and Jules Vuillemin (b. 1920), whose philosophical interests and style are much closer to analytic than to existentialist or poststructuralist philosophy, and whose work can, moreover, be seen as continuations of a French tradition of logic and philosophy of mathematics that extends from Louis Couturat

---

[57] *Reduction and Givenness*, 204.
[58] Jean-Luc Marion, *Dieu sans l'être*. The religious ramifications of phenomenology are also pursued by Michel Henry and Jean-François Courtine. See Dominique Janicaud, *Le tournant théologique de la phénoménologie française*.
[59] See his *Sur l'ontologie grise de Descartes* and *Sur la théologie blanche de Descartes*.
[60] See in particular his *La philosophie chez les autophages* and *Rationalité et cynisme*. While Bouveresse's objections to the often pretentious and unfathomable style of poststructuralist philosophers is surely on target, his arguments that their key claims can be readily dismissed as self-refuting forms of relativism or skepticism do not seem to me to be based on sufficiently careful readings of their texts.

(1868–1914) to Jean Nicod (1893–1924), Jacques Herbrand (1908–31), and Jean Cavaillès (1903–44).[61] However, this "indigenous" line of French analytic philosophy never became seriously tied to the wider international movement and remained a distinctly minor force within France, partly because of the early deaths of its main representatives during the first half of the century.[62]

Much of Bouveresse's earlier work was on Wittgenstein and combined perceptive exposition and commentary with creative rethinking of fundamental problems of epistemology and philosophy of mind from a broadly Wittgensteinian perspective. More recently, he has placed himself in the line of what he calls "Austrian philosophy", a sequence beginning with Bolzano's critique of Kant and proceeding – on a path that avoided the post-Kantian idealism and existential phenomenology from which postwar French philosophy arose – through Brentano and Meinong to Schlick, the Vienna circle, and Wittgenstein. Bouveresse sees this Continental line of analytic philosophy (supplemented, for ethical and political perspectives, by Robert Musil, for whose thought Bouveresse has an extraordinary affinity and reverence) as the most fruitful basis for contemporary philosophizing. His main current concerns are to develop a coherent realist account of perception and truth and to extend his thought to ethical and political issues.

Bouveresse has not yet succeeded in establishing a strong school of French analytic philosophers, although there are a greater number of young philosophers setting out on the analytic path. In recent years the Centre de Recherche en Epistémologie Appliquée (CREA) at the École Polytechnique has gathered together a number of analytic philosophers with special interests in philosophy of mind based on cognitive science. Perhaps the best known is Pascal Engel (now a professor at the Sorbonne), whose book in dialogue form, *La dispute*, is a lively introduction to analytic philosophy. It remains to be seen whether there will emerge a relatively unified, distinctively French analytic school or whether French analytic philosophers will

---

[61] Vuillemin is a historian of philosophy who has written important books on Descartes and Kant and has also written on Russell, Goodman, and Carnap. His major study of philosophical systems, *Nécessité ou contingence*, makes extensive use of contemporary modal logic. Granger works on the philosophy of science and of language, and he published the first French book on Wittgenstein (*Wittgenstein*).

[62] For some helpful background on analytic philosophy in France, see Pascal Engel, "Contemporary French Analytic Philosophy", in A. Phillips Griffiths (ed.), *Contemporary French Philosophy*.

remain individual contributors to debates that are defined by Anglo-American interests.

In any case, even philosophers not committed to an analytic program have exhibited a concern for clarity and for communication across the Channel and the Atlantic which was for many years in short supply among French thinkers. So, for example, reading the professionally cool and lucid prose of Renaut and Ferry produces a distinct feeling that the stylistic fever, which has so long ravaged the Left Bank, has finally begun to break. Moreover, they and other liberal political philosophers are directly engaged in dialogue with Anglophone liberal political thinkers such as John Rawls. In another vein, Michèle Le Doeuff (b. 1946), a philosopher of science with strong feminist commitments, is equally at home discussing British empiricist thought (e.g., that of Francis Bacon) and developing an acute metaphilosophical critique of Sartre through reflections on his relationship with Beauvoir – and always in accessible and directly effective prose. Her work continues the tradition of Bachelard, which is the ultimate origin of her central undertaking to articulate the images that dominate systems of scientific and philosophical thought, but develops it in a manner that can readily engage Anglo-American philosophers.[63]

For the last twenty-five years or so, observers of the French scene have been awaiting the arrival of the next Sartre, Foucault, or Derrida – a new master-thinker who would erect the barricades of the next French philosophical revolution. Recently, these long-frustrated hopes have given way to the conclusion that French philosophy is simply in a fallow period. Writing the history of the very recent past runs a high risk of disdain from future generations, who may well smile at our failure to see the obvious greatness of some name we have passed over lightly or not even mentioned. But we should also remember that good philosophy does not require great philosophers and that our romantic model of heroic master-thinkers may itself not have an eternal future. In any case, there are good reasons to think that, at the end of the twentieth century, French philosophy returned to the kind of competent stability that characterized the previous fin-de-siècle, and in that thought there is, if nothing else, a pleasant symmetry.

---

[63] See, in particular, *Recherches sur l'imaginaire philosophique*, *Étude et le rouet*, and *Le sexe du savoir*.

Conclusion: the philosophy of freedom

> ... that sense of relief which one has in reading Kant when, after the most rigorous demonstration of determinism, one finds that above the world of necessity there is the world of freedom.
>
> (Marcel Proust, *In Search of Lost Time*, III, 654)

In looking back over my account of French philosophy during the twentieth century, I have been struck by the centrality of discussions of individual freedom. Of course, this focus may have been the unconscious result of my own predilections, and there surely are other themes (perhaps consciousness or science) that would nicely unify the story. But it is hard to deny that French philosophers of the last hundred years have produced a remarkably broad and deep body of work on freedom, and, by way of conclusion, I offer some brief reflections on the general significance of this theme and on the way it has developed over the century.

The concern with individual freedom as a concrete, lived reality has, more than anything else, maintained the distinctiveness of French philosophy throughout the century. It lay behind the French resistance to German idealism, which was always read as tending to swamp individual freedom in the flood of the absolute. The focus on freedom also explains the insulation of French philosophers from epistemological foundationalism, whether that of Husserl's phenomenological "philosophy as a rigorous science" or that of logical empiricism. From Bergson through the existentialists to the poststructuralists, individual human freedom was itself a radical starting-point that required no philosophical foundation. The focus on freedom did converge with certain themes of Hegel, Husserl and, especially, Heidegger. But, as we have seen, it also restricted French interest to quite specific aspects of German thought. Hegel was exciting when he concretized his dialectic through historical perspectives on the vicissitudes of human freedom, but not when he subsumed individuals into the absolute's synthesis. The realist thrust of Husserl's doctrine of intentionality and the concrete richness of his phenomenological descriptions were fascinating, but the French had no interest in the aspects of his thought that tended to foundationalism and idealism. Heidegger loomed large for the dramatic anti-idealist vision in *Being and Time* of *Dasein* thrown into the world, but there was little charm in his larger ontological project. The French importation of German philosophy was a matter not of translation but of selective appropriation.

Individual freedom, particularly since it was increasingly approached through concrete experience, led to strong connections between philosophy and literature. It is no accident that two of France's leading philosophers, Bergson and Sartre, have been awarded the Nobel Prize for literature (although Sartre refused it). Since Bergson, almost every major French philosopher has had a distinctive philosophical identity as a reader if not also a writer of literature. Conversely, there is reason to think that concerns about freedom helped motivate the branching off of French philosophy of science as an autonomous subdiscipline (and the similar separating of the positivist social sciences). These splits expressed in methodological terms a commitment to the irreducibility of freedom in the face of scientific determinism. Accordingly, the philosophical mainstream, after Bergson and Brunschvicg, turned away from questions that science might pose or answer. This led to the development of the history and philosophy of natural science, particularly by Bachelard and Canguilhem, as an essentially autonomous subdiscipline. Mainline philosophers acknowledged its authority in its own domain, and some (notably Althusser and Foucault) drew on some of its results for their own purposes. But no major figure was a philosopher of natural science. The social sciences, insofar as they aspired to be rigorous empirical disciplines, became further and further separated from the philosophy in which they had their roots. Philosophers themselves maintained an interest primarily in the less empirical, "humanistic" domains of social science, such as psychoanalysis and ethnology. The brief upsurge of fascination with the structuralist social sciences doubtless involved attraction to an aura of rigor surrounding their penchant for technical terminology and formalization. But, as we have seen, both the rigor and philosophers' attraction to it proved superficial. The scientific (and scientistic) tendencies that motivated much analytic philosophy were present in France, but they were channeled along paths outside of philosophy. (This, however, is not to deny that much French social science, from Durkheim through Lévi-Strauss to Bourdieu, has had major philosophical significance.)

The philosophical root of the French focus on freedom was its distinctive national tradition, spiritualism. Initially, spiritualism was a philosophy to complement an optimistic bourgeois Catholicism, for which human life was a matter of individuals freely working out their salvation in a comfortable socio-economic world itself embedded in a providentially benevolent cosmos. In the course of the century, both the religion and the optimism lost their central place in French thought, but there remained the focus on understanding individual freedom and on concrete experience as the locus of this understanding.

The ultimate explanation of this emphasis on individual freedom may well lie in France's religious and revolutionary heritage. But the specific instrument of transmission for this heritage was the philosophical educational system. Here the two salient features of this system were its centralism and its institutionalism. Almost every important French philosopher was trained in Paris, and of those, the great majority studied at the École Normale. Further, this education was dominated by the institutional demands of the lycée's *classe de philosophie*, implemented by the crucial *agrégation* examination. Philosophers were trained to be purveyors of a syllabus; and it was this syllabus, with its emphasis on French philosophy (and French interpretations of non-French classics) that transmitted the emphasis on individual freedom as the core of philosophizing.

The French centering of philosophical education around a historical syllabus contrasts with the Anglo-American and the German models contemporary with it. The analytic philosophy dominant in the English-speaking world produced solvers of philosophical problems, guided much less by their formation in a national tradition or in the more general history of philosophy than by their conceptual quickness and imagination. German philosophy favored history over problems, but initiated the young philosopher into a tradition as the disciple of one of its master-thinkers. Twentieth-century French philosophy produced its share of master-thinkers, but they typically remained at some distance from the university system, either, like Bergson, Merleau-Ponty, and Foucault, moving to the Collège de

France or, like Marcel, Sartre, and Beauvoir, operating as independent intellectuals.

The leitmotiv of individual freedom is obvious from the beginning in the spiritualism of Ravaisson, the finalism of Lachelier, and the indeterminism of Renouvier and of Boutroux. Lachelier and Boutroux, in particular, are concerned to make sense of freedom in the context of a world of scientific causality. They insist from the outset on freedom as a fact, but their focus is not on explicating the fact in its own terms but on finding a place for it in a general ontological scheme compatible with a scientific worldview. Thus Lachelier, after establishing that a knowable world must be a system of efficient causes, goes on to argue that this system itself must, for parallel transcendental reasons, be embedded in a more concrete system of final causes. This latter system is the locus of the creative goals of action in terms of which Lachelier understands freedom. Boutroux, however, argues that Lachelier's comprehensive system of efficient causes cannot consistently mesh with the finality of free agents. Referring to our experience of the moral significance of freedom, he maintains that freedom is incompatible with universal causal determinism and concludes that its reality requires an indeterministic universe. His multi-layered analysis of the various forms of necessity claims to discover, beneath every necessity, a fundamental contingency.

The disagreement between Lachelier and Boutroux is, to an important extent, an instance of the classic division between compatibilism (so-called soft determinism) and libertarianism. Contemporary analytic philosophy has taken this dispute to the limit of conceptual rigor and ingenuity, seeking to reconcile, under one or the other banner, our common-sense "intuitions" regarding freedom. Can the compatibilist, who thinks free actions are causally determined, do justice to our sense that a free action is one that I could have done otherwise? Can the libertarian, who thinks free actions must be uncaused, make sense of our belief that there are always explanations of why I act as I do? Without losing all interest in the progress of this still lively discussion, we may well worry that it is not sufficiently grounded in an adequate description of the concreteness and nuance of our lived experience of freedom. Perhaps the common-sense intuitions from which it seeks to extract a finally adequate solution to the "problem of freedom" are not ultimately reliable guides to the phenomenon. At the least, we should acknowledge that a full understanding of freedom is likely to require experiential descriptions as complex and subtle as the analytic conceptual clarifications.

Bergson, the greatest figure of the early period, begins with such descriptions in his *Essai sur les données immédiates de conscience*. As we have seen, he thought that the concrete reality of freedom undermined the premise shared by both sides of the libertarian–determinist debate: that the free self is a series of distinct psychological states that are (or even could be) causally connected. To the contrary, according to Bergson, the self is an organic continuity of duration that cannot, except by a misleading abstraction, be divided into distinct states. Its freedom, therefore, is not a matter of the determination or indetermination of its states but of its creative self-extension into a novel future.

Although, unlike his Kantian predecessors, Bergson starts from a careful description of our immediate experience of freedom, he still follows them in placing this experience in the context of a larger metaphysical scheme. His subsequent books situate the lived experience of duration in relation to, successively, the general union of mind and body, the cosmic force of the *élan vital*, and the connection of this force to the divine. This combination of descriptive concreteness and systematic scope is one of the signal merits that make Bergson a great philosopher.

The iconoclasm of the young philosophers who emerged between the wars did not extend to their predecessors' focus on freedom, which they did not reject but rather intensified. The Catholics, Blondel and Marcel, situated freedom in the concrete world of lived experience and practical action. (And even Maritain's neo-Thomism led to a defense of the individual's political freedom.) Atheistic existentialism went even further, radicalizing freedom by undermining the objective meanings and values to which it was traditionally subordinated. Nonetheless, the young existential philosophers who emerged in the 1920s and 1930s did not find Bergson's vision compelling. We saw how Merleau-Ponty rejected his description of our lived experience of freedom on the grounds that it ignores essential phenomenological structures, such as the subject–object differentiation and the three irreducible temporal modalities. Nor, of course, is it merely Bergson and Merleau-Ponty who disagree over the content of immediate experience. Even within the phenomenological camp, Sartre's descriptions differ from Merleau-Ponty's in at least some significant details; and we saw how Marcel (and, before him, Blondel) found essential dimensions of hope, community, and transcendence that had no place in Sartre's and Merleau-Ponty's phenomenologies. Broadening our temporal and geographical horizon will, of course, lead to a much wider range of characterizations of what we most directly experience; for example, the classical sense-data account of Hume and the positivists, Reid's common-sense realism, even the pantheistic sensibility of certain mystics – and with these we remain within our own Western tradition, taking no account of the lived experiences of less accessible cultures.

It might be maintained that this diversity merely shows how complex must be the philosophical project of discovering just what is given in immediate experience. But can we in fact even imagine carrying out this project? Recent philosophy on both sides of the Channel has devastated the idea that immediate experience is an *epistemic* given that can serve as the ultimate ground of our cognitive structures. I suggest that the very idea of a unique experiential given is equally vulnerable – and to many of the same considerations. For example, the critiques of the idea of interpretation-free observation, combined with arguments for the historically contingent nature of interpretative categories, refute not only foundationalism but also the claim to have discovered the unique character of immediate experience.

Accordingly, there is no point in trying to determine a uniquely correct description of our lived experience. Experiential immediacy is a well from which many buckets may draw. The "immediate givens of consciousness" are an irrefutable and inevitable starting point of any inquiry. But while the sheer experience itself is certainly given, no preferred or controlling description or interpretation of it is. Experience can be read in many different ways, each with its own plausibility, self-consistency, and limitations. Some of these readings may be mutually incompatible, but many are literally consistent, tensions arising only when we ask which is the most comprehensive or most concrete. It is these latter questions I suggest we eschew, at least in their general form. On the whole, questions of superiority make sense only given a specific context, perspective, or purpose. Experience as such is no doubt an absolute, but there is nothing absolute that follows from it. There is good reason to suspect that, for a domain as complex and elusive as experience, no one formulation will be comprehensively and exhaustively adequate. In appreciating and evaluating the great philosophies of experience, we should rather think, in Nietzschean terms, of each as a particular vocabulary, with its own strengths and limitations, which we can expect to be of varying value for different purposes. In this regard, philosophies are like novels, not alternative absolutes among which we must choose the "right one" but different perspectival visions (perhaps complementary, but perhaps incompatible or even incommensurable), all of which have their relative values and uses.

From this standpoint, the new philosophies of existence that arose in France after World War I represent not a refutation of Bergson but an exploration of new aspects of our experience of freedom, aspects that came to the fore in virtue of a new orientation toward human existence. Specifically, the philosophers of existence were no longer content with Bergson's optimistic holism, according to which our species is continuous with nature and assured a central role in its creative advance. They sought instead a philosophy consistent with their tragic vision of human beings thrown into a world of contingency and conflict, in which salvation requires either the intrusion of divine grace or our own creation of authentic meanings.

This transformation of vision is not a refutation of Bergson's philosophy, because philosophies are instruments for focusing and elaborating fundamental visions of the human condition, not foundationalist justifications of such visions. We inevitably begin with fundamental perspectives on our lives that themselves define what we require of our philosophical reflection. Past philosophies are relevant or irrelevant to our concerns depending on the degree to which they share our fundamental perspectives. The young philosophers of existence shared their neo-Kantian teachers' commitment to the centrality of individual freedom and, at least in the case of Sartre, even their commitment to situating this freedom in a comprehensive ontological scheme. Their perspective differed from that of the neo-Kantians and agreed with Bergson's in its demand for a detailed philosophical explication of our concrete experience of freedom. But their explication of this experience was driven by their own distinctive tragic vision of human existence. The split between theistic and atheistic existentialism turned on pre-philosophical differences regarding the ultimate absoluteness of human freedom.

The great achievement of French existentialism is its penetrating descriptions of just what it means to be free in a world in which we are, nonetheless, so integrally implicated that we must speak of our being as "being-in-the-world". Sartre is the philosopher of freedom par excellence, not only for the unparalleled detail and subtlety of his phenomenological descriptions and ontological explications of it, but also for his continuing struggle to embed it in the realities of society and history. It is precisely because Sartre brings thinking about freedom to a peak of intensity that he remains the central French philosopher of this century. His *L'être et le néant*, whatever the limitations of its ontological categories, provides a powerful account of our lived experience of freedom as an irreducible reality in our engagement with the world. And all his work, both philosophical and literary, even if it does not achieve a comprehensive ethical vision, establishes the centrality of freedom as a moral value. Merleau-Ponty's appreciation of our embodiment provides an essential correction to the dualistic tendencies of Sartre's ontology. Beauvoir's *Deuxième sexe* goes even further, describing the significance of female embodiment as a biological and historical reality and connecting it to a specific ethical and political project. We may readily question details of these descriptions and, even more, the network of ontological and political commitments to which Sartre and company connected them. But no one who seeks a philosophy of freedom rooted in the concreteness of daily life should ignore the rich starting-point the existentialists have provided.

We have seen that what often appears as an overthrow of existentialism from the outside by structuralism in fact originated, in the work of Merleau-Ponty, from the internal logic of existential phenomenology. Unless it recognizes human structures (social and psychological) inaccessible to consciousness, phenomenology cannot avoid collapsing into idealism. Accordingly, phenomenological experience requires supplementation by "ethnological experience", of which Lévi-Strauss's structuralism was a paradigm example. As Merleau-Ponty saw it, a proper understanding of freedom, one that avoided an unacceptable gap between subject and object, required a synthesis of these two perspectives. Sartre's own responses to Lévi-Strauss and Foucault, as well as the ontology of *Critique de la raison dialectique*, show that he also accepted the need for such a synthesis.

Why then did structuralism come to be instead regarded as a stark alternative to existential phenomenology? A first level of explanation lies in the rivalry between Lévi-Strauss and Sartre for the position of reigning French master-thinker. Lévi-Strauss's explicit, sometimes virulent challenge to Sartre's dominant position (as in the concluding chapter of *La pensée sauvage*) left no room for cooperative inquiry. If Merleau-Ponty, with his close ties to Lévi-Strauss, had lived long enough and succeeded Sartre (whose interests were becoming much less philosophical) as the leading existential phenomenologist, the relations between structuralism and phenomenology may well have been very different. Moreover, with the death of Merleau-Ponty and Sartre's relative withdrawal from philosophy, the vitality of French phenomenology was sapped and its energy flowed into the new poststructuralist direction.

Poststructuralism strongly challenged the privileged role of phenomenological consciousness, speaking of the "death of man" and insisting on the subject's domination by social and linguistic structures. But it would be a gross error to conclude that this challenge was a break with the twentieth-century French focus on individual freedom. With the possible exception of Althusser's Marxism, French philosophy after 1960 strongly opposed the suggestion that individual freedom could find no purchase in a structuralist world. Such opposition was part of what made this philosophy *post*structuralist.

The poststructuralists rejected the philosophical apparatus through which existential phenomenology had explicated freedom, questioning its descriptive and ontological methods as well as its central category of consciousness. But this very rejection expressed their commitment to individual freedom. (Indeed, one reason structuralist social science so quickly collapsed as a philosophical framework was its incompatibility with freedom.) Foucault's archaeologies and genealogies, for example, are explicitly developed to free us from the limitations of specific conceptual and social structures. His critique is merely of philosophical conceptions of freedom that threaten its historical reality. Similarly, Derridean deconstruction and the other philosophies of difference attack philosophical constructions – the subject, identity, the masculinist self – through which the tradition has conceptualized freedom. But this attack is itself for the sake of freeing us from the constraints of those constructions. The justice sought by Derrida and Lyotard, like the ethical and political goals of Deleuze and Irigaray, flows from a prephilosophical commitment to individual freedom. The fin-de-siècle "return to the subject" is in the name of a freedom that thinkers such as Ferry and Renaut see as destroyed by the radical individualism of poststructuralism. But this claim is a significant challenge to Derrida, Nancy, and

Lacoue-Labarthe precisely because, if correct, it effects a genuine reductio of their thought, which becomes incoherent if it is truly incapable of maintaining individual freedom.

Nonetheless, poststructuralism contributed little to our philosophical understanding of freedom. Foucault made us aware of how various popular and scientific (or pseudo-scientific) conceptions of the self – particularly in terms of modern notions of "normality" – could be instruments of domination. And his genealogy and Derrida's deconstruction can show how what we regard as essential limitations on thought and action are often historically contingent constraints. But, as we have seen, Foucault's critique of "man" in *Les mots et les choses* does not demonstrate that traditional philosophical conceptions of the subject are as such part of oppressive social power. Moreover, it is not at all obvious that the core existentialist understanding of freedom, particularly in terms of Sartrean negation, is susceptible to poststructuralist critiques of Cartesian, Kantian, or Husserlian subjectivity. The freedom of Sartrean consciousness, which "is what it is in the mode of not being it", is not very far from a manifestation of Derridean *différance*.[1] At the very least, *L'être et le néant* and *Critique de la raison dialectique* would be excellent starting-points for a serious poststructuralist exploration of freedom.

Unfortunately, few poststructuralists have been interested in developing a positive philosophical understanding of freedom (although Jean-Luc Nancy, whose work picks up Sartrean themes, has been an important recent exception). They remain content with a naive, prereflective commitment to the unquestionable status of transgression, novelty, plurality, and difference as absolute ethical ideals. There is, accordingly, no inclination to ask difficult questions about the roots and limits of human freedom; the consuming task is to expose and overcome all obstacles to its unrestricted expansion. So, for example, Lyotard's philosophy of difference and Deleuze's ontology unqualifiedly endorse the most radical liberation without stopping to ask just what it would consist in and why it is so important.

In this respect at least, poststructuralism is an interlude rather than a decisive turning-point in the history of French philosophy. It

---

[1] On the similarity of Sartrean and poststructuralist views of subjectivity, see Christina Howells, "Conclusion: Sartre and the Deconstruction of the Subject", in Christina Howells (ed.), *The Cambridge Companion to Sartre*.

has been important for its questioning of limits and, especially, for its rejection of traditional philosophical claims to ultimate truth. But, once its critiques are properly acknowledged, there remains the fundamental twentieth-century project of articulating the individual as a locus of freedom. The recent return of French thought to the ethical philosophies of Kant and Levinas is an effort to revive the project of this articulation. In this retrospective mood, current French philosophers of freedom could also fruitfully revive – as some have begun to do – an interest in Bergson and Sartre.

But philosophical progress is never a matter of mere returns or revivals, and there is a real possibility that the twentieth-century French problematic of freedom has finally worked itself out. It has, after all, thoroughly developed the topic through embedding freedom in general systems of thought, describing our lived experience of it, and deconstructing the forces that act against it. Perhaps the theme has, for the foreseeable future, been essentially exhausted. Further, there are signs that French philosophy is losing its distinctive national character and may be splitting into a variety of elements (phenomenology, analytic philosophy, feminism) that will each make its own contribution to corresponding international discussions. At the same time, the ever-increasing prestige of the social sciences has drawn considerable talent out of philosophy and undermined its status as the leading intellectual discipline. It may not be long before we look back on twentieth-century French philosophy as a vanished golden age.

Appendix:
Philosophy and the French educational system

Since Napoleon, the base of French education has been the lycée, a state-funded and -controlled secondary school (the equivalent of American high school), which awards the *baccalauréat* degree. There are also a number of non-state secondary schools, now generally run by the Catholic Church, which are called *collèges*. (State schools for children at the junior high level are now also called *collèges*.) All students in the final year of the lycée take at least two hours of philosophy per week, and there are, accordingly, about 8000 teachers of philosophy in the lycées.

Undergraduate university studies begin with two years of work in a broadly defined area of specialization (for example, philosophy), followed by two or three years of more advanced study in the same area. Students completing the third year receive a *licence* in their area of specialization, and those completing the fourth year receive a *maîtrise*. (The first two years are now called the *premier cycle* and lead to a Diplôme d'Études Universitaires Générales (DEUG); the next two years constitute the *deuxième cycle*.) Graduate education (now called the *troisième cycle*) has taken various forms over the twentieth century. Currently, the first year of graduate studies leads to a Diplôme d'Études Approfondies (DEA), the rough equivalent of an American master's degree, which is where most graduate students end their studies. Further work is directed toward a doctoral degree. Until recently, there was the university doctorate (*doctorat d'université*), which, however, carried little prestige, and the state doctorate (*doctorat d'état*), which was the standard requirement for a position as a full professor in a university (as opposed to a *maître de conférences*, the equivalent of an associate professor). The latter degree required two theses, a primary one written in French and a shorter "complementary" thesis (which, until the beginning of the twentieth century, had to be written in Latin), typically on a historical topic related to the main thesis. In 1966, a third doctoral degree, a *doctorat du troisième cycle*, was added as a preliminary to the *doctorat d'état*. In 1984 the three doctorates were replaced by a single doctorate (itself called the *doctorat du troisième cycle*), but there is now also a *habilitation* (modelled on the German degree) required for a position as full professor, which is awarded following a candidate's defense of a set of scholarly writings (often already published).

The *agrégation* is a competitive exam for positions as teachers in lycées. It is not a necessary condition for lycée teaching, and today the majority of lycée teachers are not *agrégés*. (The alternative path to lycée teaching is a Certificat d'aptitude au professorat de l'enseignement du second degré [CAPES].) But the few who pass the *agrégation* (ranked in strict numerical order) are a very elite group, with the best chances for positions at top lycées. Moreover, university teachers, particularly in the humanities, typically are *agrégés*, although this is not an official requirement.

The usual – and surest – preparation for the *agrégation* is study at the École Normale Supérieure (ENS) in Paris, a super-elite institution, acceptance to which depends on success in a fiercely competitive (written and oral) examination. Candidates for the ENS spend two years beyond their *baccalauréat* degree studying at elite lycées for the test. (The second year is called *khâgne*, from the Greek for "lazy" and the first *hypokhâgne* ["before *khâgne*"].) Corresponding to its privileged position in the general educational system, philosophy was for a long time the most prestigious concentration at the École Normale, and most of the leading philosophers were (and still are) *normaliens*. The school is located in the heart of the Latin Quarter on the rue d'Ulm. (A branch for women was established in 1881 at Sèvres, just outside of Paris, but since the 1930s women have been admitted at the rue d'Ulm.) *Normaliens* can follow courses at the Sorbonne, and Sorbonne students preparing for the *agrégation* can sit in on ENS courses. The ENS is just one of several *grandes écoles* established after the Revolution to train French elites for various areas of government service. Currently, the most important *grandes écoles* include the ENS, the École Polytechnique, the École des Hautes Études Commerciales (for business), and the École Nationale d'Administration (for government officials).

Most influential philosophers have had positions at the University of Paris (specifically, at the Sorbonne, the University's College of Arts and Sciences), although some few have remained at provincial universities, the top Parisian lycées, or the ENS. For centuries, the University of Paris was simply the famous medieval institution on the Left Bank, but today there are numerous branches, at various locations in and around the capital.

Another important part of the French intellectual scene is a variety of multi-disciplinary centers, independent of the university system. The most famous of these is the Collège de France, roughly similar to the Princeton Institute for Advanced Study, whose professors have no formal students and are merely required to give a series of public lectures each year. A chair at the Collège is a high honor, often bitterly fought for, but it can also mean fewer disciples and much less influence on university education. Bergson, Merleau-Ponty, and Foucault all held chairs at the Collège de France. Also deserving mention are the École Pratiques des Hautes Études, founded under Napoleon III and, especially, the École des Hautes Études en Sciences Sociales, which split off from it after World War II, where major figures of the structuralist movement in the 1950s and 1960s (e.g., Claude Lévi-Strauss, Georges Dumézil, and Roland Barthes) held positions. Since World War II, the Centre National de la Recherche Scientifique (CNRS) has been a major source of facilities and support for research in numerous academic disciplines, including philosophy.

On another level, the Collège International de Philosophie has, since its founding in 1983, been an important center of philosophical activity. It has no permanent members and is not part of the official educational system. Nonetheless, led successively by directors such as Jacques Derrida, Jean-François Lyotard, and Philippe Lacoue-Labarthe, it has been an exciting locus of teaching and research for philosophers from both France and abroad and has encouraged work outside the conventional boundaries of the universities and the *grandes écoles*.

References

Aeschliman, J.-C. (ed.), *Répondre d'autrui: Emmanuel Levinas*, Neuchâtel: Baconnière, 1989.

Althusser, Louis, *L'avenir dure longtemps*, Paris: Stock/IMEC, 1992 (*The Future Lasts Forever*, translated by Richard Veasey, New York: The New Press, 1993).

Armstrong, T. J. (ed.), *Michel Foucault: Philosopher*, New York: Routledge, 1991.

Bachelard, Gaston, *L'engagement rationaliste*, Paris: Presses Universitaires de France, 1972.

Le nouvel esprit scientifique, Paris: Alcan, 1934 (*The New Scientific Spirit*, translated by Arthur Goldhammer, Boston: Beacon, 1984).

"La philosophie scientifique de Léon Brunschvicg", *Revue de métaphysique et de morale* 50 (1945), 77–84; reprinted in *L'engagement rationaliste*, 169–77.

La poétique de l'espace, Paris: Presses Universitaires de France, 1961 (*The Poetics of Space*, translated by Maria Jolas, New York: Orion, 1964).

La poétique de la rêverie, Paris: Presses Universitaires de France, 1960 (*The Poetics of Reverie*, translated by Daniel Russell, Boston: Beacon, 1969).

La psychoanalyse de feu, Paris: Gallimard, 1938 (*The Psychoanalysis of Fire*, translated by G. C. Waterston, New York: Orion, 1969).

La valeur inductive de la relativité, Paris: Vrin, 1929.

Barthes, Roland, *Mythologies*, Paris: Seuil, 1957 (*Mythologies*, selections, translated by Annette Lavers, London: Cape, 1972).

Le plaisir du texte, Paris: Seuil, 1973 (*The Pleasure of the Text*, translated by Richard Miller, New York: Hill and Wang, 1975).

Système de la mode, Paris: Seuil, 1967 (*The Fashion System*, translated by M. Ward and R. Howard, New York: Hill and Wang, 1983).

S/Z, Paris: Seuil, 1970 (*S/Z*, translated by Richard Miller, New York: Hill and Wang, 1974).

Bataille, Georges, *Oeuvres complètes*, Paris: Gallimard, 1988.

Sur Nietzsche, Paris: Gallimard, 1945 (*On Nietzsche*, translated by Bruce Boone, New York: Paragon, 1992).

Visions of Excess, edited and translated by Alan Stoekl, Minneapolis: University of Minnesota Press, 1985.

Beauvoir, Simone de,
 La cérémonie des adieux, Paris: Gallimard, 1981 (*Adieux: A Farewell to Sartre*, translated by Patrick O'Brian, New York: Pantheon Books, 1984).
 Le deuxième sexe, 2 vols., Paris: Gallimard, 1949 (*The Second Sex*, translated by H. M. Parshley, New York: Vintage, 1989).
 La force de l'âge, Paris: Gallimard, 1960 (*The Prime of Life*, translated by Peter Green, Cleveland: World Publishing, 1962).
 La force des choses, Paris: Gallimard, 1963 (*Force of Circumstance*, translated by Richard Howard, New York: Putnam, 1965).
 L'invitée, Paris: Gallimard, 1943 (*She Came to Stay*, translated by Peter Green, London: Secker & Warburg, 1949).
 "Littérature et métaphysique", in *L'existentialisme et la sagesse des nations*, Paris: Nagel, 1948.
 Mémoires d'une jeune fille rangée, Paris: Gallimard, 1958 (*Memoirs of a Dutiful Daughter*, Cleveland: World Publishing, 1959).
 "Merleau-Ponty et le pseudo-sartrisme", *Les temps modernes* 10 (1955), 2072–122.
 Pour une morale de l'ambiguïté, Paris: Gallimard, 1947 (*Ethics of Ambiguity*, translated by Bernard Frechtman, New York: Philosophical Library, 1948).
 Le sang de autres, Paris: Gallimard, 1945 (*The Blood of Others*, translated by R. Senhouse & Y. Moyse, New York: Knopf, 1948).
 Tous les hommes sont mortels, Paris: Gallimard, 1946 (*All Men are Mortal*, translated by Leonard Friedman, New York: World Publishing, 1955).
 La vieillesse, Paris: Gallimard, 1970 (*The Coming of Age*, translated by Patrick O'Brian, New York: Putnam, 1972).
Bennington, Geoffrey, *Lyotard: Writing the Event*, New York: Columbia University Press, 1988.
Bennington, Geoffrey and Derrida, Jacques, *Jacques Derrida*, Chicago: University of Chicago Press, 1993.
Benrubi, Isaac, *Les sources et les courants de la philosophie contemporaine en France*, Paris: Alcan, 1933.
Bergson, Henri, *Les deux sources de la morale et de la religion*, in Henri Bergson, *Oeuvres* (*The Two Sources of Morality and Religion*, translated by R. Audra and C. Brereton, Notre Dame, IN: University of Notre Dame Press, 1977).
 Durée et simultanéité, 2nd edn., Paris: Alcan, 1923 (*Duration and Simultaneity*, translated by Leon Jacobson, Indianapolis: Bobbs-Merrill, 1965).
 L'énergie spirituelle, in Henri Bergson, *Oeuvres*.
 Essai sur les données immédiates de la conscience, in Henri Bergson, *Oeuvres* (*Time and Free Will*, translated by F. L. Pogson, London: Sonnenschein, 1910).
 L'évolution créatrice, in Henri Bergson, *Oeuvres* (*Creative Evolution*, translated by Arthur Mitchell, New York: Modern Library, 1944).

Matière et mémoire, in Henri Bergson, *Oeuvres* (*Matter and Memory*, translated by N. M. Paul and W. S. Winter, New York: Zone Books, 1988).
Oeuvres, Paris: Presses Universitaires de France, 1959.
La pensée et le mouvant, in Henri Bergson, *Oeuvres* (*The Creative Mind*, translated by Mabelle Andison, New York: Greenwood, 1968).
Bernasconi, Robert and Simon Critchley (eds.), *Re-Reading Levinas*, Bloomington, IN; University of Indiana Press, 1997.
Blanchot, Maurice, *L'écriture du désastre*, Paris: Gallimard, 1980 (*The Writing of the Disaster*, translated by Ann Smock, Lincoln, NE: University of Nebraska Press, 1986).
L'espace littéraire, Paris: Gallimard, 1955 (*The Space of Literature*, translated by Ann Smock, Lincoln, NE: University of Nebraska Press, 1982).
Le pas au-delà, Paris: Gallimard, 1973 (*The Step not Beyond*, translated by Lycette Nelson, Albany: State University of New York Press, 1992).
Blondel, Maurice, *L'action*, Paris: Presses Universitaires de France, 1963 (*Action*, translated by Olivia Blanchette, Notre Dame, IN: University of Notre Dame Press, 1984).
L'être et les êtres, Paris: Presses Universitaires de France, 1963.
La pensée, Paris: Alcan, 1934.
La philosophie et l'esprit chrétien, Paris: Presses Universitaires de France, 1944.
Boutroux, Émile, *De l'idée de loi naturelle dans la science et la philosophie contemporaine*, Paris: Alcan, 1895 (*Natural Law in Science and Philosophy*, translated by Fred Rothwell, London: Open Court, 1914).
La contingence de les lois de la nature, Paris: Alcan, 1874 (*Natural Law in Science and Philosophy*, translated by Fred Rothwell, London: Open Court, 1914).
Nouvelles études d'histoire de la philosophie, Paris: Alcan, 1927.
Philosophy and War, translated by Fred Rothwell, New York: E. P. Dutton, 1916.
Bouveresse, Jacques, *La philosophie chez les autophages*, Paris: Minuit, 1984.
Le philosophe et le réel, Paris: Hachette, 1998.
Rationalité et cynisme, Paris: Minuit, 1985.
"Why I am so very UnFrench", in Alan Montefiore (ed.), *Philosophy in France Today*, 9–33.
Bruns, Gerald, *Maurice Blanchot*, Baltimore: Johns Hopkins University Press, 1997.
Brunschvicg, Léon, *Les étapes de la philosophie mathématique*, Paris: Alcan, 1912.
L'expérience humaine et la causalité physique, Paris: Alcan, 1922.
L'idéalisme contemporain, Paris: Alcan, 1921.
La modalité du jugement, Paris: Presses Universitaires de France, 1964.
Le progrès de la conscience dans le philosophie occidentale, Paris: Presses Universitaires de France, 1953.
"Vie intérieure et vie spirituelle", *Revue de métaphysique et de morale* 32 (1925), 139–48.

Burchell, Graham, et al. (eds.), *The Foucault Effect*, Chicago: University of Chicago Press, 1991.
Canguilhem, Georges, *Idéologie et rationalité*, Paris: Vrin, 1977 (*Ideology and Rationality in the History of the Life Sciences*, translated by Arthur Goldhammer, Cambridge, MA: MIT Press, 1988).
　Le normal et le pathologique, Paris: Presses Universitaires de France, 1966 (*On the Normal and the Pathological*, translated by Carolyn R. Fawcett, Dordrecht: Reidel, 1978).
　A Vital Rationalist: Selected Writings from Georges Canguilhem, edited by François Delaporte, translated by Arthur Goldhammer, New York: Zone Books, 1994.
Čapek, Milic, *Bergson and Modern Physics*, Dordrecht: Reidel, 1971.
Caputo, John, *The Prayers and Tears of Jacques Derrida*, Bloomington, IN: Indiana University Press, 1997.
Caputo, John (ed.), *Deconstruction in a Nutshell*, New York: Fordham University Press, 1997.
Cavaillès, Jean, *Méthode axiomatique et formalisme*, Paris: Hermann & cie, 1938.
　"On Logic and the Theory of Science", in Kockelmans and Kisiel (eds.), *Phenomenology and the Natural Sciences*, 353–409.
　Remarques sur la formation de la théorie abstraite des ensembles, Paris: Hermann & Cie, 1938.
Caws, Peter, *Sartre*, London: Routledge, 1979.
Cohen-Solal, Annie, *Sartre: A Life*, translated by Anna Cancogni, New York: Pantheon, 1987.
Collins, James, *The Existentialists*, Chicago: Regnery, 1952.
Comte, Auguste, *The Essential Comte*, edited by Stanislav Andreski, translated by Margaret Clarke, London: Croom Helm, 1974.
Cornell, D., Rosenfeld, M., and Carlson, D. (eds.), *Deconstruction and the Possibility of Justice*, London: Routledge, 1992.
Courtine, Jean-François, *Heidegger et la phénoménologie*, Paris: Vrin, 1986.
Creech, J., Kamuf, P., and Todd, J., "Deconstruction in America: An Interview with Jacques Derrida", *Critical Exchange* 14.
Culler, Jonathan, *Roland Barthes*, Oxford: Oxford University Press, 1983.
　On Deconstruction, Ithaca, NY: Cornell University Press, 1982.
　Ferdinand de Saussure, revised edition, Ithaca, NY: Cornell University Press, 1986.
Curtius, Ernst, *Die Französische Kultur*, Bern: Francke, 1975 (first published 1930) (*Civilization of France*, translated by Olive Wyon, New York: Macmillan, 1932).
Davis, Colin, *Levinas: An Introduction*, Notre Dame, IN: University of Notre Dame Press, 1991.
Deleuze, Gilles, *Bergsonisme*, Paris: Presses Universitaires de France, 1965 (*Bergsonism*, translated by Hugh Tomlinson and Barbara Habberjam, New York: Zone Books, 1988).

"La conception de la différence chez Bergson", *Les études bergsoniennes* 4 (1956), 76–112.
Différence et répétition, Paris: Presses Universitaires de France, 1968 (*Difference and Repetition*, translated by Paul Patton, New York: Columbia University Press, 1994).
Foucault, Paris: Minuit, 1986 (*Foucault*, translated by Séan Hand, Minneapolis: University of Minnesota Press, 1988).
"L'immanence: une vie . . .", *Philosophie* 47 (1995), 3–7.
Logique du sens, Paris: Minuit, 1969 (*The Logic of Sense*, translated by M. Lester and C. Stivale, New York: Columbia University Press, 1990).
Nietzsche et la philosophie, Paris: Presses Universitaires de France, 1962 (*Nietzsche and Philosophy*, translated by Hugh Tomlinson, New York: Columbia University Press, 1983).
La philosophie critique de Kant, Paris: Presses Universitaires de France, 1963 (*Kant's Critical Philosophy*, translated by H. Tomlinson and B. Habberjam, Minneapolis, MN: University of Minnesota Press, 1984).
Pourparlers, Paris: Minuit, 1990 (*Negotiations*, translated by Martin Joughin, New York: Columbia University Press, 1995).
Spinoza et le problème de l'expression, Paris: Editions de Minuit, 1968 (*Expressionism in Philosophy: Spinoza*, translated by Martin Joughin, New York: Zone Books, 1990).
Deleuze, Gilles, and Félix Guattari, *L'anti-oedipe*, Paris: Minuit, 1972 (*Anti-Oedipus*, translated by R. Hurley, M. Seem, and H. Lane, Minneapolis: University of Minnesota Press, 1983).
Mille Plateaux, Paris: Minuit, 1980 (*A Thousand Plateaus*, translated by Brian Massumi, Minneapolis: University of Minnesota Press, 1987).
Qu'est-ce que la philosophie?, Paris: Minuit, 1991 (*What is Philosophy?*, translated by H. Tomlinson and G. Burchell, New York: Columbia University Press, 1994).
Derrida, Jacques, *La carte postale*, Paris: Flammarion, 1980 (*The Post Card*, translated by Alan Bass, Chicago: University of Chicago Press, 1987).
De la grammatologie, Paris: Minuit, 1967 (*Of Grammatology*, corrected edition, translated by Gayatri Spivak, Baltimore, MD: Johns Hopkins University Press, 1998).
De l'esprit, Paris: Gallimard, 1987 (*Of Spirit: Heidegger and the Question*, translated by G. Bennington and R. Bowlby, Chicago: University of Chicago Press, 1989).
La dissémination, Paris: Seuil, 1972 (*Dissemination*, translated by Barbara Johnson, Chicago: University of Chicago Press, 1981).
Donner la mort, Paris: Galilée, 1999 (*The Gift of Death*, translated by David Wills, Chicago: University of Chicago Press, 1995).
Du droit à la philosophie, Paris: Galilée, 1990.
L'écriture et la différence, Paris: Seuil, 1967 (*Writing and Difference*, translated by Alan Bass, Chicago: University of Chicago Press, 1978).

References

Éperons: les styles de Nietzsche, Venice: Corbo e Fiori, 1976 (*Spurs: Nietzsche's Styles*, translated by Barbara Harlow, Chicago: University of Chicago Press, 1979).

Force de loi: le "fondement mystique de l'autorité", Paris: Galilée, 1994 ("Force of Law", translated by Mary Quaintance in Cornell et al., *Deconstruction and the Possibility of Justice*).

Glas, Paris: Galilée, 1974 (*Glas*, translated by J. Leavey, Jr. and R. Rand, Lincoln, NE: University of Nebraska Press, 1986).

Introduction à "L'origine de la géometrie" de Husserl, Paris: Presses Universitaires de France, 1962 (*Edmund Husserl's* Origin of Geometry: *An Introduction*, translated by J. P. Leavey, Jr., Lincoln, NE: University of Nebraska Press, 1989).

Limited Inc., translated by Elizabeth Weber, Paris: Galilée, 1990 (*Limited Inc.*, Evanston, IL: Northwestern University Press, 1988).

"La loi du genre", *Glyph* 7 (1980), 176–201 (English translation following, 202–29).

Marges de la philosophie, Paris: Minuit, 1972 (*Margins of Philosophy*, translated by Alan Bass, Chicago: University of Chicago Press, 1982).

Otobiographies: L'enseignement de Nietzsche et la politique du nom propre, Paris: Galilée, 1984 (*The Ear of the Other*, translated by Peggy Kamuf, et al., New York: Schocken, 1985).

Parages, Paris: Galilée, 1984.

Points, edited by Elizabeth Weber, Paris: Editions Gallilée, 1992 (*Points*, translated by Peggy Kamuf, et. al., Stanford, CA: Stanford University Press, 1995).

Politiques de l'amitié, Paris: Galilée, 1994 (*Politics of Friendship*, translated by George Collins, London: Verso, 1997).

Positions, Paris: Minuit, 1972 (*Positions*, translated by Alan Bass, Chicago: University of Chicago Press, 1981).

Psyché: inventions de l'autre, Paris: Gallimard, 1987.

Spectres de Marx, Paris: Galilée, 1993 (*Specters of Marx*, translated by Peggy Kamuf, London: Routledge, 1994).

"'To Do Justice to Freud': The History of Madness in the Age of Psychoanalysis", in Arnold Davidson (ed.), *Foucault and His Interlocutors*, Chicago: University of Chicago Press, 1997, 57–96.

La voix et le phénomène, 3rd edn., Paris: Presses Universitaires de France, 1976 (*Speech and Phenomena*, translated by David Allison, Evanston, IL: Northwestern University Press, 1973).

Descombes, Vincent, *Le même et l'autre*, Paris: Minuit, 1979 (*Modern French Philosophy*, Cambridge: Cambridge University Press, 1980).

Dews, Peter, *Logics of Disintegration: Post-Structuralist Thought and the Claims of Critical Theory*, London: Verso, 1987.

Dosse, François, *History of Structuralism*, 2 vols., translated by Deborah Glassman, Minneapolis: University of Minnesota Press, 1997.

Paul Ricoeur: les sens d'une vie, Paris: Éditions la Découverte, 1997.

Duhem, Pierre, *La théorie physique: son objet, sa structure*, 2nd edn., Paris: Rivière, 1914 (*The Aim and Structure of Physical Theory*, translated by Philip Wiener, New York: Atheneum, 1962).

Dupont, Christian, *Receptions of Phenomenology in French Philosophy and Religious Thought, 1889–1939*, dissertation, University of Notre Dame, 1997.

Elliot, Gregory (ed.), *Althusser: A Critical Reader*, Oxford: Blackwell, 1994.

Engel, Pascal, *La dispute*, Paris: Minuit, 1997.

Eribon, Didier, *Michel Foucault*, 2nd edn., Paris: Flammarion, 1991 (*Michel Foucault*, translated by Betsy Wing, Cambridge, MA: Harvard University Press, 1991).

Fabiani, Jean-Louis, *Les philosophes de la république*, Paris: Minuit, 1988.

Farias, Victor, *Heidegger et le nazisme*, Paris: Verdier, 1987 (*Heidegger and Nazism*, translated by P. Burrell and G. Ricci, Philadelphia, PA: Temple University Press, 1989).

Ferry, Luc, *Homo Aestheticus*, Paris: Grasset, 1990 (*Homo Aestheticus*, translated by Robert de Loaiza, Chicago: University of Chicago Press, 1993).

Ferry, Luc and Renaut, Alain, *La pensée 68*, Paris: Gallimard, 1988 (*French Philosophy of the Sixties*, translated by Mary Cattani, Amherst, MA: University of Massachusetts Press, 1990).

ffrench, Patrick, and Lack, Roland-François (eds.), *The Tel Quel Reader*, London: Routledge, 1998.

Flynn, Thomas, *Sartre and Marxist Existentialism*, Chicago: University of Chicago Press, 1984.

Foucault, Michel, *L'archéologie du savoir*, Paris: Gallimard, 1969 (*The Archaeology of Knowledge*, translated by A. Sheridan Smith, New York: Harper and Row, 1972).

Essential Works of Foucault, 1954–1984, 3 vols., edited by Paul Rabinow, New York: The New Press, 1997–9.

Folie et déraison, Paris: Gallimard, 1966 (*Madness and Civilization*, translated by Richard Howard, New York: Pantheon, 1965).

Histoire de la sexualité, 3 vols.: *La volonté de savoir*, *L'usage des plaisirs*, and *Le souici de soi*, Paris: Gallimard, 1976, 1984 (*History of Sexuality*, 3 vols.: *Introduction*, *The Uses of Pleasure*, and *Care of the Self*, translated by Robert Hurley, New York: Vintage Books, 1988–90).

"L'homme est-il mort?" interview in *Arts* 30 (1966).

Language, Counter-Memory, and Practice, edited by Donald Bouchard, Ithaca, NY: Cornell University Press, 1977.

Maladie mentale et personnalité, Paris: Presses Universitaires de France, 1954.

Maladie mentale et psychologie, Paris: Presses Universitaires de France, 1962 (*Mental Illness and Psychology*, translated by Alan Sheridan, New York: Harper and Row, 1976).

"Michel Foucault répond à Sartre", *Quinzaine Littéraire*, March 1, 1968.

Les mots et les choses, Paris: Gallimard, 1966 (*The Order of Things*, New York: Vintage, 1973).

"My Body, this Paper, this Fire", *Oxford Literary Review* 4 (1979), 5–28.

Naissance de la clinique, Paris: Presses Universitaires de France, 1963 (*The Birth of the Clinic*, translated by A. Sheridan Smith, New York: Pantheon, 1973).
Politics, Philosophy, Culture, edited by L. Kritzman, translated by A. Sheridan, et al., London: Routledge, 1988.
Power/Knowledge, edited and translated by Colin Gordon, New York: Pantheon, 1980.
Raymond Roussel, Paris: Gallimard, 1963 (*Death and the Labyrinth: The World of Raymond Roussel*, translated by Charles Ruas, Garden City, NY: Doubleday, 1986).
Surveiller et punir, Paris: Gallimard, 1975 (*Discipline and Punish*, translated by Alan Sheridan, New York: Pantheon, 1977).
Foucault, Michel, and Binswanger, Ludwig, *Dream and Existence*, edited by Keith Hoeller, New Jersey: Humanities Press, 1993.
Frank, Manfred, *What is Neostructuralism?*, translated by S. Walker and R. Gray, Minneapolis: University of Minnesota Press, 1989.
Fry, Christopher, *Sartre and Hegel: The Variation of an Enigma in L'être et le néant*, Bonn: Bouvier, 1988.
Fullbrook, Edward and Kate, *Simone de Beauvoir and Jean-Paul Sartre: The Remaking of a Twentieth-Century Legend*, New York: Harvester Wheatsheaf, 1993.
Galois, Philippe and Forzy, Gérard, *Bergson et les neurosciences*, Institut Synthélabo pour le Progrès de la Connaissance, 1997.
Gilson, Etienne, *La liberté chez Descartes et la théologie*, Paris: Alcan, 1913.
Granger, Gilles-Gaston, *Wittgenstein*, Paris: Seghers, 1968.
Griffiths, A. Phillips (ed.), *Contemporary French Philosophy*, Cambridge: Cambridge University Press, 1987.
Guattari, Félix, *Psychoanalyse et transversalité*, Paris: Maspero, 1972.
Guitton, Jean, *Regards sur la pensée française, 1870–1940*, Paris: Beauchesne, 1968.
Gunn, J. Alexander, *Modern French Philosophy*, London: T. Fisher Unwin, 1922.
Gurvitch, Georges, *Les tendances actuelles de la philosophie allemande*, Paris: Vrin, 1930.
Gutting, Gary, *Michel Foucault's Archaeology of Scientific Reason*, Cambridge: Cambridge University Press, 1989.
Gutting, Gary (ed.), *The Cambridge Companion to Foucault*, Cambridge: Cambridge University Press, 1994.
Hahn, Lewis (ed.), *The Philosophy of Paul Ricoeur* (Library of Living Philosophers, 22), LaSalle, IL: Open Court, 1995.
Hamelin, Octave, *Essai sur les éléments principaux de la représentation*, Paris: Alcan, 1907.
Le système de Renouvier, Paris: Vrin, 1927.
Hardt, Michael, *Gilles Deleuze: An Apprenticeship in Philosophy*, Minneapolis: University of Minnesota Press, 1993.

Hegel, G. W. F., *La phénoménologie de l'esprit*, translated by Jean Hyppolite, Paris: Aubier, 1941.
Henry, Michel, *L'essence de la manifestation*, Paris: Vrin, 1986.
Hering, Jean, *Phénoménologie et philosophie religieuse*, Strasbourg: Alsacienne, 1925.
Höffding, Harald, *A History of Modern Philosophy*, translated by B. E. Meyer, London: Macmillan, 1924.
Holland, Eugene, *Deleuze and Guattari's* Anti-Oedipus: *Introduction to Schizoanalysis*, New York: Routledge, 1999.
Hollier, Denis (ed.), *A New History of French Literature*, Cambridge, MA: Harvard University Press, 1989.
Howells, Christina, *Derrida: Deconstruction from Phenomenology to Ethics*, Cambridge: Polity Press, 1999.
Howells, Christina (ed.), *The Cambridge Companion to Sartre*, Cambridge: Cambridge University Press, 1992.
Husserl, Edmund, *Ideas Pertaining to a Pure Phenomenology and to a Phenomenological Philosophy, First Book*, translated by Frederick Kersten, The Hague: Nijhoff, 1972.
  Méditations cartésiennes, Paris: Vrin, 1947 (*Cartesian Meditations*, translated by Dorion Cairns, The Hague: Nijhoff, 1960).
Hyppolite, Jean, *Figures de la pensée philosophique*, Paris: Presses Universitaires de France, 1971.
  Génèse et structure de la Phénoménologie de l'esprit *de Hegel*, Paris: Aubier, 1946.
Irigaray, Luce, *Ce sexe qui n'en est pas un*, Paris: Minuit, 1977 (*This Sex Which Is Not One*, translated by C. Porter with C. Burke, Ithaca, NY: Cornell University Press, 1985).
  Le corps-à-corps avec la mère, Montreal: Éditions de la Pleine Lune, 1981.
  Éthique de la différence sexuelle, Paris: Minuit, 1984 (*An Ethics of Sexual Difference*, translated by C. Burke and G. Gill, Ithaca, NY: Cornell University Press, 1993).
  Sexes et parentés, Paris: Minuit, 1987 (*Sexes and Genealogies*, translated by Gillian Gill, New York: Columbia University Press, 1993).
  Speculum de l'autre femme, Paris: Minuit, 1977 (*Speculum of the Other Woman*, translated by Gillian Gill, Ithaca, NY: Cornell University Press, 1985).
Janicaud, Dominique, *Une généalogie du spiritualisme français*, The Hague: Nijhoff, 1969.
  La tournant théologique de la phénoménologie française, Combas: L'Éclat, 1991.
Jankélévitch, Vladimir, *Le je-ne-sais-quoi et le presque-rien*, Paris: Seuil, 1980.
  "Léon Brunschvicg", in Vladimir Jankélévitch, *Sources*.
  Sources, Paris: Seuil, 1984 (first published 1969).
  Traité des vertus, Paris: Bordas, 1949. *Henri Bergson*, 3rd edn., Paris: Presses Universitaires de France, 1975.
Judt, Tony, *Past Imperfect: French Intellectuals, 1944–1956*, Berkeley: University of California Press, 1992.

Kaufmann, Walter (ed.), *Existentialism from Dostoevsky to Sartre*, New York: New American Library, 1975.
Kearney, Richard (ed.), *Dialogues with Contemporary Continental Thinkers*, Manchester, UK: Manchester University Press, 1984.
Kitcher, Philip, *Abusing Science: The Case Against Creationism*, Cambridge, MA: MIT Press, 1982.
Kockelmans, J. J., and Kisiel, T. J. (eds.), *Phenomenology and the Natural Sciences*, Evanston, IL: Northwestern University Press, 1970.
Kojève, Alexandre, *Introduction à la lecture de Hegel*, edited by Raymond Queneau, Paris: Gallimard, 1947 (*Introduction to the Reading of Hegel*, translated by James Nichols Jr., New York: Basic Books, 1969).
Kristeva, Julia, *La révolution du langage poétique*, Paris: Seuil, 1974 (*Revolution in Poetic Language*, translated by Margaret Waller, New York: Columbia University Press, 1984).
  Samouraïs, Paris: Fayard, 1990 (*The Samurai*, translated by Barbara Bray, New York: Columbia University Press, 1992).
Lacan, Jacques, *Écrits*, Paris: Seuil, 1966 (*Ecrits: A Selection*, translated by Alan Sheridan, New York: Norton, 1977).
Lacey, A. R., *Bergson*, London: Routledge, 1989.
Lachelier, Jules, *Du fondement de l'induction*, 7th edn., Paris: Alcan, 1916 ("The Foundation of Induction", translated by Edward Ballard, in Jules Lachelier, *The Philosophy of Jules Lachelier*).
  Études sur le syllogisme, Paris: Alcan, 1907.
  Oeuvres, Paris: Alcan, 4th edn., 1902.
  The Philosophy of Jules Lachelier, translated by Edward Ballard, The Hague: Martinus Nijhoff, 1960. (Contains translations of "The Foundation of Induction", "Psychology and Metaphysics", "Notes on Pascal's Wager", and some of Lachelier's comments in Lalande's *Vocabulaire*.)
  "Rapport sur la personnalité", in *Séances et travaux de l'Académie des sciences morales et politiques*, NS, 54 (1900).
Lacoue-Labarthe, Philippe and Nancy, Jean-Luc, *Absolu littéraire*, Paris: Seuil, 1978 (*The Literary Absolute*, translated by P. Barnard and C. Lester, Albany, NY: State University of New York Press, 1988).
  "The Nazi Myth", *Critical Inquiry* 16 (1989–90), 291–312.
Lacroix, Jean, *Maurice Blondel*, Paris: Presses Universitaires de France, 1963.
Ladrière, Jean, *Les limitations internes des formalismes*, Louvain: Nauwelaerts, 1957.
Lalande, A., *Vocabulaire technique et critique de la philosophie*, 15th edn., 1985, Paris: Presses Universitaires de France.
Laruelle, François (ed.), *Textes pour Emmanuel Levinas*, Paris: Jean-Michel Place, 1980.
Le Doeuff, Michèle, *L'étude et le rouet*, Paris: Seuil, 1989 (*Hipparchia's Choice*, translated by Trista Selous, Oxford: Blackwell, 1991).

Recherches sur l'imaginaire philosophique, Paris: Payot, 1980 (*The Philosophical Imaginary*, translated by Colin Gordon, Stanford, CA: Stanford University Press, 1989).
Le sexe du savoir, Paris: Aubier, 1998.
Lefebvre, H. and Gutterman, N. (eds.), *Morceaux choisis d'Hegel*, Paris, 1936.
Leo XIII, *Aeterni Patris*, translated in *The Great Encyclical Letters of Pope Leo XIII*, Rockford, IL: TAN Books, 1995.
Le Roy, Édouard, "Science et philosophie", *Revue de métaphysique et de morale* 7 (1899), 708–31.
"La science positive et la liberté", in *Bibliothèque du Congrès International de Philosophie de 1900*, vol. I, Paris: Colin, 1900.
"Un positivisme nouveau", *Revue de métaphysique et de morale* 9 (1901).
Lévinas, Emmanuel, *Autrement qu'être*, The Hague: Nijhoff, 1974 (*Otherwise than Being*, translated by Alphonso Lingis, The Hague: Nijhoff, 1981).
De Dieu qui vient à l'idée, Paris: Vrin, 1982 (*Of God Who Comes to Mind*, translated by Bettina Bergo, Stanford, CA: Stanford University Press, 1998).
Difficile liberté, Paris: Michel, 1963 (*Difficult Freedom: Essays on Judaism*, translated by Séan Hand, Baltimore: The Johns Hopkins University Press, 1991).
Éthique et infini, dialogues with Philippe Nemo, Paris: Fayard, 1982 (*Ethics and Infinity*, translated by Richard Cohen, Pittsburgh, PA: Duquesne University Press, 1985).
Théorie de l'intuition dans la phénoménologie de Husserl, Paris: Alcan, 1930 (*The Theory of Intuition in Husserl's Phenomenology*, translated by André Orianne, Evanston, IL: Northwestern University Press, 1973).
Totalité et infini, The Hague, Nijhoff, 1961 (*Totality and Infinity*, translated by Alphonso Lingis, Pittsburgh, PA: Duquesne University Press, 1969).
Lévi-Strauss, Claude, *La pensée sauvage*, Paris: Plon, 1962 (*The Savage Mind*, Chicago: University of Chicago Press, 1966).
Lévy, Bernard-Henri, *La barbarisme à visage humain*, Paris: Grasset, 1977 (*Barbarism with a Human Face*, translated by George Holoch, New York: Harper and Row, 1979).
Le siècle de Sartre, Paris: Grasset, 2000.
Lilla, Mark (ed.), *New French Political Philosophy*, Princeton, NJ: Princeton University Press, 1994.
Logue, William, *Charles Renouvier: Philosopher of Liberty*, Baton Rouge: Louisiana State University Press, 1993.
Lyotard, Jean-François, *Chambre sourde*, Paris: Galilée, 1998.
La condition postmoderne, Paris: Minuit, 1979 (*The Postmodern Condition*, translated by G. Bennington and B. Massumi, Minneapolis: University of Minnesota Press, 1984).
La confession d'Augustin, Paris: Galilée, 1998.

Le différend, Paris: Minuit, 1983 (*The Differend*, translated by Georges van den Abbeele, Minneapolis: University of Minnesota Press, 1988).
Discours, figure, Paris: Klincksieck, 1971.
Économie libidinale, Paris: Minuit, 1974 (*Libidinal Economy*, translated by Iain Hamilton Grant, Bloomington, IN: Indiana University Press, 1993).
La phénoménologie, Paris: Presses Universitaires de France, 1954 (*Phenomenology*, translated by Brian Beakley, Albany: State University of New York Press, 1991).
Marcel, Gabriel, *De refus à l'invocation*, Paris: Gallimard, 1940.
Être et avoir, Paris: Aubier, 1935 (*Being and Having*, translated by Katherine Farrer, New York: Harper and Row, 1965).
Homo Viator, Paris: Aubier, 1944 (*Homo Viator*, translated by Emma Crawford, Chicago: Regnery, 1951).
Journal métaphysique, Paris: Gallimard, 1927 (*Metaphysical Journal*, translated by Bernard Wall, Chicago: Regnery, 1952).
Mystère de l'être, Paris: Aubier, 1951 (*The Mystery of Being*, translated by Rene Hague, Chicago: Regnery, 1951).
Marion, Jean-Luc, *Dieu sans l'être*, Paris: Fayard, 1982 (*God Without Being*, translated by Thomas Carlson, Chicago: University of Chicago Press, 1991).
Réduction et donation, Paris: Presses Universitaires de France, 1989 (*Reduction and Givenness*, translated by Thomas Carlson, Evanston, IL: Northwestern University Press, 1998).
Sur l'ontologie grise de Descartes, Paris: Presses Universitaires de France, 1981.
Sur la théologie blanche de Descartes, Paris: Presses Universitaires de France, 1981.
Maritain, Jacques, *Court traité de l'existence et de l'existant*, Paris: Hartmann, 1944 (*Existence and the Existent*, translated by L. Galantiere and G. Phelan, New York: Pantheon, 1948).
Distinguer pour unir, ou, les degrés du savoir, Paris: Brouwer, 1932 (*Distinguish to Unite, or, The Degrees of Knowledge*, translated under the supervision of Gerald Phelan, Notre Dame, IN: University of Notre Dame Press, 1995).
Du régime temporel de la liberté, Paris: Brouwer, 1933 (*Freedom in the Modern World*, translated by Richard O'Sullivan, New York: Gordian, 1971).
L'homme et l'état, translated from the English by R. Davril and F. Davril, Paris: Presses Universitaires de France, 1953 (*Man and the State*, Chicago: University of Chicago Press, 1951).
La philosophie Bergsonienne, Paris: Rivière, 1930 (*Bergsonian Philosophy and Thomism*, translated by Mabelle Andison, New York: Philosophical Library, 1955).
Primauté du spirituel, Paris: Plon, 1927 (*The Things that are not Caesar's*, translated by J. F. Scanlan, London: Sheed and Ward, 1932).

Ransoming the Time, translated by Harry Binnse, New York: Scribner's, 1941.

Sept leçons sur l'être, Paris: Tequi, 1934 (*Preface to Metaphysics: Seven Lessons on Being*, New York: Sheed and Ward, 1948).

Martin, Jean-Clet, *Variations: la philosophie de Gilles Deleuze*, Paris: Payot, 1993.

Mauss, Marcel, *Essai sur le don*, Paris: Alcan, 1925 (*The Gift*, translated by W. D. Halls, New York: Norton, 1990).

McBride, William, "Sartre: les premiers comptes-rendus de *L'être et le néant*", in Ingrid Galster (ed.), *La naissance du phénomène Sartre, 1938–1945 (Actes du Colloque d' Eichstätt)*, Paris: Seuil, 2000.

McCool, Gerald, *The Neo-Thomists*, Milwaukee: Marquette University Press, 1994.

McNeill, John, *The Blondelian Synthesis*, Leiden: Brill, 1966.

Merleau-Ponty, Maurice, *Les aventures de la dialectique*, Paris: Gallimard, 1955 (*Adventures of the Dialectic*, translated by Joseph Bien, Evanston, IL: Northwestern University Press, 1973).

Humanisme et terreur, Paris: Gallimard, 1947 (*Humanism and Terror*, translated by John O'Neill, Boston: Beacon Press, 1969).

L'oeil et l'esprit, Paris: Gallimard, 1964 ("Eye and Mind", translated by Carleton Dallery, in Maurice Merleau-Ponty, *The Primacy of Perception*).

Phénoménologie de la perception, Paris: Gallimard, 1945 (*The Phenomenology of Perception*, translated by Colin Smith, London: Routledge, 1962).

The Primacy of Perception, edited by James Edie, Evanston: Northwestern University Press, 1964.

Sens et non-sens, Paris: Nagel, 1948 (*Sense and Non-Sense*, translated by Hubert and Patricia Dreyfus, Evanston, IL: Northwestern University Press, 1964).

Signes, Paris: Gallimard, 1960 (*Signs*, translated by Richard McCleary, Evanston, IL: Northwestern University Press, 1964).

La structure du comportement, Paris: Presses Universitaires de France, 1942 (*The Structure of Behavior*, translated by Alden Fisher, Boston: Beacon Press, 1963).

Texts and Dialogues, edited by H. Silverman and J. Barry, Jr., translated by Michael Smith, et al., Atlantic Highlands, NJ: Humanities Press, 1992.

Le visible et l'invisible, edited by Claude Lefort, Paris: Gallimard, 1964 (*The Visible and the Invisible*, translated by Alfonso Lingis, Evanston: Northwestern University Press, 1964).

Meyerson, Émile, *La déduction relativiste*, Paris: Payot, 1925 (*The Relativistic Deduction*, translated by David Sipfle and Mary-Alice Sipfle, Dordrecht: Reidel, 1985).

De l'explication dans les sciences, Paris: Payot, 1927 (*Explanation in the Sciences*, Dordrecht: Kluwer, 1991).

Identité et réalité, Paris: Alcan, 1908 (*Identity and Reality*, translated by Kate Loewenberg, New York: Macmillan, 1930).
Moi, Toril, *Simone de Beauvoir: The Making of an Intellectual Woman*, Oxford: Blackwell, 1994.
Montefiore, Alan (ed.), *Philosophy in France Today*, Cambridge: Cambridge University Press, 1983.
Moore, F. C. T., *Bergson: Thinking Backwards*, Cambridge: Cambridge University Press, 1996.
Nabert, Jean, *Eléments pour une éthique*, Paris: Presses Universitaires de France, 1943 (*Elements for an Ethic*, translated by William Petrek, Evanston, IL: Northwestern University Press, 1969).
Essai sur le mal, Paris: Presses Universitaires de France, 1955.
L'expérience intérieure de la liberté, Paris: Presses Universitaires de France, 1924 (reissued in an edition edited by Paul Ricoeur, Paris: Presses Universitaires de France, 1994).
Nancy, Jean-Luc, *Communauté désoeuvrée*, Paris: Bourgeois, 1990 (*The Inoperative Community*, translated by P. Connor, et al., Minneapolis, MN: University of Minnesota Press, 1991).
Expérience de la liberté, Paris: Galilée, 1988 (*The Experience of Freedom*, translated by Bridget McDonald, Stanford, CA: Stanford University Press, 1993).
Nizan, Paul, *Aden Arabie*, with a preface by Jean-Paul Sartre, Paris: Maspero, 1960 (*Aden Arabie*, translated by Joan Pinkham, New York: Monthly Review Press, 1968).
Antoine Bloyé, Paris: Grasset, 1971 (*Antoine Bloye*, translated by Edmund Stevens, New York: Monthly Review Press, 1973).
Les chiens de garde, Paris: Maspero, 1960 (*The Watchdogs*, translated by Paul Fittingoff, New York: Monthly Review Press, 1971).
Ott, Hugo, *Martin Heidegger: éléments pour une biographie*, Paris: Payot, 1990 (*Martin Heidegger: A Political Life*, translated from the original German by Allan Blunden, New York: Basic Books, 1993).
Parodi, Dominique, *La philosophie contemporaine en France*, Paris: Alcan, 1919.
En quête d'une philosophie, Paris: Alcan, 1935.
Peperzak, Adriaan, *To the Other*, West Lafayette, IN: Purdue University Press, 1993.
Poincaré, Henri, *The Foundations of Science*, translated by George Bruce Halstead, New York: The Science Press, 1913.
La science et l'hypothèse, Paris: Flammarion, 1900 (English translation in Henri Poincaré, *The Foundations of Science*).
La valeur de la science, Paris: Flammarion, 1914 (English translation in Henri Poincaré, *The Foundations of Science*).
Poster, Mark, *Existential Marxism in Postwar France*, Princeton: Princeton University Press, 1975.
Proust, Marcel, *À la recherche du temps perdu*, Paris: Gallimard, 1954 *(In Search*

of Lost Time, translated by C. K. Scott Moncrieff, Terence Kilmartin, and Andreas Mayor, revised by D. J. Enright, New York: Modern Library, 1993).

Regan, Charles, *Paul Ricoeur: His Life and Work*, Chicago: University of Chicago Press, 1996.

Renaut, Alain, *L'ère de l'individu*, Paris: Gallimard, 1989 (*The Era of the Individual*, translated by M. B. DeBevoise and F. Philip, Princeton, NJ: Princeton University Press, 1997).

Sartre, le dernier philosophe, Paris: Grasset, 1993.

Le système du droit, Paris: Presses Universitaires de France, 1986.

Renouvier, Charles, *Essais de critique générale*, Paris: Librairie Philosophique de Ladrange, 1854–64.

Rey, Abel, "La philosophie scientifique de M. Duhem", Revue de métaphysique et de morale 12 (1904), 699–744.

Ricoeur, Paul, *À l'école de la phénoménologie*, Paris: Vrin, 1986.

Le conflit des interprétations, Paris: Seuil, 1969 (*The Conflict of Interpretations*, edited by Don Ihde, Evanston, IL: Northwestern University Press, 1974).

De l'interprétation: essai sur Freud, Paris: Le Seuil, 1965 (*Freud and Philosophy: An Essay on Interpretation*, translated by D. Savage, New Haven, CT: Yale University Press, 1970).

Gabriel Marcel et Karl Jaspers: philosophie du mystère et philosophie du paradoxe, Paris: Temps Présent, 1948.

Hermeneutics and the Human Sciences, edited and translated by J. B. Thompson, Cambridge: Cambridge University Press, 1981.

Interpretation Theory, Fort Worth, TX: Texas Christian University Press, 1976.

La métaphore vive, Paris: Seuil, 1975 (*The Rule of Metaphor*, translated by R. Czerny with K. McLaughlin and J. Costello, Toronto: University of Toronto Press, 1977).

Philosophie de la volonté, 3 vols.: *L'homme faillible*, *La symbolique du mal*, and *Le volontaire et l'involontaire*, Paris: Aubier, 1960–3 (*Freedom and Nature: The Voluntary and the Involuntary*, translated by E. V. Kohák, Evanston, IL: Northwestern University Press, 1966; *Fallible Man*, translated by C. A. Kelbley, Chicago: Regnery, 1965; *The Symbolism of Evil*, translated by E. Buchanan, New York: Harper and Row, 1967).

Soi-même comme une autre, Paris: Seuil, 1990 (*Oneself as Another*, translated by Kathleen Blamey, Chicago: University of Chicago Press, 1992).

Temps et récit, 3 vols., Paris: Seuil, 1983–5 (*Time and Narrative*, 3 vols., translated by K. McLaughlin and D. Pellauer, Chicago: University of Chicago Press, 1984–8).

Ringer, Fritz, *Fields of Knowledge: French Academic Culture in Comparative Perspective, 1890–1920*, Cambridge: Cambridge University Press, 1992.

Roth, Michael, *Knowing and History: The Resurgence of French Hegelianism from the 1930's through the Post-War Period*, Ithaca, NY: Cornell University Press, 1988.

Rousseau, Jean-Jacques, *Confessions*, London: Dent, 1960.
Santayana, George, *Egotism and German Philosophy*, London: J. M. Dent, 1916 (reissued: New York: Scribner, 1940).
Sartre, Jean-Paul, *L'âge de raison*, Paris: Gallimard, 1945 (*The Age of Reason*, translated by Eric Sutton, Harmondsworth: Penguin, 1961).
  Cahiers pour une morale, Paris: Gallimard, 1983 (*Notebook for an Ethics*, translated by David Pellauer, Chicago: University of Chicago Press, 1992).
  Critique de la raison dialectique, vol. I, Paris: Gallimard, 1960 (*Critique of Dialectical Reason*, vol. I, translated by Alan Sheridan-Smith, London: New Left Books, 1976).
  Critique de la raison dialectique, vol. II, Paris: Gallimard, 1985 (*Critique of Dialectical Reason*, vol. II, translated by Quinton Hoare, London: Verso, 1991).
  L'espoir maintenant (interviews with Benny Lévy), Lagasse: Verdier, 1991 (*Hope Now*, translated by Adrian van den Hoven, Chicago: University of Chicago Press, 1996).
  L'être et le néant, Paris: Gallimard, 1943 (*Being and Nothingness*, translated by Hazel Barnes, New York: Washington Square Press, 1956).
  L'existentialisme est un humanisme, Paris: Nagel, 1947 ("Existentialism Is a Humanism", translated by P. Mairet, in Walter Kaufmann (ed.), *Existentialism from Dostoevsky to Sartre*).
  Huis-clos, Paris: Gallimard, 1947 (*No Exit*, translated by Stuart Gilbert, New York: Knopf, 1948).
  "Une idée fondamentale de la phénoménologie de Husserl: l'intentionalité", in *Nouvelle revue française* 52 (1939), 129–32; reprinted in *Situations I*, 31–5 ("Intentionality: A Fundamental Idea of Husserl's Phenomenology", translated by Joseph Fell, *Journal of the British Society for Phenomenology* 1 (1970), 4–5).
  L'idiot de la famille, Paris: Gallimard, 1971 (*The Family Idiot*, translated by Carol Cosman, Chicago: University of Chicago Press, 1981).
  L'imaginaire, Paris: Gallimard, 1940 (*The Psychology of Imagination*, translated by Bernard Frechtman, New York: Philosophical Library, 1948).
  L'imagination, Paris: Alcan, 1936 (*Imagination*, translated by Forrest Williams, Ann Arbor, MI: University of Michigan Press, 1962).
  "Jean-Paul Sartre répond", *L'Arc* 30 (1966), 87–96.
  Mallarmé, Paris: Gallimard, 1986 (*Mallarmé, or, The Poet of Nothingness*, translated by Ernest Sturm, University Park, PA: Pennsylvania State University Press, 1988).
  La mort dans l'âme, Paris: Gallimard, 1949 (*Troubled Sleep*, translated by Gerald Hopkins, New York: Knopf, 1951).
  Les mots, Paris: Gallimard, 1964 (*The Words*, translated by Bernard Frechtman, New York: Braziller, 1964).
  Les mouches, Paris: Bordas, 1974 (*The Flies*, translated by Stuart Gilbert, New York: Knopf, 1948).

La nausée, Paris: Gallimard, 1938 (*Nausea*, translated by Lloyd Alexander, New York: New Directions, 1964).
Qu'est-ce que la littérature?, Paris: Gallimard, 1948 (*What is Literature?*, translated by Bernard Frechtman, New York: Philosophical Library, 1949).
"Question de méthode", in *Critique de la raison dialectique* (*The Problem of Method*, translated by Hazel Barnes, London: Methuen, 1963; also published as *The Search for a Method*, New York: Knopf, 1963).
Saint Genet, Paris: Gallimard, 1952 (*Saint Genet*, translated by Bernard Frechtman, New York: Braziller, 1963).
Sartre par lui-même, transcript of a documentary film directed by Alexandre Astruc and Michel Contat, Paris: Gallimard, 1977 (*Sartre by Himself*, translated by Richard Seaver, New York: Urizen Books, 1980).
Situations (10 vols.), Paris: Gallimard, 1947–72 (volume IV: *Situations*, translated by Benita Eisler, New York: Braziller, 1965; volumes VIII and IX: *Between Existentialism and Marxism*, translated by John Mathews, New York: Morrow, 1974).
Le sursis, Paris: Gallimard, 1945 (*The Reprieve*, translated by Eric Sutton, New York: Knopf, 1947).
La transcendence de l'égo, Paris: Vrin, 1966 (*Transcendence of the Ego*, translated by F. Williams and R. Kirkpatrick, New York: Noonday, 1957).
Saussure, Ferdinand de, *Cours de linguistique général*, Paris: Payot, 1980 (*Course in General Linguistics*, translated by Wade Baskin, New York: Philosophical Library, 1959).
Scheler, Max, *Wesen und Formen der Sympathie*, Bonn: Cohen, 1923 (*The Nature of Sympathy*, New Haven: Yale University Press, 1954).
Schilpp, Paul (ed.), *The Philosophy of Jean-Paul Sartre* (Library of Living Philosophers 16), LaSalle, IL: Open Court, 1981.
Schyns, Mathieu, *La philosophie d'Émile Boutroux*, Paris: Fischbacher, 1924.
Serres, Michel, *Le contrat naturel*, Paris: Bourin, 1990 (*The Natural Contract*, translated by E. MacArthur and W. Paulson, Ann Arbor, MI: University of Michigan Press, 1995).
Hermès, 5 vols., Paris: Editions Minuit, 1968–80 (*Hermes*, edited by J. Harari and D. Bell, Baltimore: Johns Hopkins, 1982).
La légende des anges, Paris: Flammarion, 1993.
Le tiers-instruit, Paris: Bourin, 1991.
Serres, Michel and Bruno Latour, *Conversations on Science, Culture, and Time*, translated by Roxanne Lapidus, Ann Arbor, MI: University of Michigan Press, 1995.
Simons, Margaret, *Beauvoir and the Second Sex: Feminism, Race, and the Origins of Existentialism*, New York: Rowman & Littlefield, 1999.
Spiegelberg, Herbert, *The Phenomenological Movement*, 2nd edn., 2 vols., The Hague: Nijhoff, 1965.

Steward, Jon (ed.), *The Debate Between Sartre and Merleau-Ponty*, Evanston, IL: Northwestern University Press, 1998.
Teilhard de Chardin, Pierre, *L'apparition de l'homme*, Paris: Seuil, 1956 (*The Phenomenon of Man*, London: Collins, 1959).
Thibaudet, Albert, *La république des professeurs*, Paris: Grasset, 1927.
Vadée, Michel, *Gaston Bachelard*, Paris: Éditions Sociales, 1975.
Van Breda, H.L., "Merleau-Ponty and the Husserl Archives at Louvain", translated by Stephen Michelman, in Maurice Merleau-Ponty, *Texts and Dialogues*.
Virgoulay, René, *"L'action" de Maurice Blondel*, Paris: Beauchesne, 1992.
Vuillemin, Jules, *Nécessité ou contingence*, Paris: Minuit, 1984.
Wahl, Jean, *Études kierkegaardiennes*, Paris: Aubier, 1938.
   Le malheur de la conscience de Hegel, 2nd edn., Paris: Presses Universitaires de France, 1951 (first published in 1929).
   Vers le concret, Paris: Vrin, 1932.
Weber, Louis, *Vers le positivisme absolu par l'idéalisme*, Paris: Alcan, 1903.
Weil, Simone, *L'enracinement*, Paris: Gallimard, 1949 (*The Need for Roots*, translated by Arthur Wills, NY: Putnam, 1952).
Whitford, Margaret, *Luce Irigaray: Philosophy in the Feminine*, London: Routledge, 1991.
Wilcocks, Robert (ed.), *Critical Essays on Jean-Paul Sartre*, Boston: G. K. Hall, 1988.
Worms, Frédéric, *Introduction à* Matière et mémoire *de Bergson*, Paris: Presses Universitaires de France, 1997.

Index

action, 89–93, 370
adversity, coefficent of, 149, 375
aesthetic experience, Bergson on, 72; Lacoue-Labarthe on, 376; Lyotard on, 319; Maritain on, 96
agrégation, 5, 82, 113, 158, 236, 382, 392
Alain (Émile Chartier), 6, 43 n18
Alexander, M., 22
Alquié, F., 122 n5
Althusser, L., 40, 85, 88 n8, 113, 230, 235–8, 250, 259, 381, 388
Amiel, H.-F., 98 n23
anguish, 107, 115; Sartre on, 140–1
Annales school, 260
anthropology, 152; Lévi-Strauss's, 221–7, 250; Merleau-Ponty on, 209–11
Aquinas, T., 91, 94, 95, 97
archaeology of knowledge, 264, 268, 285–8
Aristotle, 12, 37, 36, 42, 52, 53, 81, 166, 247, 294, 295, 304, 335, 346, 355, 370
Aron, R., 43 n18, 107–8, 119 n46, 374
Aronson, R., 128
Augustine, 94; and Blondel, 91 n14
Austrian philosophy, 378

baccalauréat, 4, 391
Bachelard, G., 9, 39, 40 n17, 84, 85–9, 149, 233, 236, 260–1, 379, 381; and Canguilhem, 228-32
Bachelard, S., 28
Bacon, F. (painter), 339
Bacon, F. (philosopher), 278, 379
bad faith, 140–4
Balibar, E., 236
Balzac, H., 247–9
Barthes, R., 222 n3, 244-9, 253, 290, 342, 393
Bataille, G., 103, 110, 122, 252–3, 254–5
Baudelaire, C., 90, 127
Beaufret, J., 252, 255
Beauvoir, S. de, 105, 107, 121, 124, 158–80, 379; and Irigaray, 352 n31; and Merleau-Ponty, 206; and Sartre, 158-60, 161 n10, 163; works: autobiography, 162-3; novels, 160–1; *Philosophy of Ambiguity*, 160; *The Second Sex*, 163–80
Beckett, S., 260
being, Boutroux on, 22; Deleuze on, 332–6; Derrida on, 256; Foucault on, 257; Heidegger on, 109, 256–7, 356, 376, 377; Levinas on, 356; Maritain on, 95–6; Marcel on, 101–2; Merleau-Ponty on, 207–8, 209; Marion, on, 377; Nancy on, 376; Sartre on, 130–3
being-for-itself, 133, 136–7, 252, 330
being-for-others, 144–7
being-in-itself, 133, 136–7
being-in-the-world, 137, 190–2, 355, 387
Bennington, G., 313 n27, 320
Benrubi, I., 9 n15
Benveniste, E., 368
Berdyaev, N., 105
Bergson, H., 6, 9, 12, 20, 27, 33, 49–83, 84, 91, 94–5, 138, 228, 380, 381, 384, 386, 390, 393; and existential philosophy, 113–17; Deleuze on, 333, 335; Marcel and, 115 n58; Merleau-Ponty on, 113–7; Sartre on, 114–15; works: *Creative Evolution*, 51–6, 66–74; *Matter and Memory*, 60–6; *Time and Free Will*, 56–60; *Two Sources of Religion and Morality*, 75–82
binary division, Derrida on, 293–4
Binswanger, L., 256
Blanchot, M., 252–3, 254–5, 260, 317, 354
Blondel, M., 14, 20, 84, 89–93, 94, 97, 98, 102, 384
body, Beauvoir on, 170; Foucault on, 273, 280; Marcel on, 99–100; Merleau-Ponty on, 190–2, 195–6, 200; Sartre on, 142; *see also* mind–body problem
Bolzano, B., 378
books, Derrida on, 295–6
Bourdieu, P., 7, 9 n15, 382

Index

Boutroux, E., 6, 9, 20–5, 26, 29, 84, 85, 89, 383
Bouveresse, J., 236 n19, 377–8
Bradley, F. H., 104 n28
Braudel, F., 260
Brentano, F., 378
Breton, A., 102, 103, 110
Bruns, G., 252 n34
Brunschvicg, L., 6, 7, 9, 40–8, 84, 381; and Bachelard, 86–8; and Bergson, 73–4; and Merleau-Ponty, 104–5, 114, 186; and Nizan, 104; and Sartre, 108
Buber, M., 101, 360
Butor, M., 260

Calvez, J., 235
Camus, A., 126, 183, 374
Canguilhem, G., 37, 39 n16, 85, 228–32, 260–1, 381
Čapek, M., 67 n14
capitalism, Deleuze and Guattari on, 339–41
Caputo, J., 313 n27, 316 n29
Carnap, R., 378 n61
Castoriadis, C., 320 n2
Catholicism, Althusser and, 237 n21; Beauvoir and, 158; Bergson and, 82, 114; Blondel and, 84, 93; Boutroux and, 89; Duhem and, 37; Lachelier and, 20; Le Roy and, 37 n12; Marcel and, 102; Marion and, 377; Maritain and, 84, Merleau-Ponty and, 102 n24, 114, 181–2; Renouvier and, 14; spiritualism and, 12, 14; *see also* Maritain, neo-Thomism
causality, 58–9; and Derrida's difference, 299; efficient, 15–20; final, 15–20
Cavaillès, J., 228, 378
Caws, P., 155 n41
Centre de Recherche en Epistémologie Appliquée (CREA), 378
Centre Nationale de la Recherche Scientifique (CNRS), 393
Certificat d'aptitude au professorat de l'enseignement du second degré (CAPES), 392
Char, R., 255
Chartier, E., *see* Alain
Chisholm, R., 59
Chomsky, N., 216
classe de philosophie, 3-4, 382
Classical Age, Foucault on, 265–6, 270–1, 279
Cohan-Solal, A., 159 n1
Collège de France, 382–3, 393
Collège de Philosophie, 290 n3, 354
Collège de Sociologie, 103

Collège International de Philosophie, 289–90, n2, 393
Collins, J., 128 n18
communism, Althusser and, 235, 238; Foucault and, 259; Merleau-Ponty and, 183-4, 206–7; "new philosophers" and, 371–2; Sartre and, 125–6, 183–4, 206–7; *see also* Marxism
community, 76, 79, 101, 167–8, 308–9, 375, 376
Comte, A., 8, 11, 27, 45
concept, Deleuze on the, 336–7; philosophy of the, 227–34
concrete, the, 50, 102–17, 252, 259
Condillac, E., 10
consciousness, 47, 58–9, 68, 71, 74, 92, 108, 111, 129, 133–7, 152, 166, 194–5; and freedom, 147; and negation, 139–40; planes of, 65; *see also* being-for-itself, being-for-others, freedom, idealism
couple, the, 179–80, 352
Courtine, J.-F., 376
Courturat, L., 377
Cousin, V., 4, 10
creative evolution, 66–74
Culler, J., 215 n1, 244 n26, 304 n17
Curtius, E., 5, 6

Darlu, A., 6
Dasein, 256, 356, 372, 377
Davidson, D., 370
Davis, C., 361 n17
De Waehlens, A., 122 n5
deconstruction, 291–7, 374
Defert, D., 285 n21
Delacour, J., 64 n9
Deleuze, G., 113, 234, 250, 255, 331–41, 388, 389; and Guattari, 339–41
democracy, 97, 334, 373
Derrida, J., 113, 123 n7, 250, 289–317, 354 n2, 388, 393; and Bataille, 252-3; and Blanchot, 252-3; and Foucault, 289–90, 308; and Heidegger, 254, 256; and Husserl, 289, 291, 296, 297 n10, 301–2; and Irigaray, 350–1; and Levinas, 354 n2; and Ricoeur, 369 n36; and Sartre, 129 n19, 389; and Saussure, 293, 300–1, 302, 303; and skepticism, 304–8; works: "La différance", 291, 299–301; *The Gift of Death*, 313–7; *Glas*, 254, 291, 297 n10; *Limited Inc.*, 305–7; *Of Grammatology*, 303, 307; *Speech and Phenomena*, 291, 301
Descartes, R., 9, 11, 54, 186, 233, 252, 355, 377
Descombes, V., 209, 232–3, 363 n21

desiring-machines, 341
determinism, 21–5, 58, 92, 147–8, 383; *see also* causality
Dews, P., 236 n20, 320 n4
différance, Derrida on, 298–302
difference, Deleuze on, 334–36; sexual, in Irigaray, 341–2
differend, 321–31
Diplôme d'Études Approfondies (DEA), 391
Diplôme d'Études Universitaires Générales (DEUG), 391
discipline, Foucault on, 278–82
discourse vs. figure, 319–20
doctorat d'état, 391
doctorat d'université, 391
Dosse, F., 210 n19, 364 n27, n29
Dreyfus affair, 7–8
Dreyfus, H., 256–7
Dufrenne, Mikel, 364
Duhem, E., 9, 27, 33-8,
Dumézil, G., 261 n9, 393
Dupont, C., 105 n32
duration, 51, 53, 55–6, 64, 73–4
Durkheim, E., 9, 20, 78, 210, 382

École Normale Supérieure, 8, 105 n31, 181 n1, 236 n18, 382, 392
École Pratiques des Hautes Études, 393
educational system, French, 3–5, 382–3, 391–3
élan vital (vital impetus), 66, 68, 70, 75, 80, 115 n58
emotions, moral and religious, 76; Sartre on, 129–30
Engel, P., 378
enjoyment, 357, 359
epistemological break, 86–7, 229–30, 236
Esprit, *see* Mounier, E.
essence, Beauvoir on, 165, 177; Maritain on, 95; Merleau-Ponty on, 186, 187–8, 199–200; Nancy on, 374–5; Sartre on, 131–2, 142; *see also* existence
ethics, Bergson on, 75–8; Brunschvicg on, 47; Derrida on, 308-13; Ferry and Renaut on, 373; Foucault on, 286–8; Irigaray on, 347–8; Lyotard on, 327–9; Levinas on, 356, 357–8, 361–2; Ricoeur on, 370; Sartre on, 124–5
ethnology, *see* anthropology
event, Deleuze on, 338
evil, Ricoeur on, 365–6
evolution, Bergson on, 68-70, 78, 81; *see also* creative evolution
Ewald, F., 285 n21
existence, Beauvoir on, 165, 177; Marcel on,

101; Maritain on, 95; Nancy on, 374–5; Sartre on, 133, 142; *see also* essence
existence, philosophy of, 114–5, 117, 181, 235, 284, 286, 386; *see also* existentialism
existentialism, 98, 102–3, 113, 122, 124, 386–7, 389; and Marxism, 126, 151-2, 155, 235, 238; Beauvoir and, 160, 161-3, 164, 165, 169–70, 177; Foucault and, 260; Heidegger and, 252, 255–6; Marcel and, 386–7; Nancy and, 374–5; *see also* existence, philosophy of
experience, 385–6
exteriority, 355; *see also* interiority

Fabiani, J.-L., 4 n5, 5 n7, 90 n12
face, 357-8
facts, *see* scientific facts
Farias, V., 376
feminism, and Levinas, 363 n21; Beauvoir on, 175–80, Derrida and Irigaray on, 351–2; *see also* Beauvoir, Irigaray, Le Doeuff
Ferry, L., 354 n1, 372–4, 379, 388
Fichte, J., 43, 373 n46
figure, *see* discourse
Flaubert, G., 126, 127
fluids, Irigaray on, 347
Flynn, T., 152 n39
Foucault, M., 39, 85, 113, 123 n7, 227–8, 230, 232, 234, 250, 258–88, 381, 389; and Bataille, 252–3; and Bachelard and Canguilhem, 260–1; and Blanchot, 252–3; and Deleuze, 339; and Heidegger, 256–7, 273; and Marxism, 259; and phenomenology, 259–60; and Sartre, 260, 261, 358–60; works: *Discipline and Punish*, 278–82; *History of Madness*, 264–7; *History of Sexuality*, 282–8; *The Order of Things*, 267–78
foundationalism, 39, 294–5, 370–1, 380, 385
France, A., 5
Frank, M., 339
fraternity, 180
freedom, 11, 13, 380–90; and poststructuralism, 388–9; Beauvoir on, 387; Bergson on, 56–60, 384; Boutroux on, 21–5; Brunschvicg on, 47; Ferry and Renaut on, 373; Lachelier on, 19–20; Levinas on, 359–60; Merleau-Ponty on, 203–8, 387–8; Nancy on, 374–5; Sartre on, 147–51, 359–60, 387–8
Freud, S., 174, 186, 238–44, 339–41, 365; Sartre on, 141 n30, 149; *see also* psychoanalysis
Fry, C., 113 n52
Fullbrook, E. and K., 161 n10
fundamental project, 148–9

Index

Gadamer, H.-G., 367 n33
Garaudy, R., 235
Garrigou-Lagrange, R., 94, 96
genealogy, 278, 285-6, 288
Genet, J., 125, 127
German philosophy, 5-6, 21, 380-1, 382
Gewirth, A., 77 n27
Gide, A., 6
gift, Derrida on, 310, 313; Marion on, 377; Mauss on, 210-11
Gilson, E., 94, 96, 97
Glucksmann, A., 371-2
God, Bergson on, 79, 81-2; Blondel on, 90, 91, 92-3; Brunschvicg on, 48; Derrida on, 313-17; Irigaray on, 349-50; Levinas on, 360-1; Marcel on, 100-1, 102; Marion on, 377; Maritain on, 95, 96, 97; Renouvier on, 13-14; spiritualism and, 11, 14; *see also* religion
Goldman, L., 235 n17
Goodman, N., 338 n61
grammatology, 293
grandes écoles, 392, 393
Granger, G.-G., 377, 378 n61
Guattari, F., 339-41
Guitton, J., 6 n9
Gunn, J. Alexander, 14 n25
Gurvitch, G., 106
Gurwitsch, A., 105 n32

habit, 12, 75
Hamelin, O., 14, 15 n27
Hardt, M., 334 n15
Hegel, G., 109-13, 115, 236, 254, 335, 355, 380-1
Heidegger, M., 102 n24, 106, 107, 108, 115, 140, 252, 350, 353-4, 372-3, 380-1; and Derrida, 254, 256; and Foucault, 256-7, 273; French translations of, 36; and Nazism, 256, 376; and poststructuralism, 255-7; and Sartre, 129-31
Henry, M., 376
Herbrand, J., 378
Hering, J., 105
hermeneutics, Ricoeur on, 366-9, 371
Hocking, W. E., 115 n58
Höffding, H., 8 n13
Holland, A., 339 n23
Hollier, D., 107, n37
homosexuality, 283, 287, 348
hospitality, Derrida on, 309
Howells, C., 254 n44, 389 n1
Hume, D., 10, 385
humor, Bergson on, 72
Husserl, E., 102 n24, 115, 228, 380-1; and Foucault, 27; and Levinas, 353-4; and Merleau-Ponty, 182, 184, 186-8; and Nazism, 376; and Sartre, 129-31, 132-3; early influence in France, 105, 106, 107-8; recent French interest in, 376-7; *see also* phenomenology
hypokhâgne, 392
hypotheses, scientific, 28-30
Hyppolite, J., 89 n11, 110 n48, 113, 115 n 57, 258

idealism, and Bachelard, 87-8; and Brunschvicg, 40, 42-3; and Lachelier, 20; and Marcel, 98; and spiritualism, 14-15; Bergson on, 61-2; German, 5-6, 109-13, 380; Merleau-Ponty on, 196, 197-203; 380; *see also* Boutroux, Brunschvicg, Hegel, Lachelier
Idéologues, 10
imagination, 88-9, 129-30
immanence, 171-2, 178; *see also* transcendence
indeterminism, 21-5; *see also* causality
induction, 15-20
infinity, 355
intellectual, specific vs. universal, 263
intelligence, 71-4
intentionality, 108, 134-5
interiority, 356-7, 358; *see also* exteriority
intuition, 71-4, 95, 100
Irigaray, L., 179, 341-52, 388

Jakobson, R., 222
James, W., 14
Janet, P., 9, 50
Janicaud, D., 50 n2, 377 n58
Jankélévitch, V., 74 n26, 82-3
Jaspers, K., 102 n24, 363
Jaurès, J., 50
Joan of Arc, 173
judgment, 41-3, 46-7; regulative vs. determinate, 329
Judt, T., 126 n14
justice, 311-13, 320-1

Kant, I., 29, 252, 329, 390; Bergson and, 54-6; Boutroux and, 21; Brunschvicg and, 45, 46, 74, 77; Deleuze and, 329, 337-8; Ferry and Renaut and, 372-3; Foucault and, 261-2, 270, 272-3; Lachelier and, 15-18; Merleau-Ponty and, 116, 186; Renouvier and, 13; Sartre and, 132
Kearney, R., 361
khâgne, 392
Kierkegaard, S., 90, 109 n44, 140, 360; and Derrida, 313-16

Kitcher, P., 69 n17
Kleutgen, J., 94
knowledge/power, 278–9, 284
Kojève, A., 103, 110–13, 235
Kosakievicz, O., 161
Koyré, A., 110
Kristeva, J., 243–4, 253, 254 n40
Kuhn, T., 39 n16, 86, 232

La Fontaine, J. de, 233
Lacan, J., 110, 238–43, 250, 275, 344, 346; and Lyotard, 318–19; and Ricoeur, 260 365
Lacey, A. R., 59 n4, 67 n14
Lachelier, J., 14–20, 25, 26, 27, 74, 89, 91, 383; and Ricoeur, 368 n33; on Hegel, 109
Lacoix, J., 92 n15
Lacoue-Labarthe, P., 376, 388, 393
Ladrière, J., 200 n13, 228
Lagneau, J., 368 n33
Lalande, A., 7
language, and phenomenology, 226; Derrida and, 252, 292, 300–2; Foucault and, 252–3, 257, 260, 268–71, 277; Lyotard on, 318–9, 326–7; Merleau-Ponty on; 192–5, 202–3; Ricoeur on, 368–70; the unconscious as (Lacan), 240–4; *see also* linguistics, phrases, Saussure
Latour, B., 9 n15
Lavelle, L., 84
law, Derrida on, 311–12; scientific, Boutroux on, 22–4; Duhem on, 34–5; Poincaré on, 28–30;
Le Dantec, F., 9 n14
Le Doeuff, M., 143 n31, 379
Le Roy, E., 3–32, 37 n12, 89
Le Saulchoir, 94
Lefebvre, H., 113 n52, 235
Lefort, C., 184 n7, 320 n2
Leibniz, G., 54, 233
LeSenne, R., 84
Levinas, E., 106, 107, 353–63, 390; and Descartes, 355; and feminism, 363 n21; and Heidegger, 353, 354, 355–6, 357; and Husserl, 353, 354; and Judaism, 354, 361; and Marxism, 354
Lévi-Strauss, C., 123 n7, 209, 210, 211, 221–7, 250, 368, 382, 393; and Merleau-Ponty, 208–10, 224–5, 387–8; and Sartre, 225–7, 387–8
Lévy, Benny, 128 n18
Lévy, Bernard-Henri, 371–2, 374 n48
Lévy-Bruhl, 78
Liberatore, M., 94
licence, 234 n15, 391
Lilla, M., 373 n47

linguistics, 215–21
literature, Sartre and, 121, 123–4; Beauvoir on, 161–2; Derrida on, 296–7; and philosophy, 102–3, 252–4, 296–7, 381
Locke, J., 10
logocentrism, 294, 369, 374
Logue, C., 13 n23
Lucretius, 233
Lukács, G., 235 n17
lycée, 4, 391
Lyotard, J.-F., 318–31, 388, 389, 393

Mach, E., 27
Macherey, P., 236
madness, Foucault on, 264–7
Main de Biran, F., 4 n4, 10, 84, 91
maître de conférences, 391
maîtrise, 391
Mallarmé, S., 127 n16
Malraux, A., 6
Marcel, G., 98-102, 105, 115, 123 n7, 354, 360, 363, 384; and Bergson, 115 n58; and Brunschvicg, 104, n28; and Merleau-Ponty, 102 n24; on Sartre, 122 n5
Marion, J.-L., 376–7
Maritain, J., 84, 94–8, 384
Marx, K., 110–13, 152, 186, 235–8; *see also* Marxism
Marxism, 151–7, 250, 339–41, 354, 372, 388; *see also* communism, Marx
materialism, 61–2, 91–2
Maurras, C., 97
Mauss, M., 210–11
May 1968, 238, 253, 320, 371, 372
McBride, W., 122 n5
McCool, G., 94 n17
McNeill, J., 91 n14
Mehl, R., 364 n27
Meinong, A., 378
memory, 61, 63–6
Mercier, D., 94
Merleau-Ponty, M., 3, 102 n24, 104-5, 109, 110, 121, 181–212, 251, 258, 355, 384–5, 387–8, 393; and Beauvoir, 161 n10; and Bergson, 113–17, 384; and Lévi-Strauss, 208–10, 224–5, 387–8; and Lyotard, 325 n7; and Marcel, 102 n24; and Sartre, 123, 126, 181–4, 195, 196, 197, 203–8, 384–5; Foucault on, 273–4; works: *Phenomenology of Perception*, 185, 186–208; *The Structure of Behavior* 184–5; *The Visible and the Invisible*, 185, 207–8, 209–10
metaphor, 242, 297, 369
Meyerson, E., 37–8, 84, 85, 108
Mill, J., 16

Index

mimesis, 276
mind–body problem, 60–6
Moi, T., 143, n31, 163
Moore, F. T. C., 71 n19
morality, *see* ethics
Mounier, E., 102 n24, 181, 363
multiplicity, Deleuze on, 332–4
Musil, R., 378
mysteries, 100
mythologies, 244–7

Nabert, J., 368 n33
Nancy, J.-L., 374–6, 388, 389
narrative, 369–70
nausea, 107, 137
negation, 138–40, 147
neo-Thomism, 94–6, 102, 384
new philosophers (*nouveaux philosophes*), 371–2
Nicod, J., 378
Nietzsche, F., 186, 234, 253 n39, 254–5, 386; Deleuze on, 333
Nizan, P., 103–4, 106, 107, 123
Nobel Prize, 51, 381
norms, Canguilhem on, 231–2; Foucault on, 266, 280–1; Lacan on, 239; Lyotard on, 328; *see also* ethics
nothing, 68 n15, 91; *see also* negation, nothingness
nothingness, 138–9

objectivity, scientific, 30–3
Ollé-Laprune, L., 91
ontology, *see* being
order, Foucault on, 267–78
other, the, 144–7, 165–8, 195–7, 355–9
Ott, H., 376

Parodi, D., 3, 9, 11, 43, 84–5
Pascal, B., 40, 89
Péguy, C., 50
Peperzak, A., 356 n4, 359 n9, 362 n19
perception, 61–3
Pfeiffer, G., 106
phenomenology, 129–31, 186–90, 228, 376–7; and ontology, 121–3, 150–1, 206–8; and Ricoeur, 365–6, 370–1; and structuralism, 208–12, 224–7, 251; Foucault on, 273–4, 276; *see also* Heidegger, Husserl
philosophy, analytic, 7, 27, 321, 370, 378–9, 382, 383, 390; Derrida on, 293–4, 295–7; in French education, 3–5, 382–3, 391–3; poststructuralist critique of, 390
phrases, Lyotard on, 322–8
Piaget, J., 50
Pius X, 37

Pius XI, 97
Plato, 293, 346–7, 355
Poincaré, H., 6, 9, 26, 27–33, 85
politics, 329–31, 375; *see also* political theory
political theory, 373–4; *see also* politics
positivism, 8-9, 10–11, 251; Boutroux and, 25; Brunschvicg and, 43, 45; French philosophy of science and, 26, 39–40
Poster, M., 235 n16
poststructuralism, 249–57, 372–4, 377, 388–90
power/knowledge, 278–9, 284
problems, 100
Protagoras, 322
Proust, M., 6, 50, 108, 131, 339
psychoanalysis, 342–4; *see also* Freud, Kristeva, Lacan

Queneau, R., 107, 110
Quine, W., 50 n1, 302 n14

Rabinow, P., 257
Ravaisson, F., 10–12, 13, 14, 15, 25, 27, 84, 91, 383
Rawls, J., 379
realism, 62, 87–8, 132–3, 197–8
reduction, phenomenological, 187, 273, 376–7; eidetic, 187–8
reflection, primary vs. secondary (Marcel), 99–101
Reid, T., 385
relativity theory, 30 n2, 38 n14, 53 n3; Bergson on, 67 n14
religion, 12, 20, 37, 47–8, 89, 93, 377; Bergson on, 78–82; Derrida on, 313–17; Irigaray on, 349–50; Levinas on, 360–1; Ricoeur on, 364–5; Sartre on, 128 n18; *see also* God
Renaissance, Foucault on, 265, 269–70
Renan, E., 9, 90
Renaut, A., 354 n1, 379, 388
Renouvier, C., 12–14, 383
repetition, Deleuze on, 336
representation, Bergson on, 61–4; Deleuze on, 331, 336–8, 341; Derrida on, 256; Duhem on, 33–4; Foucault on, 270–2, 275; Irigaray on, 347, 350, 351; Lévi-Strauss on, 222; Saussure on, 217–18
resemblance, Foucault on, 269–70; Irigaray on, 347
Revue de métaphysique et de morale, 7
Rey, A., 37
Richir, M., 364 n29
Ricoeur, P., 102 n24, 106, 234, 363–71; and Husserl, 364, 365–6, 371; and Jaspers, 363; and Levinas, 370; and Marcel, 363; and

Ricoeur, P. (cont.)
  Merleau-Ponty, 364; and Sartre, 364, 365; on hermeneutics, 366–9; on psychoanalysis, 367
Rimbaud, A., 241
Robbe-Grillet, A., 260
Rorty, R., 308
Roth, M.,110 n45–7
Rousseau, J.-J., 293, 298, 302, 303
Roussel, R., 260
Royce, J., 104 n28
Russell, B., 136 n27
Ryle, G., 188 n12

same, the, 354–5
Santayana, G., 21 n32
Sartre, J.-P., 33, 43 n18, 47, 59–60, 92, 98, 105, 106, 107–8, 109, 110 n46, 121–57, 251, 374 n48, 379, 381, 384–5, 387–8, 390; and Bergson, 114–15; and Foucault, 276–7; and Freud, 141 n30, 149; and Heidegger, 129–31; and Husserl, 129–31, 132–3; and Lévi-Strauss, 225–7, 387–8; and Levinas, 354, 358–60, 387–8; and Marxism, 125–6, 151–7; and Merleau-Ponty, 123, 126, 181–4, 195, 196, 197, 203–8; and Nancy, 374 n48, 375–6; and structuralism, 225–7, 276–7; works: *Being and Nothingness*, 122, 128–51, 358, 387; Critique of Dialectical Reason, 126, 151–7, 387; *The Family Idiot*, 126, 127–8; *The Flies*, 151 n37; *Nausea*, 107; *No Exit* 146 n33; *Saint Genet*, 125; *What Is Literature?*, 123–4; *The Words*, 127
Saussure, F., 209, 215–21, 222
Scheler, M., 106, 189
schizophrenia, Deleuze and Guattari on, 339–41
Schlick, M., 378
Schopenhauer, A., 90, 91
Schyns, M., 22 n34
science, limitations of, 51–4, 134, 188–9; objectivity of, 30–3; philosophy of, 9, 26–40, 229–34, 260–1, 381; progress of, 44–6,
sciences, human, 267–8, 274–6
sciences, social, 9 n15, 381–2; see also anthropology, Durkheim, Lévi-Strauss, Mauss, structuralism
scientific facts, 31–3, 34–5, 37–8
Searle, J., 290, 291, 370
self-deception, see bad faith
Sellars, W., 302 n14
Serres, M., 8 n8, 232–4, 234 n15
Sertillanges, A.-D., 94, 114
sexual difference, Irigaray on, 341–2

sexuality, history of, 282–8
Shakespeare, W., 369
Shestov, L., 105
Simons, M., 160 n8
situation, 149
skepticism, Derrida and, 304–8
social sciences, see sciences, social
Socialisme ou Barbarie, 320
Société Français de la Philosophie, 7
Sollers, P., 243, 253
Sorbonne, 392
Sorel, G., 50
speech, Derrida on, 292–3, 298, 302–3; Lacan on, 241–2; Levinas on, 357; Saussure on, 216, 217; see also writing
Spencer, H., 230
Spiegelberg, H., 106 n33–5, 133, 137 n28, 182 n4
Spinoza, B., 40, 54, 78; Deleuze on, 333–4
spiritualism, 9–14, 25, 91, 382, 383
Steiner, G., 39 n16
Steward, J., 182 n2
structuralism, 208–12, 215–57, 381; and phenomenology, 224–7, 387–8; Ricoeur on, 367–8; see also Lévi-Strauss; sciences, social
supplement, 302–3
surrealism, 102–3
"suspicion, masters of", 367 n33

Taine, H., 6, 9, 90
Teilhard de Chardin, P., 82 n29
Tel quel, 238, 253–4
temps modernes, Les, 123, 126, 181, 182, 183–4, 345
text, Derrida on, 305–6; see also books
Thao, Tran Duc, 110
Thibaudet, A., 3, 5
Thomism, see neo-Thomism
totality, 355–6
totems, 222–4
trace, 303–4, 311, 361 n15
transcendence, 170–1, 178, 349, 355; see also immanence
Troubetzkoy, N., 222
truth, and poststructuralism, 250–1, 255; Brunschvicg on, 43; Deleuze on, 331, 336; Derrida on, 304–8, 311; Foucault's history of, 285; Lyotard on, 320–1; Merleau-Ponty on, 201–2; vs. mimesis, 376

unconscious, Foucault on, 260, 261, 275; Lacan on, 240–2, 318–19; Lévi-Strauss on, 224; Lyotard on, 318–19; Ricoeur on, 367; Sartre on, 149; see also Freud, psychoanalysis

Vadée, M., 86 n4
Valéry, P., 6, 50, 253 n39
Van Breda, H. L., 184
Veyne, P., 260 n8
Vienna Circle, 188, 378
Virgoulay, R., 91 n13
vital force, see *élan vital*
Vuillemin, J., 377, 378 n61

Wahl, J., 105, 108 n40, 109–10, 290 n3, 354
Weber, L., 43 n18
Weil, S., 43 n18, 105 n31, 164 n14

Whitford, M., 350 n27, 351 n29
will, Blondel on, 92–3; Ricoeur on, 365–6, 370
Wittgenstein, L., 378
women, 164–5, 165–80; and biology, 169–70, 170–2, 178; as other, 165–8; *see also* feminism
Worms, F., 65 n11
writing, Derrida on, 291–3, 295–7, 298, 302–3; see also *speech*

Zeno, 51, 304
Zola, E., 5